Biosimilars Litigation and Client Counseling

Kenneth L. Dorsney and
Cortlan S. Hitch, Editors

AMERICAN BAR ASSOCIATION
Intellectual Property
Law Section

Cover design by Amy Mandel, ABA Section of Intellectual Property Law; Jill Tedhams, ABA Design

Printed in the United States of America.

28 27 26 25 24 5 4 3 2 1

A catalog record for this book is available from the Library of Congress.

Contents

PART II

CHAPTER 6
Preparing the Client for the Commitment and Costs 107

CHAPTER 7
"First Wave" Infringement Actions 133

CHAPTER 10
Post-Issuance Review and Reexamination of Patents 185

CHAPTER 11
Antitrust Litigation and Product Liability Considerations 225

PART III

CHAPTER 12
Product Case Studies (Humira®, Neupogen®/Neulasta®, and Herceptin®) 251

CHAPTER AUTHORS

Chapter 1

Kenneth L. Dorsney
Cortlan S. Hitch
Morris James LLP
Wilmington, DE

Chapter 2

Dennies Varughese, Pharm.D.
Christopher M. Gallo, Ph.D.
Alex Alfano
Zach Jacobs
Sterne, Kessler, Goldstein & Fox PLLC
Washington, D.C.

Chapter 3

Sara W. Koblitz
Hyman, Phelps & McNamara P.C.
Washington, D.C.

Chapter 4

Mark J. Feldstein, Ph.D.
William B. Raich, Ph.D.
Alissa K. Lipton
Yieyie Yang, Ph.D.
Finnegan, Henderson, Farabow, Garrett & Dunner, LLP
Washington, D.C.

Amanda K. Murphy, Ph.D.
Finnegan, Henderson, Farabow, Garrett & Dunner, LLP
London, UK

Chapter 5

Stephen R. Auten
Luke T. Shannon
Taft Stettinius & Hollister LLP
Chicago, IL

Chapter 6

Aziz Burgy
Ricardo Camposanto
Darpan Singh
Axinn, Veltrop & Harkrider LLP
Washington, D.C.

Chapter 7

Jennifer H. Wu
Peter Sandel
Stephen A. Maniscalco
Naz Wehrli
Jennifer Rea Denault
Allison Penfield
Groombridge, Wu, Baughman & Stone LLP
New York, NY

Chapter 8

Louis Fogel, Ph.D.
Shaun M. Van Horn
Fish and Richardson, P.C.
Chicago, IL

Jacob Wentzel
Jenner & Block LLP
Chicago, IL

Chapter 9

Rebecca J. Cantor
Brooks Kushman P.C.
Southfield, MI

Chapter 10

Nicholas Mitrokostas
Shaobo Zhu
A&O Shearman
Boston, MA

Mena Gaballah
A&O Shearman
New York, NY

Chapter 11

Daryl L. Wiesen
Goodwin Procter LLP
Boston, MA

Alexandra D. Valenti
Goodwin Procter LLP
New York, NY

Alison Siedor
Eric Levi
Goodwin Procter LLP
Washington, D.C.

Chapter 12

Deepro R. Mukerjee
Lance A. Soderstrom
Katten Muchin Rosenman LLP
New York, NY

Matthew M. Holub
Jillian M. Schurr
Katten Muchin Rosenman LLP
Chicago, IL

Chapter 13

Lisa M. Ferri
Richard J. McCormick
Mayer Brown LLP
New York, NY

Chapter 14

Kent Walker
Retired, formerly of Crowell & Moring LLP

Shannon Lentz
Debbie Yellin
Crowell & Moring LLP
Washington, D.C.

Laura Lydigsen
Crowell & Moring LLP
Chicago, IL

Joanna Fuller
Crowell & Moring LLP
Irvine, CA

Chapter 15

Hassen A. Sayeed, M.D.
O'Melveny & Myers LLP
New York, NY

Chapter 16

David S. Bloch
Greenberg Traurig, LLP
San Francisco, CA

Melissa Hunter-Ensor, Ph.D.
Greenberg Traurig, LLP
Boston, MA

Chapter 17

John E. Norman, Ph.D.
Andrew Medico
Gowling WLG (Canada) LLP
Ottawa, Ontario, Canada

Preface

It's been more than ten years since the release of our first book, *ANDA Litigation: Strategies and Tactics for Pharmaceutical Patent Litigators.* Since then, we have released multiple editions of *ANDA Litigation* and its partner, *Pre-ANDA Litigation: Strategies and Tactics for Developing a Drug Product and Patent Portfolio.* During the development of these editions, there was a new realm of law developing beneath our feet that we did not have the opportunity to discuss—the laws and regulations governing biologics and biosimilar products.

In 2010, the Biologics Price Competition and Innovation Act (BPCIA) was signed into law as part of the Affordable Care Act, providing a legal framework for the approval and litigation of these fascinating products. Much like the Hatch-Waxman Act that came before it, the BPCIA endeavored to strike a balance between encouraging innovative companies to develop new biologic products, while still providing generic companies the ability and incentive to manufacture and market biosimilar products, with the ultimate goal of lowering the costs to the American consumer.

Because this is still a relatively novel niche of law—with only 40 cases brought under the BPCIA as of the time of writing—we recognized the need for a practitioner's quick reference for the BPCIA as well as a guide through the complex litigation and pre-litigation tactics a litigator might encounter. The biosimilars field is just starting to take off and experts expect it to continue its trajectory of 12 percent annual growth for years to come. Now is the perfect time to dive into this extraordinary area of patent law and prepare oneself for the multitude of BPCIA litigations that are sure to sprout up over the next few decades.

The need for a robust biosimilar market could not be more apparent. Biologics are some of the most expensive medications available, accounting for nearly 50 percent of prescription medicine spending even though they only represent 3 percent of U.S. prescriptions. This disparity in cost can be alleviated by a healthy level of competition, which can only be achieved by the manufacturing of biosimilar products. With the production of biologic products only expected to expand, both the innovative companies and biosimilar manufacturers need competent professionals who can shepherd them through BPCIA litigation, both pre-suit and post-suit.

This book examines the perspective of both the innovative companies (the reference product sponsors) and the biosimilar applicants. We hope this guide will be a useful tool regardless of which entity you represent and make this complex and evolving area of law a little easier to navigate.

Kenneth L. Dorsney
Cortlan S. Hitch

Foreword

Like the Hatch-Waxman Act that is directed to small molecule–based drugs, the Biologics Price Competition and Innovation Act (BPCIA) directed to biological products seeks to balance patent rights (which incentivize innovation by granting temporary periods of exclusivity on inventions) with follow-on market competition (which exerts downward pressure on prices). But the two systems are not the same. Key procedural differences, as well as key underlying differences between small-molecule drugs and biologics themselves, pose unique considerations for parties and practitioners engaged in BPCIA litigation. These differences have also raised, and will continue to raise, issues of first impression that BPCIA litigants should bear in mind as they navigate the complex landscape of this unique niche of the judicial system. As one example, unlike small molecules that often are chemically synthesized, biological products are large, complex molecules generally produced by or derived from living organisms, through sometimes intricate and patented manufacturing processes. Thus, the BPCIA contemplates and provides for patent litigation involving the patents on these manufacturing processes, while the Hatch-Waxman system does not. As another example, the BPCIA does not provide for a 30-month stay of FDA regulatory approval of the biosimilar application. As a result, BPCIA litigation may involve biosimilar launches during the litigation, which may give rise to damages claims and jury trials.

In addressing the BPCIA, the Federal Circuit has commented, "Winston Churchill once described Russia as 'a riddle wrapped in a mystery inside an enigma.' That is this statute. In these opinions, we do our best to unravel the riddle, solve the mystery, and comprehend the enigma."[1]

---

1. Amgen Inc. v. Sandoz Inc., 794 F.3d 1347, 1351 (Fed. Cir. 2015), *rev'd in part, vacated in part*, 582 U.S. 1 (2017) (citing Winston Churchill, The Russian Enigma (BBC radio broadcast Oct. 1, 1939), http://www.churchill-society-london.org.uk/RusnEnig.html.).

Given the high costs and scientific risks already inherent in biopharmaceutical research and development (R&D), post-launch predictability is important for both biologic originators and biosimilar makers. With a cost of billions of dollars and an average R&D timeline of ten to 15 years to develop a single new drug, originators rely on the sales of the few candidates that become FDA-approved products to fund R&D for future products. Biosimilar makers, for their part, must invest $100 million to $300 million, with an R&D timeline of five to ten years, to develop a biosimilar and obtain approval of the biosimilar maker's biologics license application with the FDA. Against these dynamics, post-development uncertainties, including the complexities, novel questions, and unsettled legal issues entwined in the still-new BPCIA, can act as disincentives to the development of future products. On the other hand, practitioners who invest in learning and understanding the intricacies of this unique type of litigation can help increase business certainty for their clients through strategic counseling, informed advice, and sound arguments aimed at clarifying those aspects of the BPCIA that remain unsettled.

We commend the authors and editors of this book for demystifying the BPCIA, from its historical origins and regulatory framework (Chapters 2 to 5) to BPCIA litigation in practice (Chapters 6 to 10) to related Patent Office, antitrust, and products liability actions (Chapters 10 and 11) to case studies and product strategies (Chapters 12 to 15) to global considerations and the future (Chapters 16 and 17).

Jennifer H. Wu (Groombridge, Wu, Baughman & Stone LLP)
Ryan M. Daniel (Fresenius Kabi, LLC)
Corey Salsberg (Novartis)

chapter 1

Introduction*

I. The Biologics Price Competition and Innovation Act

Since 1938, every new drug in the United States has been regulated through approval of a new drug application (NDA) before it could be released into commerce.[1] The NDA is intended to provide the U.S. Food and Drug Administration (FDA) enough information to determine whether the drug is safe and effective, whether the labeling is appropriate, and whether the manufacturing methods are adequately designed to preserve the drug's strength and purity.[2] The NDA also details the results of clinical testing and animal studies to demonstrate how the drug behaves in the body.[3] However, the cost of clinical testing and the threat of being sued for patent infringement discouraged many companies from attempting to introduce cheaper generic versions of drugs into the marketplace.[4] This resulted in less than 20 percent of prescriptions being filled with generic drugs and many generics not even entering the market until three to five years after the patents for brand-name pharmaceuticals had expired.[5] As such, U.S. citizens were paying hefty prices for the brand-name drugs without any other choices on the market, and the brand-name companies effectively had a monopoly over their drugs for an additional three to five years after their patents for those drugs expired.

---

*Kenneth L. Dorsney and Cortlan S. Hitch, Morris James LLP.

1. *New Drug Application (NDA)*, U.S. Food & Drug Admin., https://www.fda.gov/drugs/types-applications/new-drug-application-nda (last updated Jan. 21, 2022).

2. *Id.*

3. *Id.*

4. Pharmaceutical Research and Manufacturers of America, What Is Hatch-Waxman? (2018), https://www.phrma.org/-/media/Project/PhRMA/PhRMA-Org/PhRMA-Org/PDF/D-F/Fact-Sheet_What-is-Hatch-Waxman_June-2018.pdf.

5. *Id.*

In 1984, the Drug Price Competition and Patent Term Restoration Act, more commonly known as the Hatch-Waxman Act (HWA), was enacted to streamline the process for approving generic pharmaceutical products, while still preserving the incentives for developing new drugs.[6] The HWA provided a legal framework for generic pharmaceutical companies to submit an abbreviated new drug application (ANDA) that generally does not require preclinical or clinical data to establish safety and effectiveness.[7] Rather, ANDA applicants can demonstrate the safety of the drug by showing that their product performs in the same way as a drug that has already been approved.[8] The HWA also includes a "safe harbor" provision that exempts generic companies from patent infringement liability when conducting research and development necessary for FDA approval.[9] It further provides a statutory mechanism for initiating patent infringement litigation based on an ANDA filing so that pharmaceutical companies can protect their rights to market their innovative drug products.[10] While the HWA was a groundbreaking statutory and regulatory scheme that has provided benefits to pharmaceutical companies on both the brand and generic sides, it did not encompass the growing world of biological products and their generic equivalent, "biosimilars."

In 2010, the Affordable Care Act, signed into law by President Obama, included an amendment to the Public Health Service Act that provided this long-missing abbreviated approval pathway for biological products that was intended to be comparable to the HWA's framework for drugs.[11] These new statutory provisions are referred to as the Biologics Price Competition and Innovation Act (BPCIA).

To understand the need for the BPCIA, it is important to know the distinction between a "drug" and a "biologic." A "drug," as defined by the FDA, is an "article intended for use in the diagnosis, cure, mitigation, treatment, or prevention of disease," and "articles (other than food) intended to affect the structure of any function of the body of man or other animals."[12] On the other hand, a "biologic" is defined as "a virus, therapeutic serum, toxin, antitoxin, vaccine, blood, blood component or derivative, allergenic product, protein, or analogous product, or arsphenamine or derivative of arsphenamine (or any other trivalent organic arsenic compound) applicable

6. *See, e.g.*, H.R. Rep. No. 98-857(II), at *11 (1984) (summary of the "Drug Price Competition and Patent Term Restoration Act of 1984").

7. *Abbreviated New Drug Application (ANDA)*, FDA, https://www.fda.gov/drugs/types-applications/abbreviated-new-drug-application-anda (last updated Dec. 16, 2022).

8. *Id.*

9. 35 U.S.C. § 271(e)(1).

10. *Id.* § 271(e)(2)(A).

11. 75 Fed. Reg. 76,472 (Dec. 8, 2010).

12. 21 U.S.C. § 321(g).

to the prevention, treatment, or cure of a disease or condition of human beings."[13] An easier way to think of a biologic is as a product that is manufactured in a living system.

To begin introducing a biologic product into interstate commerce, a biologics license application (BLA) must be submitted to the FDA.[14] Similar to an NDA for drugs, the BLA must include all data necessary to demonstrate safety and potency of the proposed product, including "substantial evidence of effectiveness."[15] After submitting a proper Form FDA 356h to the Center for Biologics Evaluation and Research (CBER), the FDA will conduct multiple reviews and request any necessary additional information from the filer.[16] After submission of the BLA to the FDA, it can take up to two years to gain approval.[17]

A "biosimilar" is the term used for a product that is highly similar to a biological medication already approved by the FDA—which is often referred to as the "reference product."[18] A biosimilar has no clinically meaningful difference from the reference product, will have the same safety and effectiveness, and will be made from the same types of sources.[19] However, a biosimilar is not exactly the same as the reference product, as the complex structure of the proteins in biological products cannot be precisely duplicated by a biosimilar.[20]

An application for a biosimilar product is submitted as an "abbreviated" BLA—an "aBLA." The BPCIA provides the framework to submit an aBLA. As suggested by the term "abbreviated," the aBLA does not require submission of all the elements of the BLA. The aBLA largely relies on the FDA's existing understanding of the safety and purity of the reference product.[21] However, the aBLA still must contain several of the same elements as a BLA in order to satisfy the FDA. For example, the aBLA must

---

13. 42 U.S.C. § 262(i)(1).

14. *Biologics License Applications (BLA) Process (CBER)*, FDA, https://www.fda.gov/vaccines-blood-biologics/development-approval-process-cber/biologics-license-applications-bla-process-cber (last updated Jan. 27, 2021).

15. FDA, Draft Guidance for Industry: Demonstrating Substantial Evidence of Effectiveness for Human Drug and Biological Products 4 (2019), https://www.fda.gov/media/133660/download.

16. *The Biologics License Application (BLA) Process Explained*, FDA Grp. LLC (Mar. 28, 2022), https://www.thefdagroup.com/blog/2014/07/test-the-biologics-license-application-bla-process/.

17. *The Biologics License Application Timeline—A Long, Long Road*, LeanRAQA, https://leanraqa.com/biologics-license-application-timeline/ (last visited Feb. 2, 2024).

18. 42 U.S.C. § 262(i)(2)(A).

19. *Id.* § 262(i)(2)(B).

20. FDA, Overview of Biosimilar Products, https://www.fda.gov/media/151058/download.

21. FDA, Guidance for Industry: Scientific Considerations in Demonstrating Biosimilarity to a Reference Product 3–4 (2015), https://www.fda.gov/media/82647/download.

include clinical studies and contain a Chemistry, Manufacturing, and Controls section to ensure safety, purity, and potency.[22]

The BPCIA also defines another type of product—an "interchangeable biosimilar." This is a biosimilar designation unique to the United States. An interchangeable biosimilar is not only expected to produce the same clinical result as the reference product, but is also able to be substituted for the reference product without prescriber intervention.[23] The safety and efficacy risk of switching or alternating between a biological product and its interchangeable is no higher than using the reference product alone.[24]

Like other biosimilars, an interchangeable requires an aBLA or a supplement to an already-approved aBLA. However, the interchangeable application unsurprisingly requires more information than a typical biosimilar's aBLA. Some of the additional information includes an identification of analytical differences between the reference product and the interchangeable biosimilar, an analysis of differences in the expected pharmacokinetics and biodistribution in different patient populations, and an analysis of differences in expected toxicities in each condition of use and patient population.[25]

II. A Need for Alternative Biological Products

Biologics can be composed of sugars, proteins, or nucleic acids or complex combinations of these substances, or may even be living entities such as cells or tissues.[26] Some common biologics include Humira®, Lantus®, Enbrel®, and Botox®. These well-known products work to control blood sugar levels, prevent joint inflammation, and treat cancer.[27] Unlike many drugs, it has been challenging to make biologics in a form that can be taken orally; at this time, they are mostly available as injections and infusions—with some being inhalable as well.[28]

22. 42 U.S.C. § 262(k)(2)(A)(i)(V).

23. *Id.* § 262(i)(3).

24. *Biosimilar Interchangeability: 9 Things to Consider*, AM. J. MANAGED CARE: CTR. FOR BIOSIMILARS (Apr. 2, 2018), https://www.centerforbiosimilars.com/view/biosimilar-interchangeability-9-things-to-consider.

25. 42 U.S.C. § 262(k)(4)(B).

26. *What Are "Biologics" Questions and Answers*, FDA, https://www.fda.gov/about-fda/center-biologics-evaluation-and-research-cber/what-are-biologics-questions-and-answers (last updated Feb. 6, 2018).

27. Benita Lee, *What Are Biologics? 5 Examples of Biological Drugs You May Already Be Taking*, GOODRX (June 16, 2022), https://www.goodrx.com/healthcare-access/medication-education/biologics-biological-drugs-examples.

28. *Id.*

Unfortunately, biologics are among the most expensive medications available today. In fact, the three most expensive medications in the United States in 2021 were all biologics, and were more than 40 percent more expensive than the next-most expensive product.[29] Moreover, while biologics only constitute about 3 percent of all prescriptions in the United States, they account for almost half of prescription medicine spending.[30] Much like in the days before the HWA when it came to drugs, the steep cost of biologics underscores the need for biosimilar alternatives that can be marketed at a more affordable cost.[31]

Without a healthy level of biosimilar competition in the market, the imbalance of U.S. patients' expenses on biologic products as compared to other medications will only increase. Indeed, the global biologics market is expected to grow from an estimated $382.04 billion in 2022 to $540.66 billion in 2026.[32] Experts have further noted the biologics market's consistent growth of 12–13 percent annually for the past decade—a trend that is expected to continue for years to come.[33] Also notable is that the approval of biologics outpaced small-molecule new molecular entities for the first time in 2022.[34]

III. Brief Summary of the BPCIA

The BPCIA was enacted on March 23, 2010, as part of the Patient Protection and Affordable Care Act and can be found under 42 U.S.C. § 262.

29. Anna Wells, *The Top 10 Most Expensive Popular Brand-Name Drugs in the U.S. (and How to Save)*, GoodRx (July 14, 2021), https://www.goodrx.com/healthcare-access/drug-cost-and-savings/top-10-most-expensive-popular-brand-name-drugs-us-how-to-save.

30. Patrizia Cavazzoni, *FDA and FTC Collaborate to Advance Competition in the Biologic Marketplace*, FDA (Mar. 2, 2023), https://www.fda.gov/news-events/fda-voices/fda-and-ftc-collaborate-advance-competition-biologic-marketplace.

31. Biosimilars Forum, Report: Biosimilars Have Significantly Lowered Prices of All Biologics (2021), https://biosimforum.wpengine.com/wp-content/uploads/Xcenda-ASP-One-Pager.pdf ("The report found that every brand name reference biologic was on track to have a higher average sales price in the absence of biosimilars—with an average sales price estimated to be 56% higher without biosimilar competition.").

32. Press Release, Research and Markets, Global Biologics Market Report 2022: A $540.66 Billion Market in 2026—Leading Products & Services, Key Features & Differentiators, and Development Products (May 18, 2022), https://www.businesswire.com/news/home/20220518005999/en/Global-Biologics-Market-Report-2022-A-540.66-Billion-Market-in-2026---Leading-Products-Services-Key-Features-Differentiators-and-Development-Products---ResearchAndMarkets.com.

33. *An Experienced CDMO Can Be a Differentiator in the Rapidly Growing Biologics Market*, Pharma's Almanac (Jan. 31, 2023), https://www.pharmasalmanac.com/articles/an-experienced-cdmo-can-be-a-differentiator-in-the-rapidly-growing-biologics-market-1.

34. Melanie Senior, *Fresh from the Biotech Pipeline: Fewer Approvals, but Biologics Gain Share*, 41 Nature Biotech. 174 (2023), https://www.nature.com/articles/s41587-022-01630-6.

The main subsections are (a), (i), (k), and (*l*). Subsection (a) contains the basis for granting a license to a biological product and requirements for a license. Subsection (i) defines the terms the BPCIA revolves around: "biological product," "biosimilar," "interchangeable," and "reference product." Subsections (k) and (*l*) hold the majority of the BPCIA's statutory scheme.

Subsection (k) provides the legal framework for applying for a biosimilar license. This includes the application requirements, general rules, exclusivity periods, as well as the Secretary's[35] public listing requirements. Subsection (*l*) includes the interactions between the biosimilar applicant (BA) and the sponsor of the application for the reference product (RP sponsor). For example, subsection (*l*) includes terms of providing confidential information, as well as the process for exchanging information about the biosimilar application and the patents that are allegedly covered by the reference product.

The BPCIA provides a unique mechanism where the BA and RP sponsor engage in a dispute-resolution procedure that involves an elaborate exchange of information.[36] This information exchange process is often termed the "patent dance." The patent dance begins with the BA providing information to the RP sponsor regarding the manufacturing process as well as any other information that may be requested by the RP sponsor.[37] After the manufacturing information is provided, the BA and RP sponsor engage in good faith negotiations to settle on a list of the patents that will be the subject of an infringement action.[38]

During the negotiations over the patent list, the parties also share detailed competing statements on the infringement and validity of the patents and products.[39] If the parties cannot agree to a list of patents for an infringement action, then the RP sponsor must bring an action for each patent listed on both parties' lists.[40] This spawns the immediate patent infringement action, which is sometimes referred to as "first wave" litigation.

A BA must provide a notice of commercial marketing to the RP sponsor no later than 180 days before commercial marketing begins for the licensed product.[41] The notice of commercial marketing, also called the "180-day notice," triggers a second wave of patent litigation for a declara-

35. Throughout this book will be references to a "Secretary." Unless stated otherwise, this will refer to the Secretary of Health and Human Services.

36. Amgen Inc. v. Sandoz Inc., 794 F.3d 1347 (Fed. Cir. 2015).

37. 42 U.S.C. § 262(*l*)(2)(A), (B).

38. *Id.* § 262(*l*)(4)–(5).

39. *Id.* § 262(*l*)(3)(B)–(C).

40. *Id.* § 262(*l*)(6)(B).

41. *Id.* § 262(*l*)(8)(A).

tory judgment action.[42] This second-wave litigation permits suit on any of the patents exchanged during the patent dance that were not included in a "first wave" litigation. After receiving the 180-day notice, and before the date of the first commercial marketing, the RP sponsor may seek a preliminary injunction on any patent in the second-wave litigation.[43]

For more information on the history of the BPCIA and its statutory and regulatory scheme, see Part I of this book. In Chapters 2 through 4 we take a deep dive into the BPCIA's history, the approval and regulatory process of biologics and biosimilars, and the patent dance. In Chapter 5 we examine the BPCIA as compared to the HWA and note the differences and similarities between these two remarkable schemes and differences in litigation tactics.

The United States is not alone in developing a statutory and regulatory system governing biologics and other drugs. Canada follows a similar approval process as the United States. Innovative pharmaceutical companies file a new drug submission that demonstrates its safety and efficacy, while a generic drug company can file an abbreviated new drug submission. For biosimilar products, the generic companies must also provide clinical trial data to support its safety and efficacy. For more information on the Canadian process for drug and biologic approval, as well as the statutory and regulatory framework governing litigation, and a guide on advising Canadian clients, see Chapter 17.

IV. Patent Litigation under the BPCIA

The hard work and substantial investments into developing biological products are protected through the filing and prosecution of patent applications. If granted, the owner of a U.S. patent has the right to bring an infringement action against anyone who, without authority, makes, uses, offers to sell, or sells any patented invention within the United States, or imports into the United States any patented invention during the term of the patent.[44] Under the BPCIA, it is deemed an act of infringement to submit an application seeking approval of a biological product as to all patents identified during the patent dance.[45] Additionally, if the BA fails to provide the RP sponsor a copy of the application or information on the manufacturing process of the biological product, this is an act of infringement as

42. *Id.* § 262(*l*)(9)(A).
43. *Id.* § 262(*l*)(8)(B).
44. 35 U.S.C. § 271(e)(1).
45. *Id.* § 271(e)(2)(C)(i).

to any patents that *could* be identified through the patent dance.[46] Once the litigation field has been set by the patent dance, or a BA's refusal to "dance," the patent holder can bring suit in an appropriate district court.

At the time of publishing this book, there have been 40 patent infringement actions filed in the United States under the BPCIA, with only six of them still being active. Table 1 is a list of the district courts where BPCIA litigations have been filed and the number of litigations filed in each district.

TABLE 1. BPCIA Litigations in District Courts

District Court	# of BPCIA Litigations
District of Delaware	15
District of New Jersey	9
Southern District of Florida	3
Northern District of West Virginia	3
Northern District of California	2
Southern District of California	2
District of Massachusetts	2
Northern District of Illinois	1
Western District of Pennsylvania	1
Eastern District of Texas	1
Eastern District of Virginia	1

Under the BPCIA it is commonly understood that there are two "waves" of litigation. The first wave is an immediate action under § 262(*l*)(6) that stems from the patent dance's exchange of information and contentions. The patent dance can provide significant control to the BA regarding which patents will be addressed in the first wave, as they can choose the number of patents to include.[47]

If the applicant refuses to participate in the patent dance, the RP sponsor must file a declaratory judgment action in order to protect its patents.[48] A declaratory judgment action is also appropriate when a BA fails to inform the RP sponsor of its biosimilar application.[49] Only the RP sponsor is permitted to seek a declaratory judgment—a BA cannot. Additionally, an RP sponsor can only bring a declaratory judgment action after it has been provided with a notice of commercial marketing.[50]

46. *Id.* § 271(e)(2)(C)(ii).
47. 42 U.S.C. § 262(*l*)(5)(A).
48. *Id.* § 262(*l*)(9)(B).
49. *Id.* § 262(*l*)(9)(C).
50. *Id.* § 262(*l*)(9)(A).

In Part II, we hear from some of the top litigators across the country on how to handle a BPCIA case from start to finish. This will include trial and pretrial strategies before the U.S. district courts (Chapters 6 through 9), as well as procedures before the U.S. Patent and Trademark Office and Patent Trial and Appeal Board to challenge biosimilar patents after they have been issued (Chapter 10). Part II concludes by examining the connection of biologics to non-patent legal areas, focusing in particular on product liability and antitrust issues (Chapter 11).

V. Patents of Biological Products

There are several types of patent claims that inventors can pursue to cover the various aspects of biologics and the processes for making or using them. For example, claims could be directed to methods of use, formulations, cell lines, cell culture medium, methods of manufacture, methods of purification, delivery devices, packaging, therapeutic agents, and starting materials.[51] The FDA keeps track of all licensed biological products regulated by the Center for Drug Evaluation and Research and the CBER. The FDA's "List of Licensed Biological Products with Reference Product Exclusivity and Biosimilarity or Interchangeability Evaluations" is also called the "Purple Book"—similar to the HWA's equivalent, the "Orange Book."[52]

The Purple Book is updated very frequently, and an approved product's information will generally be added within ten business days of approval.[53] Along with other important information, the Purple Book is required to list each reference product's exclusivity period and each first interchangeable exclusivity period when there is an eligible product.[54] The Purple Book also includes the patent lists for any biologic products and must be updated

51. April Abele Isaacson, *Biologics Price Competition & Innovation Act (BPCIA): Litigation Considerations*, Thomas Reuters Prac. L. (2022), https://content.next.westlaw.com/practical-law/document/I9884a5178e1111ec9f24ec7b211d8087/Biologics-Price-Competition-Innovation-Act-BPCIA-Litigation-Considerations.

52. *Purple Book: Lists of Licensed Biological Products with Reference Product Exclusivity and Biosimilarity or Interchangeability Evaluations*, FDA, https://www.fda.gov/drugs/therapeutic-biologics-applications-bla/purple-book-lists-licensed-biological-products-reference-product-exclusivity-and-biosimilarity-or (last updated Aug. 3, 2020).

53. *Purple Book Database of Licensed Biological Products: FAQs*, FDA, https://purplebooksearch.fda.gov/faqs (last visited Feb. 2, 2024).

54. Biological Product Patent Transparency (BPPT) Section of the Consolidated Appropriations Act of 2021, div. BB, § 325(a)(9)(A)(iv), Pub. L. No. 116-260, 134 Stat. 1182 (2020); *Purple Book Database of Licensed Biological Products: FAQs*, *supra* note 53 (see FAQ 5, What Purple Book listing requirements were added by the Biological Product Patent Transparency section of the Consolidated Appropriations Act of 2021 enacted December 27, 2020?).

to include any patents provided to the BA during the patent dance.[55] For more information on the Purple Book, see Chapter 4 where we take a closer look at its contents and how it is updated.

Typically, a patent will provide protection to the owner's invention rights until 20 years after the date on which the application was filed.[56] However, the wide range of patentable features of biologics and their manufacturing processes have led to an anticompetitive strategy used by RP sponsors called "patent thickets." A "patent thicket" may refer to a situation where multiple parties have overlapping patent rights on one product, requiring a manufacturer to negotiate licenses with multiple patent owners.[57] It may also refer to a situation where an RP sponsor files for many patents related to a single product to increase the infringement risks to a competitor entering the market. The more patents covering a product, the harder it is to overcome accusations of infringement and/or to establish sufficient bases for invalidity.

Relatedly, an RP sponsor may also engage in a scheme called "evergreening" where they continually tack on additional patents after their original patents and stagger the application filings. This can effectively extend the RP sponsor's monopoly over the patented biologic for much longer than intended by Congress. The FDA commissioner has lamented patent thickets and evergreening as "purely designed to deter the entry of approved biosimilars."[58] This barrier to biosimilars has a direct impact on patients in need of a less-expensive alternative. It is estimated that delayed entry of biosimilars due to patent thickets alone has cost the U.S. health care system $7.6 billion in lost savings between 2015 and 2019.[59]

VI. Litigation Management and Client Relations

Beyond providing an overview of the BPCIA and related cases, this book also aims to guide a litigant through the legal and nonlegal challenges of litigation brought under the BPCIA. In Chapter 6 we learn how to set

55. BPPT div. BB, § 325(a)(9)(A)(iii); *Purple Book Database of Licensed Biological Products: FAQs*, *supra* note 53 (see FAQ 5).

56. 35 U.S.C. § 154(a)(2).

57. Stu Woolman et al., *Evidence of Patent Thickets in Complex Biopharmaceutical Technologies*, 53 IDEA 1, 2 (2013); Carl Shapiro, *Navigating the Patent Thicket: Cross Licenses, Patent Pools, and Standard Setting*, 1 Innovation Pol'y & Econ. 119, 119 (2001).

58. Statement, FDA, Remarks from FDA Commissioner Scott Gottlieb, M.D., as Prepared for Delivery at the Brookings Institution on the Release of the FDA's Biosimilars Action Plan (July 18, 2018), https://www.fda.gov/news-events/press-announcements/remarks-fda-commissioner-scott-gottlieb-md-prepared-delivery-brookings-institution-release-fdas.

59. *Patent Abuse Blocks Access to Biosimilars for Patients*, Biosimilars Council (June 25, 2019), https://biosimilarscouncil.org/resource/failure-to-launch-white-paper/.

realistic expectations and budgets for a client. This involves a discussion of the expectations of success, the approximate time to trial, as well as the likely costs a party would expend.

Patent litigation can cost an average of $1.6 to $2.8 million if it extends past the discovery stage.[60] Due to the high prices of biologic products, it is no surprise that any damages award obtained, if a defendant is found to infringe, will also be high. The damages can skyrocket even further upon a finding of willful infringement. In one instance, a defendant owed $1.2 billion in damages after a willful infringement finding—although this was later reversed on appeal.[61] In addition to the length of litigation, the litigation's cost will also vary depending on the number of patents involved, the number of parties involved, as well as several other factors. It is thus necessary for both the RP sponsor and the BA to have a strategy from the outset on how to either draft a strong patent that can be enforced, or to design a biosimilar product that can withstand a claim for infringement.

Due to the high cost of litigation and risks of being unsuccessful at trial, parties with a dispute under the BPCIA often reach agreement during or even before litigation commences. Indeed, the majority of BPCIA cases have resulted in settlement or a stipulated or voluntary dismissal.[62] The parties may also choose to engage in certain alternative dispute resolution procedures, such as mediation or arbitration, to limit litigation costs.

In Chapters 13 and 14, we take a look at client counseling and strategies specific to the RP sponsor and the BA, respectively. The authors provide an in-depth analysis into not only strategic litigation issues, such as the venue to bring suit in and which corporate entities should be targeted, but also into pre-litigation strategies such as legal team assembly, preliminary witness interviews and fact investigation, and how to prepare for the patent dance and develop your patent portfolio or biosimilar product. The authors provide an inside look at both sides of the patent dance and the perspectives of the RP sponsor and BA.

Chapter 15 provides the reader a look into the negotiation and settlement process, the licensing contents, and discussions that typically result from settlement. This includes practice tips regarding the most frequently debated provisions such as entry date of the biosimilar product and any acceleration clauses, pre-launch stockpiling clauses, and royalty clauses. Because the majority of BPCIA cases reach settlement before trial, it is

---

60. *How Much Does Patent Litigation Cost?*, Copperpod (May 11, 2022), https://www.copperpodip.com/post/how-much-does-patent-litigation-cost.

61. *See* Juno Therapeutics, Inc. v. Kite Pharma, Inc., 10 F.4th 1330 (Fed. Cir. 2021).

62. *See* April Breyer Menon & Ha Kung Wong, Biologics HQ, The State of Biosimilars in 2023 (2023), https://www.venable.com/-/media/files/publications/2023/03/thestateofbiosimilarsin2023venable.pdf.

especially important to be aware of these sticking points and to know how to get the best outcome for your client.

VII. Future of Biosimilars and the BPCIA

The biosimilars industry is still in its nascent stage. The first approved biosimilar product was Zarxio in March 2015, and the first interchangeable product was not approved until Semglee in July 2021.[63] As of February 2023, there have only been 36 approved biosimilar products and four interchangeable products.[64] However, beginning in 2015 with Zarxio, the approvals of biosimilars increased every year until 2020 when the COVID-19 pandemic put much of the world on hold. Since then, approvals of biosimilars and interchangeables have been steadily increasing again. In fact, there are more than 100 biosimilars being developed today for more than 50 different reference products.[65]

The low number of approved biosimilar products has thus resulted in only a handful of related patent litigation cases involving the BPCIA. As such, the interpretations of the BPCIA's provisions and other legal issues have yet to be fully fleshed out. In Chapter 16, we provide a look into the expected future developments of the BPCIA. For example, there are already proposals from senators to eliminate the separate interchangeability requirement and deem all FDA-approved biosimilars "interchangeable" for purposes of the BPCIA.[66] Aside from proposed amendments to the statutory scheme of the BPCIA, there will likely be many changes stemmed from court interpretations that are sure to shape the BPCIA for years to come.

---

63. *Biosimilar Product Information*, FDA, https://www.fda.gov/drugs/biosimilars/biosimilar-product-information (last updated Dec. 8, 2023).

64. *Id.*

65. Cavazzoni, *supra* note 30.

66. S. 2305, 118th Cong. (2023).

Part I

chapter 2

BPCIA History and Overview*

"Biosimilar" refers generally to a generic alternative to a branded biological medical treatment. For those unfamiliar with this scientific landscape, it is important to understand the difference between "biologics" compared to what are known as "small-molecule drugs." Small-molecule drugs—well-known examples of which are drugs such as acetaminophen or ibuprofen—are based on relatively simple and small molecular weight synthetic organic compounds and are typically sold at neighborhood pharmacy counters. Biologics, on the other hand, are much larger protein-based drugs such as recombinant proteins or monoclonal antibodies that are made from cell cultures and typically administered in hospitals or acquired from specialty pharmacies. Biologics, given their complexity, usually have stringent storage requirements, and tend to be significantly more expensive than small-molecule drugs. The passage of the Hatch-Waxman Act in 1984 created a streamlined and abbreviated regulatory pathway for generic manufacturers to introduce low-cost alternatives to branded small-molecule drugs. But a similar abbreviated pathway for generic biologics, or biosimilars, was not enacted for nearly *30* years after.

President Obama signed into law the Biologics Price Competition and Innovation Act (BPCIA) as an amendment to the Public Health Service (PHS) Act on March 23, 2010. Congress designed the law with the dual purpose of establishing an abbreviated pathway for the licensure (i.e., U.S. Food and Drug Administration (FDA) approval) of biosimilar products to facilitate entry of lower priced alternatives to expensive biological treatments and also to incentivize innovation of newer biological treatments in the life sciences space.[1] Enacted as part of the Patient Protection and

---

*Dennies Varughese, Pharm.D., is a director within the Trial and Appellate Practice Group at Sterne Kessler. Christopher M. Gallo, Ph.D., is a director within Sterne Kessler's Biotechnology and Chemical Practice Group. Alex Alfano and Zach Jacobs are associates within Sterne Kessler's Trial and Appellate Practice Group.

1. Krista Hessler Carver et al., *An Unofficial Legislative History of the Biologics Price Competition and Innovation Act of 2009*, 65 Food & Drug L.J. 671, 671 (2010).

Affordable Care Act (ACA), the BPCIA contains several key provisions governing the development of biosimilar products. At its core, the BPCIA creates an abbreviated approval pathway—similar to but not the same as the abbreviated new drug application (ANDA) created by the Hatch-Waxman Act[2] for small-molecule drugs, for highly complex biological products shown to be "highly similar" to or "interchangeable" with the branded biologic, aka "licensed reference product."[3]

The BPCIA marked a major milestone. Before 2010, a company seeking to introduce a generic alternative to an existing biologic treatment had to file its own full biologics license application (BLA[4]), independently demonstrating safety and efficacy. This meant lengthy and expensive clinical studies.[5] And, before 2015, FDA had not approved any biosimilar product, aside from one therapeutic protein in 1997.[6]

I. History Leading Up to BPCIA Passage

Prior to U.S. enactment of a biosimilar approval pathway, the European Union and Canada implemented their own versions of biosimilar approval pathways in 2004 and 2006, respectively.[7] Part of the reason for this is that, whereas the United States has a bifurcated system (e.g., CDER[8] versus CBER[9]), Europe has a centralized structure.[10]

In the United States, it was debated whether FDA had the expertise to effectively review biosimilar applications. Other scientific questions that came up are:

---

2. Drug Price Competition and Patent Term Restoration (Hatch-Waxman) Act, Pub. L. No. 98-417, 98 Stat. 1585 (1984).

3. 42 U.S.C. § 262(k).

4. Though beyond the scope of this chapter, FDA has some authority to approve certain protein biological products under the new drug application (NDA) pathway typically used for small-molecule drugs. FDA's ability to approve generic biological products under the abbreviated ANDA and section 505(b)(2) pathways is more limited, but FDA at times has done so. *See* Pergonal® and Fortical®. Hessler Carver et al., *supra* note 1, at 671.

5. *What Are "Biologics" Questions and Answers*, FDA, https://www.fda.gov/about-fda/center-biologics-evaluation-and-research-cber/what-are-biologics-questions-and-answers (last updated Feb. 6, 2018).

6. Letter from Janet Woodcock, M.D., Director, FDA Center for Drug Evaluation and Research, to A. Peter Frank, Serono Laboratories, Inc., Docket 92P-0487, at 11–13 (June 17, 1997).

7. Noel Courage & Ainslie Parsons, *The Comparability Conundrum: Biosimilars in the United States, Europe, and Canada*, 66 Food & Drug L.J. 203, 209–12 (2011).

8. Center for Drug Evaluation and Research.

9. Center for Biologics Evaluation and Research.

10. Hessler Carver et al., *supra* note 1, at 691.

- Was it possible for a manufacturer to duplicate a reference product using a different manufacturing process?
- Would available analytical techniques for characterizing protein structure and biological activity sufficiently allow FDA to declare a biosimilar is "highly similar" to an innovative reference product?
- Could FDA deem a biosimilar interchangeable with a reference product without clinical trials?
- Could one determine whether there would be serious immunological effects of a biosimilar without clinical testing?

Due to the scientific questions raised above, FDA Commissioner Andrew von Eschenbach suggested in March 2007 that biosimilar legislation was "premature," and any case-by-case evaluation could require clinical trials and immunogenicity studies.[11] Despite this skepticism, a Democrat-majority Congress moved forward with the BPCIA in 2010 with the stated intent of "balancing innovation and consumer interests" by creating an abbreviated pathway for the approval of biological products demonstrated to be biosimilar to, or interchangeable with, an FDA-licensed reference product.[12]

The Hatch-Waxman framework served as a starting point for the BPCIA drafters. Under Hatch-Waxman, approval of generic drugs under the ANDA pathway requires only that a manufacturer demonstrate its product is pharmaceutically bioequivalent to its branded counterpart (i.e., reference listed drug).[13] Manufacturers of biologics were unable to utilize this statutory regime because the complexity involved in producing a biologic product results in heterogeneity in the final product—variations across various manufacturing batches are expected. Colloquially, the saying goes that for biologics the "product is the process." This disqualifies biosimilars from approval under the framework for generics requiring only pharmaceutical equivalence, which is relatively easily demonstrated for small-molecule compounds and drug products.

Debate on proposed biosimilar legislation began in 2006. A first iteration of the legislation would have allowed FDA to license biological products if they were "comparable" to a reference product and there was an "absence of clinically meaningful differences . . . in terms of the safety, purity, and potency of the product."[14] The legislation would not have pro-

11. *US FDA Eyes "Similarity" for Follow-on Biologicals*, Scrip News, Mar. 23, 2007, at 13; *Von E Opposes Generic Biologics Legislation*, Dickinson's FDA Rev., Mar. 2007, at 10.

12. BPCIA, Pub. L. No. 111-148, § 7001(b), 124 Stat. 804 (2010) ("It is the sense of the Senate that a biosimilars pathway balancing innovations and consumer interests [i.e., accessibility] should be established.").

13. 21 U.S.C. § 355(j)(2)(A)(iv).

14. H.R. 6257, 109th Cong. § 3(a)(2) (2006) (proposed PHS Act § 351(k)(1)).

vided marketing exclusivity to biosimilar product innovators unless they made a showing of interchangeability with the reference product.[15] Developing an interchangeable biosimilar product can be advantageous because it allows the biosimilar product to be substituted for the reference product by a pharmacy without the intervention of the prescribing physician. This is similar to what occurs for generic small-molecule drugs. A biosimilar that is not interchangeable could still be used as an alternative to the branded counterpart, but will not be automatically substituted.

Moreover, as discussed in more detail later, resolution of any patent disputes between the branded company and biosimilar sponsor played a central role both in the early proposed legislation as well as the final enacted version. The patent resolution process in the initial legislation largely mirrored the final process in the BPCIA. This process, discussed in Section II.A, is commonly referred to as the "patent dance," where biosimilar applicants and branded product owners identify patents relevant to the biosimilar and collaboratively narrow issues for a first phase of litigation.[16]

After a political realignment in Congress, elected officials continued to debate biosimilar legislation over the next several years. The second iteration of the legislation—H.R. 1038—substituted "comparable" with "highly similar" for purposes of determining whether a biosimilar can serve as a generic alternative or substitute for a branded biological product.[17] This version also required a structural comparison of the products on information generally deemed necessary by FDA.[18] It further expanded the scope of what is "interchangeable" by defining the requirement as "comparable" without regard to the principle molecular structural features.

Interchangeability was a contentious issue at hearings on the various legislation. This is because it can be expected that biologics and biosimilars will have minor differences between batches of the same product.[19] In fact, while a small-molecule drug may contain, for example, only 21 atoms, the small molecule will be chemically synthesized and not be expected to vary from batch to batch. In contrast, biologics are manufactured using living cells and may contain more than 25,000 atoms, resulting in a greater expectancy of natural variations.[20] These variations may not affect efficacy, but it forces manufacturers to dedicate significant resources to

15. *Id.*
16. *Id.*
17. H.R. 1038, 110th Cong. § 3(a)(2) (2007).
18. *Id.*
19. *Biosimilar and Interchangeable Biologics: More Treatment Choices*, FDA, https://www.fda.gov/consumers/consumer-updates/biosimilar-and-interchangeable-biologics-more-treatment-choices (last updated Aug. 17, 2023).
20. *Understanding Biologic and Biosimilar Drugs*, Am. Cancer Soc'y (July 27, 2018), https://www.fightcancer.org/policy-resources/understanding-biologic-and-biosimilar-drugs.

ensure their products behave predictably. This predictability was a concern among elected officials and stakeholders.

The length of data and marketing exclusivity for branded biologics was also a hotly contested issue across versions of the legislation.[21] Drafts of the legislation carved out different periods of exclusivity in the interest of satisfying key stakeholders. For example, one version provided 12 years of data exclusivity and two years of market exclusivity, other versions provided four years of data exclusivity followed by eight years of market exclusivity, and yet another version provided five years of market exclusivity for original products and three years for some modified versions of existing drugs.[22] Legislators sought to strike a balance between rewarding reference biologic manufacturers while encouraging follow-on products to reduce drug costs for patients.

As biologics tend to require a lengthy research and development commitment, the length of exclusivity is an important policy consideration in biosimilar legislation. For example, the Biotechnology Innovation Organization advocated for no less than a 14-year exclusivity period in the interest of protecting investments and preserving incentives for biologic innovation.[23] On the other hand, the Obama administration proposed reducing biologic exclusivity to seven years in its budget for fiscal year 2017, as well as including a prohibition on "additional periods of exclusivity for brand biologics due to minor changes in product formulations."[24]

II. Overview of Key Provisions of the BPCIA

The BPCIA reshaped the biosimilar landscape by creating a statutory pathway for FDA to approve follow-on versions of biological reference products.[25] After a 12-year period of market exclusivity for a reference product, FDA may approve a biosimilar product if it has the same primary amino acid sequence and mechanism of action as the reference product,

21. H.R. 1956, 110th Cong. § 2(a)(2) (2007) (proposed PHS Act § 351(k)); S. 1505, 110th Cong. § 2(a)(2) (2007) (proposed PHS Act § 351(k)).

22. Donald Zuhn, *Waxman Introduces Follow-on Biologics Bill*, Patent Docs (Mar. 11, 2009), https://www.patentdocs.org/2009/03/waxman-introduces-followon-biologics-bill.html.

23. *Why Is a Significant Period of Data Exclusivity Necessary in a Pathway for Biosimilars?*, Biotech. Innovation Org., https://archive.bio.org/articles/why-significant-period-data-exclusivity-necessary-pathway-biosimilars (last visited Feb. 2, 2024).

24. Office of the White House, Meeting Our Greatest Challenges: Opportunity for All—The Budget for Fiscal Year 2017, https://obamawhitehouse.archives.gov/sites/default/files/omb/budget/fy2017/assets/opportunity.pdf.

25. FDA, Biosimilars Action Plan: Balancing Innovation and Competition (2018).

and there are no clinically meaningful differences between the reference product and the biosimilar.[26]

The term "reference product" means a biological product licensed by FDA against which FDA evaluates the biological product in a biosimilar application.[27] This is similar to the "reference listed drug" in the Hatch-Waxman context for small-molecule drugs.

The term "biosimilar" or "biosimilarity" means a biological product that is "highly similar" to a reference product "notwithstanding minor differences in clinically inactive components" and a product where there are "no clinically meaningful differences between the biological product and the reference product in terms of the safety, purity, and potency of the product."[28]

The term "interchangeable" or "interchangeability" means a biological product that may be "substituted for the reference product without the intervention of the health care provider who prescribed the reference product."[29] The sponsor of an interchangeable product must demonstrate the biosimilar will produce the same clinical result as the reference product in any given patient and the risk of switching between use of the interchangeable product and a reference product will not be greater than the risk of using the reference product without switching.[30]

Key provisions of the BPCIA include those related to (1) ensuring the relevant product is safe for use based on its similarity to a reference product; and (2) a streamlined litigation process by which to resolve any disputes over patent infringement. As explained above, grappling with the safety of complex biosimilar products was a significant hurdle to adopting a regulatory scheme that mirrors approval of small-molecule generics.

The BPCIA ensures biosimilar products are safe for marketing by requiring studies demonstrating similarity to a reference product on the market. An application filed using this accelerated pathway is termed an "abbreviated biological license application," or "aBLA." Any person may submit an aBLA if the application includes information demonstrating the proposed product (1) is biosimilar to a reference product; (2) utilizes the same "mechanism or mechanisms of action" as the reference product for the condition or conditions prescribed; (3) treats the condition or conditions previously approved for the reference product; (4) has the same route of

---

26. Hannah Koyfman, *Biosimilarity and Interchangeability in the Biologics Price Competition and Innovation Act of 2009 and FDA's 2012 Draft Guidance for Industry*, 32 BIOTECH. L. REP. 238 (2013), https://doi.org/10.1089/blr.2013.9884.

27. 42 U.S.C. § 262(k)(2)(A)(i)(I).

28. *Id.* § 262(i)(2)(A)–(B) (2010).

29. *Id.* § 262(k)(4)(A) (2010).

30. *Id.*

administration and strength of dose as the reference product; and (5) is manufactured in a facility that meets adequate safety standards.[31]

FDA evaluates the first factor—similarity to the reference product—through analytical studies demonstrating the new product is "highly similar" to the reference product "notwithstanding minor differences in clinically inactive components."[32] Sponsors of a biosimilar application, in addition to analytical studies, must also provide animal studies on the assessment of toxicity and a clinical study or studies sufficient to demonstrate "safety, purity, and potency" in one or more appropriate conditions of use for which the reference product is licensed. FDA, however, may determine that an analytical study, animal study, or clinical study is unnecessary to lessen the burden on applicants depending on the biosimilar.[33]

Market exclusivity is a key feature of the BPCIA. As with small-molecule branded and generic products, market exclusivity serves as a substantial incentive for manufacturers to be the first to develop a branded biologic product or a biosimilar product. For instance, small-molecule compounds governed by the Hatch-Waxman Act are entitled to a new chemical entity exclusivity after approval, during which period a generic applicant cannot file an ANDA referencing its data.[34] Similarly, the BPCIA grants branded biologic products a four-year period of data exclusivity during which a biosimilar applicant cannot file an aBLA relying on that product's research and development data to establish the safety of their product. The BPCIA also includes a longer 12-year total period of market exclusivity from the date of licensure of the branded product during which the FDA, although allowed to receive an aBLA, will not approve another biosimilar application.[35]

The Hatch-Waxman Act provides a special incentive—a period of 180 days of exclusive marketing rights—to the first generic to challenge patents and succeed in entering the market early. The BPCIA, likewise, offers special protection to sponsors who demonstrate their biosimilar is interchangeable with a reference product. If deemed interchangeable, the biosimilar will receive up to one year of exclusivity over subsequent biosimilar applicants,[36] and likely higher profits as pharmacies can substitute the interchangeable biosimilar without consulting a health care provider.[37] Congress instructed FDA to not approve another biosimilar product as

31. *Id.* § 262(k)(2)(A)(i)–(v).
32. *Id.* § 262(i)(1).
33. *Id.* § 262(k)(2)(A)(ii).
34. 21 U.S.C. § 355(c)(3)(E)(ii).
35. 42 U.S.C. § 262(k)(7)(A).
36. *Id.* § 262(k)(6).
37. *Id.* § 262(i)(3).

interchangeable until the earlier of (1) one year after the first commercial marketing of the first relevant interchangeable biosimilar biological product; (2) 18 months after a final court decision or dismissal with or without prejudice against the applicant of the first approved interchangeable biosimilar biological product; (3) 42 months after approval of the first interchangeable biosimilar product where the applicant is in ongoing litigation; or (4) 18 months after approval of the first interchangeable biosimilar product if the applicant has not been sued.

This means the first interchangeable biosimilar on the market has exclusivity among competing biosimilar developers from one year to three and a half years depending on whether they are challenged through litigation. This ensures a manufacturer will not lose their exclusivity due to litigation.

Although FDA has provided guidance to address some aspects of biosimilar approvals, it has adopted a "totality of evidence" approach to provide flexibility in the requirements for specific biosimilar applications. This results in a case-by-case evaluation of whether a biosimilar is in fact "highly similar" to the original product. The Secretary of FDA has significant authority to issue guidance documents regarding biologic licensing after a period of public comment, and FDA has issued several guidance documents regarding different aspects of the biosimilar regulatory pathway.

A. The Patent Dance

The filing of a biosimilar application is considered a technical act of infringement that gives rise to a cause of action for patent infringement if the application seeks approval of the biosimilar for the commercial manufacture, use, or sale of the biosimilar prior to the expiration of the reference product's patents. Of course, a suit must be filed and an ultimate adjudication of actual infringement must occur before there is any liability determined or relief granted.

The Hatch-Waxman Act requires NDA holders to identify any relevant patents covering a branded drug in an electronic database the FDA operates, called Approved Drug Products with Therapeutic Equivalence Evaluations (aka the "Orange Book"), where relevant patents are every patent that claims the "drug" or "method of using [the] drug" and for which a claim of patent infringement could reasonably be asserted. The BPCIA has no such provision or such repository of information.[38] And while FDA does publish an online database called the "Purple Book," more formally called Lists of Licensed Biological Products with Reference Product Exclusivity and Biosimilarity or Interchangeability Evaluations, this Purple

38. 21 U.S.C. § 355(b)(1).

Book does not always contain any of the patent and non-patent exclusivity information provided in the Orange Book. One exception to the lack of a requirement to list relevant patents is that patents that have been identified by the reference product sponsor during the patent dance, discussed in this section, are now required to be listed in the Purple Book. Consequently, the first aBLA applicants to develop a biosimilar for a given reference product often have to engage in patent landscape analyses ahead of product development to determine what patents may be asserted against it by the reference product sponsor. This puts aBLA applicants at a disadvantage compared to ANDA applicants, as there is uncertainty regarding the number and types of patents the aBLA applicant may face in an infringement suit filed by the reference product sponsor.

The Hatch-Waxman Act also requires ANDA applicants to send notice to the NDA holder and patent(s) owner of Orange Book-listed patents when an ANDA includes a challenge to one or more of the Orange Book-listed patents as being invalid and/or not be infringed by the proposed ANDA product.[39] That challenge is commonly called a "Paragraph IV certification." The valuable 180-day generic exclusivity is awarded to the first generic company to file an ANDA containing a Paragraph IV certification. FDA publishes an online database that tracks all first ANDA filings containing a Paragraph IV certification for a given branded drug. This list allows stakeholders to gain insight into the potential number of generics that could initially enter the market with 180-day marketing exclusivity. The BPCIA does not have a similar Paragraph IV certification provision, nor does FDA publish any list identifying how many aBLAs it has received for a given reference product. Biosimilar applicants, therefore, can be left guessing how many potential biosimilar competitors may enter the market, unless aBLA applicants have made any of their clinical studies related to their aBLA public.[40]

Those Hatch-Waxman Act provisions discussed earlier that are not found in the BPCIA are possible areas that Congress could consider amending into the BPCIA to provide further harmonization with the Hatch-Waxman Act that would aid aBLA filers in the future.

And while the BPCIA does not have a patent-listing requirement, like that provided in the Hatch-Waxman Act, to streamline infringement litigation over biosimilar marketing, the BPCIA provides a framework—colloquially known as the "patent dance"—for biosimilar applicants and

39. *Id.* § 355(j)(2)(A)(vii)(IV).

40. Clinical trials are listed at clinicaltrials.gov. Biosimilar applicants may also announce their progress with clinical trials and when they submit their aBLA or when their aBLAs are accepted for review.

reference product sponsors to exchange confidential information concerning a biosimilar application, address infringement issues, and set the stage for potential litigation to clear uncertainties early in the approval process. The patent dance is discussed in detail in Chapter 4.

Although the patent dance is not mandatory,[41] there are several advantages to this bifurcated infringement litigation system. First, the system exists to encourage the parties to settle their dispute without infringement litigation. The collaborative exchange of patent lists and defenses prior to the filing of an action furthers this objective. Second, if a biosimilar applicant opts out of the system, they lose several beneficial protections like a damages clock and ability to bring their own action in the second phase of litigation. The reference product sponsors must bring the first phase of litigation within 30 days after the end of the patent dance information exchange process or risk a limitation on damages that follow,[42] and the biosimilar applicant may not start the second round of litigation with a declaratory judgment action if they opt out of this resolution system.[43]

B. Impact of the BPCIA

The BPCIA has had a considerable impact on the development and approvals of biologics. FDA released a Biosimilars Action Plan in 2018 with the goal of encouraging innovation and competition among biologics.[44] Key elements of the plan included:

1. Developing and implementing new FDA review tools, such as standardized review templates that are tailored to marketing applications for biosimilars and interchangeable products, to improve the efficiency of FDA review and enhance the public information about FDA's evaluation of these products.
2. Creating information resources and development tools for sponsors of biosimilar applications to maximize the scientific and regulatory clarity for the biosimilar product development community. This includes enhancing the Purple Book to include more information about approved biological products, including information relating to reference product exclusivity.
3. Developing effective communications to improve understanding of biosimilars among patients, clinicians, and insurers.

---

41. Sandoz Inc. v. Amgen Inc., 582 U.S. 1 (2017).
42. 35 U.S.C. § 271(e)(6).
43. 42 U.S.C. § 262(l)(9)(C).
44. *Biological Product Innovation and Competition*, FDA, https://www.fda.gov/drugs/biosimilars/biological-product-innovation-and-competition (last updated Mar. 7, 2023).

4. Publishing final or revised draft guidance on biosimilar product labeling to assist sponsors in determining what data and information should be included in the labeling.

Since release of this plan, FDA has expanded access to biosimilar information in its Purple Book. Under the Biological Product Patent Transparency amendments to the BPCIA passed as part of the Consolidated Appropriations Act in 2021,[45] FDA began listing the patents owned or licensed exclusively by the reference product sponsor and previously identified as part of the patent dance. Publication of the Purple Book by FDA is also now mandatory.[46]

Analysts have observed several trends in biosimilar development and approval since passage of the BPCIA. The rate of biosimilar approval has modestly increased in recent years as developers see biosimilars as a lucrative investment opportunity. In 2022, FDA approved seven biosimilar products, up from one in 2015 and three in 2016.[47] To date, FDA has approved 45 biosimilars within the product classes of (1) insulin; (2) granulocyte colony-stimulating factor; (3) monoclonal antibodies; and (4) tumor necrosis factor-alpha (TNF-α).

---

45. Pub. L. No. 116-260, 134 Stat. 1182 (2020).
46. 42 U.S.C. § 262(k)(9)(A)(iii)–(iv).
47. *Biosimilar Product Information*, FDA, https://www.fda.gov/drugs/biosimilars/biosimilar-product-information (last updated Dec. 8, 2023).

chapter 3

FDA Approval and Regulatory Process*

Biological products—or "biologics"—meet the statutory definition of "drug" and thus are subject to strict regulation to ensure that a product both is safe to administer to and provides some therapeutic benefit for patients. The term "biologic" is broad, encompassing a wide range of products, including many of the newest cutting-edge technologies, and both new biological products and follow-on biologics, called "biosimilars," and their substitutable counterparts, "interchangeable biosimilars," fall under the biologic rubric. There are, however, very different licensing requirements for each type of biologic application. With those licensing requirements come certain data exclusivity and intellectual property considerations, which again differ depending on the type of biologic application, and which differ significantly from the parallel process for small molecules. Consequently, understanding the application process for biological products, the requirements for licensure, the related regulatory scheme for both new and biosimilars, and the available exclusivities is critical to understanding a client's needs and considerations with respect to the biosimilar litigation practice.

I. Background

Biologics fall under the purview of the U.S. Food and Drug Administration (FDA). FDA has authority to regulate any products that meet the definition of "drug," which includes both products that are subject to the Federal Food, Drug, and Cosmetic Act (FDC Act) and the Public Health Service Act (PHS Act).[1] The FDC Act defines the broader category of drugs as follows:

*Sara Koblitz, Hyman, Phelps & McNamara P.C.

1. Pub. L. No. 75-717, 52 Stat. 1040 (1938); Pub. L. No. 78-410, ch. 373, 58 Stat. 682 (1944).

> (A) articles recognized in the official United States Pharmacopoeia, official Homoeopathic Pharmacopoeia of the United States, or official National Formulary, or any supplement to any of them; and (B) articles intended for use in the diagnosis, cure, mitigation, treatment, or prevention of disease in man or other animals; and (C) articles (other than food) intended to affect the structure or any function of the body of man or other animals; and (D) articles intended for use as a component of any article specified in clause (A), (B), or (C).[2]

Any product meeting this definition is subject to FDA regulation under title 21 of the *Code of Federal Regulations*, which houses all of the regulations implementing the agency's governing statutes.

While FDA's general regulatory authority arises from the FDC Act, the PHS Act sets forth the agency's authority to regulate a subset of products that meet the FDC Act definition of "drug." Those drugs are known as "biological products" or "biologics," defined as "a virus, therapeutic serum, toxin, antitoxin, vaccine, blood, blood component or derivative, allergenic product, protein, or analogous product, or arsphenamine or derivative of arsphenamine (or any other trivalent organic arsenic compound), applicable to the prevention, treatment, or cure of a disease or condition of human beings."[3]

FDA regulations and policies have established that biological products include blood-derived products, vaccines, in vivo diagnostic allergenic products, immunoglobulin products, products containing cells or microorganisms, and most protein products.[4] These drugs are typically larger, more complex molecules than other drugs regulated by FDA and are made from living sources, like bacteria, yeast, and animal cells.[5] Because they are made from living sources, there often are many variations from batch to batch, rendering them more complicated to purify, process, and manufacture.[6] And because each variation can dramatically affect the characteristics of a given biologic, FDA regulates and licenses both the biological product itself, as well as its manufacturing process.

Rather than assess biologics for "safety and effectiveness," as it does for small-molecule drugs, FDA assesses biologics based on their safety,

---

2. 21 U.S.C. § 321(g).
3. 42 U.S.C. § 262(i).
4. *Frequently Asked Questions about Therapeutic Biological Products*, FDA, https://www.fda.gov/drugs/therapeutic-biologics-applications-bla/frequently-asked-questions-about-therapeutic-biological-products (last updated July 7, 2015).
5. *Overview for Health Care Professionals*, FDA, https://www.fda.gov/drugs/biosimilars/overview-health-care-professionals (last updated Jan. 1, 2024).
6. *Id.*

purity, and potency.[7] To that end, biological products are evaluated and licensed by FDA on the basis of a demonstration that the biological product is, and the facility used in its manufacture meets standards to ensure that the product is, "safe, pure, and potent."[8] While not defined by statute, FDA regulations define each of these terms in turn. "Safety" is the "relative freedom from harmful effect to persons affected, directly or indirectly, by a product when prudently administered."[9] "Purity" is defined as "relative freedom from extraneous matter in the finished product, whether or not harmful to the recipient or deleterious to the product."[10] "Potency" is akin to efficacy, "interpreted to mean the specific ability or capacity of the product, as indicated by appropriate laboratory tests or by adequately controlled clinical data obtained through the administration of the product in the manner intended, to effect a given result."[11] FDA requires extensive data submitted in an application for licensure to assess safety, purity, and potency of both biologics and follow-on biosimilars.[12]

II. Types of Biological Products

As noted, the PHS Act defines "biological product" as "a virus, therapeutic serum, toxin, antitoxin, vaccine, blood, blood component or derivative, allergenic product, protein, or analogous product, or arsphenamine or derivative of arsphenamine (or any other trivalent organic arsenic compound), applicable to the prevention, treatment, or cure of a disease or condition of human beings."[13] This definition has been integrated into FDA regulations, which provide more detail on each of the aforementioned types of biological product.[14]

At the outset, a product only meets the definition of a "biological product" if that product is "deemed *applicable to the prevention, treatment, or cure of diseases or injuries of man*."[15] FDA's implementing regulations explain that the mode of administration or application of the product is irrelevant; in other words, the product need not be specifically used to *treat* disease or injury. It can still be a biological product even if the product only is "intended . . . as an aid in diagnosis, or in evaluating the degree of

7. 42 U.S.C. § 262(a)(2).
8. *Id.*
9. 21 C.F.R. § 600.3(p) (2024).
10. *Id.* § 600.3(r).
11. *Id.* § 600.3(s).
12. 42 U.S.C. § 262(a)(2).
13. *Id.* § 262(i).
14. 21 C.F.R. § 600.3 (2024).
15. *Id.* § 600.3(j) (emphasis added).

susceptibility or immunity possessed by a person, and including also any other use for purposes of diagnosis," assuming a biological product is used to either prepare or aid in the preparation of the diagnostic substance.[16]

Because the statutorily enumerated types of biological products are open to interpretation, FDA has adopted specific definitions of several of these types. Under FDA's implementing regulations:

- A *virus* is interpreted to be a product containing the minute living cause of an infectious disease and includes but is not limited to filterable viruses, bacteria, rickettsia, fungi, and protozoa.[17]
- A *therapeutic serum* is a product obtained from blood by removing the clot or clot components and the blood cells.[18]
- A *toxin* is a product containing a soluble substance poisonous to laboratory animals or to man in doses of 1 milliliter or less (or equivalent in weight) of the product, and having the property, following the injection of nonfatal doses into an animal, of causing to be produced therein another soluble substance which specifically neutralizes the poisonous substance and which is demonstrable in the serum of the animal thus immunized.[19]
- An *antitoxin* is a product containing the soluble substance in serum or other body fluid of an immunized animal which specifically neutralizes the toxin against which the animal is immune.[20]
- *Blood* means a product that is a fluid containing dissolved and suspended elements which was collected from the vascular system of a human.[21]
- *Blood component* means a product containing a part of blood separated by physical or mechanical means.[22]
- *Allergenic Products* are products that are administered to man for the diagnosis, prevention or treatment of allergies.[23]
- *Trivalent organic arsenicals* means arsphenamine and its derivatives (or any other trivalent organic arsenic

16. *Id.*
17. *Id.* § 600.3(h)(1) (emphasis added).
18. *Id.* § 600.3(h)(2) (emphasis added).
19. *Id.* § 600.3(h)(3) (emphasis added).
20. *Id.* § 600.3(h)(4) (emphasis added).
21. *Id.* § 630.3(a).
22. *Id.* § 630.3(b).
23. *Id.* § 680.1(a) (emphasis added).

> compound) applicable to the prevention, treatment, or cure of diseases or injuries of man.[24]

FDA has not promulgated a regulatory definition of "vaccine," and while FDA has codified definitions of "protein" and "analogous product," these definitions are somewhat more complicated.

A. Protein

Until the passage of the Biologics Price Competition and Innovation Act (BPCIA)[25] in 2010, a "protein" could be regulated as either a small molecule under section 505 of the FDC Act (21 U.S.C. § 355) or section 351 of the PHS Act (42 U.S.C. § 262). Though the majority of proteins were licensed as biologics, the dividing line between drug or biologic was unclear.[26] With the BPCIA, lines were drawn, as Congress amended the definition of "biological product" specifically to include a "protein (except any chemically synthesized polypeptide)."[27] "Protein," in turn, was defined as "any alpha amino acid polymer with a specific, defined sequence that is greater than 40 amino acids in size."[28] In 2020, however, Congress removed the exception for chemically synthesized polypeptides, such that now *all* polypeptides with 40 or more amino acids, regardless of how they are made, are regulated as a biological product.[29]

The BPCIA provided a ten-year transition period during which proteins could be approved either under the FDC Act or the PHS Act unless FDA had already approved the proposed product under the PHS Act.[30] At the end of that ten-year period, all new drug applications (NDAs) for proteins approved under the FDC Act transitioned to biologics license applications (BLAs) approved under the PHS Act, called "deemed BLAs," and all new protein products were required to seek approval as biologics under a BLA pursuant to the PHS Act.[31]

---

24. *Id.* § 600.3(h)(6)(i).

25. Pub. L. No. 111-148, §§ 7001–7003, 124 Stat. 119, 804–21 (2010).

26. *See* Definition of the Term "Biological Product," 85 Fed. Reg. 10,057, 10,058 (Feb. 21, 2020) ("The BPCI Act clarified the statutory authority under which certain protein products are to be regulated.").

27. Pub. L. No. 11-148, § 7002(b)(1).

28. Definition of the Term "Biological Product," 83 Fed. Reg. 63,817, 63,817 (proposed Dec. 12, 2018).

29. Further Consolidated Appropriations Act, Pub. L. No. 116-94, § 605, 133 Stat. 2534, 3127 (2019).

30. Pub. L. No. 11-148, § 7002(e)(1)–(3). If a molecule was already approved under the PHS Act, any application for the same molecule must have been filed under the PHS Act.

31. *Id.* § 7002(e)(4).

On March 23, 2020, that transition occurred and approximately 85 products previously approved under the FDC Act were "deemed" biologics.[32] That transition was not without issue, however. Several manufacturers sued FDA over its interpretation of the term "protein." Immediately after the transition date, Teva Pharmaceuticals Industries Ltd. and Teva Pharmaceuticals USA, Inc. sued FDA in the District Court of the District of Columbia challenging the agency's failure to transition its Copaxone (glatiramer acetate) to a deemed BLA on the transition date.[33] Teva argued that Copaxone meets the statutory definition of "biological product" given that the product is a chemically synthesized polypeptide with an average length of 40 to 100 amino acids. FDA, however, noted that the regulations define "protein" to have more than 40 amino acids in "specific, defined sequence"; because Copaxone does not have such a sequence, it could not be a protein, argued FDA.[34] The court deferred to FDA's interpretation.[35]

Three years later, Ipsen sued FDA over the same provision. This time, Ipsen argued that the agency's decision to regulate Ipsen's Somatuline Depot (lanreotide acetate) as a drug under the FDC Act rather than a biological product under the PHS Act was arbitrary and capricious because its *finished drug product* had more than 40 amino acids; in contrast, FDA made its assessment of "protein" based on the *active ingredient*.[36] A synthetic octapeptide available as ready-to-use prefilled syringes for deep subcutaneous injection, Somatuline Depot consists of only eight amino acids linked in a polypeptide chain, but it contains multiple copies of its active ingredient that are linked together "in a manner that occurs in nature" to form a "nanotube" greater than 40 amino acids long.[37] Ipsen argued that FDA should look to the nanotube—not the individual active ingredient—to determine whether a given product meets the 40 amino acid definition of "protein." FDA disagreed with Ipsen's approach to defining a protein and took the position that the finished product form (i.e., the nanotube) is irrelevant because it is the "active ingredient" that is the relevant peptide for consideration of a "protein." Because the active ingredient of Somatuline Depot is *not* the nanotube but is the eight amino acids linked in the polypeptide chain, FDA argued that Somatuline Depot is not a protein and is

32. FDA, List of Approved NDAs for Biological Products That Were Deemed to Be BLAs on March 23, 2020, https://www.fda.gov/media/119229/download.

33. Complaint, Teva Pharms. USA, Inc. v. FDA, No. 1:20-cv-00808 (D.D.C. Mar. 24, 2020), ECF No. 1.

34. Memorandum Opinion, Teva Pharms. USA, Inc. v. FDA, No. 1:20-cv-00808 (D.D.C. Dec. 31, 2020), ECF No. 54 [hereinafter Teva Opinion].

35. *Id.*

36. Memorandum Opinion, Ipsen Biopharms., Inc. v. Becerra, No. 1-22-cv-00860 (D.D.C. May 8, 2023), ECF No. 42 [hereinafter Ipsen Opinion].

37. *Id.*

appropriately regulated as a drug product under the FDC Act. Ultimately, the court agreed with FDA.

The court found that FDA's determination that Ipsen's Somatuline Depot is not a biologic was consistent with the regulation's plain language and reflects rational decision-making. The court explained that "neither the statute nor the regulatory definition of a 'protein' *requires* the FDA to consider the size of the active ingredient as it appears in the final drug product, rather than standing alone."[38] Instead, FDA's decision to assess the active ingredient based on what "confers [its] pharmacologic activity" "was unambiguously correct"—and even if it were not, the court stated it would "defer to the FDA's interpretation as reasonable" because it falls within FDA's area of special expertise.[39]

As a result of these two cases, a protein unambiguously requires the *active ingredient* to contain a *specific*, *defined sequence* of 40 or more amino acids.

B. Analogous Product

Finally, under FDA's implementing regulations, whether a product is "analogous" for purposes of determining whether it is a biologic depends on the type of product used as the comparator.[40] A product is analogous to a virus if it is "prepared from or with a virus or agent actually or potentially infectious, without regard to the degree of virulence or toxicogenicity of the specific strain used."[41] It is analogous to a therapeutic serum "if composed of whole blood or plasma or containing some organic constituent or product other than a hormone or an amino acid, derived from whole blood, plasma, or serum."[42] If a product is intended to be analogous to a toxin or antitoxin, it must be, "irrespective of its source of origin," "applicable to the prevention, treatment, or cure of disease or injuries of man through a specific immune process."[43]

FDA has not promulgated regulations describing what it means to be "analogous" to a "protein" and specifically did not do so when updating its regulations to include a definition of a "protein."[44] At that time, in response to a comment urging FDA to "propose a regulatory definition of products that are 'analogous' to a protein and therefore are biological products,"

38. *Id.* at 21.
39. *Id.* at 21, 23.
40. 21 C.F.R. § 600.3(h)(5) (2024).
41. *Id.* § 600.3(h)(5)(i).
42. *Id.* § 600.3(h)(5)(ii).
43. *Id.* § 600.3(h)(5)(iii).
44. Definition of the Term "Biological Product," 85 Fed. Reg. 10,057, 10,057 (Feb. 21, 2020).

FDA declined, noting that it was "outside the scope of this rulemaking."[45] All FDA said on the issue is that "it would not be appropriate for the statutory term 'analogous product' to be interpreted in a way that would include products that are specifically excluded by this final rule."[46]

With no definition of "analogous product" for proteins, the same litigation that challenged the meaning of the term "protein" also challenged FDA's *lack* of definition of an analogous protein. As arguments in the alternative (i.e., if the courts upheld FDA's determination that neither product met the definition of a protein), both Teva and Ipsen asserted that their products—a product without a "specific, defined sequence" and a nanotube with eight amino acids in repetition respectively—were "analogous" to a protein.[47] In both cases, FDA took the position that the products at issue could not be analogous to proteins because such an interpretation would include amino acid polymers that are specifically excluded by the interpretation of the term "protein" in FDA's final rule.[48]

The courts agreed with FDA: a product that was decisively *not a protein* could not be considered a protein under the "analogous" provision. In the Copaxone case, FDA stated that it "would not consider an amino acid polymer that does not have a specific, defined sequence to be 'analogous' to a protein."[49] Instead, FDA explained that the term "analogous" was intended to address substances and mixtures composed "at least in part of a protein with a specific, defined sequence" even if the "protein component" is in "low levels or unknown amounts."[50] The District Court for the District of Columbia distilled that explanation to mean that FDA "appears to understand the 'analogous product' category as a narrow residual provision" for products that satisfy the regulatory definitions of each category in *most* ways but are not an *exact* fit.[51] One example, the court cited, is a protein that includes one or more non-biological products that contribute to the product's activity.[52] Such products are "analogous" to proteins "because their protein components are 'necessary . . . to achieving the intended therapeutic effect,' but they are not simply 'proteins' because their non-biological product components also contribute to their efficacy."[53] In the case at hand, FDA determined that Copaxone does not contain any component with a "specific, defined sequence," and therefore it could not

45. *Id.* at 10,061.
46. *Id.*
47. Teva Opinion, *supra* note 34, at 20; Ipsen Opinion, *supra* note 36, at 27.
48. Teva Opinion, *supra* note 34, at 20.
49. *Id.* at 65.
50. *Id.* at 65–66.
51. *Id.* at 71–72.
52. *Id.* at 72.
53. *Id.*

be considered either a protein or "analogous" to one.[54] In turn, the court held that, though FDA's definition of the "analogous product" provision is "not well-defined or well-explained," the determination that an analogous protein must have a "specific, defined sequence" of amino acids is reasonable and thus could stand.[55]

In the case of Somatuline Depot, the District Court for the District of Columbia reiterated the same conclusion: "it would not be appropriate to interpret the statutory term . . . in a way that would include amino acid polymers that are specifically excluded by the interpretation of the term 'protein' set forth in FDA's [Biological Product Definition Final Rule]."[56] Thus, the court held that Somatuline Depot, based on its active ingredient with only eight amino acids, is "in no way comparable or 'analogous' to a protein, which is 40 or more amino acids in size."[57] Notably, in this case, Ipsen implicitly took the position that the term "analogous product" in the statute must be defined to include at least one product analogous to each and every discrete type of biological product in the statute. The court flatly rejected that position.[58]

While FDA has not clearly established what it means to be "analogous" to a protein, it has firmly established what it does not mean: if expressly excluded from the definition of protein, a product cannot be "analogous" to one.

III. Licensure of Biologics, Biosimilars, and Interchangeables

FDA licenses under the statute (or, more colloquially, approves) a given biological product pursuant to a BLA for a new product, often called a "reference product," or an abbreviated BLA (aBLA) for a biosimilar.[59] Biosimilars, in turn, can include both biosimilars, which are "highly similar" to a product licensed under a BLA, and "interchangeable" biosimilars, which have been demonstrated to be so similar to its reference product that it can be substituted for that product without the intervention of a health care provider.[60] Each has its own requirements for submission.

54. *Id.*
55. *Id.* at 67.
56. Ipsen Opinion, *supra* note 36, at 27.
57. *Id.* at 29–30.
58. *Id.*
59. 42 U.S.C. § 262(a), (k), (i)(4).
60. *Id.* § 262(i)(2), (3).

A. BLAs

Novel products that fall under the statutory definition of a "biological product," which became known as reference products after the passage of the BPCIA, require licensure of a BLA under section 351 of the PHS Act, which serves as a "request for permission to introduce, or deliver for introduction, a biologic product into interstate commerce."[61] Pursuant to 21 C.F.R. § 601.2, a manufacturer must submit a BLA and all its requisite parts to FDA through its Center for Biologics Evaluation and Research (CBER) or the Center for Drug Evaluation and Research (CDER) based on the type of product approval that is sought.[62] CDER has responsibility for monoclonal antibodies for in vivo use, cytokines, growth factors, enzymes, immunomodulators, thrombolytics, proteins intended for therapeutic use that are extracted from animals or microorganisms (including recombinant versions of these products with the exception of clotting factors), and other non-vaccine therapeutic immunotherapies. Other biological products, including blood products and vaccines, are the responsibility of CBER.[63]

In addition to administrative documents like an application form, a BLA must include all data necessary to demonstrate safety and potency of the proposed product. This includes data derived from nonclinical studies performed in accordance with FDA's requirement for Good Laboratory Practices[64] and clinical studies that demonstrate the proposed product is safe and effective.[65] FDA expects to see "substantial evidence of effectiveness" in order to support BLA licensure, which typically requires at least two adequate and well-controlled clinical investigations, which usually are conducted under an investigational new drug application (IND).[66] Financial certifications and/or disclosure statements for clinical investigators must be included as part of the BLA, and each human clinical study should comply with FDA regulations for institutional review and informed consent.[67]

---

61. *Biologics License Applications (BLA) Process (CBER)*, FDA, https://www.fda.gov/vaccines-blood-biologics/development-approval-process-cber/biologics-license-applications-bla-process-cber (last updated Jan. 27, 2021).

62. *Transfer of Therapeutic Biological Products to the Center for Drug Evaluation and Research*, FDA, https://www.fda.gov/combination-products/jurisdictional-information/transfer-therapeutic-biological-products-center-drug-evaluation-and-research (last updated Mar. 7, 2022).

63. *Id.*

64. *See* 21 C.F.R. pt. 58 (2024).

65. *Id.* § 601.2(a).

66. FDA, Draft Guidance for Industry: Demonstrating Substantial Evidence of Effectiveness for Human Drug and Biological Products 4 (2019), https://www.fda.gov/media/133660/download.

67. 21 C.F.R. § 601.2(a) (2024); *see also id.* pt. 56; *id.* pt. 50.

Equally important as clinical studies demonstrating safety and potency is the Chemistry, Manufacturing, and Controls section of a BLA, which is used to assess purity. There, FDA requires the submission of a full description of all manufacturing methods, data establishing the stability of the product through the proposed dating period, summaries of testing results, and representative samples of the proposed product for introduction into interstate commerce.[68] BLAs must also include samples of product labeling, enclosures, and containers.[69] The manufacturing process is subject to significant scrutiny because changes or inconsistencies in the manufacturing process can cause changes to the biological product. In addition to data review, FDA performs an inspection of the manufacturing facility to ensure that the relevant establishments comply with the standards established in the BLA and the requirements prescribed in applicable regulations.[70]

Finally, under the Pediatric Research Equity Act (PREA),[71] BLAs for new active ingredients, new indications, new dosing regimens, or new routes of administration are required to contain a pediatric assessment to support administration of the product to pediatric patients.[72] Specifically, a pediatric assessment contains data from pediatric studies for various pediatric age groups to assess the safety and effectiveness of the proposed biological product for the claimed indications in relevant pediatric subpopulations, and to support dosing and administration for each pediatric subpopulation for which the biological product has been assessed to be safe and effective.[73] Such studies are mandatory unless the requirement is waived, deferred, or inapplicable.[74]

B. Biosimilars and aBLAs

Statutorily created in 2010 under the BPCIA,[75] biosimilar applications are "abbreviated" BLAs in that they do not require submission of all of the elements of a BLA. This is because a biosimilar application, or an aBLA, relies on FDA's existing knowledge about the safety, purity, and potency

68. *Id.* § 601.2(a).

69. *Id.*

70. *Id.* § 601.20(c), (d).

71. Pub. L. No. 108-155, 117 Stat. 1936 (2003).

72. 21 U.S.C. § 355c(a)(1)(A)(ii).

73. FDA, Draft Guidance for Industry: Pediatric Drug Development: Regulatory Considerations—Complying with the Pediatric Research Equity Act and Qualifying for Pediatric Exclusivity under the Best Pharmaceuticals for Children Act 10–11 (2023), https://www.fda.gov/media/168201/download.

74. 21 U.S.C. § 355c(a)(4), (5).

75. Pub. L. No. 111-148, §§ 7001–7003.

of the reference product to support licensure.[76] An aBLA therefore must reference a biologic approved under a BLA pursuant to section 351(a) of the PHS Act—again, the "reference product"—and include information "to show that the [proposed product] is biosimilar to the reference product."[77] Biosimilarity means that the proposed product is "highly similar to the reference product notwithstanding minor differences in clinically inactive components" and that "there are no clinically meaningful differences between the [proposed product] and the reference product in terms of the safety, purity, and potency of the product."[78] A biosimilar, however, is not substitutable for its reference product unless it is "interchangeable," which requires additional testing.[79]

Biosimilars are licensed under section 351(k) of the PHS Act, which requires the submission of an application including data demonstrating biosimilarity to the reference product to the FDA division that reviewed and approved the corresponding reference product.[80] While FDA has not defined the key terms "highly similar" or "clinically meaningful" in regulation, FDA has set forth various factors that it uses to determine whether products meet the statutory requirements.[81] Importantly, the showing needed to demonstrate biosimilarity to a reference product is significantly more rigorous than the bioequivalence standard used for generic drugs under the FDC Act. Rather than demonstrating mere equivalence in terms of bioavailability, equivalent safety and effectiveness must be demonstrated for approval of a biosimilar product.

Though the aBLA need not include "substantial evidence of effectiveness," it still must include clinical studies sufficient to demonstrate safety,

---

76. FDA, Guidance for Industry: Scientific Considerations in Demonstrating Biosimilarity to a Reference Product 3–4 (2015) [hereinafter Scientific Considerations in Demonstrating Biosimilarity Guidance], https://www.fda.gov/media/82647/download.

77. 42 U.S.C. § 262(k)(3).

78. *Id.* § 262(i)(2).

79. *Id.* § 262(i)(3).

80. *Id.* § 262(k)(2)(A); *id.* § 262(k)(5)(B).

81. *See, e.g.*, FDA, Guidance for Industry: Quality Considerations in Demonstrating Biosimilarity of a Therapeutic Protein Product to a Reference Product (2015), https://www.fda.gov/media/135612/download; Scientific Considerations in Demonstrating Biosimilarity Guidance, *supra* note 76; FDA, Guidance for Industry: Clinical Pharmacology Data to Support a Demonstration of Biosimilarity to a Reference Product (2016), https://www.fda.gov/media/88622/download; FDA, Draft Guidance for Industry: Development of Therapeutic Protein Biosimilars: Comparative Analytical Assessment and Other Quality-Related Considerations (2019), https://www.fda.gov/media/159261/download; FDA, Draft Guidance for Industry: Biosimilars and Interchangeable Biosimilars: Licensure for Fewer Than All Conditions of Use for Which the Reference Product Has Been Licensed (2020) [hereinafter Biosimilars and Interchangeable Biosimilars Guidance], https://www.fda.gov/media/134932/download; FDA, Draft Guidance for Industry: Biosimilarity and Interchangeability: Additional Draft Q&As on Biosimilar Development and the BPCI Act (rev. 1, 2023) [hereinafter Biosimilars Additional Q&A Guidance], https://www.fda.gov/media/172169/download.

purity, and potency in one or more conditions of use for which the reference product is licensed.[82] To that end, an aBLA must include data derived from analytical studies, toxicity assessments, clinical studies, or, where necessary, animal studies, all of which are at FDA's discretion.[83] These studies however are more limited in nature than a full BLA and may consist only of assessments of immunogenicity and pharmacokinetics or pharmacodynamics.[84] The aBLA must also include publicly available information regarding FDA's determination that the reference product relied on for approval is safe and effective[85] and may include "any additional information in support of the application, including publicly-available information with respect to the reference product or another biological product."[86]

It is important to note that the proposed biosimilar need not be exactly the same as its reference product, but it must be the same as its reference product in specific ways. The proposed product must "utilize the same mechanism or mechanisms of action" as the reference product.[87] The conditions of use in the labeling must have been approved for the reference product—though the biosimilars need not be approved for every use that its reference product is.[88] Additionally, the proposed product must have the same route of administration, dosage form, and strength as its reference product, and changes to any of those elements is not approvable as part of an aBLA; a new BLA or supplement to a BLA would be required to make any such changes.[89] And, after years of debate, FDA now requires biosimilars to have the same root name as their reference product with the addition of a distinctive suffix of four lower case letters to avoid confusion.[90]

Like the BLA, the aBLA must contain a Chemistry, Manufacturing, and Controls section, which demonstrates that the facility in which the

---

82. 42 U.S.C. § 262(k)(2)(A)(i)(I)(cc).

83. *Id.* § 262(k)(2)(A)(i)(I); FDA, Guidance for Industry: Questions and Answers on Biosimilar Development and the BPCI Act 3 (rev. 2, 2021) [hereinafter Q&A on Biosimilar Development Guidance], https://www.fda.gov/media/119258/download.

84. 42 U.S.C. § 262(k)(2)(A)(i)(I)(cc).

85. *See id.* § 262(k)(2)(A)(iii)(I). FDA has commented that "publicly available information" includes, but is not limited to, the types of information found in the so-called "action package," *see* FDC Act § 505(*l*)(2)(C), 21 U.S.C. § 355(*l*)(2)(C), for a section 351(a) BLA. *See* Biosimilars Additional Q&A Guidance, *supra* note 81, at 11.

86. PHS Act § 351(k)(2)(A)(iii)(II), 42 U.S.C. § 262(k)(2)(A)(iii)(II).

87. 42 U.S.C. § 262(k)(2)(A)(i)(II).

88. Q&A on Biosimilar Development Guidance, *supra* note 83, at 21.

89. 42 U.S.C. § 262(k)(2)(A)(i)(IV); Q&A on Biosimilar Development Guidance, *supra* note 83, at 20.

90. *See* Designation of Official Names and Proper Names for Certain Biological Products, 80 Fed. Reg. 52,224 (proposed Aug. 28, 2015); FDA, Guidance for Industry: Nonproprietary Naming of Biological Products (2017), https://www.fda.gov/media/93218/download.

biosimilar is manufactured meets applicable standards to ensure safety, purity, and potency.[91] FDA will also perform a pre-licensure inspection.

Finally, biosimilars, like BLAs, are subject to PREA, assuming the aBLA is not interchangeable with the reference product. Under PREA, a biosimilar product (that is not interchangeable) is considered to have a "new active ingredient," which requires a pediatric assessment unless waived or deferred.[92] Such requirements apply only to the extent that compliance with PREA would not result in a condition of use that has not been previously approved for the reference product or a dosage form, strength, or route of administration that differs from the reference product.[93] Thus, when the reference product does not have pediatric use information in its labeling or an age-appropriate formulation for a relevant pediatric population, the biosimilar applicant would not be expected to obtain licensure for a pediatric use (or describe that use in product labeling).[94]

Additional requirements applicable to the conditions of use are also relevant for an aBLA. For example, if the reference product is subject to a Risk Evaluation and Mitigation Strategy, the aBLA will be as well.[95] And Congress currently is exploring whether there is a pathway for aBLAs to differ to some extent from their reference products through "bio-betters," which would allow for the development of new biologics based on FDA's findings for licensed biologics.[96]

Without all required elements of a BLA or an aBLA, FDA will "refuse to file" the license application, which means that FDA will not review the application until it has been resubmitted with all of the required information.[97] This slows down FDA's review process and may require payment of an additional user fee.[98]

C. Interchangeable Biosimilars

While biosimilar products only need to meet a "highly similar" standard, the threshold is higher for "interchangeable" biosimilars, which are biosimilars that "may be substituted for the reference product without the intervention of [a] health care provider."[99] Thus, applications for

---

91. 42 U.S.C. § 262(k)(2)(A)(i)(V).

92. Q&A on Biosimilar Development Guidance, *supra* note 83, at 12; 21 U.S.C. § 355c(a)(1)(A)(ii).

93. Q&A on Biosimilar Development Guidance, *supra* note 83, at 13.

94. *Id.* at 15.

95. *See* PHS Act § 351(k)(5)(C), 42 U.S.C. § 262(k)(5)(C).

96. This pathway would be similar to the 505(b)(2) regulatory pathway set forth in FDC Act § 505(b)(2), 21 U.S.C. § 355(b)(2).

97. CDER, FDA, Manual of Policies and Procedures (MAPP), 6025.4 (2018).

98. *See infra* Section IV.

99. 42 U.S.C. § 262(i)(3).

interchangeable biosimilars require data to demonstrate that the biosimilar "can be expected to produce the same clinical result as the reference product in any given patient."[100] Where the reference product is administered more than once to a patient, an applicant must provide sufficient information to show that the risks in terms of safety or efficacy of alternating and switching between the proposed product and the reference product are no greater than using the reference product without such a switch.[101]

Because an interchangeable biosimilar is a biosimilar, an aBLA or a supplement to an approved aBLA under PHS Act section 351(k) is required, but an interchangeable application contains additional data than the typical aBLA. Regardless of whether the interchangeable product is submitted in an aBLA or a supplement, the same evidence will be necessary for licensure. Such evidence might include:

- Identification and analysis of the critical quality attributes
- Identification of analytical differences between the reference product and the proposed interchangeable product with an analysis of the potential clinical impact of the differences
- Analysis of the mechanism of action in each condition of use for which the reference product is licensed, which may include analysis of the target receptor for each relevant activity/function of the product; binding, dose/concentration response, and pattern of molecular signaling upon engagement of target receptor or receptors; the relationship between product structure and target/receptor interactions; and the location and expression of target receptor or receptors
- Analysis of any differences in the expected pharmacokinetics and biodistribution of the product in different patient populations for which the reference product is licensed
- Analysis of any differences in the expected immunogenicity risk of the product in different patient populations for which the reference product is licensed
- Analysis of any differences in expected toxicities of the product in each condition of use and patient population
- Any other information that goes to the safety or efficacy of the product in each condition of use and patient population for which the reference product is licensed[102]

The data and information necessary to meet the interchangeability standard varies depending on the nature of the proposed interchangeable

100. *Id.* § 262(k)(4)(A).
101. *Id.* § 262(k)(4)(B).
102. *Id.*

product.[103] Not all factors will be relevant to every proposed interchangeable product. Product complexity and characterization capability and product-specific immunogenicity risk will dictate much of the information required to demonstrate interchangeability.[104] If applicable, the application should include scientific justification for any differences between the reference product and proposed interchangeable explaining that they can be expected to produce the same clinical result as the reference product in any given patient notwithstanding such differences.[105]

Switching studies, which assess the risks of alternating or switching between the reference product and the proposed product, are a critical element of the interchangeable biosimilar application for products that are intended to be administered more than once.[106] These studies should evaluate changes in treatment that result in two or more alternating exposures to the proposed interchangeable product and the reference product.[107] The design of such studies will depend on the product and its use in clinical practice, but they must assess whether switching results in differences in immunogenicity and pharmacokinetic and/or pharmacodynamics as compared to use only of the reference product.[108] FDA highly encourages sponsors to meet with the agency to discuss the planned development approach before commencing studies.[109]

Though an interchangeable aBLA may contain more data than a typical aBLA, interchangeable biosimilars are exempt from PREA requirements. This is because an interchangeable product is not considered to contain a new "active ingredient" for purposes of required pediatric testing.[110] However, if an applicant first seeks licensure of its proposed product as a biosimilar product (rather than an interchangeable biosimilar product), the applicant must address applicable PREA requirements in its non-interchangeable biosimilar product, even if the applicant ultimately intends to later seek licensure of the product as an interchangeable product.[111]

---

103. FDA, Guidance for Industry: Considerations in Demonstrating Interchangeability with a Reference Product 4 (2019), https://www.fda.gov/media/124907/download.

104. *Id.* at 5–7.

105. *Id.*

106. *Id.* at 9.

107. *Id.*

108. *Id.* at 9–10.

109. *Id.* at 10.

110. *See* 21 U.S.C. § 355c(*l*)(2). A non-interchangeable biosimilar product is considered to contain a new active ingredient, and, therefore, is subject to pediatric testing requirements. *See id.* § 355c(*l*)(1).

111. Q&A on Biosimilar Development Guidance, *supra* note 83, at 12.

As of August 2023, only 42 biosimilars, four of which are interchangeable, have been approved in the United States.[112]

IV. User Fees

In order to seek approval of a BLA or an aBLA, the submission of a "user fee" is required. First implemented in 1992 to generate revenue in exchange for FDA's agreement to improve upon its historically slow review times, the Prescription Drug User Fee Act (PDUFA) requires NDA and BLA applicants to pay fees of a million dollars or more to simply to submit an application.[113] In turn, FDA has agreed to "performance goals," which are timeframes by which FDA agrees to review applications. Over time, Congress, with input from FDA, has adopted user fees for generic drugs, medical devices, and, after passage of the BPCIA, biosimilars. These user fees are reauthorized every five years under User Fee Acts, which, because they are "must-pass legislation," often are hosts for other bills that the agency wants Congress to pass. And each user fee bill seems to change its respective user fee program to some degree.

Under the current PDUFA, PDUFA VII, BLA sponsors must pay the agency an application fee for each application submitted, as well as program fees for ongoing support of approved applications. Application fees are assessed for each human drug application, including an original BLA, in amounts based on the types of data included in the application for approval. If the BLA contains clinical data (other than bioavailability or bioequivalence studies) with respect to safety or effectiveness, the entire PDUFA fee of $4,048,695 for fiscal year (FY) 2024 must be paid before FDA will review the application; if the BLA contains none of the aforementioned clinical data, the user fee assessed is $2,024,348.[114] If FDA refuses to file the BLA, 75 percent of the application fee will be refunded.[115] And while there are some exemptions and some waivers and reductions available, most applications require this user fee. Failure to pay an application fee will preclude FDA from reviewing that application.

FDA also assesses a program fee annually for all prescription drug products identified in an approved BLA or NDA. Program fees for FY 2024

---

112. *See Biosimilar Product Information*, FDA, https://www.fda.gov/drugs/biosimilars/biosimilar-product-information (last updated Dec. 8, 2023).

113. Pub. L. No. -571, 106 Stat. 4491 (1992).

114. Prescription Drug User Fee Rates for Fiscal Year 2024, 88 Fed. Reg. 48,881, 48,882 (July 28, 2023).

115. *Prescription User Fee Amendments*, FDA, https://www.fda.gov/industry/fda-user-fee-programs/prescription-drug-user-fee-amendments (last updated Dec. 14, 2023).

are set at $416,429,[116] and sponsors must pay a separate program fee for each strength or potency of a drug product up to five strengths included in a single application (in addition to the application fee).[117] Again, there are some exemptions to the program fee, but most sponsors are required to pay. Failure to pay program fees deems an applicant "in arrears."[118] FDA maintains an "arrears list," and FDA will refuse to review any applications submitted by a sponsor on that list, even if the application fee has been paid for the given application.[119]

Biosimilars are subject to a similar, but much more recent, user fee scheme. The Biosimilar User Fee Act (BsUFA), enacted under the Food and Drug Administration Safety and Innovation Act, first established a biosimilar user fee in 2012.[120] Like PDUFA, it provides additional revenue so that FDA can hire staff, improve systems, and manage the biological review process smoothly.[121]

Under the current iteration of BsUFA, BsUFA III, Congress has imposed three types of user fees: biosimilar biological product development (BPD) fees, application fees, and program fees. The BPD fee is a one-time fee assessed to a sponsor who submits a meeting request to FDA for a BPD meeting or submits an IND intended to support a biosimilar biological product application. There is an initial BPD fee and annual BPD fee for each product under development. Like PDUFA fees, FDA assesses a user fee for each aBLA submission and an annual fee for each product that has been approved up to five program fees.[122] Both the initial BPD fee and annual BPD fee are $10,000 for FY 2024. The BsUFA application fee where clinical data is required is $1,018,753; where it is not, the fee is $509,377 for FY 2024. The program fee for FY 2024 is $177,397.[123]

Failure to pay BsUFA fees has similar consequences to PDUFA. If a sponsor fails to pay any BPD fee, FDA will refuse to provide a BPD meeting for the product for which fees are owed and may put a clinical investigation on hold.[124] If an application fee is not paid, FDA will refuse

116. 88 Fed. Reg. at 48,882.

117. *Id.* at 48,887.

118. CDER, FDA, Manual of Policies and Procedures (MAPP), 6050.1 (rev. 2, 2021).

119. *Id.* at 3.

120. Pub. L. No. 112-144, 126 Stat. 993 (2012).

121. *See* Reauthorization of the Biosimilar User Fee Act; Public Meeting; Request for Comments, 86 Fed. Reg. 52,685, 52,686 (Sept. 22, 2021).

122. *Biosimilar User Fee Amendments*, FDA, https://www.fda.gov/industry/fda-user-fee-programs/biosimilar-user-fee-amendments (last updated Oct. 3, 2023).

123. Biosimilar User Fee Rates for Fiscal Year 2024, 88 Fed. Reg. 48,855, 48,856 (July 28, 2023).

124. FDA, Guidance for Industry: Assessing User Fees under the Biosimilar User Fee Amendments of 2022 (2023), https://www.fda.gov/media/170634/download.

to review the application.[125] And failure to pay program fees gets an applicant on the arrears list.

V. Biologic and Biosimilar Approval Process

While FDA licenses a biological product under either a BLA or an aBLA, granting the application holder permission to introduce a biologic product into interstate commerce, the applicable requirements differ depending on the type of licensing application filed.[126] The timing for review also depends on the type of licensing application filed. But the process is the same: FDA reviews the application and either approves the application or comes back to the sponsor for additional information.[127]

Both BLAs and aBLAs must be "filed"—or accepted—by FDA to commence review. FDA will only file a BLA that includes sufficient information, on its face, to facilitate a complete review; in other words, it must contain all information required under the PHS Act.[128] FDA reviews the file for any deficiencies and will either refuse to file the BLA or aBLA or will accept the application and commence review. In certain cases, where the deficiencies appear to be correctable, FDA may work with the applicant to rectify these issues, but FDA has no obligation to do so.[129] FDA will notify an applicant within 60 days whether the application has been filed successfully.[130]

Once FDA has filed the application, the Review Division—assigned based on proposed therapeutic use—divides the application amongst different disciplines, such as clinical, pharmacology, product quality, biometrics, and manufacturing.[131] After submission and while the disciplines are reviewing the Review Division hosts the sponsors for various meetings, including filing/planning meetings, mid-cycle meetings, and wrap-up meetings, which may differ depending on whether the application is a BLA

---

125. CDER, FDA, Manual of Policies and Procedures (MAPP), 6050.2 (2021).

126. 21 C.F.R. § 601.2(a) (2024).

127. Theoretically, FDA could deny a license application, but this rarely happens.

128. FDA, Draft Guidance for Industry: Refuse to File: NDA and BLA Submissions to CDER 2 (2017) [hereinafter Guidance for Industry: Refuse to File: NDA and BLA Submissions], https://www.fda.gov/media/109758/download.

129. FDA, CDER 21st Century Review Process Desk Reference Guide: New Drug Application and Biologics License Application Reviews 20 [hereinafter CDER 21st Century Review Process Desk Reference Guide], https://www.fda.gov/media/78941/download.

130. Guidance for Industry: Refuse to File: NDA and BLA Submissions, *supra* note 128, at 2.

131. There are many more. *See* CDER 21st Century Review Process Desk Reference Guide, *supra* note 129, at 3.

or an aBLA.[132] Reviewers will also communicate with the applicant during the review cycle by asking for additional information through information requests or discipline review letters.[133] As part of the review, the reviewers may seek expert advice from other FDA divisions or centers, through an Advisory Committee meeting, or through other means.[134] Finally, FDA and the applicant engage in labeling and post-marketing requirement negotiations.[135]

FDA approval also requires an assessment of the manufacturing facilities for a given biological product. This is because manufacturing is key to the safety and efficacy of a biologic, and thus licenses for biologics will not be issued unless the manufacturing establishment complies with FDA regulations for the applicable current Good Manufacturing Practices.[136] FDA determines whether a pre-license or pre-approval inspection is necessary based on the risk profile of a given facility, and such inspections generally are necessary where FDA has not recently inspected the facility; the facility is new; there is a new production suite or significant manufacturing change within an existing facility; or the facility does not have a compliance history.[137]

FDA, as part of PDUFA and BsUFA, has committed to review schedule "goals" in which it will review an application. Under PDUFA, FDA has committed to reviewing 90 percent of original BLA submissions within ten months of the 60-day filing date—or within a year of submission—and to 90 percent of original BLA submissions that have been granted "priority review" within six months of the 60-day filing date—or within eight months.[138] Supplements to BLAs are expected to be reviewed within ten months for standard efficacy supplements and six months for priority efficacy supplements.[139] "Major amendments" to pending applications

---

132. *Id.* at 6.

133. *Id.* at 26.

134. *Id.* at 32.

135. *Id.* at 36–37.

136. CBER, FDA, SOP 8410: Determining When Pre-License/Pre-Approval Inspections Are Necessary 1–2 (2020).

137. *Id.* at 3.

138. FDA, PDUFA Reauthorization Performance Goals and Procedures Fiscal Years 2023 through 2027 [hereinafter PDUFA Commitment Letter FY 2023–2027], https://www.fda.gov/media/151712/download. "Priority review" is a designation awarded to a proposed product that treats a serious condition and, if approved, would provide a significant improvement in safety or effectiveness over available therapies. FDA, Guidance for Industry: Expedited Programs for Serious Conditions—Drugs and Biologics 24 (2014), https://www.fda.gov/media/86377/download. Alternatively, priority review can be obtained through use of a priority review voucher, which is an incentive provided under the FDC Act for a variety of programs.

139. PDUFA Commitment Letter FY 2023–2027, *supra* note 138.

can extend the timeline by as many as three months.[140] For aBLAs, FDA commits to reviewing 90 percent of original aBLAs within ten months of the 60-day filing date (again, one year), and resubmitted aBLAs within six months of receipt (which does not include an additional 60-day filing date).[141] Like for BLAs, a "major amendment" may extend the review cycle.[142]

At the end of the review cycle—on or near the PDUFA or BsUFA goal date—FDA will either issue an approval letter or send an applicant a "complete response letter" (CRL), which lists all the deficiencies that are preventing the application from being approved.[143] Technically, FDA has the authority to deny a license, but, practically, the agency rarely does so.[144] Instead, FDA issues CRLs until the applicant either perfects or withdraws the application. Those CRLs state that an application cannot be approved in its current state and describe all of the deficiencies the agency has identified and provide agency recommendations of actions the applicant might take to facilitate approval.[145] In response, an applicant may resubmit the application, addressing all deficiencies identified in the CRL; withdraw the application; or take no action, which is treated as a withdrawal.[146] CRLs are incredibly common; many applications receive multiple before securing approval.

With small molecules, there would be patent considerations for both applications and abbreviated applications, but patents have no role in the regulatory approval process for biologics. Though patents are integral to the biologic development process and to the balance between innovation (usually considered the BLA) and access (typically the aBLA), patents on a given reference product do not block FDA from approving an aBLA. Patents may eventually be listed in FDA's "Purple Book"—its list of all biological products licensed under the PHS Act[147]—but that process is separate from the BLA and aBLA approval process.

---

140. *Id.*

141. FDA, Biosimilar Biological Reauthorization Performance Goals and Procedures Fiscal Years 2023 through 2027, https://www.fda.gov/media/152279/download.

142. *Id.*

143. 21 C.F.R. § 601.3(a) (2024).

144. *See id.* § 601.4(b) ("If the Commissioner determines that the establishment or product does not meet the requirements established in this chapter, the biologics license application shall be denied. . . .").

145. *Id.* § 601.3(a).

146. *Id.* § 601.3(b), (c).

147. *See* Chapter 4.

VI. Available Exclusivities

As an incentive to innovate, Congress built in to the BPCIA regulatory exclusivities for eligible BLAs and interchangeable aBLAs.[148] Though built off the model set forth in the FDC Act, which provides exclusivity for new chemical entities, new clinical studies, and first-to-file generic drugs, the available exclusivities for biologics are very different than those for small molecules. For full BLAs, the BPCIA provides for 12 years of data exclusivity for a reference product—"reference product exclusivity"—precluding biosimilars from relying on that reference product for approval for 12 years. For interchangeable biosimilars, the BPCIA provides one year during which FDA cannot approve another interchangeable biosimilar. Notably, no exclusivity is available for biosimilars that are not interchangeable.

A. Reference Product Exclusivity

Under the BPCIA, reference products are protected by a 12-year period of reference product exclusivity. Under the statute, FDA cannot accept for review an aBLA—interchangeable or otherwise—relying on a given reference for four years after the date of "first licensure" or approve an aBLA relying on that reference product for 12 years.[149] Due to the way the statute is written, FDA explains exclusivity for a reference product in terms of "a prohibition on acceptance or approval of an application for a biosimilar or interchangeable product for a period of time starting from the date of first licensure."[150] Put another way, reference product exclusivity protects a new biological product from biosimilar competition for 12 years. Importantly, the reference product's exclusivity does not block approval of a BLA for the same molecule—meaning that any sponsor can file a BLA under section 351(a) of the PHS Act—but merely precludes approval of an application relying on that reference product's data for approval.[151]

Not all reference products are eligible for reference product exclusivity, however. Under the act, supplements to BLAs are not eligible for reference product exclusivity.[152] In practice, this means that new indications and new formulations do not qualify for reference product exclusivity even if completely new clinical trials were required for approval. Thus, each

148. 42 U.S.C. § 262(k)(6), (7).

149. *Id.* § 262(k)(7).

150. FDA, Draft Guidance for Industry: Reference Product Exclusivity for Biological Products Filed under Section 351(a) of the PHS Act 2 (2014) [hereinafter Guidance for Industry: Reference Product Exclusivity], https://www.fda.gov/media/89049/download.

151. *See* 42 U.S.C. § 262(k)(7)(A).

152. *Id.* § 262(k)(7)(C).

product is provided with a single period of reference product exclusivity, and, unlike with small molecules, there is no opportunity for a second period of exclusivity based on tweaks to the original formulation even if that tweak results in new, innovative features.

The statute further excludes from eligibility for reference product exclusivity "subsequent application[s] filed by the same sponsor or manufacturer of the biological product that is the reference product (or a licensor, predecessor in interest, or other related entity)" for a change to the product, even if that change results in a new indication, route of administration, dosing schedule, dosage form, delivery system, delivery device, or strength.[153] The exception to the exclusion from reference product exclusivity eligibility is for a supplement from the same manufacturer that results in a "modification to the structure of the biological product that does not result in a change in safety, purity, or potency."[154] This means that unless a subsequent application for an approved biologic filed by the same sponsor has a different structure from the previously approved drug product, the new application is not eligible for exclusivity.

Notably, a subsequent BLA under section 351(a) of the PHS Act filed *by a different applicant for the same molecule* is also eligible for reference product exclusivity,[155] which makes the definition of the "same sponsor or manufacturer" important. While the "same sponsor or manufacturer" is clear—it means the same applicant as the approved BLA—FDA also interprets it to include a "licensor, predecessor in interest, or other related entity." These terms are subject to agency interpretation.

FDA examines the relationships between business entities involved in each BLA to determine eligibility of that BLA for reference product exclusivity.[156] FDA further elucidates in guidance how it will assess "licensor, predecessor in interest, or other related entity."[157] Specifically, FDA defines a "licensor" as any entity that has granted the sponsor a license to market the reference product, regardless of whether such license is exclusive.[158] A licensor includes a party that retains intellectual property rights over the biological product or otherwise has the right to develop, manufacture, or market the biological product.[159] FDA further defines a "predecessor in interest" as any entity that the sponsor has "taken over, merged

153. *Id.*
154. *Id.*
155. *See id.* (excluding from reference product exclusivity eligibility only subsequent applications filed by the "same sponsor or manufacturer" of a given product).
156. Guidance for Industry: Reference Product Exclusivity, *supra* note 150, at 4.
157. *See generally id.*
158. *Id.* at 5.
159. *Id.*

with, or purchased," has granted the sponsor exclusive rights to market the biologic under the BLA, or had exclusive rights to the data upon which the BLA was approved.[160] Thus, not only is FDA looking at the parties who currently own the intellectual property or other rights to market a product but also to any party that *previously* had such rights.

More complicated is the agency's examination of a "related entity." That ambiguous term is not defined anywhere in the PHS Act, so the agency has decided to look to control and ownership.[161] FDA will consider an entity a "related entity" to an applicant for purposes of reference product exclusivity where one party owns, controls, or has the power to own or control the other, either directly or through other entities.[162] If the parties are under common ownership or control, they are also considered "related entities."[163] Alternatively, the agency may consider two parties related entities if they were engaged in commercial collaboration to develop the product at issue, excluding "service contracts" like contract research organizations.[164] However, it is not clear exactly what FDA is looking for and the extent of collaboration necessary to meet the threshold for a "related entity": FDA assesses this on a case-by-case basis.

A subsequent application *could* be eligible for another period of reference product exclusivity but only where there is a "modification to the structure of the biological product" and that modification results in a "change in safety, purity, or potency."[165] FDA therefore reviews each product submitted in a subsequent application to determine whether it constitutes a modification to the structure of a previously licensed product.[166] As part of that review, FDA examines, based on both materials provided by the sponsor and its own scientific analysis, the structural similarities and differences between its proposed product and any previously licensed biological product that was the subject of a section 351(a) application filed by the same sponsor or manufacturer (or its licensor, predecessor in interest, or other related entity).[167] For protein products, structural differences assessed include, as appropriate, any differences in amino acid sequence, glycosylation patterns, tertiary structures, post-translational events (including any chemical modifications of the molecular structure such as pegylation), and infidelity of translation or transcription, among others.[168]

160. *Id.*
161. *Id.*
162. *Id.*
163. *Id.*
164. *Id.*
165. 42 U.S.C. § 262(k)(7)(C)(ii).
166. GUIDANCE FOR INDUSTRY: REFERENCE PRODUCT EXCLUSIVITY, *supra* note 150, at 5–6.
167. *Id.* at 5.
168. *Id.* at 5–6.

FDA also will consider the principal structural molecular features of two related products, as well as the molecular target.[169] Importantly, modification of a structure will not be presumed; it requires a sponsor to submit to the BLA an explanation of the change.[170] Each assessment of such a modification is made on a case-by-case basis.[171]

Once FDA determines there is a modification to the structure of a biologic, it then looks to see whether that structural modification has resulted in a change in safety, purity, or potency such that the proposed product has a different safety or efficacy profile than the previously licensed product.[172] That determination is also made on a case-by-case basis as supported by data submitted to the BLA by the sponsor.[173] FDA will look at measurable effects (typically demonstrated in preclinical or clinical studies) describing how the *modification resulted in a change* in safety, purity, or potency compared to the previously licensed product.[174] FDA will presume a change to the proposed product's safety, purity, or potency if the proposed product affects a different molecular target—a molecule whose activity is modified by the product—than the original product, as long as it results in a *desirable* therapeutic effect.[175] Such molecular targets can include receptors, enzymes, ion channels, structural or membrane transport proteins, nucleic acids, and pathogens, among others.[176] That the change will provide a meaningful benefit to public health is also supportive of such a change.[177] If FDA determines that there is such a modification, the modified product will be eligible for its own period of reference product exclusivity.[178]

An applicant should include a request for reference product exclusivity in its BLA. That request should include a list of all licensed biological products structurally related to the reference product, including products that share some of the same principal molecular structural features and products that affect the same molecular target.[179] If any of those products were sponsored by affiliates, licensors, predecessors in interest, or related entities of the applicant, such parties should be identified in the request. FDA also expects to see a description of the structural differences between the proposed product and any structurally similar products identified in

169. *Id.* at 6.
170. *Id.* at 5–6.
171. *Id.*
172. *Id.* at 6–7.
173. *Id.* at 6.
174. *Id.*
175. *Id.*
176. *Id.*
177. *Id.*
178. *Id.* at 7.
179. *Id.* at 7–8.

the list. Finally, FDA requests any information supporting a change in the safety, purity, or potency of the proposed product, including a description of how structural differences relate to such changes.[180]

Once FDA has reviewed a request for exclusivity and made a final determination about whether a given product is eligible for reference product exclusivity, FDA notifies sponsors by publication in the Purple Book. To do so, FDA assigns a date of "first licensure" in the Purple Book, which serves as the start of the 12-year exclusivity period. The listing of such date signifies that the product qualifies for reference product exclusivity and the date on which the exclusivity will expire.[181] In most instances, the date of first licensure will be the initial date the BLA for a particular product at issue was first licensed in the United States.[182]

B. Biosimilar Exclusivity

While the BPCIA created a pathway for biosimilars under section 351(k), it did not provide exclusivity for biosimilar application absent a determination that a particular biosimilar is interchangeable with its reference product.[183] Thus, biosimilar exclusivity does not exist; however, exclusivity for the first *interchangeable* biosimilar for such a reference product is available, reflecting Congress's intent to encourage development of biosimilars that could be substituted for the reference product without intervention of a health care professional.

"Interchangeable exclusivity" is awarded to the first applicant that obtains FDA approval of its product as an interchangeable product.[184] That exclusivity prevents FDA from approving another interchangeable application for the same reference product until the earlier of:

- One year after commercial marketing of the interchangeable biosimilar protected by exclusivity
- 18 months after a final court decision—defined as a decision of a court from which no appeal (other than to the U.S. Supreme Court) has been or can be taken—on or dismissal of any and all patent infringement litigation brought by the reference product sponsor against the interchangeable product sponsor
- 42 months after approval of the first interchangeable product if the patent infringement action brought against the first interchangeable product applicant is still ongoing

180. *Id.* at 8.
181. *Id.* at 1.
182. *Id.* at 3.
183. *See* 42 U.S.C. § 262(k)(6) (providing exclusivity only for interchangeable biosimilars).
184. *Id.*

- 18 months after approval of the first interchangeable product if the applicant has not been sued by the reference product sponsor[185]

The "first interchangeable biosimilar biological product" is defined as any interchangeable biosimilar biological product that is approved on the first day on which such a product is approved as interchangeable with the reference product.[186] Under the statute, therefore, the first interchangeable biosimilar referencing a given reference product is eligible for one year of exclusivity, but that exclusivity can be forfeited if the product is not marketed within 18 months or 42 months, depending on the status of patent litigation under the "patent dance" established under the BPCIA.[187]

Like reference product exclusivity, interchangeable exclusivity is marked in the Purple Book.[188] A date or the term "Date TBD" indicates that FDA has determined that the interchangeable product is eligible for interchangeable exclusivity, but FDA has not yet determined the period of exclusivity or if that exclusivity has been forfeited. The absence of a date, however, cannot be interpreted to mean that FDA has decided that a given interchangeable *is not eligible* for interchangeable exclusivity; FDA may not have made that determination yet.[189] And indeed, FDA is often slow to make such a determination.

C. Other Exclusivities

In addition to the BPCIA-enacted exclusivities, BLAs are eligible for orphan drug exclusivity and pediatric exclusivity. Technically, these exclusivities arise under the FDC Act rather than the PHS Act, but they apply to biological products as well. These exclusivities, as they are intended to reward development of new drugs in specific patient populations, are available only to full BLAs rather than biosimilars or interchangeable biosimilars.

To incentivize the development of drug products, including biological products, to treat rare medical conditions, the Orphan Drug Act provides, among other benefits like tax breaks and development assistance, seven years of exclusivity for a reference product indicated for a rare disease or condition during which FDA cannot approve a biosimilar or

---

185. *Id.*

186. *Id.*

187. *Id.*; *see* Chapter 4.

188. *Purple Book Database of Licensed Biological Products FAQs*, FDA, https://purplebooksearch.fda.gov/faqs (last visited Feb. 6, 2024) (Q3: What does the first interchangeable exclusivity date indicate?).

189. *Id.*

interchangeable biosimilar that references this product.[190] To qualify for this exclusivity, the agency must designate the drug product proposed as a drug to treat a rare disease or condition prior to the submission of an NDA or BLA.[191] To be designated a treatment for a "rare disease or condition," FDA must find either that the disease or condition that the BLA product's therapeutically active component is intended to treat "affects less than 200,000 persons in the United States" or that the targeted disease or condition affects more than 200,000 people and "there is no reasonable expectation that the cost of developing and making available in the United States a drug for such disease or condition will be recovered from sales in the United States of such drug" (the "cost-recovery clause").[192] While FDA "shall designate the drug as a drug for such disease or condition" in either of those situations, FDA has rarely—and not recently—designated products by way of the cost-recovery clause.[193]

Once a drug with orphan drug designation is approved, FDA awards the application orphan drug exclusivity.[194] Orphan drug exclusivity prohibits FDA from approving for seven years "the same drug for the same disease or condition" for which the orphan-protected drug product is approved.[195] In assessing "same drug," FDA looks at the therapeutically active component, which, for large molecules like biological products, is the product's "principal molecular structural features," in order to ensure that small differences in macromolecules do not circumvent exclusivity.[196] FDA regulations establish sameness standards specifically for protein drugs, polysaccharide drugs, polynucleotide drugs, and "closely related, complex partly definable drugs with similar therapeutic intent."[197] Sameness, however, can be overcome by a showing that a drug is "clinically superior" to the previously approved drug by way of greater safety, greater

190. Pub. L. No. 97-414, § 1(b), 96 Stat. 2049, 2049 (1983); *see also* H.R. Rep. No. 97-840, at 1 (1982); 21 U.S.C. § 360cc(a).

191. 21 U.S.C. § 360bb(a)(1) ("A request for designation of a drug shall be made before the submission of an [NDA or BLA] for the drug.").

192. *Id.* § 360bb(a)(2).

193. *Id.* § 360bb(a)(1).

194. *Id.* § 360cc(a).

195. *Id.*

196. 21 C.F.R. § 316.3(b)(14)(ii) (2024); *see also* Orphan Drug Regulations, 56 Fed. Reg. 3,338, 3,341 (proposed Jan. 29, 1991) (explaining that FDA focuses on the designated large molecule's principal structural features because "it is possible to make changes in macromolecules that are very likely to have no pharmacologic effect (e.g., a substitution of one amino acid for another similar one at an unimportant site in the molecule), but that could nonetheless defeat exclusive marketing if any structural difference were sufficient to make drugs different for purposes of orphan-drug exclusive marketing" and noting that "small differences may affect the function of macromolecules much less than that of small molecules").

197. 21 C.F.R. § 316.3(b)(14) (2024).

effectiveness, or a major contribution to patient care.[198] A product may have both orphan drug exclusivity and reference product exclusivity, but the exclusivities run concurrently.[199]

Importantly, Orphan drug exclusivity—unlike reference product exclusivity—can be "carved out" or omitted from labeling of a biosimilar or interchangeable biosimilar relying on an exclusivity-protected orphan reference product.[200] This is because orphan drug exclusivity is condition-specific—it blocks applications for the same molecule for the same disease or condition—meaning that an application referencing a reference product that has a non-orphan-protected indication can still be approved but not for the protected indication.[201] When that exclusivity expires, the biosimilar or interchangeable applicant may submit a supplement to add the orphan indication to its labeling.

VII. Pediatric Exclusivity

Reference products are also eligible for a six-month extension of reference product exclusivity or orphan drug exclusivity as a reward for performing certain clinical studies on pediatric patient populations.[202] To be eligible for such exclusivity, FDA must issue a written request for pediatric studies, the study must be completed, and FDA must determine that the product meets the requirements set forth in the written request.[203] Pediatric exclusivity only extends existing exclusivities; thus, if a given product has no reference product exclusivity or orphan drug exclusivity, no pediatric exclusivity can be awarded.[204]

198. *Id.* § 316.3(b)(14)(ii); *id.* § 316.3(b)(3).

199. Guidance for Industry: Reference Product Exclusivity, *supra* note 150, at 2–3.

200. Biosimilars and Interchangeable Biosimilars Guidance, *supra* note 81, at 3.

201. *See id.* at 3–4 ("FDA may be able to license a biosimilar or interchangeable product for one or more indications of the reference product that are not protected by orphan-drug exclusivity.").

202. 42 U.S.C. § 262(m).

203. *Qualifying for Pediatric Exclusivity under Section 505A of the Federal Food, Drug, and Cosmetic Act: Frequently Asked Questions on Pediatric Exclusivity (505A)*, FDA, https://www.fda.gov/drugs/development-resources/qualifying-pediatric-exclusivity-under-section-505a-federal-food-drug-and-cosmetic-act-frequently (last updated Mar. 1, 2022).

204. *See* 42 U.S.C. § 262(m) (limiting pediatric exclusivity to extension of existing exclusivities). This differs from the FDC Act, which adds the six months of pediatric exclusivity both to patents and to exclusivities. This is because patents play a more limited role in the approval process for biological products.

VIII. Patent Considerations

While patents play a much more limited role in the approval process for biosimilars and interchangeable biosimilars than in small-molecule generic drug approval, they remain relevant. There is no patent listing or certification process, meaning that the patents for a given reference product do not serve as a regulatory block to approval; FDA can approve an aBLA at any time regardless of whether there is existing patent protection for a given reference product. In other words, FDA leaves the patents to the parties and the courts to sort out, as explained in Chapter 4. Other than affecting eligibility for interchangeable exclusivity, related patent litigation does not delay FDA approval.

BLAs are eligible for patent term extensions, which increase a patent's life, to make up for the time lost during which the product was in development or under FDA review. A patent term extension extends the patent term by half of the time the product spent in the testing process and all of the time the product was in review, up to five years.[205] The patent term extension cannot extend the remaining term of a patent beyond 14 years of the date of approval.[206] Only one patent per BLA can be extended.[207]

Even though patents are not part of the FDA approval or licensure process, patents covering a biological product do need to be listed in the Purple Book when the patent has been asserted by the applicant as part of the exchange of patent lists described in Chapter 4.[208] The Purple Book thus contains a list of patents and their expiration dates.[209] FDA's role in maintaining that patent list, however, is ministerial, and the patents listed do not affect timing of FDA approval or licensure of a given biosimilar or interchangeable biosimilar.

IX. Conclusion

Biological products and biosimilars are complex and licensure of both takes a significant investment in scientific data, which costs both time and money. Biological products are rewarded for that investment with a 12-year period of reference product exclusivity, and interchangeable biosimilars with one year of interchangeable exclusivity. This system is intended to benefit patients by encouraging access to both innovative new

---

205. 35 U.S.C. § 156.
206. *Id.*
207. *Id.*
208. *See* Chapter 4 (explaining the exchange of patent lists).
209. 42 U.S.C. § 262(k)(9)(A)(iii).

medicines and affordable substitutable versions of older ones. And biosimilar applications, which may not be eligible for exclusivity, can take advantage of an abbreviated pathway to market. The BPCIA and the biosimilar pathway thus has something for everyone.

FDA approval or licensure, however, is not the end of the story. Access to, and launch of, biosimilars and interchangeable biosimilars is also dependent on the outcome of the complicated “patent dance,” as discussed in the next chapter.

chapter 4

Patent Dance and the Purple Book*

The abbreviated regulatory pathway for biosimilar products under the Biologics Price Competition and Innovation Act (BPCIA) includes a process codified in 42 U.S.C. § 262(*l*)(2)–(9) to address patent disputes, which is nicknamed the "patent dance." This chapter introduces the exchange and subsequent negotiation steps between a reference product sponsor (RPS) and a biosimilar applicant (BA) during the patent dance under these statutory provisions. This chapter then discusses notable court rulings that provide insight into how the steps of the BPCIA patent dance play out in practice. Finally, the chapter discusses the U.S. Food and Drug Administration's (FDA's) "Purple Book" for all FDA-licensed biological products, the RPS's obligation to submit patent list(s) to the FDA once it participates in the patent dance, and the FDA's publication of information in the Purple Book.

I. Patent Dance

As part of its patent dispute-resolution regime, the BPCIA "established a unique and elaborate process for information exchange between the biosimilar applicant and the RPS"[1] commonly referred to as the "patent dance." As shown in Figure 1, the patent dance starts with a BA's abbreviated biologics license application (aBLA) filing followed by a series of steps with the RPS to complete the requirements of 42 U.S.C. § 262(*l*)(2)–(5).[2] The patent dance contemplates two possible waves of litigation: a first

*Mark Feldstein, William Raich, Amanda Murphy, Alissa Lipton, and Yieyie Yang, Finnegan, Henderson, Farabow, Garrett & Dunner, Washington, D.C.; Amanda K. Murphy, Finnegan, Henderson, Farabow, Garrett & Dunner, London.

1. Amgen Inc. v. Sandoz Inc., 794 F.3d 1347 (Fed. Cir. 2015).

2. Common shorthand abbreviations (e.g., "section 2(A)," "section 3(A)") used in Figure 1 and this chapter refer to the respective BPCIA statutory sections (e.g., §§ 262(*l*)(2)(A), 262(*l*)(3)(A)).

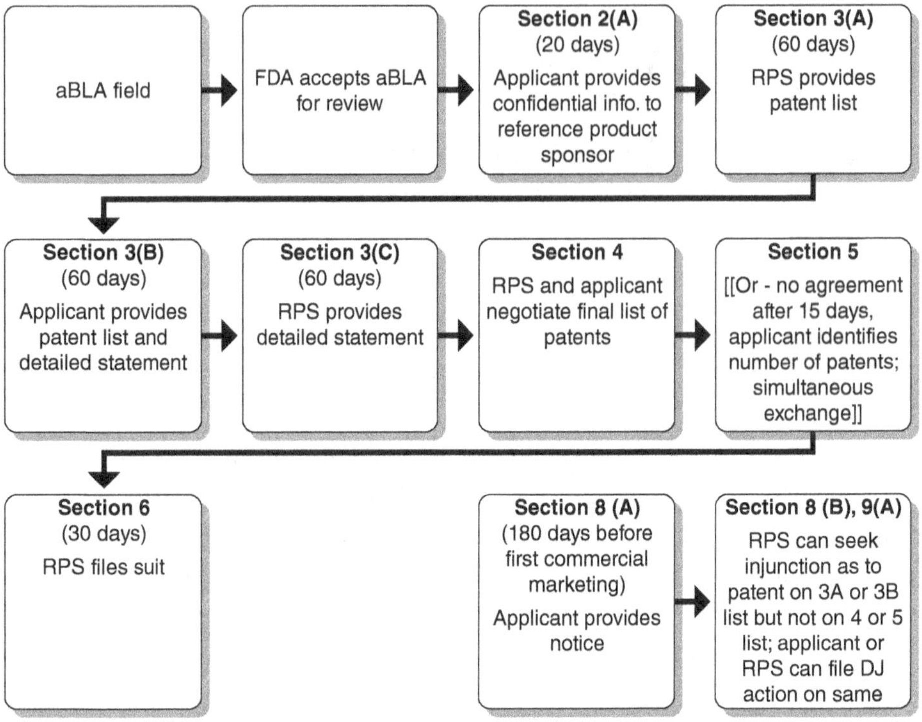

FIGURE 1. A Schematic Depiction of 42 U.S.C. § 262(*l*), Including the Patent Dance

wave under § 262(*l*)(6) (section 6), and a second wave under § 262(*l*)(9) (section 9).

The subsections below further discuss the statutory language and courts' interpretation of the requirements for each step under the respective BPCIA statutory provisions.

A. Information Exchange, § 262(l)(2)–(3)

Under 42 U.S.C. § 262(*l*)(2), within 20 days of being notified by the FDA that its section 351(k) aBLA has been accepted for review, the BA

> (A) shall provide to the reference product sponsor a copy of the application submitted to the Secretary under subsection (k), and such other information that describes the process or processes used to manufacture the biological product that is the subject of such application; and
>
> (B) may provide to the reference product sponsor additional information requested by or on behalf of the reference product sponsor.[3]

3. 42 U.S.C. § 262(*l*)(2)(A), (B).

Despite the statutory language of § 262(*l*)(2)(A) that the BA "shall provide" the RPS with a copy of its aBLA, the U.S. Supreme Court has held that a BA can withhold its aBLA "subject only to the consequences set forth in 42 U.S.C. § 262(l)(9)(C)."[4] Under the statute, the consequences include the BA losing the opportunity for bringing a declaratory judgment action against the RPS under section 9 and, as discussed later, being unable to limit remedies available to the RPS. Withholding its aBLA thus "vest[s] in the [RPS] the control that the [BA] would otherwise have exercised over the scope and timing of the patent litigation and depriv[es] the [BA] of the certainty it could have obtained by bringing a declaratory-judgment action prior to marketing its product."[5]

By contrast, under § 262(*l*)(2)(B), the BA *may* provide to the RPS additional information requested by or on behalf of the RPS, meaning the BA can choose to provide or not to provide additional information requested by the RPS. The BA can refuse to provide such information without penalty under the BPCIA.

Under 42 U.S.C. § 262(*l*)(3)(A), no later than 60 days after the RPS receives the application and required information under § 262(*l*)(2), the RPS *shall* provide the BA with:

1. A list of patents for which the RPS believes "a claim of patent infringement could reasonably be asserted" by the RPS or a patent owner who granted the RPS an exclusive license for the reference product, *if a person not licensed by the RPS engaged in the making, using, offering to sell, selling, or importing of the reference product for which the BLA is filed, into the United States*[6]
2. An identification of the patents on the list that the RPS would be prepared to license to the BA[7]

Under section 3(A), an RPS should include in its initial patent list any patent that "could reasonably be asserted." The patent list provided by the RPS during this step is also called the "section 3(A) list." As further discussed later in this chapter, an RPS's failure to list all such patents on its section 3(A) list could prevent it from requesting information relevant to the unlisted patents in litigation or otherwise asserting those patents against the BA.[8] Thus, for an RPS, it is prudent to be inclusive when considering which patents to include on its section 3(A) list. Provided that the RPS has a good faith belief that the patent could be asserted, even if the

4. Sandoz Inc. v. Amgen Inc., 137 S. Ct. 1664, 1667–68 (2017).
5. *Id.*
6. 42 U.S.C. § 262(*l*)(3)(A)(i).
7. *Id.* § 262(*l*)(3)(A)(ii).
8. Amgen Inc. v. Hospira Inc., 866 F.3d 1355 (Fed. Cir. 2017).

BA does not provide sufficient information during the patent dance to fully evaluate that belief, the RPS can include that patent on its section 3(A) list and ultimately assert it in litigation. Traditional tools of discovery can then be used to obtain evidence needed to prove infringement.[9]

As further discussed in more detail later in this chapter, the Biological Product Patent Transparency Act (BPPT), which was included into the 2021 Consolidated Appropriations Act, requires an RPS engaged in a patent dance to notify the FDA of the patent numbers and expiration dates for all patents identified on its section 3(A) list within 30 days of providing the list to the BA.[10] Under the BPPT, the FDA should then publish these patent details in the "Purple Book," which contains information about all FDA-licensed biological products.[11]

No later than 60 days after the BA receives the section 3(A) list from the RPS, § 262(*l*)(3)(B) states that the BA *may* provide the RPS with a list of patents for which it believes "a claim of patent infringement could reasonably be asserted" by the RPS if a person not licensed by the RPS engaged in the making, using, offering to sell, selling, or importing of the reference product for which the biologics license application (BLA) is filed, into the United States.[12]

Within the same time period, the BA *shall* provide to the RPS, for every patent listed by the RPS on its section 3(A) list as well as any patents identified by the BA, (1) detailed statements, on a claim-by-claim basis, describing the factual and legal bases for invalidity, unenforceability, or noninfringement; *or* (2) a statement that it does not intend to market its biosimilar before the RPS's listed patents expire.[13] Thus, during this stage of the patent dance, the BA is required to provide its positions on invalidity, unenforceability, and/or noninfringement for each section 3(A)-listed patent. These detailed statements are also known as section 3(B) statements. However, at least one court has determined that the BA is not limited by its patent dance contentions in the ensuing litigation.[14] For example, the U.S. District Court for the District of Delaware concluded

---

9. *Id.*

10. BPPT Section of the Consolidated Appropriations Act of 2021, § 325(a)(9)(A)(iii), Pub. L. No. 116-260, 134 Stat. 1182 (2020); *see also Purple Book Database of Licensed Biological Products FAQs*, FDA, https://purplebooksearch.fda.gov/faqs (last visited Feb. 2, 2024) (FAQ #12).

11. *Background Information: List of Licensed Biological Products with Reference Product Exclusivity and Biosimilarity of Interchangeability Evaluations (Purple Book)*, FDA, https://www.fda.gov/drugs/biosimilars/background-information-list-licensed-biological-products-reference-product-exclusivity-and (last updated Aug. 3, 2020).

12. 42 U.S.C. § 262(*l*)(3)(B)(i).

13. *Id.* § 262(*l*)(3)(B).

14. *See, e.g.*, Genentech, Inc. v. Amgen Inc., No. CV 17-1407-CFC, 2020 WL 636439, at *4 (D. Del. Feb. 11, 2020).

in *Genentech v. Amgen* that nothing in the BPCIA or corresponding case law interpreting the BPCIA supports "barring a biosimilar applicant from making in a BPCIA case contentions not disclosed in the patent dance."[15]

Under 42 U.S.C. § 262(*l*)(9)(B), if a BA fails to provide its section 3(B) statements during the patent dance, the RPS "may bring an action under section 2201 of title 28 for a declaration of infringement, validity, or enforceability of any patent included in the list described in paragraph (3)(A), including as provided under paragraph (7)."[16] Thus, similar to a BA's nondisclosure of its aBLA, the consequence of failing to provide its section 3(B) statement is again the potential for the BA to be immediately sued by the RPS in a declaratory judgment action. However, in that suit, the BA can still raise invalidity, unenforceability, and/or noninfringement contentions in RPS-initiated litigation.[17]

Under § 262(*l*)(3)(C), no later than 60 days after receiving the BA's proposed list of patents and section 3(B) statements, the RPS *shall* provide to the BA (1) a detailed statement, on a claim-by-claim basis, describing the factual and legal bases for the RPS's opinion that such patent will be infringed by the marketing of the reference product that is the subject of the BLA; *and* (2) a response to the statement concerning validity and enforceability provided under § 262(*l*)(3)(B)(ii)(I).[18] As such, in the section 3(C) statement, the RPS provides its infringement positions and responses to the BA's invalidity challenges.

B. Resolution Negotiations, § 262(*l*)(4)–(5)

Under § 262(*l*)(4), after the exchange of their detailed statements, the BA and the RPS *shall* engage in good faith negotiation to resolve which patents among those listed by the RPS or the BA shall be the subject of an action for patent infringement under § 262(*l*)(6).[19] Under § 262(*l*)(4)(B) and (*l*)(5)(A), if no agreement is reached by the parties within 15 days of initiating good faith negotiations, the BA shall notify the RPS of the number of patents it will provide to the RPS under § 262(*l*)(5)(B)(i)(I).[20]

On a date agreed to by the BA and the RPS, but in no case later than five days after the BA notifies the RPS of the number of the patents to be litigated under § 262(*l*)(6), the BA and the RPS *shall* simultaneously exchange the lists of patents that each party believes should be the subject

15. *Id.*
16. 42 U.S.C. § 262(*l*)(9)(B).
17. *See* Sandoz Inc. v. Amgen Inc., 137 S. Ct. 1664, 1676 (2017); *Genentech*, 2020 WL 636439, at *4.
18. 42 U.S.C. § 262(*l*)(3)(C).
19. *Id.* § 262(*l*)(4)(A).
20. *Id.* § 262(*l*)(5)(A).

of the infringement action under § 262(*l*)(6).[21] The number of patents listed by the RPS *cannot exceed* the number of patents chosen by the BA under § 262(*l*)(5)(A), unless the BA does not list any patents, in which case the RPS can list one patent.[22] In other words, under the BPCIA, the BA, not the RPS, controls the number of patents to be litigated under § 262(*l*)(6). As explained by the Supreme Court, the "applicant has substantial control over the timing and scope of" the first phase of litigation under the BPCIA.[23]

Under § 262(*l*)(9)(B), if a BA fails to complete an action required under paragraph (5), the RPS may bring a declaratory judgment action for infringement of any patent in the section 3(A) list.[24] Indeed, attempts to skip the resolution negotiation steps required by § 262(*l*)(4)–(5) have been rejected by courts. For example, in *Celltrion v. Genentech*, the U.S. District Court for the Northern District of California dismissed Celltrion's argument that it should have been permitted to skip several negotiation steps because it told Genentech it wished to litigate all patents on Genentech's 3(A) disclosure.[25] According to Celltrion, its statement fulfilled Celltrion's obligations to engage in "good faith negotiations" under section (*l*)(4) and nullified the requirements under (*l*)(5)(A) and (*l*)(5)(B) as "redundant."[26] The district court concluded that Celltrion had improperly conflated sections (*l*)(4)–(5), and that, based on the statute's plain language and the relationship between the sections, "no single statement or gesture can satisfy the requirements of both sections simultaneously."[27] The court reasoned that "Celltrion's assertion that it 'wished' to litigate all the patents on Genentech's 3(A) Disclosure was merely a response to Genentech's initial proposition," and that "the 3(A), (B), and (C) Disclosures" "are, in fact, distinct statutory steps which the parties must complete before commencing the Section (1)(4) negotiations."[28] To the court, "[t]he statutory procedures do not allow an applicant to collapse its multiple distinct obligations into one or two perfunctory actions."[29] Accordingly, the court dismissed Celltrion's declaratory judgment action against Genentech.[30] Thus, a BA's failure to comply with the steps of § 262(*l*)(4)–(5) can result

21. *Id.* § 262(*l*)(5)(B)(i)(I)–(II).
22. *Id.* § 262(*l*)(5)(B)(ii)(I)–(II).
23. Sandoz Inc. v. Amgen Inc., 137 S. Ct. 1664, 1666 (2017).
24. 42 U.S.C. § 262(*l*)(9)(B).
25. No. 18-CV-00274-JSW, 2018 WL 2448254, at *5 (N.D. Cal. May 9, 2018).
26. *Id.*
27. *Id.* at *6.
28. *Id.*
29. *Id.*
30. *Id.* at *8.

in its loss of rights to declaratory judgment relief in later patent infringement litigation.

C. First-Wave Litigation, § 262(l)(6)

If the BA and RPS agree on the list of patents under § 262(*l*)(4), no later than 30 days after such agreement, the RPS *shall* bring an action for patent infringement with respect to each patent on the list under § 262(*l*)(6)(A).[31] If the BA and RPS were unable to agree on a negotiated set of patents to litigate, then under § 262(*l*)(6)(B), no later than 30 days after the exchange of the lists under (5)(B), the RPS *shall* bring an action for patent infringement with respect to each patent on the lists.[32] This immediate patent infringement action under § 262(*l*)(6) is sometimes referred to as "first wave" litigation.

The remedies available to the RPS can be limited if the (*l*)(6) suit is untimely, dismissed without prejudice, or not prosecuted to judgment in good faith. For example, if a patent owner files its suit *more than 30 days* after the exchange of the patent lists provided for under § 262(*l*)(4) or (5)(B), the "sole and exclusive remedy that may be granted by a court, upon a finding that the making, using, offering to sell, selling, or importation into the United States of the biological product that is the subject of the action infringed the patent, shall be a reasonable royalty."[33] Similarly, if the (*l*)(6) suit is timely brought, but the suit was dismissed without prejudice, the same limitation on remedy applies.

The BA should comply with the requirements of the patent dance for these limitations on potential remedies to apply. For example, the U.S. District Court for the District of Massachusetts held that "the alleged infringer must comply with each step of the BPCIA process in order to limit the [RPS or patent owner] to a reasonable royalty if [the RPS or patent owner] does not sue within 30 days of the end of that process."[34] Further, "[i]t is only the list of patents that emerge from the properly completed BPCIA procedure that are potentially subject to the reasonable royalty damages limitation."[35]

31. 42 U.S.C. § 262(*l*)(6)(A).

32. *Id.* § 262(*l*)(6)(B).

33. 35 U.S.C. § 271(e)(6); Janssen Biotech, Inc. v. Celltrion Healthcare Co., 239 F. Supp. 3d 328, 331 (D. Mass. 2017); Amgen Inc. v. Sandoz Inc., No. 14-CV-04741-RS, 2015 WL 1264756, at *3 (N.D. Cal. Mar. 19, 2015), *aff'd in part, vacated in part, remanded,* 794 F.3d 1347 (Fed. Cir. 2015), *rev'd in part, vacated in part,* 137 S. Ct. 1664 (2017), *and aff'd,* 877 F.3d 1315 (Fed. Cir. 2017) ("Should the sponsor elect not to [bring suit within 30 days], it may collect only a reasonable royalty.").

34. *Janssen Biotech,* 239 F. Supp. at 332.

35. *Id.*

Within 30 days after a complaint in a patent infringement action is served on the BA, the BA must provide the FDA with notice and a copy of the complaint.[36] The FDA will then publish the notice in the *Federal Register*.[37] Unlike a Hatch-Waxman action, however, BPCIA litigation does not automatically trigger a stay of FDA approval for the biosimilar product. Instead, consistent with traditional patent litigation, the RPS may seek an injunction in the litigation. Note, however, that under section 351(k)(7) of the Public Health Service (PHS) Act, approval of an aBLA may not be made effective until the date that is 12 years after the date on which the reference product was first licensed.[38] Thus, an RPS need only seek an injunction in BPCIA litigation if the 12-year regulatory exclusivity is expected to end before the conclusion of the litigation.

D. Newly Issued or Licensed Patents, § 262(*l*)(7)

The BPCIA has provisions addressing patents that are newly issued to or licensed by the RPS following initial exchange of the section 3(A) list. If the RPS reasonably believes that it could assert such a patent against the BA, it can add the patent to its section 3(A) patent list as a supplement no later than 30 days after the patent issues or is licensed.[39] No later than 30 days after being provided with the supplement, the BA shall provide a section 3(B) statement against the new patent.[40] The newly listed patents are then potentially subject to the second wave of patent litigation governed by § 262(*l*)(8), discussed in the following subsection.[41]

Because newly issued patents may have claims dissimilar to the original patents in the section 3(A) list, they may present additional challenges to a BA even if they are related to the already litigated patents. For example, in *Amgen Inc. v. Apotex Inc.*, the U.S. District Court for the Southern District of Florida noted that it had previously affirmed noninfringement of a patent in Amgen's original section 3(A) list, but decided that because the limitations of a newly issued and asserted patent were different from those of the earlier litigated patent, the patent issues needed to be reviewed independently, and collateral estoppel did not automatically apply.[42] Thus, a BA should continue monitoring ongoing patent prosecution of potentially relevant patents after commencement of (*l*)(6)

36. 42 U.S.C. § 262(*l*)(6)(C)(i).
37. *Id.* § 262(*l*)(6)(C)(ii).
38. PHS Act § 351(k)(7).
39. 42 U.S.C. § 262(*l*)(7).
40. *Id.*
41. *Id.*
42. No. 18-61828-CIV-WPD/LSS, 2019 WL 13061848, at *5 (S.D. Fla. Apr. 5, 2019).

litigation, as subsequently issued patents may be asserted by the RPS in "second wave" BPCIA litigation.

E. Second-Wave Litigation, § 262(l)(8) and § 262(l)(9)(A)

Under § 262(*l*)(8)(A), a BA must provide notice of commercial marketing to the RPS no later than 180 days before commercial marketing begins for the licensed product.[43] This notice of commercial marketing is thus also called the "180-day notice," and triggers the potential for a second wave of patent litigation under the BPCIA. The Supreme Court has clarified that "the [biosimilar] applicant may provide [the 180-day] notice either before or after receiving FDA approval" of its biosimilar product.[44] As further explained later in this chapter, the BA can provide the 180-day notice well before actual or even anticipated approval.

Under § 262(*l*)(9)(A), neither the BA nor the RPS "may, prior to the date notice is received under paragraph (8)(A) [for commercial marketing], bring any action under section 2201 of title 28, for a declaration of infringement, validity, or enforceability of any patent that is described in clauses (i) and (ii) of paragraph 8(B)."[45] The patents described in § 262(*l*)(8)(B) clauses (i) and (ii) are those (1) included in the section 3(A) list or the list provided by the BA under section 3(B), and (2) not included, as applicable, on the list of patents described in section (4) or the lists of patents described in section (5)(B).[46] As such, § 262(*l*)(8)(B) encompasses the remaining patents from the section 3(A) list not yet litigated during the first-wave litigation under section (*l*)(6). Thus, the BA's 180-day notice permits suit on any patent included in the section 3(A) list (including as supplemented under § 262(*l*)(7)) that was not litigated during the (*l*)(6) suit.[47]

If both the BA and the RPS completed the patent dance, the BA's 180-day notice can trigger declaratory judgment actions by the BA and/or the RPS.[48] However, as explained, if the BA fails to provide its aBLA and manufacturing information as required by section 2(A) and/or otherwise fails to complete the patent dance as required by sections (3)(B), (5), (6)(C)(i), and/or (7), the RPS, but not the BA, may bring a declaratory judgment action.[49]

43. 42 U.S.C. § 262(*l*)(8)(A).

44. Sandoz Inc. v. Amgen Inc., 582 U.S. 1 (2017).

45. 42 U.S.C. § 262(*l*)(9)(A).

46. *Id.* § 262(*l*)(8)(B).

47. Amgen Inc. v. Genentech, Inc., No. CV 17-7349-GW(AGRX), 2018 WL 910198, at *3 (C.D. Cal. Jan. 11, 2018) ("The BPCIA is thus structured so that after the applicant provides notice of commercial marketing, either party can bring suit with respect to any of the leftover patents that were not selected for litigation through the parties' exchanges and negotiations.").

48. *See* 42 U.S.C. § 262(*l*)(9).

49. *Id.* § 262(*l*)(9)(B), (C).

After receiving the 180-day notice and before the date of the first commercial marketing of the biosimilar product, the RPS may seek a preliminary injunction for any patent that is (1) included in the section 3(A) list or the list provided by the BA under section 3(B), and (2) not included, as applicable, on the list of patents described in section (4) or the lists of patents described in section (5)(B).[50] As the Supreme Court and Federal Circuit explained, under § 262(*l*)(8)(B), the RPS may seek a preliminary injunction based on any patent in the second-wave litigation.[51] Moreover, the RPS may also seek injunctive relief under 35 U.S.C. § 271(e)(4) for patents in the first-wave litigation, provided that it initiated suit within 30 days after the negotiation steps under § 262(*l*)(4)–(5).[52] The BA then must reasonably cooperate with the RPS to expedite discovery in conjunction with these preliminary injunction motions.[53]

As the Federal Circuit explained in *Amgen*, the 180-day period triggered by the notice of commercial marketing "gives the parties and the district court the time for adjudicating such matters without the reliability-reducing rush that would attend requests for relief against immediate market entry that could cause irreparable injury."[54]

The RPS should seek a preliminary injunction as early as practically possible during the second-wave litigation, as undue delay could preclude such opportunity. For instance, the Delaware District Court denied Genentech's delayed motion for a preliminary injunction that was filed more than a year after receiving Amgen's 180-day notice and almost a month after Amgen's biosimilar product had received FDA approval.[55]

---

50. *Id.* § 262(*l*)(8)(B).

51. Sandoz Inc. v. Amgen Inc., 137 S. Ct. 1664, 1672 (2017) ("prior to the date of first commercial marketing, the sponsor may 'seek a preliminary injunction . . . with respect to any patent that' was included on the § 262(*l*)(3) lists but not litigated in the first phase"); Amgen Inc. v. Apotex Inc., 827 F.3d 1052, 1057 (Fed. Cir. 2016), *cert. denied*, 137 S. Ct. 591 (2016) ("(8)(B) then declares that, after receiving the (8)(A) post-licensure notice but before the applicant's commercial marketing begins, the reference product sponsor may seek a preliminary injunction based on any patent within either of two classes. The first class, expressly described in (8)(B), consists of the patents that appeared on any of the original paragraph (3) lists, minus patents that were the subject of paragraph (6) litigation (by agreement under (4) or by the narrowing process under (5)). § 262(*l*)(8)(B). The second class consists of certain patents that were issued to or exclusively licensed by the reference product sponsor after it gave the applicant its (3)(A) list.").

52. *See* 35 U.S.C. § 271(e)(4), (6).

53. 42 U.S.C. § 262(*l*)(8)(C).

54. *Amgen*, 827 F.3d at 1063.

55. Genentech, Inc. v. Amgen Inc., No. CV 18-924-cfc, 2019 WL 3290167, at *1 (D. Del. July 18, 2019), *aff'd*, 796 F. App'x 726 (Fed. Cir. 2020).

Under § 262(*l*)(9)(B), if the BA fails to provide the 180-day notice, the RPS can bring a declaratory judgment action for infringement of any patent in the section 3(A) list.[56]

F. Notable BPCIA Patent Dance Court Decisions

Since the BPCIA was enacted in 2010, only a handful of BPCIA cases have been filed. The limited number of BPCIA cases—especially as compared to the hundreds of abbreviated new drug application (ANDA) cases filed each year—correlates with the relatively small numbers of approved biological products and BAs. The BPCIA patent dance may also have reduced patent disputes such that the parties reached agreements and eliminated the need for litigation.

Still, courts' decisions in the small number of cases to date provide valuable insight into how the steps of the BPCIA patent dance play out in practice. Courts' interpretations of the BPCIA statute and rulings on practical issues are also instructive for both BAs and RPSs to make strategic business and litigation decisions. Below are some particularly significant lessons.

1. A BA Is Permitted to Withhold Its Application or Manufacturing Data (*Amgen Inc. v. Sandoz Inc.*)

As explained earlier in this chapter, a BA is permitted under § 262(*l*)(2) to withhold its aBLA and other information during the patent dance but with certain legal consequences. Multiple decisions have confirmed this interpretation of the BPCIA statutory framework.

This issue was addressed most significantly in a case that began with Sandoz filing in July 2014 an aBLA for its filgrastim biosimilar to Amgen's Neupogen®.[57] Although Sandoz notified Amgen of the aBLA filing, Sandoz did not provide its application and manufacturing information to Amgen pursuant to § 262(*l*)(2) of the patent dance, as described above.[58] Amgen sued Sandoz in the U.S. District Court for the Northern District of California in October 2014, seeking declaratory judgment and injunctive relief, arguing, inter alia, that Sandoz behaved unlawfully by failing to comply with the § 262(*l*)(2) disclosure and negotiation procedures.[59] Rejecting Amgen's argument and ruling in Sandoz's favor, the district court held

56. 42 U.S.C. § 262(*l*)(9).

57. Amgen Inc. v. Sandoz Inc., No. 14-CV-04741-RS, 2015 WL 1264756, at *1 (N.D. Cal. Mar. 19, 2015).

58. *Id.*

59. Amgen Inc. v. Sandoz Inc., 794 F.3d 1347, 1356 (Fed. Cir. 2015) ("Moreover, 35 U.S.C. § 271(e)(4) provides 'the *only* remedies which may be granted by a court for an act of infringement described in paragraph (2)' (emphasis added).").

that "[t]he BPCIA renders permissible . . . not to provide its BLA and/or manufacturing information to the reference product sponsor, subject only to the consequences set forth in 42 U.S.C. § 262(*l*)(9)(C)," precluding the BA from filing a declaratory injunction action for patent infringement, validity, or enforceability under the BPCIA.[60]

The Federal Circuit concluded that Sandoz "did not violate the BPCIA by not disclosing its aBLA and the manufacturing information by the statutory deadline."[61] Specifically, the court agreed that the language of § 262(*l*)(2)(A) should not be read in isolation and that "[a]s a direct consequence of failing to comply with paragraph (*l*)(2)(A), paragraph (*l*)(9)(C) bars the subsection (k) applicant from bringing a declaratory judgment action on patents that claim the biological product or its use."[62] The court further reasoned that "filing a subsection (k) application and failing to disclose the required information under paragraph (*l*)(2)(A) is an artificial 'act of infringement'" under 35 U.S.C. § 271(e)(2), the remedies for which are expressly limited under § 271(e)(4).[63] Thus, "when a subsection (k) applicant fails the disclosure requirement, 42 U.S.C. § 262(*l*)(9)(C) and 35 U.S.C. § 271(e) expressly provide the only remedies as those being based on a claim of patent infringement."[64]

The Supreme Court ultimately affirmed the Federal Circuit's holding that Sandoz did not violate the BPCIA and that no injunctive relief was available to Amgen, but disagreed with the reasoning of the Federal Circuit that relied on infringement and remedies under 35 U.S.C. § 271(e). The Supreme Court first explained that "Section 262(*l*)(2)(A)'s requirement that an applicant provide the sponsor with its application and manufacturing information is not enforceable by an injunction under federal law."[65] It further reasoned that "§ 262(*l*)(9)(C) [] provides a remedy for an applicant's failure to turn over its application and manufacturing information," and Sandoz's failure to disclose the application and manufacturing information required by § 262(*l*)(2)(A) "was not an act of artificial infringement remediable under § 271(e)(4)."[66] The Court concluded that "Sandoz failed to disclose the requisite information under § 262(*l*)(2)(A), and was accordingly

---

60. *Amgen*, 2015 WL 1264756, at *11, *8 ("as Sandoz's decision to forego the benefits of subsection (*l*)'s disclosure and negotiation procedures and instead open itself up to immediate suit for patent infringement was entirely permissible under 42 U.S.C. § 262, Sandoz has committed no wrongful act").

61. *Amgen*, 794 F.3d at 1356.

62. *Id.*

63. *Id.*

64. *Id.* at 1356–57.

65. Sandoz Inc. v. Amgen Inc., 137 S. Ct. 1664, 1667 (2017).

66. *Id.*

subject to the consequence specified in § 262(*l*)(9)(C)."[67] According to the Court, "[t]he presence of this remedy [under § 262(*l*)(9)(C)], coupled with the absence of any other textually specified remedies, indicates that Congress did not intend sponsors to have access to injunctive relief, at least as a matter of federal law, to enforce the disclosure requirement."[68]

Thus, despite the statutory language "shall" in § 262(*l*)(2)(A), the BA is permitted to withhold its aBLA and manufacturing information during the patent dance, with the consequence of losing its right to file a declaratory judgment action against the RPS during the second wave of litigation under § 262(*l*)(9)(C). The BA's failure to provide information, by itself, does not provide the RPS with certainty that it will obtain injunctive relief.

2. A BA Can File Its 180-Day Notice before FDA Approval of Its Biosimilar Product (*Amgen Inc. v. Sandoz Inc.*)

As explained earlier in this chapter, under § 262(*l*)(8)(A), a BA must provide a 180-day notice to trigger the second wave of litigation under the BPCIA. In the *Amgen* case discussed previously, the Supreme Court confirmed that the BA can provide its 180-day notice before FDA approval of its biosimilar product.

As background, Sandoz—just one day after the FDA had accepted its aBLA for review—notified Amgen that it had submitted an aBLA and that it intended to market Zarxio immediately upon receiving FDA approval.[69] In other words, Sandoz simultaneously provided both its section 2(A) notice and its 180-day notice of commercial marketing under § 262(*l*)(8)(A) immediately after its aBLA was accepted for review and prior to FDA approval. In its suit in the U.S. District Court for the Northern District of California, Amgen argued that Sandoz's notice of commercial marketing prior to FDA approval violated the BPCIA as premature and ineffective, such that Sandoz should be enjoined from launching its aBLA product after FDA approval.[70]

The district court rejected Amgen's argument and concluded that it is "not wrongful for Sandoz to give Amgen its 180 days' notice prior to first commercial marketing pursuant to subparagraph (*l*)(8)(A) in July 2014, in advance of receiving FDA approval."[71] The court reasoned that "[b]ecause the FDA cannot license a biosimilar until twelve years after approval of a reference product, Amgen's reading would tack an unconditional extra

67. *Id.*
68. *Id.* at 1668.
69. *Id.*
70. Amgen Inc. v. Sandoz Inc., No. 14-CV-04741-RS, 2015 WL 1264756, at *1 (N.D. Cal. Mar. 19, 2015).
71. *Id.* at *8.

six months of market exclusivity onto the twelve years reference product sponsors already enjoy under 42 U.S.C. § 262(k)(7)(A)."[72]

On appeal, the Federal Circuit reversed the district court on this issue based on interpreting the statutory language of § 262(*l*)(8)(A) to require that the aBLA product must have been "licensed" (i.e., approved by the FDA) before the BA can provide its 180-day notice.[73] Accordingly, the Federal Circuit held, inter alia, that "under paragraph (*l*)(8)(A), a subsection (k) applicant may only give effective notice of commercial marketing after the FDA has licensed its product" and that Sandoz was prohibited from marketing its aBLA product until at least 180 days after FDA approval.[74]

The Supreme Court reversed the Federal Circuit on this notice issue. Focusing on the language of § 262(*l*)(8)(A), the Court explained "[b]ecause the phrase 'of the biological product licensed under subsection (k)' modifies 'commercial marketing' rather than 'notice,' 'commercial marketing' is the point in time by which the biosimilar must be 'licensed.'"[75] Thus, the Court concluded that the plain language of the statute determines that "the applicant may provide notice either before or after receiving FDA approval."[76]

As a result, as long as a BA provides notice to an RPS that it will commercialize its biosimilar product at least 180 days before its commercialization—even if it provides the notice well in advance of actual approval of its aBLA—the BA satisfies the requirement of § 262(*l*)(8)(A). As further explained in this chapter, whether a BA has standing to file a declaratory judgment immediately after providing its 180-day notice is a separate issue.

3. An RPS Can File Multiple Suits and Assert Newly Issued Patents against the BA (Multiple Cases)

As explained previously, § 262(*l*)(7) allows an RPS to assert newly issued patents not included on the original section 3(A) list separately from those litigated during the first-wave litigation. When a newly issued patent is litigated, courts consider invalidity and infringement issues concerning the new patent separately from those for patents already litigated during the first-wave litigation under the BPCIA.

During a patent dance related to Apotex's aBLA for biosimilars to Amgen's recombinant proteins pegfilgrastim (Neulasta®) and filgrastim (Neupogen®) products, Amgen identified one patent on its section 3(A) list

72. *Id.*
73. Amgen Inc. v. Sandoz Inc., 794 F.3d 1347, 1358 (Fed. Cir. 2015).
74. *Id.* at 1357.
75. Sandoz Inc. v. Amgen Inc., 137 S. Ct. 1664, 1677 (2017).
76. *Id.*

and then sued Apotex under the BPCIA for infringement of this patent.[77] In November 2017, the Federal Circuit affirmed the district court's holding that Amgen failed to meet its burden to show that Apotex infringes claim 1 reciting a "refold mixture," which is construed to require a "high protein concentration [] . . . at or above about 1 [gram/liter (g/L)]."[78]

In January 2018, a new Amgen patent issued that was related to the previously litigated patent.[79] Amgen asserted this new patent against Apotex in a second litigation under § 262(*l*)(7).[80] Apotex moved to dismiss, alleging that Amgen's infringement claims were barred by collateral estoppel based on the prior litigation.[81] Denying Apotex's motion, the district court explained that the claim language of the newly issued patent differed from that of the previously litigated patent, and for this reason refused to apply collateral estoppel "at this stage of the proceedings."[82] The court further explained that collateral estoppel does not necessarily apply merely because two patents are related.[83] Thus, the court confirmed the appropriateness of Amgen's second suit asserting the newly issued patent and considered arguments for that patent independently from the earlier case.

In the context of second-wave litigation, courts have confirmed that the RPS may seek injunctive relief because the submission of an aBLA is an "artificial" act of infringement under 35 U.S.C. § 271(e)(2).[84] For instance, in *AbbVie v. Alvotech*, AbbVie brought a first-wave suit against Alvotech hf., a BA developing a biosimilar of AbbVie's Humira®, for infringement of certain patents.[85] When AbbVie subsequently filed a second patent infringement suit against Alvotech hf. for infringement of the remaining patents from the original section 3(A) list, Alvotech moved to dismiss, arguing that § 262(*l*)(8)–(9) second wave is limited to a declaratory judgment action, precluding 35 U.S.C. § 271(e)(2)(C)(i) infringement claims and injunctive relief.[86] The district court rejected Alvotech's arguments, explaining that "under § 271(e)(2), the submission of a BLA application creates an artificial act of infringement as to all patents identified by the RPS pursuant to § 262(*l*)(3), without regard to whether the patents

77. Amgen Inc. v. Apotex Inc., 712 F. App'x 985, 986 (Fed. Cir. 2017).

78. *Id.* at 988–93.

79. Amgen Inc. v. Apotex Inc., No. 18-61828-CIV-WPD/LSS, 2019 WL 13061848, at *1 (S.D. Fla. Apr. 5, 2019).

80. *Id.*

81. *Id.* at *3.

82. *Id.* at *4–5.

83. *Id.*

84. *See* Sandoz Inc. v. Amgen Inc., 137 S. Ct. 1664, 1670 (2017) ("Section 271(e)(4) provides remedies for artificial infringement, including injunctive relief and damages.").

85. No. 21 C 2258, 2021 WL 3737733, at *1 (N.D. Ill. Aug. 23, 2021).

86. AbbVie Inc. v. Alvotech hf., 582 F. Supp. 3d 584, 587 (N.D. Ill. 2022).

are asserted in the first phase of the litigation or the second."[87] The court further explained that "nothing in § 262(*l*)(9) indicates that its reference to an 'action . . . for a declaration of infringement, validity, or enforceability' was intended to exclude all other remedies."[88] Thus, an RPS can seek remedies for a BA's patent infringement under § 271(e)(4) not limited by the declaratory judgment scope of § 262(*l*)(9).

4. An RPS Should Not Wait Until Biosimilar Approval to Seek a Preliminary Injunction (*Genentech, Inc. v. Amgen Inc.*)

As discussed earlier in this chapter, an RPS is entitled to seek a preliminary injunction for the patents in the second-wave litigation after receiving the BA's 180day notice under § 262(*l*)(8)(B). However, undue delay in raising a motion for a preliminary injunction may result in denial of this relief. This fact pattern was addressed in *Genentech, Inc. v. Amgen Inc.*, where the U.S. District Court for the District of Delaware, affirmed by the Federal Circuit, held that Genentech was not entitled to a preliminary injunction because it waited to file its motion until after the biosimilar product had been approved.[89]

Amgen submitted an aBLA for Kanjinti, a biosimilar of Genentech's drug product Herceptin®, and started the patent dance by providing a copy of its aBLA.[90] Amgen also served Genentech its 180-day notice, although the aBLA had not yet been approved for marketing. Genentech then sued Amgen under the BPCIA in the District Court of Delaware but did not initially seek a preliminary injunction against Amgen.[91] Later during that litigation, after Kanjinti was approved by the FDA, Genentech first moved for a preliminary injunction.[92]

In denying the preliminary injunction, the district court noted that "Genentech did not file its motion for a preliminary injunction until . . . fourteen months after receiving the Notice of Commercial Marketing, three months after receiving a fairly specific launch date, and almost one month after Amgen had FDA approval to launch Kanjinti."[93] To the court, such actions are "contrary to the spirit and purpose of the BPCIA" because the 180-day period is designed to prevent exactly the circumstances that Genentech has engineered in this case—a "race to court for immediate

87. *Id.* at 591.

88. *Id.* at 592.

89. No. CV 18-924-CFC, 2019 WL 3290167, at *1 (D. Del. July 18, 2019), *aff'd*, 796 F. App'x 726 (Fed. Cir. 2020).

90. Genentech, Inc. v. Amgen Inc., No. CV 18-924-CFC, 2018 WL 5310437, ¶ 21 (D. Del. July 25, 2018).

91. *Genentech*, 2019 WL 3290167, at *1.

92. *Id.*

93. *Id.* at *2.

relief to avoid irreparable harm from market entry, and . . . the hurried motion practice that (8)(A) is designed to replace."[94] Accordingly, the court denied Genentech's motion.[95]

Thus, although even a timely submitted motion for preliminary injunction may not be granted, undue delay in seeking preliminary injunction and waiting until after FDA approval of the aBLA may be disfavored by courts.

5. It May Be Premature for a BA to File a Declaratory Judgment Action before Completing the Patent Dance (Multiple Cases)

A BA cannot file a declaratory judgment action against an RPS before it completes clinical studies for FDA approval of its biosimilar product or immediately after its aBLA submission. Moreover, even after a BA has provided the 180-day notice, it cannot file a declaratory judgment action against an RPS before completing the patent dance. The proper timing for a BA to file a declaratory judgment suit against an RPS has been addressed by multiple courts in multiple cases. In each instance, the courts have rejected attempts by the BA to initiate declaratory judgment actions as premature and failing to meet the case or controversy standard for a declaratory judgment action.

Sandoz Inc. v. Amgen Inc. was a declaratory judgment action filed by Sandoz seeking to invalidate patents of Amgen *on the same day* Sandoz had started its Phase III trial on its biosimilar of Amgen's Enbrel®.[96] The Federal Circuit concluded that Sandoz's complaint did not present a case or controversy and affirmed the district court's dismissal of the case.[97] The court explained that because Sandoz had not yet finished its clinical studies that are covered by the safe harbor under 35 U.S.C. § 271(e)(1) and had not filed an aBLA, the events exposing Sandoz to infringement liability "may not occur as anticipated, or indeed may not occur at all."[98] According to the court, its affirmance of the dismissal "is consistent with our cases under the Hatch-Waxman Act."[99]

In *Celltrion Healthcare Co. v. Kennedy Trust for Rheumatology Research*, Celltrion, as the developer of Remsima (a biosimilar version of Remicade®), filed a declaratory judgment action against the patent owner (Kennedy) after Celltrion had completed a bridging clinical study suggested by the FDA but while it was still actively communicating with the

94. *Id.* at *3.
95. *Id.*
96. 773 F.3d 1274, 1276 (Fed. Cir. 2014).
97. *Id.* at 1278.
98. *Id.*
99. *Id.*

FDA to finalize the specifics of its aBLA.[100] The U.S. District Court for the Southern District of New York concluded that while Celltrion "exhibit[ed] a true intention to bring Remsima to the U.S. market, Celltrion is simply too far from receiving FDA approval of Remsima for the exercise of declaratory judgment jurisdiction to be proper."[101] To the court, Celltrion's aBLA "approval preparations are simply not at a stage that can support a declaratory judgment action."[102]

After finding that there was no actual case or controversy to support Celltrion's declaratory judgment action, the court further emphasized it would exercise its discretion to decline to hear the case further in view of the remedies provided to Celltrion under the BPCIA.[103] The court explained that "[t]here is no reason to believe, and Celltrion has failed to demonstrate or even allege, that the dispute resolution procedure established by the BPCIA would be insufficient to resolve any patent disputes here."[104] To the court, "Celltrion's attempts to skirt the BPCIA's dispute resolution mechanisms while reaping the benefits of its approval process is improper."[105] The court also rejected Celltrion's argument that the BPCIA patent dance does not apply because Kennedy is the patent owner instead of an RPS, noting that the BPCIA does provide for a level of involvement by the patent owner.[106] The court concluded that "[s]hould Celltrion have a ripened patent dispute against Kennedy once it properly engages in the BPCIA dispute resolution procedures and once it is further along the pathway towards approval of its biosimilar, Celltrion may litigate those issues at that time."[107]

The same district court similarly dismissed Hospira's declaratory judgment action against the RPS, Janssen Biotech.[108] In this case, Hospira entered a co-licensing agreement with Celltrion to co-exclusively market the biosimilar product infliximab under the name Inflectra and filed a declaratory judgment action against Janssen Biotech within a month after Celltrion filed its aBLA.[109] The district court concluded that "the instant case presents an even more compelling reason for dismissal than that

100. No. CV 14-2256, 2014 WL 6765996, at *1 (S.D.N.Y. Dec. 1, 2014).
101. *Id.* at *3.
102. *Id.*
103. *Id.* at *4.
104. *Id.*
105. *Id.*
106. *Id.* at *5.
107. *Id.*
108. Hospira, Inc. v. Janssen Biotech, Inc., No. CV 14-7049, 2014 WL 6766263, at *1 (S.D.N.Y. Dec. 1, 2014).
109. *Id.*

presented in *Celltrion*."[110] The court explained that it was improper for Hospira to "utilize the BPCIA pathway for approval of its biosimilar drug, yet disavow[] the BPCIA's authority over patent disputes."[111] The court reiterated that "the existence of the BPCIA mechanisms for dispute resolution counsels against the exercise of jurisdiction over this complaint" and that Hospira's claims were too attenuated from any crystallized dispute to qualify as a justiciable case or controversy.[112]

In *Amgen Inc. v. Genentech, Inc.*, although Amgen provided its 180-day notice after it already received the FDA's approval of its aBLA and before commercializing its biosimilar product, the U.S. District Court for the Central District of California still declined to hear the case in view of Amgen's failure to complete the required negotiation steps under the BPCIA framework.[113] In this case, Amgen triggered the patent dance scheme on January 4, 2017, when it filed its aBLA.[114] While the parties were in the process of exchanging information and statements and negotiating the patents to be litigated, the FDA approved Amgen's aBLA on September 14, 2017, the same day on which the parties started negotiation under § 262(*l*)(4).[115] The statutory period for negotiations expired on September 29, 2017, with the parties unable to reach agreement under § 262(*l*)(4)(B).[116] After the parties' statutory period for negotiations ended, on October 6, 2017, Amgen provided its § 262(*l*)(8)(A) notice of commercial marketing.[117] Rather than proceeding with the final patent exchange procedures set out by the BPCIA for the first phase, Amgen immediately filed a lawsuit for declaratory judgment as to all patents on Genentech's § 262(*l*)(3)(A) list.[118]

The district court emphasized that "[a]llowing an applicant to sidestep the BPCIA's exchange and negotiation requirements and bring suit on any patent simply by filing its notice of commercial marketing would effectively vitiate the BPCIA's provisions."[119] Accordingly, "Amgen's argument that it was entitled to bring suit after providing its notice under § 262(*l*)(8)(A) but before completing the rest of the BPCIA's patent list exchange steps is rejected."[120]

---

110. *Id.*
111. *Id.*
112. *Id.*
113. No. 17-7349, 2018 WL 910198, at *1 (C.D. Cal. Jan. 11, 2018).
114. *Id.* at *2.
115. *Id.*
116. *Id.*
117. *Id.*
118. *Id.*
119. *Id.* at *4.
120. *Id.*

The rule from these cases is fairly clear: it is too early for a BA to file a declaratory judgment suit against the RPS during clinical studies or right after submitting its aBLA. Moreover, even after a BA provides its 180-day notice, it still should consider at least completing the required patent dance before filing a declaratory judgment suit against the RPS to avoid possible court dismissal.

6. Factual Statements Made by Parties during the Patent Dance Are Not Necessarily Dispositive during Later Litigation (*Amgen Inc. v. Apotex Inc.*)

During the patent dance, after the BA provides its aBLA and manufacturing information to the RPS under § 262(*l*)(2), each party may rely on the information provided by the putative opponents to make their respective sections 3(B) and 3(C) statements. But when later evidence during litigation shows that such information is inaccurate, the information and statements made during the patent dance are not necessarily dispositive.

In *Amgen Inc. v. Apotex Inc.*, Apotex filed aBLAs to market biosimilars of Amgen's Neulasta® and Neupogen®, and provided Amgen with copies of its aBLAs.[121] On its section 3(A) list, Amgen identified a manufacturing process patent reciting a "refold mixture," which was later construed by the district court as having a "high protein concentration[ ] . . . at or above about 1 g/L."[122] During the first-wave litigation after the patent dance, Amgen relied on Apotex's aBLA that was provided during the patent dance and certain language in Apotex's pre-litigation letters, alleging that those disclosures and statements support that Apotex's protein concentration during manufacture is 0.9–1.4 g/L, which infringes claim 1 that requires a protein concentration of at or above about 1 g/L.[123]

While the Federal Circuit agreed that Apotex's pre-litigation statements are party admissions, it also noted that other evidence presented at trial indicated that the pre-litigation information Amgen relied on was inaccurate and factually incorrect.[124] Because Amgen did not present any evidence, other than the pre-litigation letters themselves, to contradict Apotex's witness testimony supporting that the maximum protein concentration in Apotex's process is below 1 g/L, the court held that Amgen failed to show infringement.[125]

Thus, while the parties can rely on pre-litigation statements made during the patent dance, they should still actively compile additional evidence

121. 712 F. App'x 985, 986 (Fed. Cir. 2017).
122. *Id.* at 988.
123. *Id.*
124. *Id.* at 989–90.
125. *Id.* at 990.

during litigation to meet their respective burdens of proving invalidity or infringement. Inaccurate information exchanged during the patent dance may be discarded by the court for lack of probative value.

7. BPCIA Litigation Venue (Multiple Cases)

Courts' rulings have further clarified the legal standard for proper venue and confirmed that earlier court precedents on the venue for ANDA litigation apply to the first- and second-wave litigations under §§ 262(*l*)(6) and 262(*l*)(8) of the BPCIA.

In *Valeant Pharmaceuticals North America LLC v. Mylan Pharmaceuticals Inc.*, the Federal Circuit emphasized that in Hatch-Waxman litigation, venue is proper "only in districts where actions related to the submission of an Abbreviated New Drug Application ('ANDA') occur, not in all locations where future distribution of the generic products specified in the ANDA is contemplated."[126] The court held that "venue in Hatch-Waxman cases must be predicated on past acts of infringement—i.e., acts that occurred before the action alleging infringement was filed."[127] Although the *Valeant* decision discusses venue in Hatch-Waxman cases, the U.S. District Court for the Northern District of Illinois applied the same venue requirement to BPCIA cases.

In *AbbVie v. Alvotech hf.*, AbbVie initiated the first-wave litigation under § 262(*l*)(6) against Alvotech hf., an Icelandic company, in Illinois.[128] Alvotech moved to dismiss, arguing that its Virginia subsidiary, Alvotech USA, was the aBLA "submitter" and therefore a Federal Rule of Civil Procedure 19 "necessary party" for which Illinois is an improper venue.[129] The district court first considered the Federal Circuit's previous findings concerning qualification of a "submitter" of an ANDA under § 271(e), concluding that "the Federal Circuit's interpretation in *Rosuvastatin* of what it means 'to submit' an application under § 271(e)(2) controls, absent any express BPCIA provision to the contrary."[130] The court then explained that, based on earlier precedent, "[p]arties actively involved in preparing the ANDA are deemed to have submitted the ANDA, regardless of whether they are the named applicant, especially where the parties involved are in the same corporate family. Active involvement includes marketing and distributing the approved generic drugs in the United States."[131] Applying these legal standards to Alvotech hf., the court concluded that AbbVie's

126. 978 F.3d 1374, 1375 (Fed. Cir. 2020).
127. *Id.* at 1381.
128. No. 21 C 2258, 2021 WL 3737733, at *1 (N.D. Ill. Aug. 23, 2021).
129. *Id.* at *4.
130. *Id.* at *6 (citing *In re* Rosuvastatin, 703 F.3d 511 (Fed. Cir. 2012)), *8.
131. *Id.*

complaint adequately pled that Alvotech hf. is a "submit[ter]" of the aBLA within the meaning of 35 U.S.C. § 271(e)(2)(C) and denied Alvotech's motion to dismiss.[132] Thus, proper venue for BPCIA litigation, like venue in ANDA litigation, depends on identifying the appropriate "submitter" of the aBLA.

8. Conclusion

While many questions remain unanswered, the case law discussed earlier has provided a foundation for guiding BAs and RPSs through the patent dance and sheds light on the legal consequences of failing to complete certain steps of the dance. With the increasing number of BAs and new aBLA filings, new court decisions should provide additional clarification and address new issues that result from the statutory language and application of the BPCIA. Biologic drug developers should pay close attention to this developing area of the law to make informed strategic business and litigation decisions and take full advantage of the BPCIA framework to accomplish productive negotiation and resolution of patent disputes.

II. The Purple Book

Since February 2020, the FDA has started providing an online searchable database containing information about all FDA-licensed biological products, which is called the "Purple Book."[133] The Purple Book contains information about all FDA-licensed biological products regulated by the Center for Drug Evaluation and Research (CDER), including any biosimilar and interchangeable biological products, licensed (approved) by the FDA and FDA-licensed allergenic, cellular and gene therapy, hematologic, and vaccine products regulated by the Center for Biologics Evaluation and Research (CBER).[134] Such information may be useful for a variety of users in the general public, including patients, health care providers, manufacturers, and researchers.

As explained in Part I, the BPPT section of the Consolidated Appropriations Act of 2021 required that the FDA *must* publish and make available to the public in a searchable, electronic format (1) a list of biological products, by nonproprietary name, for which a biologics license under

132. *Id.* at *8–9.

133. *Purple Book Database of Licensed Biological Products*, FDA, https://purplebooksearch.fda.gov/ (last updated Jan. 29, 2024).

134. *Center for Drug Evaluation and Research/CDER*, FDA, https://www.fda.gov/about-fda/fda-organization/center-drug-evaluation-and-research-cder (last updated Aug. 14, 2023).

section 351(a) or section 351(k) of the PHS Act is in effect; (2) the date of licensure of the marketing application and the application number; (3) the licensure status; and (4) if available, marketing status.[135]

The statute also requires that the FDA revise the list every 30 days to include any additional products licensed under section 351(a) or section 351(k) of the PHS Act.[136] Indeed, the FDA's website states that "[a]n FDA-approved biological product or updates to an approved product's information will generally be added to the Purple Book within 10 business days of approval."[137] In addition, for each biological product on the list, the BPPT requires that the Purple Book list each reference product exclusivity period and each first interchangeable exclusivity period for which the FDA has determined such biological product to be eligible and for which such period has not concluded.[138]

A BLA holder can provide to the FDA a report containing information required to be listed in the Purple Book by "submitting a Cover Letter to each applicable BLA file (i.e., each approved BLA with products listed as having a status of 'Rx' in the Purple Book that is covered by such one-time report) via the Electronic Submissions Gateway."[139] If a BLA sponsor has multiple BLAs to address in the report, "the same report can be submitted to each applicable BLA file as long as the report addresses each biological product licensed under all of the sponsor's applicable BLAs."[140] "In other words, the same report can be submitted to each applicable BLA file as part of a single grouped submission or separate reports addressing individual products can be submitted to each applicable BLA file."[141] The RPS should also send an email with a copy of the cover letter to PurpleBook@fda.hhs.gov.[142]

Importantly, as explained earlier, the BPPT section of the Consolidated Appropriations Act of 2021 further requires publication in the Purple Book of patents in the RPS's section 3(A) list and any supplements added under subsection (*l*)(7) (i.e., newly issued or licensed patents) that it

---

135. BPPT Section of the Consolidated Appropriations Act of 2021, § 325(a)(9)(A)(iii), Pub. L. No. 116-260, 134 Stat. 1182 (2020); *see also Purple Book Database of Licensed Biological Products FAQs*, *supra* note 10 (FAQ #12).

136. BPPT § 325(a)(9)(A)(ii); *see also Purple Book Database of Licensed Biological Products FAQs*, *supra* note 10 (FAQ #12).

137. *Purple Book Database of Licensed Biological Products FAQs*, *supra* note 10 (FAQ #12).

138. BPPT § 325(a)(9)(A)(iv); *see also Purple Book Database of Licensed Biological Products FAQs*, *supra* note 10 (FAQ #12).

139. *Purple Book Database of Licensed Biological Products FAQs*, *supra* note 10 (FAQ #12).

140. *Id.*

141. *Id.*

142. *Id.*

has provided to the BA during the patent dance. Specifically, under section 325(a)(9)(A)(iii) of the BPPT:

> Not later than 30 days after a list of patents under subsection (*l*)(3)(A), or a supplement to such list under subsection (*l*)(7), has been provided by the reference product sponsor to the subsection (k) applicant respecting a biological product included on the list published under this subparagraph, the reference product sponsor shall provide such list of patents (or supplement thereto) and their corresponding expiry dates to the Secretary.[143]

The RPS is also required to provide to the FDA any subsequent or supplemental lists, and their corresponding expiry dates, within 30 days of the provision of such lists to a 351(k) applicant under section 351(*l*)(3)(A) or (*l*)(7) of the PHS Act.[144]

The FDA began publishing patent lists in the Purple Book in June 2021.[145] The BPPT section of the Consolidated Appropriations Act of 2021 also requires the FDA to publish the updates and supplemental information provided by the RPS along with its updates of the Purple Book every 30 days after the publication of the first list.[146] The FDA also states that it "intends to revise the published list on a monthly basis to include any additional initial lists and any updates from subsequent or supplemental lists."[147] The FDA, however, emphasizes that its role in publishing patent information is ministerial, and the FDA does not consider the applicability of patents to a biosimilar product (e.g., validity, enforceability, or potential infringement) in publishing the information described in section 351(k)(9) of the PHS Act, nor in the FDA's review of a 351(k) BLA or supplement to a 351(k) BLA.[148]

---

143. BPPT § 325(a)(9)(A)(iii); *see also Purple Book Database of Licensed Biological Products FAQs*, *supra* note 10 (FAQ #12).

144. BPPT § 325(a)(9)(A)(iii); *see also Purple Book Database of Licensed Biological Products FAQs*, *supra* note 10 (FAQ #12).

145. *Purple Book Database of Licensed Biological Products FAQs*, *supra* note 10 (FAQ #12).

146. BPPT § 325(a)(9)(A)(iii); *see also Purple Book Database of Licensed Biological Products FAQs*, *supra* note 10 (FAQ #12).

147. *Purple Book Database of Licensed Biological Products FAQs*, *supra* note 10 (FAQ #12).

148. *Id.*

III. Conclusion

The BPCIA legal framework and FDA Purple Book listing rules work in synergy to provide a balanced system for RPSs and BAs to resolve patent disputes through negotiation and litigation. This chapter summarizes case law interpreting the BPCIA as well as pertinent FDA requirements, aiming to help companies navigate these legal disputes while providing information for making more informed business decisions. Given the ever-increasing number of biologics in the marketplace and accelerating pace of BPCIA litigation, we recommend continued monitoring of this exciting area of the law.

chapter 5

Notable Differences between Hatch-Waxman and BPCIA Litigation: What Can We Learn?*

I. Introduction

The Hatch-Waxman Act and the Biologics Price Competition and Innovation Act (BPCIA) both present pathways for bringing affordable medicines to the American public, and both provide a framework within which patent owners and patent challengers can litigate to resolve patent rights and liabilities prior to launch. Given these conceptual similarities, questions arise regarding the extent to which and the ways in which BPCIA litigants can learn from the extensive history of Hatch-Waxman litigation. In 2024, Hatch-Waxman celebrates its 40th anniversary, while the BPCIA marks 14 years since its enactment. While neither can truly be considered young or new, particularly by comparison to the BPCIA, Hatch-Waxman litigation exploded in the years since its enactment and has since matured. Of course, challenges abound in every case, but considerations formerly unique to Hatch-Waxman litigation often manifest in BPCIA cases, though with notable differences. An understanding of both of these acts and the implications can assist the practitioner, and calls to mind the proverb that while experience may be the best teacher, a fool learns from no other.

*Stephen R. Auten and Luke T. Shannon, Taft Stettinius & Hollister LLP.

II. Overview of the Hatch-Waxman Act and the BPCIA

A. Overview of the Hatch-Waxman Act

The Hatch-Waxman Act created a framework within which an abbreviated new drug application (ANDA) applicant and new drug application (NDA) holder can resolve patent issues in federal court along a predictable timetable, with the goal of avoiding the risk to the ANDA applicant of patent infringement damages. In kind, because the patent issues are generally resolved before a generic drug launches, the branded pharmaceutical companies enjoy the benefit of resolving their patent disputes before generic entry erodes their markets. Under the Hatch-Waxman Act, branded drug companies identify any patents that cover the main aspects of their products (e.g., drug substance, drug product, method of use), which the U.S. Food and Drug Administration (FDA) publishes (or "lists," in industry vernacular) in the "Orange Book."[1]

When a generic drug company seeks approval to market a generic product, the generic drug company must account for each Orange Book-listed patent.[2] Notably, the generic drug company can certify—through a so-called Paragraph IV certification—that the marketing of its product will not infringe the identified Orange Book-listed patent, and/or that that patent is invalid.[3] Such a certification is deemed to be a technical act of infringement, and provides the prerequisite for the brand company to bring a patent litigation suit.[4]

Within 20 days after FDA confirms receipt of an ANDA that contains a Paragraph IV certification, the ANDA applicant must notify the owner of the patents and the NDA holder of that certification.[5] That notification must contain a "detailed statement" (often called a "notice letter") providing the bases for the ANDA applicant's belief that the Orange Book-listed patents are invalid and/or not infringed.[6]

The patent owner may then bring a patent infringement lawsuit against the ANDA applicant in federal court asserting infringement of the Orange Book–listed patents to which the ANDA applicant has submitted a Paragraph IV certification. If that patent infringement suit is initiated within 45 days of the patent owner's receipt of the notice letter, then FDA is prohibited from granting final approval to an ANDA until the earliest

1. 21 U.S.C. § 355(b)(1)(A)(viii).
2. *Id.* § 355(j)(2)(A)(vii).
3. *Id.* § 355(j)(2)(A)(vii)(IV).
4. 35 U.S.C. § 271(e)(2).
5. 21 U.S.C. § 355(j)(2)(B)(ii), (iii).
6. *Id.* § 355(j)(2)(B)(iv)(II).

of the date of the court's decision that the asserted patent is found to be invalid or not infringed, the date the asserted patent expires, or the date 30 months subsequent to the patent owner's receipt of the notice of Paragraph IV certification (a so-called "30-month stay").[7]

Under 35 U.S.C. § 271(e)(4), the relief the patent owner seeks is injunctive—i.e., an injunction preventing final approval by FDA of the ANDA until the expiration of the relevant Orange Book-listed patents.

The purpose of the 30-month stay is to provide the parties with time sufficient to resolve the patent issues prior to approval and consequent potential "at risk" launch of the generic product, which may introduce considerations relating to damages. Because an at-risk launch changes the stakes of the litigation for both sides (e.g., the possibility of lost profits-based damages, and the possibility of price erosion and other market effects), a final approval often coincides with a patent owner's motion for preliminary injunction or temporary restraining order.

B. Overview of the BPCIA

Like the Hatch-Waxman Act, the BPCIA sets forth an abbreviated process by which an applicant can seek FDA approval to market a biological product based on a previously approved biological product (called the "reference product"). Conceptually similar to bioequivalence under the Hatch-Waxman Act, the BPCIA requires the applicant's biological product to be "biosimilar" to the reference product. Also like the Hatch-Waxman Act, the BPCIA provides an avenue for the biosimilar applicant and the reference product sponsor to address (and potentially resolve) patent infringement liability concerns stemming from the biosimilar applicant's marketing of the biosimilar.

In what can be considered a first phase of (likely) litigation, the biosimilar applicant and reference product sponsor engage in what is colloquially known as the "patent dance." Under the rules, within 20 days of FDA's accepting the biosimilar application (i.e., the abbreviated biologics license application, or "aBLA"), the biosimilar applicant must notify the reference product sponsor and provide confidential access to its aBLA.[8] Within 60 days thereafter, the reference product sponsor must provide the biosimilar applicant a list of patents that the reference product sponsor believes could reasonably be asserted against the biosimilar applicant, as well as "an identification of patents on such list that the reference product sponsor would be prepared to license."[9] Within 60 days of its receipt of that list from the reference product sponsor, the biosimilar applicant, in turn, may provide its own

7. *Id.* § 355(j)(5)(B)(iii).
8. 42 U.S.C. § 262(*l*)(2).
9. *Id.* § 262(*l*)(3)(A).

list of patents that it believes "a claim of patent infringement could reasonably be asserted by the reference product sponsor"; the biosimilar applicant must also provide a detailed statement describing on a claim-by-claim basis its positions regarding invalidity, unenforceability, and noninfringement of the patents identified by it or by the reference product sponsor.[10] The reference product sponsor then has 60 days within which to provide to the biosimilar applicant a detailed statement describing, on a claim-by-claim basis, its positions regarding infringement, validity, and enforceability.[11] The BPCIA provides 15 days thereafter for the parties to "engage in good faith negotiations to agree on which, if any, patents . . . shall be the subject of an action for patent infringement" as part of the first phase of (likely) litigation.[12] The reference product sponsor may then file a patent infringement suit, asserting the agreed-upon patents,[13] and must do so within 30 days in order to preserve a right to damages other than a reasonable royalty.[14]

The BPCIA also contemplates a potential second round of litigation under 42 U.S.C. § 262(*l*)(8). Specifically, the biosimilar applicant must provide notice to the reference product sponsor no later than 180 days before commercial marketing of the biosimilar.[15] Subsequently, the reference product sponsor may sue the biosimilar applicant for infringement of all other patents that were listed by the parties as part of their exchange under 42 U.S.C. § 262(*l*)(3)(A) or (B).[16]

In 2021, Congress passed the Consolidated Appropriations Act of 2021, which included a section called Biological Product Patent Transparency (BPPT). The BPPT requires FDA to publish patent lists provided by reference product sponsors (i.e., biologics license application (BLA) holders) to FDA for certain licensed biological products. FDA does so in the so-called "Purple Book." Specifically, a reference product sponsor is required to provide to FDA, as described in section 351(k)(9)(A)(iii) of the Public Health Service (PHS) Act, the list of patents and corresponding expiry dates (also referred to as the "initial list"), not later than 30 days after the reference product sponsor has provided the initial list to a 351(k) applicant under section 351(*l*)(3)(A) or (*l*)(7) of the PHS Act. The reference product sponsor is also required to provide to FDA any subsequent or supplemental lists, and their corresponding expiry dates, within 30 days of the provision of

---

10. *Id.* § 262(*l*)(3)(B).
11. *Id.* § 262(*l*)(3)(C).
12. *Id.* § 262(*l*)(4)(A). There is an additional step if no agreement has been reached. *Id.* § 262(*l*)(4)(B).
13. *Id.* § 262(*l*)(6).
14. 35 U.S.C. § 271(e)(6)(A), (B).
15. 42 U.S.C. § 262(*l*)(8)(A).
16. *Id.* § 262(*l*)(8)(B).

such lists to a 351(k) applicant under section 351(*l*)(3)(A) or (*l*)(7) of the PHS Act. Pursuant to section 351(k)(9)(A)(iii) of the PHS Act, FDA shall include this information in the published list and revise it on a monthly basis to include any additional initial lists and any updates from subsequent or supplemental lists.

As with the Orange Book, FDA's role in publishing patent information in the Purple Book is ministerial, and FDA does not consider the applicability of patents to a biosimilar product (e.g., validity, enforceability, or potential infringement) in publishing the information described in section 351(k)(9) of the PHS Act, nor in FDA's review of a 351(k) BLA or supplement to a 351(k) BLA.

III. Pre-Suit Considerations: Where to Litigate?

A. Venue and Jurisdiction Questions

Recent case law has clarified where Hatch-Waxman cases may be brought. The result of that case law is to bring some measure of clarity as to where Hatch-Waxman cases may proceed. Much of the analysis has carried over to BPCIA litigation and, where it has not, the Hatch-Waxman analysis would seem to apply or at least to inform a court.

1. Venue

a. Hatch-Waxman Venue

Under federal statute, patent infringement cases may only be brought where the defendant resides or where the defendant has committed acts of infringement and has an established place of business.[17] In *TC Heartland LLC v. Kraft Foods Group Brands LLC*,[18] the U.S. Supreme Court ruled that a corporate defendant "resides" for purposes of § 1400(b) only in the state of incorporation. The question pertinent to Hatch-Waxman cases then became the application of the language found in § 1400(b), "where the defendant has committed acts of infringement."

The Federal Circuit addressed this question in the years following *TC Heartland*. In *Valeant Pharmaceuticals North America LLC v. Mylan Pharmaceuticals Inc.*,[19] the Federal Circuit provided clarity as to the meaning of "acts of infringement" in Hatch-Waxman cases that are based on the filing of an ANDA, before the generic product has launched. The Federal Circuit confirmed that the infringing acts supporting venue are not the likely or

17. 28 U.S.C. § 1400(b).
18. 581 U.S. 258 (2017).
19. 978 F.3d 1374 (Fed. Cir. 2020).

intended future distribution of the ANDA product, but rather the acts of infringement relevant to venue must be sufficiently related to the ANDA submission. The court held that venue in Hatch-Waxman cases must be based on past acts of infringement, reasoning that "it is the submission of the ANDA, and only the submission, that constitutes an act of infringement in this context."[20] The court concluded that venue "is proper only in those districts that are sufficiently related to the ANDA submission—in those districts where acts occurred that would suffice to categorize those taking them as a 'submitter' under § 271(e)."[21]

In concrete terms, venue in Hatch-Waxman cases based on the "acts of infringement" prong of § 1400(b) presumably includes the district(s) in which the ANDA filer prepared the ANDA and from which the ANDA was sent. Some have suggested that the U.S. District Court for the District of Maryland would also be a proper venue for Hatch-Waxman cases, on the theory that FDA—located in Maryland—receives ANDAs with Paragraph IV certifications there. Regardless of the merits of that theory, subsequent to *Valeant*, the District of Maryland has not been transformed into a Hatch-Waxman case hotbed, and the number of Hatch-Waxman cases pending there has decreased, rather than increased.

b. BPCIA Venue

The rationale of *Valeant* and other cases applying § 1400(b) would seem to apply to BPCIA, and not only to Hatch-Waxman, cases. Under 35 U.S.C. § 271(e)(2)(C), the submission of an aBLA is an act of patent infringement "if the purpose of such submission is to obtain approval . . . to engage in the commercial manufacture, use, or sale of a drug, veterinary biological product or biological product claimed in a patent or the use of which is claimed in a patent before the expiration of such patent."[22] Like Hatch-Waxman cases, BPCIA cases involve technical acts of infringement, in which sales or offers for sale of the biosimilar in question have not yet been undertaken. Under the rationale espoused in *Valeant*, future commercial activities such as the anticipated marketing and distribution of the biosimilar that is the subject of the aBLA would not be sufficient to support venue.

Based on the rationale of *Valeant*, venue under the "acts of infringement" prong of § 1400(b) would be proper where the biosimilar application was prepared and from which it was submitted to FDA (and possibly also the District of Maryland). It is unclear, however, the exact scope of additional relevant venue-supporting activities. Questions remain as to whether and the extent to which venue could be found based on the correspondence

20. *Id.* at 1381.
21. *Id.* at 1384.
22. 35 U.S.C. § 271(e)(2)(C).

relating to the patent dance, in which negotiations between the biosimilar applicant and the biological sponsor take place. Could those acts and correspondence support venue? Presumably those negotiations take place via outside counsel; by comparison, negotiations for access to an ANDA filer's ANDA under an offer of confidential access—also typically done through outside counsel—has not been used to support venue. Understood more narrowly, *Valeant* likely circumscribes the available venue options to the residence of the biosimilar applicant and the location where that applicant prepared and from which it submitted the biosimilar application.

Aggressive but prudent litigants wishing to file in a different jurisdiction (e.g., based on the correspondence comprising the patent dance) would be wise to file a protective suit in a jurisdiction where venue is indisputable, in order to preserve the benefits that come from timely filing suit to resolve BPCIA litigation.

2. Personal Jurisdiction

a. *Hatch-Waxman Personal Jurisdiction*

Case law has provided an indication as to the scope of personal jurisdiction in Hatch-Waxman cases.

General personal jurisdiction is generally straightforward, but questions arise as to specific personal jurisdiction in Hatch-Waxman cases, given that the ANDA defendant has undertaken only a technical act of infringement (i.e., filing the ANDA), and has not (or not yet) sold or offered for sale products that infringe any patent. Unlike questions of venue under the "acts of infringement" prong of § 1400(b), which the Federal Circuit has read narrowly, the Federal Circuit has applied specific personal jurisdiction relatively more broadly.

In *Acorda Therapeutics, Inc. v. Mylan Pharmaceuticals, Inc.*,[23] the Federal Circuit confirmed that defendant ANDA filers may be subject to personal jurisdiction in states in which they are not a resident, but instead based on ANDA filings. That case involved an appeal of two actions brought against Mylan in the District of Delaware, one brought by Acorda and Alkermes and the other brought by AstraZeneca, based on Mylan's ANDAs seeking approval of generic versions of Ampyra® and Onglyza®, and Kombiglyze™, respectively. Mylan moved to dismiss both cases for lack of personal jurisdiction on several grounds: that it is a West Virginia corporation with a principal place of business there; its ANDAs were submitted to FDA in Maryland; much or all of its preparatory work was done in West Virginia; and its notice letters required by 21 U.S.C. § 355(j)(2)(B) were sent to Acorda in New York and Alkermes in Ireland,

---

23. 817 F.3d 755 (Fed. Cir. 2016).

to AstraZeneca's subsidiary in Delaware, and to AstraZeneca in Sweden.[24] The Federal Circuit found the exercise of personal jurisdiction over Mylan to be proper and to comport with the Due Process Clause based on Mylan's intent to undertake activities (i.e., the sale of products generic to the plaintiffs' branded product) that allegedly would infringe the plaintiffs' Orange Book-listed patents within Delaware. The court reasoned that "the particular actions Mylan has already taken—its ANDA filings—for the purpose of engaging in that injury-causing and allegedly wrongful marketing conduct in Delaware" were sufficient to provide minimum contacts required for specific personal jurisdiction.[25] As the Federal Circuit stated, "We have pointed to the future real-world market acts as sufficiently connected to the ANDA that triggers the litigation."[26] The court also stated:

> Mylan does not meaningfully develop an argument that at rigid past/future dividing line governs the minimum-contacts standard. Specifically, Mylan does not show that a State is forbidden to exercise its judicial power to prevent a defendant's planned future conduct in the State, but must wait until the conduct occurs. Such a rule would run counter to the legal tradition of injunctive actions to prevent a defendant's planned, non-speculative harmful conduct before it occurs.[27]

Following *Acorda*, as far as personal jurisdiction is concerned, Hatch-Waxman cases may be brought in nearly any federal district. In effect, because generic ANDA products in all likelihood will be available or marketed in every jurisdiction, the filing of an ANDA subjects the ANDA applicant to specific personal jurisdiction in every federal district. Notably, the court in *Acorda* based some of its reasoning on Mylan's history of litigating Hatch-Waxman cases in Delaware, as Mylan has long been a frequent Hatch-Waxman defendant there. It is unclear whether an ANDA filer that is naïve to litigation would be able to challenge personal jurisdiction successfully, given the court's reasoning otherwise, but in view of the court's unequivocal reasoning that the submission of an ANDA renders specific personal jurisdiction proper, that consideration alone is likely not to be outcome determinative.[28]

---

24. *Id.* at 758.
25. *Id.* at 760.
26. *Id.* at 761.
27. *Id.* at 762.
28. Interestingly, prior to *Acorda*, the lower courts were split on whether compliance with Delaware's registration statute constitutes consent to specific personal jurisdiction. In a concurrence, Judge O'Malley would have found consent on those facts.

b. BPCIA Personal Jurisdiction

Personal jurisdiction questions have not arisen with the same level of frequency in BPCIA cases as they have in Hatch-Waxman cases, likely due at least in part to the sheer number of Hatch-Waxman cases over the past nearly 40 years as compared to the relatively few number of BPCIA cases, at least to date. But it stands to reason that theories of consent and specific personal jurisdiction should be equally applicable in BPCIA cases as in Hatch-Waxman cases. Like in Hatch-Waxman cases, in which an ANDA filer by its ANDA submission demonstrates intent to market the generic drug upon final approval by FDA, BPCIA cases are brought based on FDA submissions that demonstrate the intent of the biosimilar applicant to market a biosimilar upon approval by FDA. The question then becomes whether courts will apply a Hatch-Waxman type jurisdiction analysis in the BPCIA context.

This question was addressed in *AbbVie Inc. v. Alvotech hf.*[29] There, AbbVie had filed suit against Alvotech hf. (an Icelandic company) to prevent Alvotech from infringing certain patents relating to AbbVie's Humira® biologic. Alvotech hf. moved to dismiss, among other purported bases, for lack of personal jurisdiction. In denying the motion to dismiss and finding the exercise of personal jurisdiction proper, the court rested its analysis squarely on *Acorda*:

> In *Acorda*, the Federal Circuit held that the submission of an ANDA pursuant to the Hatch-Waxman Act is "'suit-related' and has a 'substantial connection' with [the forum state]" where the defendant "plans to market its proposed drugs in [the forum state] and the lawsuit is about patent constraints on such in-State marketing."[30]

The court continued:

> In *Acorda*, the Federal Circuit viewed the defendant's submission of its ANDA as a concrete step demonstrating the defendant's actual intent to market and sell the infringing drug in the forum state. Here, Alvotech hf.'s role in submitting the AVT02 aBLA demonstrates the same intent. As such, the Court finds that Alvotech hf.'s submission of its aBLA is suit-related. And, because the aBLA submission indicates Alvotech hf.'s intent to market and distribute its biosimilar drug in Illinois, the Court finds that it has specific jurisdiction over it.[31]

29. No. 21-C-2258, 2021 WL 3737733 (N.D. Ill. Aug. 23, 2021).
30. *Id.* at *12 (quoting *Acorda*, 817 F.3d at 762–63).
31. *Id.*

In short, BPCIA personal jurisdiction questions seem to be largely resolved by *Acorda* and by extension *AbbVie*. As in Hatch-Waxman litigation, these cases provide a clear pathway for litigation in the reference product sponsor's jurisdiction of choice: because, in all likelihood, a biosimilar applicant intends to market the biosimilar in virtually every state nationwide, *Acorda* and *AbbVie* would seem to support specific personal jurisdiction in any district. Although it is perhaps an open question whether compliance with state registration requirements can support consent-based personal jurisdiction (as in the Hatch-Waxman context), those questions are essentially moot as a practical matter, given that specific personal jurisdiction is likely found anywhere.

IV. Litigation Considerations

A. Applicable Local Rules and Practices

Many jurisdictions around the country have implemented local rules pertaining to patent cases, and the list continues to grow. At present, at least the following jurisdictions have local patent rules:

- Northern District of California
- District of Colorado
- Northern District of Florida
- Northern District of Georgia
- District of Idaho
- Northern District of Illinois
- Northern District of Indiana
- District of Kansas
- District of Maryland
- District of Massachusetts
- District of Minnesota
- Eastern and Western Districts of Missouri
- District of Nevada
- District of New Hampshire
- District of New Jersey
- Western, Northern, Southern, and Eastern Districts of New York
- Western, Middle, and Eastern Districts of North Carolina
- Northern and Southern Districts of Ohio
- Western District of Pennsylvania
- Western District of Tennessee
- Northern, Eastern, and Southern Districts of Texas
- District of Utah
- Eastern and Western Districts of Washington

In addition to those districts that have formal local patent rules, numerous jurisdictions have judges whose standing orders include rules pertaining specifically to patent cases.

Given this movement to adopt local patent rules and standing orders, the minority of jurisdictions do not have any local patent rules. Notable jurisdictions that presently have no local patent rules include the following:

- District of Oregon
- Central District of California
- Western District of Texas
- Southern District of Indiana
- Eastern District of Pennsylvania

These lists might be somewhat deceiving. For example, the District of Delaware does not have local patent rules per se. Yet, that district does have a Default Standard for Discovery, Including Discovery of Electronically Stored Information. That Default Standard includes a paragraph 4 titled "Initial Discovery in Patent Litigation," which sets forth the requirements and a timeline for producing core technical documents and exchanging infringement and invalidity contentions.

1. Hatch-Waxman Local Rules

In addition to local patent rules, several jurisdictions have developed local rules that pertain specifically to Hatch-Waxman cases. Perhaps the most notable is the District of New Jersey, both because of its stringent and particular requirements that pertain to Hatch-Waxman cases, and because of the fact that so many Hatch-Waxman cases have been litigated in that district.

The Hatch-Waxman local rules in the District of New Jersey require early production of the defendant's ANDA, followed by an identification by the plaintiff of the asserted patent claims. The rules also require service of invalidity contentions and noninfringement contentions by the ANDA filer, along with a production of supporting documents, the deadline for which is keyed off of the initial scheduling conference. Thereafter, the plaintiff must serve infringement contentions and responses to invalidity contentions. The local rules also automatically require the ANDA filer to

> provide a copy of all correspondence between itself and the FDA pertaining to the ANDA application to each party asserting infringement, or set forth the basis of any claim of privilege for such correspondence pursuant to [Local Civil Rule] 34.1, no later than seven days after the date it sent same to the FDA or receives same from the FDA.[32]

---

32. Loc. Pat. R. 3.5(j). Some have asserted that the application of this local rule must be read in conjunction with Federal Rule of Civil Procedure 26(a) and its standard of relevance, such that irrelevant FDA correspondence need not be produced pursuant to this local rule.

Regarding the order and timing of the exchange of contentions, the rule places the "burden" (in a chronological sense) on the ANDA filer: the ANDA filer is to go first with noninfringement and invalidity contentions, and subsequently the plaintiff (who bears the burden of proof with respect to infringement) provides infringement contentions. The Report of the Local Patent Rules Committee provides Explanatory Notes for 2011 amendments to the local rules, which explain the Committee's rationale for its rules. As they pertain to Hatch-Waxman cases, the Notes state:

> In the area of Hatch-Waxman actions under [Local Patent Rule] 3.6, the Committee concluded that in order to help narrow the focus of a generic's invalidity contentions, the patent holder should be required to provide early disclosure of each patent and patent claim for infringement to which its infringement contentions would be limited. This eliminates speculation and added work by the generics in formulating their non-infringement and invalidity contentions. Changes recommended to disclosure obligations in non-Hatch-Waxman cases as they would apply in the Hatch-Waxman context were also proposed. In addition, the Committee determined that the ANDA filer should produce its Abbreviated New Drug Application or New Drug Application shortly after filing an answer or motion as this is a fundamental element of the Hatch-Waxman action. It was also recommended that the ANDA filer be required to advise the Food and Drug Administration ("FDA") of any motion for injunctive relief and supply the parties with relevant communications with the FDA which concern the subject matter filed in the District Court. This is intended to keep the FDA and parties apprised of any proceedings that may impact the ongoing litigation. See L. Pat. R. 3.6(a), (b), (c), (i) and (j).[33]

The operation of these local rules has practical, strategic implications. First, the rules operate automatically to apply contentions deadlines, and operate relatively quickly. The fact that the ANDA filer goes first with noninfringement and invalidity contentions can keep the ANDA filer on its heels; however, given the reality that the ANDA filer has already sent a notice letter with a detailed statement, the prudent ANDA filer should already have a sense of its noninfringement and invalidity positions in the case.

Moreover, many plaintiffs find value in the local rules' automatic requirement to produce FDA correspondence within seven days. In addition to the desire to know of material changes to the ANDA that may

33. U.S. District Court District of New Jersey, Report of the Local Patent Rules Committee: Explanatory Notes for 2011 Amendments to Local Patent Rules.

impact the infringement or noninfringement aspects of the case, plaintiffs generally take the position that this rule requires production of correspondence from FDA regarding final approval, which operates as advance notice of the possibility of the ANDA filer's launch at risk. The obvious impact is that the plaintiff hopes to know as far in advance as possible whether a motion for emergency injunctive relief is warranted, prior to a launch at risk.

In addition, Local Patent Rule 3.7, titled "Amendments," provides that amendments to contentions "may be made only by order of the Court upon a timely application and showing of good cause," and lists nonexclusive examples of good cause.[34] Courts in the District of New Jersey have addressed amendment and supplementation of contentions in a hard-line fashion, generally requiring a showing of good cause as to why the amendment was not made earlier.[35] Litigants often are tempted to find the application of Local Patent Rule 3.7 draconian. In theory, the rule can help to cabin in the scope of discovery, which can often become unwieldly in the event a large number of prior art references and combinations is at play. The motivation therefore exists for ANDA filers to serve voluminous contentions, in an effort not to be foreclosed from offering positions later as fact and expert discovery proceeds. Parties frequently, whether by agreement or by order, meet and confer to limit the number of asserted claims and the number of prior art references and combinations supporting invalidity based on anticipation and/or obviousness, in advance of trial.

As another point of comparison, as noted earlier, the District of Delaware, though it does not have formal local patent rules, does contain the Default Standard for Discovery. Paragraph 4 requires "Initial Discovery in Patent Litigation," including an identification by the plaintiff of accused devices and asserted patents, production of core technical documents by the accused infringer, infringement contentions (i.e., a claim chart), and invalidity contentions. In this fashion, discovery in the District of Delaware proceeds in a manner somewhat similar to the District of New Jersey, though neither noninfringement contentions nor responses to invalidity contentions are required. In addition, Delaware does not have a local rule containing an automatic requirement to produce FDA correspondence.

---

34. Loc. Pat. R. 3.7.

35. *See, e.g.*, Eisai R&D Mgmt. Co. v. Shilpa Medicare Ltd., 656 F. Supp. 3d 515 (D.N.J. 2023) (requiring good cause shown before allowing invalidity contentions to be amended); Chiesi USA, Inc. v. Aurobindo Pharma USA, Inc., No. 19-18756, 2021 WL 6774679, at *5 (D.N.J. Mar. 26, 2021) (denying ANDA applicant's request to amend invalidity contentions to include patent prosecution information that was publicly available at the time of the original contentions).

In contrast to the District of New Jersey, amendment of contentions in the District of Delaware is generally thought to be more likely to be permitted than in the District of New Jersey. Default Standard paragraph 4 contains a footnote 3, which reads: "As these disclosures are 'initial,' each party shall be permitted to supplement." In theory, this footnote reflects a liberal or relaxed standard for amending or supplementing contentions. The prevailing case law in the Third Circuit[36] applies a standard that considers prejudice among other factors in evaluating a motion to strike:

> (1) the prejudice or surprise to the party against whom the evidence is offered; (2) the possibility of curing the prejudice; (3) the potential disruption of an orderly and efficient trial; (4) the presence of bad faith or willfulness in failing to disclose the evidence; and (5) the importance of the information withheld.[37]

2. The BPCIA

To date, the authors are aware of no district that has adopted local rules specific to BPCIA cases, or early disclosure requirements pertaining specifically to BPCIA cases. In the absence of BPCIA-specific local rules, the issue of local rules application will hinge on the existence and operation of local patent rules (or absence thereof).

It is conceivable that in a particular case a judge would be receptive to applying Hatch-Waxman local rules to a BPCIA case. The District of New Jersey's justification for its Hatch-Waxman specific local rules would seem to apply in BPCIA litigation as well, with the desire to identify asserted claims at the outset, ostensibly as a way to cabin in the scope of contentions. A question exists as to whether the rationale that a notice letter and detailed statement by the ANDA filer in Hatch-Waxman litigation suggests that the ANDA filer already has a sense of the noninfringement and invalidity issues in the case would carry over to BPCIA cases. Moreover, both an ANDA in Hatch-Waxman cases and the aBLA in BPCIA cases are pending with FDA during the pendency of the litigation; based on these parallels, a particular judge may see merit to applying local rules akin to Hatch-Waxman local rules in a BPCIA case.

It is possible as well that, in the event BPCIA litigation proliferates in a given district, that that district would introduce BPCIA local rules that track local Hatch-Waxman rules, such as those in place in New Jersey, or

---

36. Following Meyers v. Pennypack Woods Home Ownership Ass'n, 559 F.2d 894, 904–05 (3d Cir. 1977).

37. TQ Delta, LLC v. ADTRAN, Inc., No. 14-954-RGA, 2019 WL 4346530, at *1 (D. Del. Sept. 12, 2019) (citing Konstantopoulos v. Westvaco Corp., 112 F.3d 710, 719 (3d Cir. 1997)).

else early disclosure requirements such as those in Delaware. Whether a jurisdiction adopts such rules remains to be seen.

B. Experts

The past 40 years of Hatch-Waxman litigation has provided strong incentives for scientific experts in their respective fields to see the opportunities present through providing expert consulting. Litigants will recognize that, although often expert search firms are required to identify and retain the best qualified experts in any complex patent litigation, Hatch-Waxman cases often return to the same stable of experts or types of experts. Likely as a function of the fact that technical issues pertaining to one or more in a suite of patents has already been addressed in prior litigation, parties and counsel in Hatch-Waxman cases often have the luxury of turning to their preferred expert(s) to handle a given technological issue. In the event a preferred expert is unavailable or if options are limited, experts with substantial consulting and testifying experience are often available. Litigants can often vet those expert candidates thoroughly, even prior to the first point of contact, by confirming the depth of experience and track record of success (or lack thereof).

While in one sense the availability of a deep bench of expert candidates provides ample well-qualified options, pitfalls exist. Experts who have extensive testifying experience are open to the characterization of being professional experts. Similarly, experts tend to testify nearly exclusively on behalf of patentees or on behalf of ANDA filers; in that case, experts with extensive testifying experience are susceptible to being perceived as having a pro- or anti-patent bias.

In addition, given the frequency with which an expert may provide testimony, it is only a matter of time before that expert is mentioned unfavorably in a court decision questioning that expert's credibility. In that case, such an expert becomes a much less attractive candidate.

Many of these considerations pertain to the BPCIA context as well. Presently, given the nature of technology likely to be at issue in BPCIA litigation, it is likely that relatively few expert candidates may be available, though those that are available are likely to have fairly extensive experience consulting and testifying. As with Hatch-Waxman cases, litigants will need to take extra care to thoroughly vet expert candidates, and charges of pro- or anti-patent bias will pertain to BPCIA cases as they do to Hatch-Waxman cases.

C. Trends on Time to Trial

Certain jurisdictions have a reputation for providing relatively speedy resolution of cases, and are colloquially referred to as "rocket dockets." Some jurisdictions adopt local rules designed to reach resolution by some date certain. As it pertains to Hatch-Waxman case law, timing is critical in order to avoid forfeiture, as well as to resolve patent issues before expiration of the "30-month stay." In contrast, BPCIA cases have the patent dance followed by one, and possibly two, rounds of litigation.

V. Settlement Considerations

One commonality between Hatch-Waxman cases and BPCIA cases is that the majority of them settle before trial. Another is that settlement agreements concerning either are required to be filed with the Department of Justice and the Federal Trade Commission.[38] Another commonality is the fundamental purpose of settlement: to obtain as much benefit as possible while minimizing risk. For Hatch-Waxman litigants, as concerning first applicants[39] (the first ANDA applicant with a Paragraph IV certification to an Orange Book-listed patent), that benefit is preserving eligibility for the 180-day exclusivity and avoiding forfeiture of such exclusivity. For subsequent applicants, the main concern is having an open route to market and not being blocked by the first applicant's exclusivity, especially if settlement of the litigation will foreclose the opportunity to trigger forfeiture of the first applicant's eligibility for the 180-day exclusivity (by way of a final court decision, as required by the statute).[40]

As such, settlement agreements for first applicants generally include acceleration clauses for market entry, which are specifically designed to avoid any forfeiture of eligibility for the 180-day exclusivity for failure to market, as codified by 21 U.S.C. § 355(j)(5)(D)(i)(I). Other, typical accelerators permit entry upon the marketing of an authorized generic product by the branded company or other party, or upon satisfaction of a defined erosion of the branded product. After all, due to the automatic substitution at the pharmacy level of therapeutically equivalent generic products for branded products, if there is no market for the branded product, then so too it goes that there will be no market for the generic product. Or, in other words, if the market is zero, then substitution into that market is also zero. As such, settlement agreements may permit generic entry if the branded market erodes to a defined level before reaching zero.

38. Pub. L. No. 108-173, §§ 1111–1118 (codified at 21 U.S.C. § 355 note), § 1112(a), 117 Stat. 2066, 2461–64 (2003).

39. Hatch-Waxman defines a "first applicant" as "an applicant that, on the first day on which a substantially complete application containing a [Paragraph IV] certification . . . is submitted for approval of a drug, submits a substantially complete application that contains and lawfully maintains a [Paragraph IV] certification." 21 U.S.C. § 355(j)(5)(B)(iv)(II)(bb).

40. *See id.* § 355(j)(5)(D)(i)(I)(bb)(AA).

As biosimilar applicants do not have any eligibility for 180-day exclusivity, and because there are no forfeiture provisions that may motivate protracted litigation with the reference product sponsor to trigger such forfeiture, the underlying motivations for settlement may differ from Hatch-Waxman litigants. That said, there is *one* route for exclusivity for a biosimilar applicant, but that is limited to the first interchangeable biosimilar for any particular reference product.[41] The BPCIA provides that FDA shall not grant interchangeability status for any subsequent biosimilar applicant until the later of certain events, which generally speaking are one year after commercial marketing of the first interchangeable biosimilar, 18 months after a final court decision or dismissal of the litigation (with or without prejudice), and 42 months after approval of the first interchangeable biosimilar if the litigation remains ongoing.[42]

Expanding on that, and turning to the statute, FDA

> shall not make approval as an interchangeable biological product effective with respect to an application submitted under this subsection that relies on the same reference product for which a prior biological product has received a determination of interchangeability for any condition of use, until the earlier of—
>
> (A) 1 year after the first commercial marketing of the first interchangeable biosimilar biological product to be approved as interchangeable for that reference product;
> (B) 18 months after—
>
> > (i) a final court decision on all patents in suit in an action instituted under subsection (l)(6) against the applicant that submitted the application for the first approved interchangeable biosimilar biological product; or

---

41. As described by FDA in late 2023:

> To meet the standard for "interchangeability," an applicant must provide sufficient information to demonstrate biosimilarity to the reference product and also to demonstrate that the biological product can be expected to produce the same clinical result as the reference product in any given patient, and if the biological product is administered more than once to an individual, the risk in terms of safety or diminished efficacy of alternating or switching between the use of the biological product and the reference product is not greater than the risk of using the reference product without such alternation or switch (see section 351(k)(4) of the PHS Act). Interchangeable products may be substituted for the reference product without the intervention of the prescribing health care provider (see section 351(i)(3) of the PHS Act).

FDA, Draft Guidance for Industry: "Biosimilarity and Interchangeability: Additional Draft Q&As on Biosimilar Development and the BPCI Act 3 (2023).

42. *See* 42 U.S.C. § 262(k)(6)(A)–(C).

(ii) the dismissal with or without prejudice of an action instituted under subsection (l)(6) against the applicant that submitted the application for the first approved interchangeable biosimilar biological product; or

(C)

(i) 42 months after approval of the first interchangeable biosimilar biological product if the applicant that submitted such application has been sued under subsection (l)(6) and such litigation is still ongoing within such 42-month period; or

(ii) 18 months after approval of the first interchangeable biosimilar biological product if the applicant that submitted such application has not been sued under subsection (l)(6).[43]

In the most fundamental scenario, the first interchangeable biosimilar will have one year of exclusivity upon launch. Only after that year will subsequent biosimilars be approved for the same reference product and with the same interchangeability status. However, that one year of exclusivity may instead be 18 months if there is a final court decision or dismissal (with or without prejudice) on all patents asserted against the first approved interchangeable biosimilar. Or longer still, that exclusivity can last up to 42 months if the litigation remains ongoing after aBLA approval. That may motivate the parties to extend the litigation, thereby preventing any subsequent applicants from obtaining interchangeability status for three and a half years.[44]

As noted, except for the first interchangeable biosimilar, there is no market exclusivity for a biosimilar applicant. Nor do biosimilar applicants enjoy the benefit of automatic substitution at pharmacies nationwide, though an interchangeable biosimilar *may* be substituted at the pharmacy level without the prescriber's intervention. Nor do authorized generics exist in the same way for biosimilar products as for small-molecule drugs. However, as noted previously, the objective remains the same: to maximize value and minimize risk.

As such, settlement agreements for biosimilar applicants will largely mirror those for ANDA litigants but for the provisions relating to the 180-day exclusivity. Freedom to operate will remain key, and the agreement should provide that to the biosimilar applicant through a license, covenant

---

43. *Id.*

44. One commentator suggested that the innovator and biosimilar applicant could share the exclusivity period through a settlement agreement, thereby delaying competition by the 18 months contemplated by the statute. David A. Fazzolare, *Gaming the Biosimilars Act*, FDLI UPDATE, July/Aug. 2010. Time has not proven this true.

not to sue, representations and warranties, or a combination thereof. Serial litigation is to be avoided if at all possible. Market erosion triggers may remain possible, but those are difficult to define let alone enforce. The best bet is to ensure, as best possible, that there remains a biosimilar market at the time of the patent-licensed launch.

VI. Conclusion

Hatch-Waxman litigation and BPCIA litigation, though different, share notable similarities. The extensive development of a rich body of case law in the Hatch-Waxman sphere presents litigants (and courts) helpful direction. BPCIA litigants would be wise to lean on Hatch-Waxman case law and rationale where appropriate, and a thorough familiarity with Hatch-Waxman case law and strategy will benefit careful and diligent BPCIA counsel and parties.

Part II

chapter 6

Preparing the Client for the Commitment and Costs*

I. Introduction

The Biologics Price Competition and Innovation Act of 2009 (BPCIA) sets out an abbreviated approval process to encourage early market entry of biologics that are sufficiently similar to an already approved biological product (the "reference product"). Following in the footsteps of the Hatch-Waxman laws that govern generic small-molecule drugs, the core policy goals behind the BPCIA and Hatch-Waxman are essentially the same. Both sets of laws are intended to facilitate the approval and market entry of lower cost versions of older, previously approved medicines and both sets of laws arose out of a desire to create price competition—and achieve cost savings—for popular, expensive medicines that are nearing the end of market exclusivity.[1] The pathway for resolving patent disputes under the BPCIA, however, is markedly different from the Hatch-Waxman laws governing small molecules.

As of June 2023, 41 biosimilars have been approved by the U.S. Food and Drug Administration (FDA).[2] Only 27 of these are commercially available.[3] This discrepancy is mainly due to the reality that the launch of biosimilar products can be delayed due to ongoing patent litigation and settlements between brand biologic and biosimilar companies. Patent

---

*Aziz Burgy, Ricardo Camposanto, and Darpan Singh, Axinn, Veltrop & Harkrider LLP.

1. Drug Price Competition and Patent Term Restoration Act of 1984, Pub. L. No. 98-417, 98 Stat. 1585 (codified as amended in scattered sections of 15, 21, 35 & 42 U.S.C. (2012)) (Hatch-Waxman Act).

2. *Biosimilar Product Information*, FDA, https://www.fda.gov/drugs/biosimilars/biosimilar-product-information (last updated Dec. 8, 2023).

3. April Breyer Menon & Ha Kung Wong, Biologics HQ, The State of Biosimilars in 2023 (2023), https://www.venable.com/-/media/files/publications/2023/03/thestateofbiosimilarsin2023venable.pdf (analyzing BPCIA litigation through February 28, 2023).

litigation is not mandatory for biosimilar launch. Biosimilar applicants have a number of choices to make on the path to a commercial biosimilar product. For example, a biosimilar applicant can either launch at risk or try to clear the patent rights controlled by the reference product sponsor (RPS) before launch.

"At risk" launches appear more common for biosimilar products than small-molecule generics, potentially because the possible liability faced for launching a biosimilar at risk is typically less.[4] While small-molecule generics offer steep discounts as compared to their brand-name counterparts, biosimilars are typically offered at a smaller discount to the brand name list price. Thus, a biosimilar's potential liability for launching at risk may be equivalent only to its profits. Indeed, "[b]y contrast, for a small-molecule drug, which can be upwards of 60% discount to the brand list price, the generic's liability will be measured against the brand's lost profits, and that liability can potentially eclipse any profits earned by the generic for launching at risk."[5] That being said, in most cases at-risk launches eventually result in settlements.

If a biosimilar applicant chooses to clear the RPS's patent rights, it can choose to engage in a procedure commonly called the "patent dance" and optionally participate in multiple waves of litigation, as set forth in the BPCIA. With this patent dance can come a hefty commitment of time and money depending on the number of patents being asserted by the RPS. For example, the most notable case of patent litigation leading to the delayed entry of biosimilars involves adalimumab, one of the top-selling drugs in the world.[6] "From 2011 to 2021, worldwide net revenues more than doubled from $7.9 billion to $20.7 billion as the drug's market power strengthened."[7] AbbVie, adalimumab's manufacturer, had procured more than 100 patents on the product.[8] Although AbbVie's active ingredient patent on adalimumab expired in 2016, it was granted a series of patents protecting everything from the manufacturing process to new formulations of the drug.[9] One 2021 report found that 89 percent of these patent

4. *See id.* at 6; Zachary Silbersher, *When Do Biosimilars Launch at Risk?*, MARKMAN ADVISORS (Jan. 25, 2018), https://www.markmanadvisors.com/blog/2018/1/25/why-do-biosimilars-launch-at-risk; KIRKE M. HASSON & MARIA SALGADO, PILLSBURY, BIOSIMILARS ENTER THE COURTS: HOW WILL PATENT INFRINGEMENT SETTLEMENTS BE TESTED FOR VALIDITY UNDER ANTITRUST LAWS? (2016), https://www.pillsburylaw.com/images/content/1/0/109239.pdf.

5. Silbersher, *supra* note 4.

6. Jason B. Gibbons & Micaela Laber, *Humira: The First $20 Billion Drug*, 29 AM. J. MANAGED CARE 78, 78 (2023).

7. *Id.*

8. Mike Z. Zhai et al., *Why Are Biosimilars Not Living Up to Their Promise in the US?*, 21 AMA J. ETHICS 668 (2019), https://journalofethics.ama-assn.org/article/why-are-biosimilars-not-living-their-promise-us/2019-08.

9. *Id.*

applications were filed after adalimumab was on the market, and 50 percent of the applications in the United States were filed by AbbVie from 2014 onwards—more than 20 years after the initial scientific research began and more than a decade after the product was first marketed.[10] This patent strategy, known as a "patent thicket," is discussed more in-depth later in this section. AbbVie sued the manufacturers of adalimumab biosimilars, including Amgen, Boehringer Ingelheim, Mylan, Pfizer, Samsung Bioepis, and Sandoz, for patent infringement, with settlements having been reached in all but one case. As a consequence of these settlements, the first biosimilars for adalimumab did not enter the U.S. market until January 2023.[11]

II. Pre-Litigation Assessment of Patents

The cost of obtaining a patent is miniscule compared to steep costs necessary to take a new biologic through clinical safety and efficacy trials. Thus, patent rights play a paramount role in enabling innovators to protect intellectual property rights and recouping investment. An RPS may seek many kinds of patents directed to the biological drug, including patents covering drug composition, methods of manufacturing the drug, and methods of using the drug for treatment. Biologics are complicated products, thus the number of patents covering each product can be substantial. Further, as discussed more in-depth later in this chapter, RPSs have come up with a number of patent strategies to maintain the exclusivity of their drugs for as long as possible. This has resulted in patents of questionable validity, which can be used to improperly block competitors out of the market. The number of patents covering the RPS will play a significant role in determining the time and cost commitment of patent litigation.

Having early access to patent information regarding licensed biologic products is not only valuable for biosimilar applicants but also for RPSs. Given the short timing of the patent dance, it is an advantage to a biosimilar applicant to obtain as much information regarding the patents identified by the RPS before the dance begins. Such information will allow more time for a biosimilar applicant to develop noninfringement and invalidity

---

10. I-MAK, Overpatented, Overpriced Special Edition: Humira (2021), https://www.i-mak.org/wp-content/uploads/2021/09/i-mak.humira.report.3.final-REVISED-2021-09-22.pdf.

11. Press Release, AbbVie, AbbVie Announces Global Resolution of HUMIRA® (adalimumab) Patent Disputes with Sandoz. (Oct. 11, 2018), https://news.abbvie.com/2018-10-11-AbbVie-Announces-Global-Resolution-of-HUMIRA-R-adalimumab-Patent-Disputes-with-Sandoz.

positions. If, on the other hand, an RPS has strong patent coverage for its product, a biosimilar applicant may decide to wait to seek approval until after the RPS's patents expire. This would allow the RPS to avoid the costs of engaging in the patent dance and litigation.

A. The Patent Dance

The process of exchanging materials prior to the start of litigation under the BPCIA is laid out in 42 U.S.C. § 262(*l*). This process is often informally referred to as the "patent dance." It is a carefully calibrated procedure for preparing to litigate, and then litigating, claims of infringement of patents.[12]

In brief, the patent dance requires that the biosimilar applicant disclose both its abbreviated biologics licensing application (aBLA) and manufacturing process information to the RPS. The RPS will then provide a list of all patents it may assert against the applicant based on the information the applicant discloses. The parties exchange patent infringement and validity contentions regarding the listed patents. Then they can negotiate which (if any) patents they want to litigate. The parties may agree to litigate all the listed patents at one time in a first-wave litigation; otherwise, the remaining patents may be asserted in a second-wave litigation once the biosimilar applicant provides notice no later than 180 days prior to commercial launch. This notice is known as the notice of commercial marketing (NCM). The U.S. Supreme Court has clarified that a biosimilar applicant "may give such notice before or after receiving FDA approval."[13]

The biggest upside to the patent dance is that it allows for a biosimilar applicant to retain some control over the number of patents litigated in a first wave. The patent dance is not mandatory; an applicant can choose to not dance at all by choosing not to provide its aBLA and manufacturing information. If the biosimilar applicant does choose to forgo the patent dance, however, then the RPS is authorized to immediately bring a declaratory judgment action of infringement, validity, and enforceability with respect to all patents that can reasonably be asserted against the applicant.

42 U.S.C. § 262(*l*) breaks this patent dance down to a precise timeline, which follows:

Step 1 application information. Within 20 days of FDA's acceptance of the aBLA for review, the applicant "shall provide" its application and

12. *See* Tony Hagen, *BIO Attorneys Discuss the BPCIA Patent Dance*, Ctr. for Biosimilars (Sept. 15, 2021), https://www.centerforbiosimilars.com/view/bio-attorneys-discuss-the-bpcia-patent-dance (detailing the patent dance procedure).

13. Sandoz Inc. v. Amgen Inc., 582 U.S. 1, 19 (2017).

"such other manufacturing information that describes the process or processes used to manufacture the . . . product" to the "RPS." The applicant may also provide "additional information requested by . . . the reference product sponsor." The statute allows the applicant to designate any information produced during the patent dance as "confidential," and the RPS's outside counsel, in-house counsel, and experts, to have access to such information, subject to various restrictions on use and disclosure.

Step 2 list by the RPS. No later than 60 days from the receipt of the application the RPS "shall provide" a list of patents it believes "could reasonably be asserted" for patent infringement. This is often referred to as the "3(A)" list, from the section of the BPCIA that requires it. The RPS can also identify which of these patents they are willing to license to the applicant.

Step 3 list and description by applicant. Within 60 days of receipt of the patent list from the RPS, the applicant "may provide" a list of patents it believes "could reasonably be asserted" by the RPS for patent infringement. In addition, the applicant "shall provide" either a detailed statement describing the noninfringement, invalidity, and unenforceability contentions of the patents listed by the RPS on a claim-by-claim basis or a statement that commercial marketing of the biological product will not begin until the expiration of the RPS's patent. These are often referred to as the "3(B)" disclosures, from the section of the BPCIA that requires them. If the RPS identified patents they would be willing to license, the applicant "shall provide" a response at this time if it were willing to license them.

Step 4 description by the RPS. Within 60 days of receipt of the patent list and detailed statement from the applicant, the RPS "shall provide" a detailed statement of the "factual and legal basis of the opinion" that such patents will be infringed by the commercial marketing of the biological product on a claim-by-claim basis, in addition to a response to the applicant's statement concerning the validity and enforceability of the patents on the 3(A) list.

Step 5 patent resolution negotiation. The applicant and RPS shall negotiate in good faith which patents will be litigated in the first wave of litigation. There are two possible outcomes:

1. The RPS and applicant agree on the list of patents to be litigated for patent infringement.
2. If the RPS and applicant do not agree on the list of patents to be litigated within 15 days of the start of negotiations, the applicant "shall notify" the RPS "of the number of patents that such

applicant will provide to the [RPS]." No later than five days after the applicant's notification, the applicant and RPS "shall simultaneously exchange" lists of patents they believe should be the subject of immediate patent infringement action. The number of patents believed to be the subject of patent infringement action by the RPS may not exceed the number of patents listed by the applicant; the RPS may, however, list one patent if the applicant does not list any patent.

Step 6 patent infringement action. The RPS "shall" bring an action for patent infringement either (A) for the patents mutually agreed upon within 30 days of the agreement or (B), in the case of disagreement between the applicant and the RPS, for the patents included on the exchanged lists within 30 days of the simultaneous exchange.

Although the first wave of infringement litigation can be restricted in scope by the applicant, the RPS can assert the remainder of the patents on the 3(A) list in a second wave of litigation, once the applicant provides the NCM.

Applicants can choose to comply to varying degrees with the provisions of the patent dance. If the applicant does not participate in the patent dance, the RPS may "bring an action under section 2201 of title 28 for a declaration of infringement, validity, or enforceability of any patent that claims the biological product or a use of the biological product."[14] The RPS may also seek a declaratory judgment if the applicant fails to engage in subsequent steps of the patent dance.

The RPS's patents may expire before or after litigation is resolved. Even if a biosimilar applicant waits to launch until patent expiration, recent case law suggests it may still be liable for pre-launch infringing activities performed while the patents were still in force (e.g., making and stockpiling commercial batches for future commercial sale).[15]

To date, applicants have used different strategies in navigating the patent dance. For example, applicants have:

- Opted out of the dance entirely by not producing the aBLA and manufacturing information
- Opted to dance, but limited their § 262(*l*)(2)(A) disclosures to their aBLAs—in other words, they do not produce any manufacturing information beyond what is included in the aBLA
- Filed an NCM after dancing most of the way until the end, and immediately thereafter sought declaratory judgment actions

14. *See* 42 U.S.C. § 262(*l*)(9)(A).
15. *See* Amgen Inc. v. Hospira, Inc., 944 F.3d 1327, 1339–40 (Fed. Cir. 2019).

regarding noninfringement, invalidity, and unenforceability regarding the patents identified during the patent dance

- Served an NCM after the RPS serves its § 262(*l*)(3)(A) patent list, and after the RPS filed a complaint asserting all patents on that list, the parties continued to dance

B. The Purple Book

In 2014, with the development of biologics and biosimilars, FDA began publishing a "List of Licensed Biological Products with Reference Product Exclusivity and Biosimilarity or Interchangeability Evaluations," which is commonly known as the "Purple Book." Originally, the Purple Book consisted of two lists—one containing biologics regulated by the Center for Drug Evaluation and Research (CDER) and the other containing biologics regulated by the Center for Biologics Evaluation and Research (CBER). The lists included the biologic's name, biologics license application (BLA) number, licensure date, exclusivity information, biosimilar information, and whether the biologic had been withdrawn—but did not include any information about patents covering biologics. Prior to the passing of the Biological Product Patent Transparency Act (BPPT) in 2020, patents covering biologics were maintained under strict confidentiality and only disclosed to a biosimilar upon initiation of the patent dance.

The BPPT now requires an RPS to provide to FDA a list of any patents identified to a biosimilar applicant as part of the patent dance, no later than 30 days after those patents were identified to the applicant. FDA is then required to include that information in a searchable format and does so via the Purple Book.

Thus, there are limitations to the information included in the Purple Book. First, this additional patent information does not affect the first biosimilar to file an application following the implementation of the Purple Book changes. They will still be in the dark as to patents likely to be identified by an RPS during the patent dance. Until a biosimilar filing, patent information would not be posted in the FDA database. The Purple Book therefore provides a major advantage for biosimilars looking to enter the market after a first biosimilar has already begun engaging in a patent dance with the RPS. Second, the statute leaves open the question of what happens if the biosimilar sponsor decides not to engage in the patent dance. Finally, there is no obligation for product sponsors to keep patent information in the Purple Book current outside of the patent dance. A product sponsor is only required to update information each time it engages in a patent dance with a biosimilar. Accordingly, subsequent applicants should not solely rely on the Purple Book when trying to identify and understand the potential patent landscape.

C. Patent Thickets

With patenting occurring early in the drug development cycle, some of the patent term will have expired before the drug gets to market. Estimates suggest that the average remaining patent period for a new drug is 12 years after it comes to market.[16] While still a considerable reward, 12 years of exclusivity is far less than a term of 20 years that patents receive from the time of application. Pharmaceutical manufacturers have thus developed a number of strategies to extend the life of patent protection surrounding their products. One such strategy is known as "patent thickets." "This term is used in two slightly different ways, both relating to products covered by a high number of patents."[17]

First, a patent thicket may describe the situation in which multiple parties have overlapping patent rights on one product, such that a "potential manufacturer must negotiate licenses with each patent owner in order to bring a product to market without infringing."[18] Patent thickets, in this sense, raise concerns about inefficient exploitation of a technology because the multiplicity of patent owners increases transaction costs and creates coordination challenges. Second, the term may be used in a different sense to describe an RPS manufacturer's practice of amassing a large number of patents relating to a single product, with the intent of intimidating competitors from entering the market, or to make it too costly and risky to do so. With regard to biologics, concerns about patent thickets have mainly been raised with regard to the second type of patent thicket. Manufacturing a pharmaceutical using living cells is complicated, offering more opportunities for patenting relative to chemically synthesizing small-molecule drugs. As changes are implemented to either the biologic product or its manufacturing process throughout the original patent term, those changes can be claimed as inventions and used to extend the effective patent protection. For example, a company producing biologics could patent the use of a different medium for cell growth or adjustments made to the dosing.

Biosimilar companies do not only need to evaluate granted patents when assessing whether to enter the market, they must also track and review patent applications when assessing the decision to enter the market. The high volume of both filed patent applications and granted patents creates a complex web of actual and potential barriers to market entry for biosimilar competitors. There are four times as many patents granted on

16. Robin Feldman, *May Your Drug Price Be Evergreen*, 5 J. L. BIOSCIS. 590, 598 (2018).

17. CONGRESSIONAL RESEARCH SERVICE, DRUG PRICING AND PHARMACEUTICAL PATENTING PRACTICES 22 (2020), https://bit.ly/3Qsi1EY.

18. Stu Woolman et al., *Evidence of Patent Thickets in Complex Biopharmaceutical Technologies*, 53 IDEA 1, 2 (2013); Carl Shapiro, *Navigating the Patent Thicket: Cross Licenses, Patent Pools, and Standard Setting*, 1 INNOVATION POL'Y & ECON. 119, 119 (2001).

the top ten drugs in the United States compared to Europe.[19] Of the top ten drugs in the United States in 2021, one study found that drugmakers filed more than 140 patent applications on average per drug.[20] Moreover, the same study found that, on average, 66 percent of these patent applications were filed after FDA granted marketing approval.[21]

The patent portfolio that covers Humira, a biologic produced by pharmaceutical manufacturer AbbVie, is an exemplar of a patent thicket. A study found that AbbVie filed 247 patent applications on various aspects of Humira, resulting in 132 issued patents.[22] Although originally due to lose patent protection in 2016, the patent thicket that AbbVie built around Humira has allowed it to extend patent protection through 2034.[23] Attempts to introduce Humira biosimilars have been met by litigation, with one lawsuit claiming that the biosimilar would infringe 1,600 claims across 74 of AbbVie's patents.[24]

D. Evergreening

Patent "evergreening" is the practice of filing for new patents on secondary features of a particular product as earlier patents expire, thereby extending patent exclusivity past the original 20-year term. Later-filed patents may delay or prevent entry by competitors, allowing the brand-name drug manufacturer (the brand) to extend the monopoly over the market. Simple techniques can involve obtaining new protections on existing drugs by filing for additional patents, sometimes on methods of producing or manufacturing the drugs or on other aspects. More complex evergreening strategies involve developing new formulations, dosage schedules, or combinations that can be used to obtain new patents. These can be combined with attempts to move the market to the slightly altered product.

---

19. I-MAK, Overpatented, Overpriced: Curbing Patent Abuse: Tackling the Root of the Drug Pricing Crisis 6–8 (2022), https://www.i-mak.org/wp-content/uploads/2023/01/Overpatented-Overpriced-2023-01-24.pdf.

20. *Id.*

21. *Id.*

22. I-MAK, Overpatented, Overpriced: How Excessive Pharmaceutical Patenting Is Extending Monopolies and Driving Up Drug Prices 6–8 (2018), http://www.i-mak.org/wp-content/uploads/2018/08/I-MAK-Overpatented-Overpriced-Report.pdf.

23. Cynthia Koons, *This Shield of Patents Protects the World's Best-Selling Drug*, Bloomberg (Sept. 7, 2017), https://bloom.bg/2GIch7F.

24. *See* AbbVie Inc. v Boehringer Ingelheim Int'l GmbH, No. 17-cv-01065-MSG-RL, Dkt. No. 1, at 15 (D. Del. Aug. 2, 2017) ("On July 11, 2017, AbbVie provided Defendants with its detailed statement pursuant to 42 U.S.C. § 262(l)(3)(C). AbbVie's nearly 1,500-page statement shows that AbbVie has reason to believe that Boehringer's biosimilar product, BI 695501, would infringe as many as 1,600 claims from among the following 71 AbbVie patents . . . .").

III. Biosimilar versus Biosimilar Litigation

"Biosimilar makers are filing for and obtaining manufacturing patents of their own as they do not have to use the manufacturing processes of innovators to obtain approval of their products."[25] In 2019, the United States saw the first lawsuit between two biosimilar makers—both with biosimilars of AbbVie's adalimumab (Humira).[26] Coherus BioSciences, a biosimilar manufacturer, filed a complaint alleging that Amgen's biosimilar of adalimumab (Amgevita) infringed four patents for its own biosimilar version of adalimumab. This case illustrates that a biosimilar looking to enter the market must consider the patents of not only the RPS but also of other biosimilar competitors. The number of patent proceedings between biosimilar makers will likely continue to increase as more biosimilar makers compete for market share.

IV. Setting Realistic Expectations and Budgets

As of July 2023, there have been 48 BPCIA litigations.[27] In the 14 years since the BPCIA was enacted, a few trends have emerged allowing biosimilar applicants to set expectations on timing and costs.

A. The Number of Patents Asserted in a Litigation

The number of patents asserted can and does play a role in the resolution of BPCIA litigation. Twenty-seven of the 48 (56 percent) *resolved* BPCIA litigations involved five or fewer patents, 15 (31 percent) involved more than ten patents, and 11 (23 percent) involved between 20 to 65 patents. The litigation with the highest number of patents asserted was *AbbVie Inc. v. Alvotech*,[28] with 61 asserted patents.

Of the cases that have gone to resolution through either a jury or bench trial verdict, or a grant of summary judgment, all of them involved five or

25. Irena Royzman, *Biosimilar Litigation Trends and Lessons Learned in 2019*, Kramer Levin: Bio L. Blog (Jan. 9, 2020), https://www.kramerlevin.com/en/perspectives-search/biosimilar-litigation-trends-and-lessons-learned-in-2019.html.

26. *Id.*

27. This data, as well as all the data in this section, was collected using Docket Navigator searching for cases using Docket Navigator's "Complaint-Infringement-BPCIA" classification. This number is based on complaints filed in district courts. This number excludes all pending litigations as of July 2023 (i.e., filtering Docket Navigator's results for a "Case Status" of "Terminated"). This number includes, however, any litigation alleging infringement under BPCIA in a filed complaint, regardless of whether the litigation was later consolidated into another "lead" case.

28. No. 1-21-cv-02899 (N.D. Ill. filed May 28, 2021).

fewer patents. Moreover, as to cases involving five or fewer patents, the RPS won in two out of the 27 cases, whereas the biosimilar applicant prevailed in eight out of 27 cases. Thirteen of the remaining cases ended in settlements and/or voluntary dismissals.

Of the 15 cases that involved more than ten patents, 13 cases settled. In the two remaining cases, 28 patents had been asserted, and only three of those 28 patents had been resolved before the parties stipulated to a dismissal.

B. The Probability of a Settlement Remains High Although Some Biosimilars Are Avoiding Costly Patent Disputes Altogether

Thus, as demonstrated, settlements in biosimilar litigation are the most likely outcome. Thirty-one of the 48 litigations ended in settlements and/ or voluntary dismissals. Moreover, although public details of these settlements remain minimal, AbbVie's settlements relating to Humira with Sandoz, Amgen, Samsung Bioepis, and Mylan demonstrate that terms of a settlement may include a nonexclusive license to the RPS's patents.

An additional study found that, as of February 28, 2023, "there have been at least nine biosimilar settlements without a patent dispute in the patent office or district court, including Humira biosimilars Hadlima, Abrilada™, Hulio®, Idacio®, and Yuflyma™, Lucentis® (ranibizumab) biosimilars Byooviz™ and Cimerli™, Rituxan biosimilar Riabni™, and Avastin® (bevacizumab) biosimilar Vegzelma®."[29] Furthermore, "[t]here have been two additional biosimilar launches without patent disputes or announcement of a settlement agreement, including Avastin biosimilar Alymsys® and Remicade® (infliximab) biosimilar Avsola®."[30]

C. At-Risk Launches Have Been Common

"While at least 11 of the 27 launched biosimilars (40.7%) launched at-risk to at least some degree, so far, none of them have been ordered to pay any damages."[31]

Some of the at-risk launches took place after an initial decision in the biosimilar's favor, but before appeals were exhausted, but some took place

29. Menon & Wong, *supra* note 3, at 6.

30. *Id.*

31. *Id.*; *see* also Client Alert, Morrison & Foerster, FDA Approves 25th Biosimilar (Nov. 21, 2019), https://www.mofo.com/resources/insights/191121-fda-approves-biosimilar (stating that, as of November 2019, there were ten products "launched 'at risk' to varying degrees, i.e., the launches occurred while patent litigation was ongoing, although some launches occurred following favorable court decisions but before all appeals had been exhausted").

earlier in litigation. Ultimately, at-risk launches eventually resulted in settlements or voluntary dismissals in most cases.

For example, Pfizer's Inflectra®, the biosimilar for Janssen's Remicade®, was approved by FDA in April 2016. Litigation over the biosimilar remained pending before the Federal Circuit in late 2016 when Hospira and Celltrion launched Inflectra.[32]

Merck launched Renflexis® at risk, which is also a biosimilar for Remicade®.[33] The biosimilar was approved by FDA in April 2017, and Merck launched nearly immediately in July 2017. At the time of its launch, Merck's Renflexis® partner, Samsung Bioepis, was involved in BPCIA patent litigation with Janssen.[34] Janssen dropped the lawsuit shortly after the launch, in November 2017.

D. Trials in Which the RPS Won

Because of the high likelihood that BPCIA cases will settle, BPCIA trials are infrequent. Indeed, as for RPS wins at trial, our data identified four in total. These cases were *Amgen Inc. v. Hospira, Inc.*,[35] *Immunex v. Sandoz*,[36] *Juno Therapeutics, Inc. v. Kite Pharma, Inc.*,[37] and *Teva Pharmaceuticals International GmbH v. Eli Lilly & Co.*[38]

These cases are helpful in illustrating that large damages awards are likely to be at play if the RPS wins. Specifically, in *Amgen*, a jury awarded a $70 million damages award for patent infringement based on a lump-sum royalty award, which the Federal Circuit upheld on appeal.[39] Further, a jury in *Juno* found that biosimilar applicant Kite had willfully infringed Juno's patents and thus owed $1.2 billion in damages—on appeal, however, the Federal Circuit reversed this judgment and left Kite having to pay nothing.[40] Lastly, in *Teva*, the jury awarded RPS Teva approximately $180 million in lost profits and reasonable royalty damages,[41] although the parties are currently litigating post-trial motions, and thus the ultimate outcome remains uncertain.[42]

---

32. Big Molecule Watch, *Celltrion and Hospira Have Launched Inflectra® in U.S.*, GOODWIN (Dec. 8, 2016), https://www.bigmoleculewatch.com/2016/12/08/inflectra-launched-in-us/.

33. Silbersher, *supra* note 4.

34. *Id.*

35. No. 1-15-cv-00839 (D. Del. filed Sept. 18, 2015).

36. No. 16-01118 (D.N.J. filed Feb. 26, 2016).

37. No. 2-17-cv-07639 (C.D. Cal. Oct. 18, 2017).

38. No. 1-18-cv-12029-ABD (D. Mass. filed Sept. 27, 2018).

39. *See* Amgen Inc. v. Hospira, Inc., 944 F.3d 1327, 1331–32 (Fed. Cir. 2019).

40. *See* Juno Therapeutics, Inc. v. Kite Pharma, Inc., 10 F.4th 1330 (Fed. Cir. 2021).

41. Teva Pharms. Int'l GmbH v. Eli Lilly & Co., No. 1-18-cv-12029-ABD, Dkt. No. 638, at 2 (D. Mass. Dec. 30, 2022).

42. *Immunex* resulted in an injunction following a bench trial that upheld the validity of the patents-in-suit. No. 2-16-cv-01118, Dkt. No. 719 (D.N.J. Oct. 8, 2019).

E. Cases in Which the Biosimilar Won Litigation

According to our data, biosimilars applicants have won a total of ten times at the district court level. In cases where the biosimilar applicant frequently resolved via motion practice, and indeed, eight out of these ten cases resolved via either a motion to dismiss, a motion for judgment on the pleadings, or a motion for summary judgment. The remaining two related cases proceeded to a bench trial that found for the biosimilar applicant.[43]

F. Expectations on Timing

Of all the variables biosimilars in BPCIA litigation face, timing may be the largest. Although the patent dance seeks to establish predictable milestones for litigation, litigants are given discretion on how much of the patent dance they wish to partake in. Even then, the average time biosimilars spent on litigation across all 48 cases was 17 months. The shortest of these cases generally resulted in a settlement and voluntary dismissal, and these cases lasted only one or two months. On the other hand, the longest case located was *Immunex Corp. v. Sandoz Inc.*,[44] which involved Immunex's reference product ENBREL® and which lasted about three and a half years at the district court level.

G. Costs

Lastly, the costs associated with biosimilar litigation vary greatly. Cost depends on how much of the patent dance parties undertake, the number of patents associated with the RPS, the number of parties actually litigated, and the degree of aggression with which an RPS chooses to pursue the case. The vast majority of BPCIA disputes end in settlements, the details of which are not publicly disclosed.

In the event that a court finds a biosimilar applicant has infringed a patent that is valid and enforceable, the RPS may be entitled to relief, such as injunctive relief or damages. The remedies available under patent infringement are prescribed by 35 U.S.C. § 271(e)(4).

35 U.S.C. § 271(e)(6) limits an RPS's damages for infringement of a patent identified under 42 U.S.C. § 262(*l*)(4) and (5)(B) of the BPCIA to a reasonable royalty if the infringement suit is filed more than 30 days after the end of the "patent dance" information exchange process prescribed by the BPCIA.

---

43. These cases were *Amgen Inc. v. Apotex Inc.*, No. 0:15-cv-62081 (S.D. Fla.), and *Amgen Inc. v. Apotex Inc.*, No. 0:15-cv-61631 (S.D. Fla.).

44. No. 2-16-cv-01118 (D.N.J. filed Feb. 26, 2016).

V. Exploring Alternatives to BPCIA Litigation

A. Introduction

Given the high cost, complexity, and length of district court BPCIA litigation, it may be in the best interest of one or both parties to seek alternatives to litigation. These alternatives are varied and offer benefits in cost and time—benefits that often make such alternatives more preferred to litigation. Indeed, one study in 2023 found that out of 46 analyzed BPCIA cases, more than 60 percent resulted in a settlement or in a stipulated or voluntary dismissal.[45] Accordingly, a proper understanding of the alternatives to BPCIA litigation is necessary for fully counseling a client who is either considering, is participating in, or is at risk of BPCIA litigation. As such, this section will discuss various alternatives to BPCIA litigation, as well as possible implications for these alternatives.

B. Licensing and Settlements

One option to avoid BPCIA litigation is licensing, which is a contract between a patentee (i.e., the RPS) and a party seeking to use the technology (i.e., the biosimilars applicant). With regards to patents, a license equates to "an agreement not to sue the licensee of a patent for patent infringement."[46] Accordingly, should the RPS and the biosimilars applicant be able to reach an agreement on a license, the parties will be able to entirely avoid BPCIA litigation. There are, however, various aspects of licensing that attorneys and clients need to consider, which we discuss in the following sections.

C. Pre-Litigation

First, the RPS and biosimilar applicant can negotiate a license agreement *prior* to the start of any suit, thus avoiding BPCIA litigation altogether. This result will dramatically reduce, if not eliminate, the costs associated with district court litigation—depending upon the degree of pre-litigation work already completed. Pre-litigation licensing may, however, be less appropriate where a party has a particularly strong argument or defense, as such a party may be able to receive better terms once litigation progresses.

---

45. *See* Menon & Wong, *supra* note 3, at 3.

46. FTC v. Endo Pharms. Inc., 596 F. Supp. 3d 115, 121 (D.D.C. 2022) (citing United States v. Studiengesellschaft Kohle, m.b.H, 670 F.2d 1122, 1127 (D.C. Cir. 1981)).

D. During BPCIA Litigation

In the event parties proceed into BPCIA litigation, it is still often in the interests of both parties to settle the dispute prior to any dispositive court ruling (e.g., trial, motion for summary judgment, etc.). Settling and licensing during litigation gives the parties the ability to assess their opponent's argument, as well as further assess their own. Moreover, resolving ongoing litigation without a court ruling gives parties a degree of certainty (e.g., the paying party will know exactly how much they must pay), rather than the uncertainty of what a court will award. Resolving a dispute *during* litigation, however, does mean that the parties may incur substantial attorneys' fees, particularly if the case settles close to trial. Nonetheless, most BPCIA litigation resolves via settlement, rather than a court ruling.[47] Furthermore, in the event parties do settle or license outside of court, the parties will need to dismiss the case, typically through Federal Rule of Civil Procedure 41(a).[48]

E. Mediation

One method to facilitate licensing and settlements is through mediation. Generally, "[m]ediation is a flexible, non-binding, confidential process in which a neutral mediator facilitates settlement negotiations."[49] While the particular details of mediation in any case can vary, the mediator will generally meet the parties individually and jointly and will try to facilitate communication and negations. Further, mediation can occur in a handful of ways, such as through a private mediator or through a magistrate judge.

Indeed, numerous district courts mandate that parties engage in some form of alternative dispute resolution (ADR) and, more specifically,

---

47. *See* Menon & Wong, *supra* note 3 (calculating a more than 60 percent settlement rate for BPCIA litigations).

48. Federal Rule of Civil Procedure 41(a) is voluntary dismissal by plaintiff and states:

> (1) *By the Plaintiff.*
> (A) *Without a Court Order.* Subject to Rules 23(e), 23.1(c), 23.2, and 66 and any applicable federal statute, the plaintiff may dismiss an action without a court order by filing:
> (i) a notice of dismissal before the opposing party serves either an answer or a motion for summary judgment; or
> (ii) a stipulation of dismissal signed by all parties who have appeared.
> (B) *Effect.* Unless the notice or stipulation states otherwise, the dismissal is without prejudice. But if the plaintiff previously dismissed any federal- or state-court action based on or including the same claim, a notice of dismissal operates as an adjudication on the merits.

49. *Mediation*, U.S. Dist. Ct. for N. Dist. Cal., https://cand.uscourts.gov/about/court-programs/alternative-dispute-resolution-adr/mediation/ (last visited Feb. 8, 2024).

mediation.[50] For instance, in the U.S. District Court for the Northern District of California, "[m]ost civil cases are automatically assigned at filing to the ADR Multi-Option Program," and "[i]n advance of the initial case management conference, parties and counsel review and confer about several ADR options."[51] These options include early neutral evaluation, mediation, settlement conference with a magistrate judge, as well as private mediation. As such, even if the parties in a BPCIA litigation do not consider mediation at the outset, the specific venue may force the parties to engage in the mediation process.

Accordingly, while a mediator cannot force the parties to reach an agreement, and cannot unilaterally decide the dispute, the mediator may nonetheless prove helpful in facilitating settlement and license negotiations.

F. Factors to Consider in Licensing and Settlements

Regardless of how or when the parties approach licensing or settlement discussions, the parties will need to consider a variety of different terms to agree on. The following subsections discuss several of these points.

1. Size of Payment

One of the first items parties will negotiate is the cost of the license or settlement. Generally, a prospective licensee (i.e., the biosimilar applicant) will pay the prospective licensor (i.e., the RPS) to continue using the patented technology. The form of this payment can be highly varied and can include upfront payments, continuing payments, and royalties.[52]

Further, there are many factors that go into calculating the ultimate payment, including potential market size, current and projected profits, uniqueness of the patented technology, and existing and potential competitors. Indeed, the factors parties are likely to consider match closely with the *Georgia-Pacific* factors that courts use to calculate a reasonable

---

50. U.S. Department of Justice, ADR in the Federal District Courts—District-by-District Summaries (2016), https://www.justice.gov/archives/olp/file/827536/download.

51. *ADR in the Northern District*, U.S. Dist. Ct. for N. Dist. Cal., https://cand.uscourts.gov/about/court-programs/alternative-dispute-resolution-adr/ (last amended June 30, 2021).

52. *See, e.g.*, *Patent Licensing: A Closer Look*, InQuartik (Jan. 21, 2021), https://www.inquartik.com/blog/patent-licensing-a-closer-look-part-2.

royalty damages award.[53] Moreover, depending on the nature of any prior litigation, such a license or settlement may include provisions for attorneys' fees.

2. Agreement on Market Entry Dates

In addition to payments, the parties are likely to negotiate on the biosimilar product's market entry date. Specifically, the parties will discuss and

53. The *Georgia-Pacific* factors include:

1. The royalties received by the patentee for the licensing of the patent in suit, proving or tending to prove an established royalty.
2. The rates paid by the licensee for the use of other patents comparable to the patent in suit.
3. The nature and scope of the license, as exclusive or non-exclusive; or as restricted or non-restricted in terms of territory or with respect to whom the manufactured product may be sold.
4. The licensor's established policy and marketing program to maintain his patent monopoly by not licensing others to use the invention or by granting licenses under special conditions designed to preserve that monopoly.
5. The commercial relationship between the licensor and licensee, such as, whether they are competitors in the same territory in the same line of business; or whether they are inventor and promoter.
6. The effect of selling the patented specialty in promoting sales of other products of the licensee; that existing value of the invention to the licensor as a generator of sales of his non-patented items; and the extent of such derivative or convoyed sales.
7. The duration of the patent and the term of the license.
8. The established profitability of the product made under the patent; its commercial success; and its current popularity.
9. The utility and advantages of the patent property over the old modes or devices, if any, that had been used for working out similar results.
10. The nature of the patented invention; the character of the commercial embodiment of it as owned and produced by the licensor; and the benefits to those who have used the invention.
11. The extent to which the infringer has made use of the invention; and any evidence probative of the value of that use.
12. The portion of the profit or of the selling price that may be customary in the particular business or in comparable businesses to allow for the use of the invention or analogous inventions.
13. The portion of the realizable profit that should be credited to the invention as distinguished from non-patented elements, the manufacturing process, business risks, or significant features or improvements added by the infringer.
14. The opinion testimony of qualified experts.
15. The amount that a licensor (such as the patentee) and a licensee (such as the infringer) would have agreed upon (at the time the infringement began) if both had been reasonably and voluntarily trying to reach an agreement; that is, the amount that a prudent licensee—who desired, as a business proposition, to obtain a license to manufacture and sell a particular article embodying the patented invention—would have been willing to pay as a royalty and yet be able to make a reasonable profit and which amount would have been acceptable by a prudent patentee who was willing to grant a license.

Georgia-Pacific Corp. v. U.S. Plywood Corp., 318 F. Supp. 1116, 1120 (S.D.N.Y. 1970).

agree upon when the biosimilar applicant can begin to sell the biosimilar product. Upon the release of a biosimilar product, the price for that product can drop dramatically, as there are now two sellers competing for the same market (i.e., the RPS owner and now the biosimilar owner).[54] Accordingly, it is in the interest of the RPS to delay biosimilar market entry as *long* as possible, while it is in the interest of the biosimilar applicant to release as *soon* as possible. Thus, both parties will need to carefully consider whether to negotiate a market entry date for the biosimilar product.

3. Reverse-Payment Settlements

In some cases, however, an RPS may pay the biosimilar applicant in exchange for the latter delaying market entry. These "reverse payment," or "pay for delay," settlements are well-known in Hatch-Waxman litigation, wherein a new drug application (NDA) holder pays an abbreviated new drug application (ANDA) holder to delay launch of the ANDA holder's generic drug.[55] Put another way, the brand or reference product is paying the generic or biosimilar to stay off the market, which in turn will allow the brand or RPS to continue having the benefits of market exclusivity (e.g., higher prices, larger market share). With an extended exclusivity, the price of the product will likely stay high—as opposed to falling, as is expected upon release of a competitor product—enabling high profits that can justify the reverse-payment.

G. Antitrust Implications of Alternatives to Litigation

Depending on the nature of the license or settlement agreement there may be antitrust concerns. Specifically, such agreements can be anticompetitive by permitting the RPS a longer period of monopoly profits than would ordinarily occur.[56]

In 2013 the Supreme Court weighed in on such antitrust concerns, and in *FTC v. Actavis* held that the Federal Trade Commission (FTC) or private plaintiffs could sue under antitrust law, and that courts were to apply the rule of reason.[57] The rule of reason is an antitrust doctrine and

---

54. *See, e.g.*, *Generic Competition and Drug Prices*, FDA, https://www.fda.gov/about-fda/center-drug-evaluation-and-research-cder/generic-competition-and-drug-prices (last updated Oct. 5, 2023); Andrew W. Mulcahy et al., *Biosimilar Cost Savings in the United States*, 7 RAND Health Q. 3 (2018), https://www.rand.org/pubs/periodicals/health-quarterly/issues/v7/n4/03.html.

55. *See, e.g.*, John R. Thomas, Congressional Research Service, Pharmaceutical Patent-Antitrust: Reverse Payment Settlements and Product Hopping 2–4 (2015), https://crsreports.congress.gov/product/pdf/R/R44222.

56. *See, e.g.*, Max Theiler, *Pay-to-Delay for Biosimilars*, Fideres (Jan. 29, 2019), https://fideres.com/pay-to-delay-for-biosimilars.

57. *See generally* 570 U.S. 156 (2013).

analysis, under which courts weigh the positive and negative effects of an agreement to determine if the agreement violates antitrust laws. Put another way, courts will assess whether the challenged agreement promotes or suppresses market competition.

Antitrust suits of this nature are well-known in Hatch-Waxman cases,[58] but these suits remain undeveloped with regard to biosimilars. Nonetheless, one example exists in litigation surrounding AbbVie's Humira monoclonal antibody treatment.[59] There, and in relevant part, third-party payers sued AbbVie and alleged that AbbVie's settlements were anticompetitive. In particular, the third-party payers alleged that AbbVie violated antitrust laws by permitting biosimilar market entry years earlier in the European Union as compared to the United States. According to the third-party payers, the "reverse payment" for delayed United States market entry was whatever profits the biosimilars could make in the European Union. The court rejected this argument, however, and stated that "[t]he transfer of value, as large as it was, did not have the hallmarks of an unjustified and otherwise inexplicable payment because the package either increased competition or preserved an anticompetitive status quo."[60] The Seventh Circuit went on to affirm this decision.[61]

Accordingly, while antitrust law has not developed as deeply with BPCIA litigation as it has done with ANDA litigation, parties must still be cognizant of potential antitrust implications for any settlements or agreements.

VI. Arbitration

Arbitration is an additional form of ADR where the parties voluntarily agree, or are required under contract, to submit their case to an arbitrator, who are typically "lawyers, retired judges, or business professionals with expertise in a particular field."[62] Unlike mediation, however, the Federal Arbitration Act dictates that arbitration is binding.[63] As such, an arbitrator's decision will generally preclude further district court litigation. More-

58. *See generally* Mike McCaughan, *Patent Settlements*, Health Affs. (July 21, 2017), https://www.healthaffairs.org/do/10.1377/hpb20170721.583967/.

59. *See generally In re* Humira (Adalimumab) Antitr. Litig., 465 F. Supp. 3d 811 (N.D. Ill. 2020).

60. *Id.* at 841.

61. Mayor & City Council of Balt. v. AbbVie Inc., 42 F.4th 709, 716 (7th Cir. 2022).

62. *Occupational Outlook Handbook: Arbitrators, Mediators, and Conciliators*, U.S. Bureau Lab. Stat., https://www.bls.gov/ooh/legal/arbitrators-mediators-and-conciliators.htm (last modified Sept. 6, 2023).

63. *See* 9 U.S.C. § 9.

over, arbitration generally is faster to reach a decision and is generally less expensive.[64] These benefits are largely due to limited discovery and motion practice, although the particulars of arbitration proceedings will vary between arbitrators.

Because of the binding and limited nature of arbitration, parties generally disfavor arbitration, particularly for complex litigation. As such, voluntary arbitration appears to be an unlikely alternative for district court BPCIA litigation. Some interest groups, however, have suggested that mandatory arbitration may be an avenue to lower drug prices, including biologic prices.[65]

VII. Adversarial Alternatives to BPCIA Litigation

Beyond the aforementioned, parties have access to a handful of adversarial alternatives to district court BPCIA litigation. Specifically, parties can engage in adversarial administrative proceedings that could invalidate the patents-at-issue, or that could block importation of the allegedly infringing biosimilar product into the United States. These proceedings are oftentimes substantially quicker to conclude, as well as being more cost effective.[66] Sections VII.A–.B discuss various alternatives to district court litigation, namely post-grant proceedings before the Patent Trial and Appeal Board (PTAB) and before the International Trade Commission (ITC).

A. Post-Grant Proceedings at the PTAB

The America Invents Act (AIA) introduced two new post-grant proceedings for parties seeking to invalidate a patent—inter partes review (IPR) and post-grant review (PGR).[67] IPR and PGR proceedings are generally available for parties seeking to invalidate a patent and do not require that the

64. *Arbitration vs. Litigation: the Differences*, Thomson Reuters: Legal (Oct. 4, 2022), https://legal.thomsonreuters.com/blog/arbitration-vs-litigation-the-differences/.

65. John Rother, *Is Arbitration an Answer for High Drug Prices?*, Commonwealth Fund (May 3, 2019), https://www.commonwealthfund.org/blog/2019/arbitration-answer-high-drug-prices.

66. Philip Swain, *The Cost-Effectiveness of PTAB Proceedings*, PTAB Blog (Nov. 13, 2015), https://www.ptab-blog.com/2015/11/13/the-cost-effectiveness-of-ptab-proceedings/.

67. Note that the AIA also introduced covered business method review (CBM). CBMs, however, are only available to patents claiming a business method, and are thus not relevant to BPCIA litigation. *See* Thomas L. Giannetti, U.S. Patent and Trademark Office, Administrative Patent Trials before the Patent Trial and Appeal Board (2013), https://www.uspto.gov/sites/default/files/aia_implementation/Suffolk_Conference_2013_IPR-PGR-CBM.pptx; *see also* 37 C.F.R. § 42.301(a) (2024).

parties already be engaged in litigation.[68] Further, IPRs and PGRs are substantially faster than district court proceedings, with IPRs and PGRs generally concluding between 12 to 18 months after filing, as compared to the three to five years seen in district court litigation.[69] Moreover, the burden of proof for invalidating a patent in IPRs and PGRs is lower—merely preponderance of the evidence, as opposed to a district court's standard of clear and convincing evidence.[70]

Accordingly, IPRs and PGRs present an attractive avenue for biosimilar applicants who seek to invalidate patents that cover the reference product. Moreover, because a party may file a petition for IPR or PGR *before* any litigation has begun, IPRs and PGRs present a way to forestall the entire BPCIA process. As such, any biosimilars applicant anticipating, or currently engaging in, litigation should consider whether an IPR or PGR might forward their overall strategic objective.

Turning to IPRs and PGRs themselves, both follow similar procedures. Specifically, a patent challenger (i.e., the biosimilar applicant) will file a petition with the PTAB, after which the patentee (i.e., the RPS) is permitted to file a preliminary response within three months.[71] Three months after the RPS's preliminary response, the PTAB will issue a decision on whether or not to institute review based on whether there is a "reasonable likelihood" that the patent challenger will succeed as to at least one challenged claim.[72] Should the PTAB institute review, then the PTAB must issue a final written decision within one year, and within that time the parties will file opposing papers and will ultimately present an oral argument to the PTAB.[73]

IPRs and PGRs do, however, differ in terms of *when* a party may file a petition and *what grounds* that party may challenge. In particular, PGRs are only available to challenge patents within nine months of the patent's issuance[74] and "patents subject to the first-to-file provisions of the

---

68. Note, however, that IPRs and PGRs are not available for a party who has already filed a declaratory judgment action seeking invalidation of the patent at issue. *See* 35 U.S.C. § 315(a)(2); 35 U.S.C. § 325(a)(1).

69. *See* Michael J. Flibbert & Maureen D. Queler, *5 Distinctions between IPRs and District Court Patent Litigation*, Finnegan (Dec. 16, 2015), https://www.finnegan.com/en/insights/articles/5-distinctions-between-iprs-and-district-court-patent-litigation.html.

70. *See* 35 U.S.C. §§ 316(e), 326(e).

71. 37 C.F.R. § 42.120(b) (2024); *id.* § 42.207(b).

72. *Id.* § 42.100(c); 35 U.S.C. § 314(a).

73. For further explanation of IPR and PGR procedures, see, for example, *Inter Partes Review (IPR)*, Morgan Lewis (Apr. 21, 2021), https://www.morganlewis.com/pubs/2021/04/inter-partes-review-ipr-2020.

74. 35 U.S.C. § 321(c).

AIA."[75] A party can, however, base a PGR on any invalidity ground (i.e., §§ 101 subject matter eligibility, 102 novelty, 103 nonobviousness, and 112 enablement and written description). In contrast, IPRs are only available nine months *after* issuance, and a party may only challenge the patent under §§ 102 novelty and 103 nonobviousness.[76] Moreover, a party may only base IPR challenges "on the basis of prior art consisting of patents or printed publications."[77]

Further, while IPRs and PGRs present many benefits for biosimilar applicants, these proceedings can estop a party from asserting certain invalidity arguments elsewhere. Specifically, under 35 U.S.C. §§ 315(e)(2) (for IPRs) and 325(e)(2) (for PGRs), a party "may not assert . . . that [a] claim is invalid on any ground that the petitioner raised or reasonably could have raised during that post-grant review."[78] This estoppel applies in both district court litigation as well as ITC litigation, and thus any patent challenger seeking to petition for an IPR or PGR must be careful so as to not destroy promising invalidity arguments.

B. ITC Proceedings

In addition, the ITC can serve as another alternative, or complement, to BPCIA litigation. In particular, an RPS can bring an ITC case alleging patent infringement and, if successful, the ITC will issue an exclusion order preventing "importation into the United States, the sale for importation, or the sale within the United States after importation."[79] This exclusion order could apply to the patented products themselves, as well as those products made using a patented process.[80] While the ITC has yet to investigate biosimilar products, "the ITC has previously resolved Section 337 actions for other biologic products, including recombinant erythropoietin

75. Team Worldwide Corp. v. Intex Recreation Corp., No. 2020-1975, 2021 WL 4130634, at *2 n.2 (Fed. Cir. Sept. 9, 2021) ("Post-grant review is only available for patents subject to the first-to-file provisions of the AIA. In other words, post-grant review is available for patents containing at least one claim with an effective filing date after the effective date of the AIA—March 16, 2013." (citing AIA § 6(f)(2)(A))).

76. 35 U.S.C. § 311.

77. *Id.*

78. Cal. Inst. of Tech. v. Broadcom Ltd., 25 F.4th 976, 991 (Fed. Cir. 2022) ("[E]stoppel applies not just to claims and grounds asserted in the petition and instituted for consideration by the Board, but to all grounds not stated in the petition but which reasonably could have been asserted against the claims included in the petition.").

79. 19 U.S.C. § 1337(a)(1)(B).

80. *Id.*; *see also* Kinik Co. v. ITC, 362 F.3d 1359, 1362 (Fed. Cir. 2004) ("The enactment of 35 U.S.C. § 271(g) was part of the Omnibus Trade and Competitiveness Act of 1988. It was explained that § 271(g) was intended to provide 'patent owners the new right to sue for damages and seek an injunction in Federal district court when someone, without authorization, uses or sells in the United States, or imports into the United States a product made by their patented process.'" (citations omitted)).

(rEPO), recombinant factor VIII products, recombinant factor IX products, botulinum neurotoxin products, and snake antivenom."[81]

In general, the requirements for a successful ITC action include (1) that there was an unfair act; (2) that the accused product was or will be imported; (3) that there is a domestic industry; and (4) that there was injury to the patentee.[82] In particular to patents, the patentee will have to prove that the imported articles "infringe a valid and enforceable United States patent" or "are made, produced, processed, or mined under, or by means of, a process covered by the claims of a valid and enforceable United States patent."[83] Further, the patentee will have to establish that "an industry in the United States, relating to the articles protected by the patent . . . exists or is in the process of existing."[84]

Once an RPS files a complaint with the ITC, the ITC has 30 days to determine "whether the complaint is properly filed and whether an investigation should be instituted."[85] If the ITC agrees to institution, the ITC assigns the case to an administrative law judge (ALJ).[86] After institution, the responding party (i.e., the biosimilar applicant) in the ITC case then has 20 days to respond.[87] The parties then proceed through discovery, have two prehearing conferences, and then a final hearing, after which the ALJ will issue an initial determination.[88] Barring objection of at least one ITC commissioner, the ITC then adopts this initial determination as a final determination automatically after 45 days.[89]

The ITC offers several benefits to an RPS that may make the ITC a promising replacement for, or a complement to, BPCIA district court litigation. Primarily, ITC proceedings are significantly faster than district court litigation, with the final hearing typically occurring within nine to 12 months, and a final decision typically within 16 months.[90] Furthermore, the ITC offers fast temporary injunctive relief, as the ITC only has 35 days to decide whether to accept a motion for temporary relief, which are typically filed with the complaint.[91] If the ITC accepts the motion for

81. *See generally* Goodwin Procter LLP, Guide to Biosimilars Litigation and Regulation in the U.S. § 6.1 (Nov. 2022 ed.) (collecting examples of ITC biologics cases).

82. *Id.* § 6.2.

83. 19 U.S.C. § 1337(a)(1)(B)(i)–(ii).

84. *Id.* § 1337(a)(2)–(3).

85. *Id.*

86. 19 C.F.R. § 210.10 (2024); 19 U.S.C. § 1337(b)(1).

87. 19 C.F.R. § 210.13(a) (2024).

88. *Id.* § 210.42(a)(1).

89. *Id.* § 210.42(h).

90. H. Mark Lyon & Sarah E. Piepmeier, Practical Law Co., ITC Section 337 Investigations: Patent Infringement Claims (2012), https://www.gibsondunn.com/wp-content/uploads/documents/publications/Lyon-ITCSection337InvestigationsPatentInfingementClaims.pdf.

91. 19 U.S.C. § 1337(e), (f); 19 C.F.R. § 210.58 (2024).

temporary relief, the ITC refers the motion to the ALJ, who will issue an initial decision within 70 or 120 (for cases designated as complex) days.[92] The ITC will then review the initial decision, but the ITC must make a final determination within 90 or 150 (for cases designated as complex) days. Accordingly, the ITC presents an attractive option for RPSs seeking a quicker remedy than is available in traditional BPCIA district court litigation.

The ITC, however, is limited in its power. Specifically, ITC decisions with regard to patents are *not* binding on district courts.[93] Thus, an ITC decision on patent validity or invalidity is merely persuasive authority for district courts, and it is entirely possible for the ITC to hold that a patent is not invalid, only to have a district court go on to invalidate that same patent. Nonetheless, ITC proceedings present an attractive option for an RPS to seek fast relief in blocking importation of infringing products.

VIII. Establishing End Goals and Objectives

If cost, time, and regulatory approval were irrelevant, the end goal for a biosimilar applicant in BPCIA litigation would always be to get a total, unassailable victory in the district court that allowed it to launch its approved product immediately. In reality, however, all of those things *are* relevant, so an applicant must consider whether that victory would be worth the legal and other expenses, whether it is willing to wait for the litigation to play out before launching, and whether it expects to receive FDA approval in time to take advantage of the win.

It is important to keep such considerations in mind when figuring out reasonable end goals and objectives, which is an exercise that should take place early—even during the product development stages—and often. The exercise should be repeated regularly because goals and objectives may change based on, for example:

92. 19 C.F.R. § 210.66(b) (2024).

93. Tandon Corp. v. ITC, 831 F.2d 1017, 1018 (Fed. Cir. 1987) ("ITC findings neither purport to be, nor can they be, regarded as binding interpretations of the U.S. patent laws in particular factual contexts. Therefore, it seems clear that any disposition of a Commission action by a federal court should not have a res judicata or collateral estoppel effect in cases before such courts."); *see also* Eric Schweibenz & Alex Englehart, *Did You Know . . . Determinations of Patent Issues at the ITC Are for Purposes of Section 337 Only and Do Not Have Res Judicata Effect?*, ITC 337 L. Blog (Mar. 19, 2023), https://www.itcblog.com/488-did-you-know-determinations-of-patent-issues-at-the-itc-are-for-purposes-of-section-337-only-and-do-not-have-res-judicata-effect.

- **Litigation events**. As the record and legal arguments are developed, they may affect the applicant's perception of the likelihood of prevailing at trial.
- **Regulatory progress**. If the aBLA faces major hurdles at FDA, the applicant may be less inclined to spend on litigation.
- **Market forces**. Other biosimilar applicants may get approval sooner, or public demand for the drug may change.
- **Case complexity**. If a case grows more complicated and expensive due to PTAB proceedings, biosimilar versus biosimilar litigation, and/or a ballooning patent thicket, it may affect the applicant's thresholds for reverse-payment settlement and reasonable royalty amounts.
- **Settlement discussions**. Progress (or lack thereof) in negotiations may affect the decision to keep litigating.

The aforementioned considerations and others are always viewed through the lens of a given applicant's risk tolerance and resources. A 15 percent chance of winning at trial might be palatable to one company, but a different company might see that as motivation to speed up settlement talks. A large, well-established company might be able to withstand a long, drawn-out litigation, but a startup might not have the coffers for it and instead be settlement-minded from the outset. And where one company sees great conditions for launching at risk, a more risk-averse company might see reason to wait and avoid the exposure to potential damages.

Whatever a given biosimilar applicant's situation may be, to establish proper end goals and objectives, there must be an open and active discourse among its research and development (R&D) department, regulatory department, legal department, outside counsel, and corporate. Questions that should be addressed include:

- **R&D**. What challenges is the applicant facing in product development and manufacture? Could those challenges delay the applicant's readiness to launch? If so, by how long?
- **Regulatory**. What is a realistic timeline for receiving FDA approval in light of how smoothly (or not) the application process has unfolded so far?
- **Legal**. What are the strongest arguments that can be made for invalidity and/or noninfringement for each patent? What is the likelihood of prevailing on the merits?
- **Corporate**. How much is the company willing to spend on litigation for this product?

There is no one-size-fits-all approach for how to approach patent litigation against an RPS (or a fellow biosimilar applicant), especially because of the nascence of this area of law. The numerous variables discussed throughout this chapter must all be accounted for, and all plausible routes to resolving the dispute with the RPS should be considered. The more detail and discussion, the more that the applicant can develop a litigation strategy that is tailored to its appetite for risk, maximizes potential gain, and incorporates an accurate view of what an optimal—and realistic—litigation result would look like.

chapter 7

"First Wave" Infringement Actions*

I. Venue

The Biologics Price Competition and Innovation Act (BPCIA) does not set forth requirements for venue, and thus whether venue is proper is decided in accordance with federal law, which is not limited to patent cases.[1] Selecting the proper venue in BPCIA litigations is important. Because the BPCIA does not allow for an extension of time as to where to file the mandatory 42 U.S.C. § 262(*l*)(6) patent infringement action, it is important for reference product sponsors to choose the correct venue (or venues if a safety suit is filed elsewhere). Filing in an improper venue may result in loss of rights under the BPCIA with respect to the remedies set forth in 35 U.S.C. § 271(e)(6). Specifically, 35 U.S.C. § 271(e)(6) limits the potential remedies for patent infringement to a reasonable royalty where the (*l*)(6) action is

*Jennifer H. Wu, Peter Sandel, Stephen A. Maniscalco, Naz Wehrli, Jennifer Rea Denault, and Allison Penfield, Groombridge, Wu, Baughman & Stone LLP

1. *See* 28 U.S.C. § 1400(b) ("Any civil action for patent infringement may be brought in the judicial district where the defendant resides, or where the defendant has committed acts of infringement and has a regular and established place of business."); *see also id.* § 1391; *see, e.g.*, Genentech, Inc. v. Celltrion, Inc., No. 1:18-cv-01025, Dkt. No. 1, at 9 (D. Del. July 11, 2018) (relying on 28 U.S.C. §§ 1391, 1400(b) for venue); Amgen Inc. v. Tanvex BioPharma USA, Inc., No. 3:19-cv-01374, Dkt. No. 1, at 6 (S.D. Cal. July 23, 2019) (same); Hospira, Inc. v. Janssen Biotech, Inc., No. 1:14-cv-07049, Dkt. No. 1, at 6 (S.D.N.Y. Aug. 29, 2014) (same); Amgen Inc. v. Sandoz Inc., No. 1:23-cv-02406, Dkt. No. 1, at 7 (D.N.J. May 1, 2023) (same); Genentech, Inc. v. Pfizer Inc., No. 1:19-cv-00638, Dkt. No. 1, at 6 (D. Del. Apr. 5, 2019) (relying on 28 U.S.C. § 1400(b) for venue).

filed outside of a 30-day window set forth in 42 U.S.C. § 262(*l*)(6)(A)–(B).[2] 35 U.S.C. § 271(e)(6) states:

> **(6)**
>
> **(A)** *Subparagraph (B) applies, in lieu of paragraph (4), in the case of a patent—*
>
> **(i)** that is identified, as applicable, in the list of patents described in section 351(l)(4) of the Public Health Service Act or the lists of patents described in section 351(l)(5)(B) of such Act with respect to a biological product; and
>
> **(ii)** *for which an action for infringement of the patent with respect to the biological product—*
>
> **(I)** *was brought after the expiration of the 30-day period described in subparagraph (A) or (B), as applicable, of section 351(l)(6) of such Act; or*
>
> **(II)** *was brought before the expiration of the 30-day period described in subclause (I), but which was dismissed without prejudice or was not prosecuted to judgment in good faith.*
>
> **(B)** *In an action for infringement of a patent described in subparagraph (A), the sole and exclusive remedy that may be granted by a court*, upon a finding that the making, using, offering to sell, selling, or importation into the United States of the biological product that is the subject of the action infringed the patent, *shall be a reasonable royalty.*
>
> **(C)** The owner of a patent that should have been included in the list described in section 351(l)(3)(A) of the Public Health Service Act, including as provided under section 351(l)(7) of such Act for a biological product, but was not timely included in such list, may not bring an action under

2. *See* 42 U.S.C. § 262(*l*)(6)(A) ("If the subsection (k) applicant and the reference product sponsor agree on patents as described in paragraph (4), not later than 30 days after such agreement, the reference product sponsor shall bring an action for patent infringement with respect to each such patent."); *id.* § 262(*l*)(6)(B) ("If the provisions of paragraph (5) apply to the parties as described in paragraph (4)(B), not later than 30 days after the exchange of lists under paragraph (5)(B), the reference product sponsor shall bring an action for patent infringement with respect to each patent that is included on such lists.").

> this section for infringement of the patent with respect to the biological product.[3]

What this means is that filing in an improper venue, even where leave is granted to refile without prejudice elsewhere, could forfeit the reference product sponsor's ability to seek the mandatory injunction set forth in 35 U.S.C. § 271(e)(4) and other remedies such as lost profits damages. In the abbreviated new drug application (ANDA) context, product sponsors face a similar concern regarding their ability to obtain a 30-month stay if their infringement action is dismissed for lack of personal jurisdiction and they are forced to refile outside the 45-day window. In order to mitigate this risk, a number of product sponsors have filed backup or protective suits in addition to filing in their preferred forum.[4] If faced with uncertainty regarding personal jurisdiction in the forum of its choosing, a reference product sponsor may similarly consider filing a backup or protective suit.

So far, the relatively few number of venue disputes in BPCIA litigations have been informed by considerations also present in ANDA litigations.[5] For example, in *AbbVie Inc. v. Alvotech hf.*,[6] Alvotech hf. moved to dismiss for lack of venue, arguing that its U.S. subsidiary was a necessary party but not amenable to suit in the Northern District of Illinois.[7] Looking to decisions in the ANDA context in which parties involved in preparing an ANDA were deemed to be "submitters," the court concluded that the complaint adequately alleges that Alvotech hf. was a "submitter" of the

---

3. 35 U.S.C. § 271(e)(6) (emphases added).

4. *See, e.g.*, Schering Corp. v. Caraco Pharm. Lab'ys, Ltd., No. 06-cv-14386, 2007 WL 1648908, at *2–3 (E.D. Mich. June 6, 2007) (granting motion to stay second-filed "protective" action pending resolution of jurisdictional dispute in first-filed New Jersey action); Pfizer, Inc. v. Mylan, Inc., No. 1:09-cv-79, 2009 WL 10270101, at *2–3 (N.D. W. Va. Nov. 20, 2009) (granting motion to transfer second-filed protective suit to Delaware where patentee had filed first suit); Pfizer Inc. v. Mylan Inc., No. 1:15-cv-4, 2015 WL 3903386, at *3–4 (N.D. W. Va. Apr. 24, 2015) (granting motion to stay second "protective" suit pending resolution of jurisdictional dispute in first-filed Delaware case); Novartis AG v. Ezra Ventures, LLC, No. 4:15-cv-00095, 2015 WL 4197692, at *3–5 (E.D. Ark. July 10, 2015) (granting motion to stay second-filed "protective" suit in favor of first-filed Delaware action).

5. *See, e.g.*, *Venue Considerations for Hatch-Waxman and BPCIA Litigation*, JD Supra (Nov. 19, 2020), https://www.jdsupra.com/legalnews/venue-considerations-for-hatch-waxman-19700/.

6. No. 21-cv-02258, 2021 WL 3737733, at *1 (N.D. Ill. Aug. 23, 2021).

7. Alvotech hf.'s subsidiary, Alvotech USA, had filed the biologics license application (BLA) seeking approval to market a biosimilar to Humira but, based on allegations that Alvotech hf. was involved in the preparation of the BLA and would be the entity engaging in manufacturing, commercialization, marketing, and sale of the biosimilar, AbbVie named Alvotech hf. as a defendant and did not name Alvotech USA. *AbbVie Inc.*, 2021 WL 3737733, at *2–3.

biologics license application (BLA) under § 271(e)(2)(C) and that Alvotech hf. had failed to establish that its subsidiary was a necessary party.[8]

As is the case for ANDA litigations, the act of infringement in the context of BPCIA litigations is set forth in 35 U.S.C. § 271(e)(2):

> **(2)** *It shall be an act of infringement to submit—*
>
> > **(A)** an application under section 505(j) of the Federal Food, Drug, and Cosmetic Act or described in section 505(b)(2) of such Act for a drug claimed in a patent or the use of which is claimed in a patent,
> >
> > **(B)** an application under section 512 of such Act or under the Act of March 4, 1913 (21 U.S.C. 151–158) for a drug or veterinary biological product which is not primarily manufactured using recombinant DNA, recombinant RNA, hybridoma technology, or other processes involving site specific genetic manipulation techniques and which is claimed in a patent or the use of which is claimed in a patent, or
> >
> > **(C)**
> >
> > > **(i)** *with respect to a patent that is identified in the list of patents described in section 351(l)(3) of the Public Health Service Act (including as provided under section 351(l)(7) of such Act), an application seeking approval of a biological product*, or
> > >
> > > **(ii)** if the applicant for the application fails to provide the application and information required under section 351(*l*)(2)(A) of such Act, an application seeking approval of a biological product for a patent that could be identified pursuant to section 351(*l*)(3)(A)(i) of such Act,
>
> *if the purpose of such submission is to obtain approval under such Act to engage in the commercial manufacture, use, or sale of a* drug, veterinary biological product, or *biological product claimed in a patent or the use of which is claimed in a patent before the expiration of such patent.*[9]

In the ANDA context,[10] the Federal Circuit recently addressed "whether the act of infringement identified in § 1400(b) occurs only when and where

8. *Id.* at *9–10.

9. 35 U.S.C. § 271(e)(2) (emphases added).

10. *See AbbVie Inc.*, 2021 WL 3737733, at *2 ("When Congress passed the BPCIA in 2009, it was not writing on a blank slate. The BPCIA's [abbreviated biologics license application (aBLA)] procedure closely resembles one that was already available under the Hatch-Waxman Act for small molecule drugs.").

an ANDA-filer submits its ANDA to the [U.S. Food and Drug Administration (FDA)] or occurs wherever future distribution of the generic is contemplated."[11] The Federal Circuit held:

> [I]n Hatch-Waxman cases, venue is not proper in all judicial districts where a generic product specified in an ANDA is likely to be distributed. It is proper only in those districts that are sufficiently related to the ANDA submission—in those districts where acts occurred that would suffice to categorize those taking them as a "submitter" under § 271(e).[12]

Approximately a year later, in *Celgene Corp. v. Mylan Pharmaceuticals Inc.*, the Federal Circuit explained:

> While the court took care not to prematurely "define what all relevant acts involved in the preparation and submission of an ANDA might be," *Valeant*, 978 F.3d at 1384 n.8, it did make clear that it is the *submission* that infringes, *id.* at 1381–82. *Valeant*'s focus on the submission itself (along with acts involved in its "preparation") indicates that the relevant infringing acts must, at a minimum, fairly be *part of* the submission—not merely "related to" it in some broader sense. *See id.* at 1384 (considering whether "acts occurred" in the district "that would suffice to categorize those taking them as a 'submitter' under § 271(e)"). After all, the relevant prong of § 1400(b) restricts venue to "where the defendant has committed acts of infringement"—not where the defendant has committed acts related to (but not part of) acts of infringement. *See Valeant*, 978 F.3d at 1381 ("[I]t is the submission of the ANDA, and only the submission, that constitutes an act of infringement in this context.").[13]

II. Pleadings

Under the BPCIA, a reference product sponsor may bring suit against a biosimilar applicant in two ways: (1) an immediate patent infringement action under 42 U.S.C. § 262(*l*)(6), or (2), in certain instances, a declaratory judgment action under 28 U.S.C. § 2201. 35 U.S.C. § 271(e)(2)(C) creates a technical act of infringement based on the submission of an abbreviated biologics license application (aBLA) to FDA seeking approval of a biological

11. Valeant Pharms. N. Am. LLC v. Mylan Pharms. Inc., 978 F.3d 1374, 1378–79 (Fed. Cir. 2020).
12. *Id.* at 1384.
13. Celgene Corp. v. Mylan Pharms. Inc., 17 F.4th 1111, 1121 (Fed. Cir. 2021).

product. This artificial act of infringement applies to patents listed by the parties under section (*l*)(3);[14] or, if the biosimilar applicant fails to provide a copy of its BLA and information required by section (*l*)(2)(A), any patents that could be listed under section (*l*)(3)(A).[15]

As with ANDA litigations, certain venues are more popular for BPCIA litigations than others. The most popular venue for BPCIA litigation is the U.S. District Court for the District of Delaware where approximately 40 percent of such litigations are filed.[16] The next most common venues are the U.S. District Court for the District of New Jersey[17] and the U.S. District Court for the Northern District of California,[18] followed by the U.S. District Court for the Southern District of Florida[19] and the U.S. District Court for the District of Massachusetts.[20] The remainder includes the U.S. District Court for the Northern District of Illinois,[21] the U.S. District Court for the Southern District of New York,[22] the U.S. District Court for the

14. Common shorthand abbreviations (e.g., "section (*l*)(3)," "(*l*)(3)," etc.) used in this chapter refer to the respective BPCIA statutory sections (e.g., § 262(*l*)(3), etc.).

15. 35 U.S.C. § 271(e)(2)(C)(i)–(ii).

16. *See* Amgen Inc. v. Hospira, Inc., No. 1:15-cv-00839 (D. Del. 2015); AbbVie Inc. v. Amgen Inc., No. 1:16-cv-00666 (D. Del. 2016); Amgen Inc. v. Coherus BioScis. Inc., No. 1:17-cv-00546 (D. Del. 2017); AbbVie Inc. v. Boehringer Ingelheim Int'l GmbH, No. 1:17-cv-01065 (D. Del. 2017); Genentech, Inc. v. Amgen Inc., No. 1:17-cv-01407 (D. Del. 2017); Genentech, Inc. v. Amgen Inc., No. 1:17-cv-01471 (D. Del. 2017); Genentech, Inc. v. Celltrion, Inc., No. 1:18-cv-00095 (D. Del. 2018); Genentech, Inc. v. Amgen Inc., No. 1:18-cv-00924 (D. Del. 2018); Genentech, Inc. v. Celltrion, Inc., No. 1:18-cv-01025 (D. Del. 2018); Amgen Inc. v. Hospira, Inc., No. 1:18-cv-01064 (D. Del. 2018); Genentech, Inc. v. Samsung Bioepis Co., No. 1:18-cv-01363 (D. Del. 2018); Genentech, Inc. v. Immunex R.I. Corp., No. 1:19-cv-00602 (D. Del. 2019); Genentech, Inc. v. Pfizer Inc., No. 1:19-cv-00648 (D. Del. 2019); Amgen Inc. v. Hospira, Inc., No. 1:20-cv-00201 (D. Del. 2020); Amgen Inc. v. Hospira, Inc., No. 1:20-cv-00561 (D. Del. 2020); Genentech, Inc. v. Samsung Bioepis Co. Ltd., No. 1:20-cv-00859 (D. Del. 2020).

17. *See* Immunex Corp. v. Sandoz Inc., No. 2:16-cv-01118 (D.N.J. 2016); Genentech, Inc. v. Celltrion, Inc., No. 1:18-cv-00574 (D.N.J. 2018); Amgen Inc. v. Kashiv Bioscis. LLC, No. 2:18-cv-03347 (D.N.J. 2018); Genentech, Inc. v. Celltrion, Inc., No. 1:18-cv-11553 (D.N.J. 2018); Immunex Corp. v. Samsung Bioepis Co. Ltd., No. 2:19-cv-11755 (D.N.J. 2019); Amgen Inc. v. Sandoz Inc., No. 1:23-cv-02406 (D.N.J. 2023).

18. *See* Sandoz Inc. v. Amgen Inc., No. 3:13-cv-02904 (N.D. Cal. 2013); Amgen Inc. v. Sandoz Inc., No. 3:14-cv-04741 (N.D. Cal. 2014); Amgen Inc. v. Sandoz Inc., No. 3:16-cv-02581 (N.D. Cal. 2016); Celltrion, Inc. v. Genentech, Inc., No. 4:18-cv-00274 (N.D. Cal. 2018); Celltrion, Inc. v. Genentech, Inc., No. 4:18-cv-00276 (N.D. Cal. 2018); Sandoz Inc. v. Amgen Inc., No. 3:19-cv-00977 (N.D. Cal. 2019).

19. *See* Amgen Inc. v Apotex Inc., No. 0:15-cv-61631 (S.D. Fla. 2015); Amgen Inc. v. Apotex Inc., No. 0:15-cv-62081 (S.D. Fla. 2015); Amgen Inc. v. Accord BioPharma, No. 0:18-cv-61828 (S.D. Fla. 2018).

20. *See* Janssen Biotech, Inc. v. Celltrion Healthcare Co., No. 1:15-cv-10698 (D. Mass. 2015); Janssen Biotech, Inc. v. Celltrion Healthcare Co., No. 1:17-cv-11008 (D. Mass. 2017); Teva Pharms. Int'l GmbH v. Eli Lilly & Co., No. 1:18-cv-12029 (D. Mass. 2018).

21. *See* AbbVie Inc. v. Alvotech hf., No. 1:21-cv-02899 (N.D. Ill. 2021).

22. *See* Celltrion Healthcare Co., Ltd. v. Kennedy Tr. for Rheumatology Rsch., No. 1:14-cv-02256 (S.D.N.Y. 2014); Hospira, Inc. v. Janssen Biotech, Inc., No. 1:14-cv-07049 (S.D.N.Y. 2014).

Southern District of California,[23] the U.S. District Court for the Central District of California,[24] the U.S. District Court for the Western District of Pennsylvania,[25] and the U.S. District Court for the Northern District of West Virginia.[26] The popularity of Delaware as a venue for BPCIA litigations suggests that a district court's experience with BPCIA litigation and pharmaceutical litigation generally is important to the reference product sponsor's decision of where to file.

A. Immediate Patent Infringement Actions

1. The Statute

The exchange of information and contentions between the biosimilar applicant and the reference product sponsor under the BPCIA, the so-called "patent dance," culminates in an "immediate patent infringement action" under section (*l*)(6).[27] The BPCIA encourages parties to participate in the patent dance by barring the biosimilar applicant and the reference product sponsor from bringing declaratory judgment actions once the patent dance has begun.[28] Participation in the dance allows the biosimilar sponsor substantial control regarding the selection of patents to be addressed in the first wave. If the reference product sponsor and the biosimilar applicant are unable to reach agreement on the selection of patents under section (*l*)(4), then the parties must exchange lists of the patents to be the subject of the first wave. However, section (*l*)(5)(A) allows the biosimilar sponsor to determine the number of patents to be included in each party's list.[29] Once the biosimilar applicant notifies the reference product sponsor of the number of patents, the parties are to simultaneously exchange their respective lists of patents each believes should be the subject of the (*l*)(6) action. Following the determination of which patents will be the subject of the immediate action, the reference product sponsor "shall bring an action for patent infringement with respect" to patents agreed upon by the parties under section (*l*)(4), or upon the patents listed by the parties under section (*l*)(5), within 30 days.[30] If the reference product sponsor timely

---

23. *See* Amgen Inc. v. Tanvex BioPharma USA, Inc., No. 3:19-cv-01374 (S.D. Cal. 2019); Genentech, Inc. v. Tanvex BioPharma USA, Inc., No. 3:22-cv-00809 (S.D. Cal. 2022).

24. *See* Amgen Inc. v. Genentech, Inc., No. 2:17-cv-07349 (C.D. Cal. 2017).

25. *See* Amgen Inc. v. Mylan Inc., No. 2:17-cv-01235 (W.D. Pa. 2017).

26. *See* Regeneron Pharms., Inc. v. Mylan Pharms. Inc., No. 1:22-cv-00061 (N.D. W. Va. 2022).

27. A comprehensive treatment of the patent dance is provided in Chapter 4.

28. 42 U.S.C. § 262(*l*)(9)(A).

29. An exception is provided in instances in which the biosimilar applicant chooses not to list any patents, in which case the reference product sponsor may nevertheless list one patent. *See id.* § 262(*l*)(5)(B)(ii)(II).

30. *Id.* § 262(*l*)(6); *see also* Sandoz Inc. v. Amgen Inc., 137 S. Ct. 1664, 1671–72 (2017).

brings an action and prevails, it may obtain the remedies provided under § 271(e)(4) including injunctive relief and, if there has been commercial activity, monetary damages.[31] Conversely, if a reference product sponsor fails to bring an action within the prescribed 30-day period, its available remedies are limited to a reasonable royalty under § 271(e)(6)(B).

In determining whether or not to participate in the patent dance, a biosimilar applicant may wish to consider the size of the reference product sponsor's patent portfolio. As discussed earlier, a biosimilar applicant that provides its BLA and information under section (*l*)(2)(A) and participates in the steps of the patent dance is provided with substantial control over the scope of the first wave of litigation. Specifically, if negotiations under section (*l*)(4) are unsuccessful, the parties must exchange lists of patents to be included in the (*l*)(6) action and, under section (*l*)(5)(A), it is the biosimilar applicant that determines the number of patents on each party's list.[32] The ability to select the number of patents under (*l*)(5)(A) has allowed biosimilar applicants to substantially reduce the number of patents to be addressed in the first wave[33] or, in other instances, to insist that all patents be addressed in the first wave.[34]

2. Strategic Considerations

The BPCIA provides for a relatively short time frame for the reference product sponsor to evaluate the aBLA—which is usually a million or more pages—before the filing of an (*l*)(6) immediate infringement action. Specifically, section (*l*)(2) provides that the biosimilar applicant shall provide to the reference product sponsor "a copy of the [aBLA] submitted to [FDA] under subsection (k), and such other information that describes the

31. 35 U.S.C. § 271(e)(4).

32. An exception is provided in instances in which the biosimilar applicant chooses not to list any patents, in which case the reference product sponsor may nevertheless list one patent. *See* 42 U.S.C. § 262(*l*)(5)(B)(ii)(II).

33. In *AbbVie Inc. v. Amgen Inc.*, AbbVie's (3)(C) list included 61 patents. The parties were unable to agree under section (*l*)(4) and Amgen set the number of patents to be listed under (*l*)(5) as six. The parties then simultaneously exchanged lists of six patents. The listed patents overlapped with regard to two patents, bringing the total number of patents for inclusion in the (*l*)(6) to ten patents. AbbVie Inc. v. Amgen Inc., No. 1:16-cv-00666-SLR-SRF, Dkt. 1 (D. Del. Aug. 4, 2016). *See also* AbbVie Inc. v. Boehringer Ingelheim Int'l GmbH, No. 1:17-cv-01065-UNA, Dkt. No. 1 (D. Del. Aug. 2, 2017) (Seventy-one patents identified in reference product sponsor's (3)(C) statement, narrowed to eight patents for inclusion in (*l*)(6) action).

34. In *Regeneron v. Mylan*, Regeneron sought to limit the number of patents to be included in the (*l*)(6) action. Mylan disagreed and negotiations were unsuccessful under (*l*)(4). Under (*l*)(5), Mylan listed 25 patents and Regeneron listed 12, each of which was also on Mylan's list. Regeneron subsequently filed its (*l*)(6) action asserting infringement of 24 patents (one patent was removed as no longer asserted). Regeneron Pharms., Inc. v. Mylan Pharms. Inc., No. 1:22-cv-00061-TSK, Dkt. No. 1 (N.D. W. Va. Aug. 2, 2022).

process or processes used to manufacture the biological product that is the subject of such application."[35] Upon receipt of the biosimilar applicants BLA and other information under (*l*)(2)(A), the reference product sponsor has only 60 days to provide its list of patents for which the reference product sponsor "believes a claim of patent infringement could reasonably be asserted."[36]

Importantly, access to the aBLA and manufacturing information provided under the BPCIA is limited to outside counsel and a single in-house attorney who is an employee of the reference product sponsor.[37] Having only one in-house counsel access the information exchanged under the BPCIA can present issues where the reference product sponsor is a large organization in which multiple attorneys have knowledge of the potential patents to assert. This can be particularly challenging where the potentially asserted patents are manufacturing patents, which are a class of patents not included in most ANDA litigations but for which the BPCIA expressly allows assertion.

Another challenge in filing BPCIA complaints is that the default confidentiality provisions of the BPCIA require that "[n]o confidential information may be included in any publicly-available complaint or other pleading."[38] This means BPCIA complaints cannot include confidential information in the aBLA that is the basis for the patent infringement claims in the (*l*)(6) infringement action, unless the parties have come to an agreement other than the default confidentiality provisions. At the same time, the reference product sponsor's complaint must, under Federal Rule of Civil Procedure 8(a), contain "a short and plain statement of the claim showing the pleader is entitled to relief" and, to survive a motion to dismiss, the complaint must contain sufficient facts "to state a claim to relief that is plausible on its face."[39]

While a small number of BPCIA complaints have been filed under seal, the more common approach has been to include a reference to the exchange of confidential information and the reference product sponsor's provision of detailed contentions as part of its section (*l*)(3)(C) statement.[40] In at least one instance a biosimilar applicant challenged this pleading

35. 42 U.S.C. § 262(*l*)(2)(A).

36. *Id.* § 262(*l*)(3)(A)(i).

37. *Id.* § 262(*l*)(1)(B)(ii).

38. *Id.* § 262(*l*)(1)(F).

39. Bell Atl. Corp. v. Twombly, 127 S. Ct. 1955, 1974 (2007); *see also* Ashcroft v. Iqbal, 129 S. Ct. 1937, 1945 (2009).

40. *See, e.g.*, Amgen Inc. v. Mylan Inc., No. 2:17-cv-01235, Dkt. No. 1 (W.D. Pa. Sept. 22, 2017); Amgen Inc. v. Hospira, Inc., No. 1:20-cv-00201, Dkt. No. 1 (D. Del. Feb. 11, 2020); Regeneron Pharms., Inc. v. Mylan Pharms. Inc., No. 1:22-cv-00061, Dkt. No. 1 (N.D. W. Va. Aug. 22, 2022).

approach as failing to put forward sufficient information to state a claim under *Twombly* because the substance of the section (*l*)(3)(C) contentions could not be incorporated by reference into the complaint.[41] However, the motion was withdrawn before the court rendered a decision.

Yet another consideration for the reference product sponsor is whether to assert patents for which additional information, obtainable in discovery or via testing, is required to make out an infringement claim. The exchange of information under section (*l*)(2)(A) may be narrower in scope than what is available in discovery once the (*l*)(6) infringement action has commenced; however, discovery in litigation is limited to that which is relevant to the patents being asserted in that action.[42] As is often the case, in *Amgen v. Hospira*, there was a dispute regarding the adequacy of information provided under section (*l*)(2)(A).[43] During the patent dance, Amgen alleged that Hospira had failed to fully disclose the specific composition of its cell culture medium and that, without this information, Amgen could not assess the reasonableness of asserting certain patents directed to cell culture. In the subsequent (*l*)(6) action, Amgen did not assert its cell culture patents and the district court denied Amgen's efforts to compel discovery regarding Hospira's cell culture medium as it was not relevant to the patents that were asserted. On appeal, Amgen argued that unless discovery of Hospira's cell culture process was allowed it would be deprived of its right to sue under the BPCIA. The Federal Circuit disagreed. The Federal Circuit noted that a reference product sponsor can list patents it "believes . . . could reasonably be asserted" on its section (3)(A) list at which point the biosimilar applicant must come forward with additional disclosures under section (3)(B). "If the applicant fails to comply with its obligation to respond under paragraph (*l*)(3)(B), the sponsor would have a reasonable basis for asserting a claim of patent infringement."[44] While discovery will likely be required in order for the reference product sponsor to meet its burden of proving infringement at trial, in *Amgen v. Hospira*, the Federal Circuit also noted that Federal Rule of Civil Procedure 11 "expressly permits factual allegations that 'will likely have evidentiary support after a reasonable opportunity for further investigation or discovery.'"[45]

41. Genentech, Inc. v. Celltrion, Inc., No. 1:18-cv-00095-GMS, Dkt. No. 18 (D. Del. Apr. 23, 2018).
42. *See, e.g.*, Fed. R. Civ. P. 26(a).
43. 866 F.3d 1355, 1357 (Fed. Cir. 2017).
44. *Id.* at 1362.
45. *Id.*

B. Declaratory Judgment Actions

The U.S. Supreme Court has made clear that a biosimilar applicant may opt out of the BPCIA's provisions requiring exchange of information, such as under section (*l*)(2)(A), and decline to participate in the patent dance.[46] Specifically, the Supreme Court held that an injunction is not available to enforce compliance with section (*l*)(2)(A).[47] However, the BPCIA does provide a remedy for a biosimilar applicant's failure to provide its BLA and manufacturing information. When a biosimilar applicant fails to comply with section (*l*)(2)(A), section (*l*)(9)(C) authorizes the reference product sponsor, but not the biosimilar applicant, to bring an action for a declaration of patent infringement, validity, or enforceability. "Section 262(*l*)(9)(C) thus vests in the sponsor the control that the applicant would otherwise have exercised over the scope and timing of the patent litigation."[48] Similarly, if a biosimilar applicant provides information under (*l*)(2)(A) but fails to complete the actions required by sections (*l*)(3)(B)(ii), (5), (6)(C)(i), (7), or (8)(A), the reference product sponsor may bring a declaratory judgment action regarding any patent included on its section (*l*)(3)(A) list.

Since the Supreme Court's decision in *Sandoz*, only one biosimilar applicant has refused to provide a copy of its BLA.[49] Generally, district courts have rejected attempts by biosimilar applicants to file preemptive declaratory judgment actions and, to date, the ability to seek declaratory judgment regarding patent infringement or validity has been reserved for reference product sponsors. Several early attempts by biosimilar applicants to bring declaratory judgment actions were dismissed for lack of Article III controversy.[50] Based on the language of (*l*)(9)(A), several biosimilar applicants have also asserted that the bar on bringing declaratory judgment actions ends with the biosimilar applicant's notice of commercial

46. Sandoz Inc. v. Amgen Inc., 137 S. Ct. 1664 (2017).

47. *Id.* at 1674.

48. *Id.* at 1675.

49. *See* Amgen Inc. v. Kashiv Bioscis., LLC, No. 2:18-cv-03348-CCC-MF, Dkt. No. 1 (D.N.J. Mar. 3, 2018).

50. *See, e.g.*, Sandoz Inc. v. Amgen Inc., No. C-13-2904 MMC, 2013 WL 6000069, at *2 (N.D. Cal. Feb. 12, 2013) (granting motion to dismiss declaratory judgment action brought by Sandoz before filing of Sandoz's BLA for lack of Article III controversy and holding that, "even after an applicant provides a 'notice of commercial marketing,' it cannot bring an action for declaratory relief until, at a minimum, it has complied with its obligations under § 262(*l*)(2)(A)"); *see also* Hospira Inc. v. Janssen Biotech, Inc., No. 14-cv-7049-PAC, 2014 WL 6766263, at *1–2 (S.D.N.Y. Dec. 1, 2014) (granting motion to dismiss declaratory judgment action brought by Hospira based on a lack of standing and noting that "the existence of the BPCIA mechanisms for dispute resolution counsels against the exercise of jurisdiction over this complaint. The BPCIA purposefully ties the dispute resolution process to events throughout the biosimilar approval process, ensuring that full information exchange occurs at relevant and crucial times during the approval process.").

marketing under section (*l*)(8)(A) and have filed declaratory judgment actions after providing their (*l*)(8)(A) notice. In rejecting these attempts, several district courts have concluded that provision of the notice of commercial marketing may enable "second phase" litigation regarding patents that were not selected for the immediate patent infringement action under section (*l*)(6), but does not allow biosimilar applicants to sidestep the BPCIA's exchange-and-negotiation provisions and file declaratory judgment actions.[51]

III. Fact Discovery

Fact discovery in biosimilar cases is similar to that in patent infringement cases in general. During fact discovery, the reference product sponsor seeks evidence supporting its patent infringement claims and patent validity.[52] Conversely, the biosimilar applicant seeks evidence supporting its noninfringement defenses and patent invalidity defenses.[53] A party uses the typical discovery tools available in litigation, including interrogatories, requests for production, requests for admission, depositions, and subpoenas, to acquire evidence from the opposing party and third parties.[54]

Because of the limited information provided through the patent dance, it is not unusual to see large numbers of patents asserted in the complaints of biosimilar cases.[55] This leads to a broad scope of relevant information in fact discovery.[56] Fact discovery can be used to narrow the asserted patents as additional information is disclosed by the biosimilar applicant to the reference product sponsor.[57]

---

51. *See, e.g.*, Amgen Inc. v. Genentech, Inc., No. 17-cv-7349 GW, 2018 WL 910198 (C.D. Cal. Jan. 11, 2018) (rejecting the argument that a biosimilar is entitled to bring suit after providing notice of commercial marketing but before completing the patent dance and noting that the BPCIA is structured "so that after the applicant provides notice of commercial marketing, either party can bring suit with respect to any of the leftover patents that were not selected for litigation").

52. *E.g.*, AbbVie Inc. v. Boehringer Ingelheim Int'l GmbH, No. 1:17-cv-1065-MSG-RL, Dkt. Nos. 33, 39, 65, 139 (D. Del. Nov. 22, 2017, Dec. 4, 2017, Apr. 18, 2018, July 27, 2018) (notices of service of interrogatories and requests for production).

53. *E.g.*, *id.* Dkt. Nos. 34, 36, 47 (notices of service of interrogatories and requests for production).

54. *E.g.*, *id.* Dkt. No. 29 (scheduling order limiting the number of interrogatories, requests for production, and requests for admission, among other things).

55. *E.g.*, Regeneron Pharms., Inc. v. Mylan Pharms. Inc., No. 1:22-cv-61-TSK-JPM, Dkt. No. 1 (N.D. W. Va. Aug. 2, 2022) (complaint asserting 24 patents).

56. Fed. R. Civ. P. 34; *AbbVie Inc.*, No. 1:17-cv-1065-MSG-RL, Dkt. No. 58 (D. Del. Apr. 2, 2018) (granting motion to compel).

57. *Regeneron Pharms., Inc.*, No. 1:22-cv-61-TSK-JPM, Dkt. No. 1.

Certain areas of discovery are particularly important in biosimilar cases. For example, discovery of the aBLA, amendments to it, and communications between FDA and the biosimilar applicant may be particularly important if there have been changes to the manufacturing processes or product specifications. The version of the aBLA provided during the patent dance is often not in a format appropriate for court. The aBLA is often in electronic common technical document (eCTD) format, which may require specialized software to facilitate review. For trial, a Bates stamped version of the aBLA, or sections of the aBLA, is generally necessary.

Another example, and in contrast to most Hatch-Waxman litigation, is the possibility of damages discovery if the biosimilar applicant receives approval and launches during the pendency of the case. The scope of discovery on damages is similar to patent cases in general, but may be complicated by issues related to pharmaceutical pricing, rebates, reimbursement, and formulary coverage.

Depending on the scope of the asserted patents, discovery may include the biosimilar manufacturing process. The manufacturing process or other relevant information is sometimes held by entities located outside the United States and parties should consider whether discovery under the Hague Convention will be required. A potentially further complicating factor in obtaining discovery of the manufacturing process is the possibility that the approved manufacturing process and product specifications may differ from those described in the originally filed aBLA as a result of amendments made during the approval process. In addition, the product specifications in the aBLA may be broader than the biosimilar's manufacturing specifications. In the context of ANDA litigation, multiple courts have made clear that an ANDA applicant cannot avoid infringement by relying on narrower product specifications than those that are provided by its ANDA, and therefore those for which it seeks approval to market.[58] "What a generic applicant asks for and receives approval to market, if within the scope of a valid claim, is an infringement."[59]

A party can file a motion to compel when an opposing party refuses to produce information. For example, motions to compel were filed in *AbbVie Inc. v. Boehringer Ingelheim International GmbH*. They included requests to compel information addressing (1) secondary considerations; (2) interchangeability with the reference product sponsor's product; (3) productions, contentions, and settlements in litigation related to the

---

58. Exela Pharma Scis., LLC v. Eaton Pharms., Inc., No. 1:20-cv-365-MN, 2022 WL 806524, at *3 (D. Del. Feb. 8, 2022); *see* Sunovion Pharms., Inc. v. Teva Pharms. USA, Inc., 731 F.3d 1271, 1279 (Fed. Cir. 2013) (explaining the court should not look beyond the ANDA specification unless it is silent on the limitation).

59. *Sunovion Pharms.*, 731 F.3d at 1278.

same biologic product; (4) batch manufacturing records; and (5) patent prosecution documents and a privilege log for any documents withheld.[60] The court granted the motions.[61]

IV. Claim Construction

Claim construction is an issue in patent law that is not unique to BPCIA litigation, and courts have analyzed claim construction issues in BPCIA litigations as they have in other patent cases.[62] The median time to a claim construction hearing in BPCIA cases is about one year from filing of the complaint, and, like a traditional patent case, timing of and process for claim construction will vary by district. In addition, like a traditional patent case, expert discovery and parallel inter partes review proceedings are other considerations that may impact claim construction strategy.

V. Expert Witnesses

As is the case with any other patent litigation, expert witnesses play key roles in BPCIA litigation. Expert witnesses assist in investigating complex factual issues specific to the case, assist the judge or the jury in understanding complex technical and economic issues, and assist the hiring party in developing a case strategy. Expert witnesses are retained either as testifying experts who will provide opinions and testimony in the case or as consulting experts to provide specialized case support such as testing products at issue.

In a typical BPCIA litigation, each side hires at least one but more typically two or three technical experts to provide opinions on infringement and invalidity and a "damages expert" to provide opinions relating to economic issues in the case. Because there are fundamental differences between an infringing product in a Hatch-Waxman litigation and that of a BPCIA litigation, there are also additional challenges for experts hired for a BPCIA litigation. Thus, it therefore is essential that parties identify

60. *AbbVie Inc.*, No. 1:17-cv-1065-MSG-RL, Dkt. No. 58; *id.* Dkt. No. 207 (D. Del. Sept. 7, 2018).

61. *AbbVie Inc.*, No. 1:17-cv-1065-MSG-RL, Dkt. No. 58; *id.* Dkt. No. 207 (D. Del. Sept. 7, 2018).

62. *See, e.g.*, Teva Pharms. Int'l GmbH v. Eli Lilly & Co., No. 18-cv-12029-ABD, Dkt. No. 101 (D. Mass. Feb. 24, 2021); Genentech, Inc. v. Amgen Inc., Nos. 17-1407-CFC, 18-924-CFC, Dkt. No. 652 (D. Del. Mar. 9, 2020); Immunex Corp. v. Sandoz Inc., No. 16-cv-1118-CCC-MF, Dkt. No. 595 (D.N.J. Aug. 20, 2018); Amgen, Inc. v. Apotex Inc., No. 15-61631, Dkt. No. 119 (S.D. Fla. Apr. 7, 2016).

the elements of their case that may require expert testimony and retain a full contingent of experts that will support their case as early as possible.

The BPCIA provides 60 days for the reference product sponsor to evaluate the aBLA, which can be more than 1,000,000 pages long, and other manufacturing information, if provided, before identifying the patents it considers as potentially infringing in its (*l*)(3)(A) letter. The BPCIA allows experts retained by the reference product sponsor to review these materials as long as prior written consent of the biosimilar applicant is obtained.[63] According to the statute, such consent shall not be unreasonably withheld. It is advisable for the reference product sponsor to take advantage of this permissible use of its technical experts during the review of the aBLA.

A. Technical Experts in Manufacturing Processes

In BPCIA litigation there is an early need for experts, even at pre-litigation stages, compared to Hatch-Waxman cases. This is because the products at issue and patents covering these products in each type of litigation are fundamentally different. In a BPCIA litigation, the active ingredient in the accused product is a "biologic"—a large complex molecule that is produced and isolated from microorganisms or cultured cells using technologies including recombinant DNA biotechnologies and hybridoma technologies. Examples of biologics include antibodies, enzymes, immunomodulators, and growth factors. In addition, because biologics are produced in microorganisms and cultured cells, there is a foreseeable potential for variability among the various preparations of a biologic based on the choice of host cells or organisms used for production, the variations in the growth conditions used to grow the host cells or organisms, and the methods of purification used to isolate the biologic from contaminants that inevitably are formed in the production process.

In contrast, in a Hatch-Waxman litigation, the active ingredient in an accused product is a small molecule that tends to be synthesized chemically using a small number of well-characterized chemical methods. Potential for variation between each preparation is not as great as it is for a biologic. Thus, manufacturing of a biologic or its biosimilar compared to that of a small molecule or its generic is more challenging. It is often the case that the reference product sponsor engages experts even before the 12-year exclusivity period ends to ensure that these experts know their biologic product and its unique properties so that the sponsor is able to obtain strong patent protection over the biologic itself. Further, because unlike small molecules, biological molecules generally cannot be

63. 42 U.S.C. § 262(*l*)(1)(B)(ii)(I).

completely characterized, technical expertise is required when evaluating a biologic and its biosimilar. As such, it is advisable for sides to engage with technical experts at early stages of litigation to be able to establish equivalency between the biologic and its biosimilar.

Another difference is the types of patents that are obtained for patent protection in BPCIA and Hatch-Waxman litigations. In BPCIA litigation, typically a vast majority of the asserted patents are manufacturing patents, rather than the composition patents, formulation patents, or methods of treatment patents typically asserted in Hatch-Waxman litigation. This is apparent when looking at the patents listed in the "Purple Book" for biologics: a vast majority of the patent portfolio of each biologic consists of manufacturing methods, new indications, or formulations. This is partly because by the time a biosimilar applies for FDA approval after 12 years of exclusivity, any patents covering the active ingredient may be towards the end of their expiration dates. However, because producing biologics through microorganisms and cultured cells is more complex and many independent methods may be developed and used, there are more opportunities for reference product sponsors to innovate, resulting in manufacturing patents in addition to composition patents. The typical manufacturing of a biological product involves a number of steps and components relating to cell culture conditions and media, purification, filtration, and formulation of the final product.

The downside of developing alternative manufacturing methods is the possibility that any variation in the process may lead to a material change in the product's safety or efficacy. It is established that even minor changes in pH, cell culture growth medium, or growth temperature during the manufacturing process can impact how biologics form into three-dimensional complex molecules and hence how they function as therapeutics. Therefore, biosimilars strive to copy the reference product sponsor's manufacturing processes as much as possible to ensure the product's safety and efficacy, while attempting to avoid infringing patents protecting the underlying manufacturing technologies. During the patent dance, the reference product sponsor needs to ascertain the manufacturing process of a biosimilar to determine if any of its manufacturing patents are being practiced. Because the molecules at issue and the various manufacturing methods are both inherently and technically complex, technical expertise is often required at early stages of a BPCIA litigation to help in understanding the reference drug, the biologic, their properties, and all of the different possible ways to manufacture them. Another complicating factor is that the number of technical experts with the appropriate background may be limited, and parties may retain multiple experts with similar expertise to make the pool of available candidates even smaller.

As such, it is advisable for the parties to identify and retain experts even before the patent dance.

In at least one BPCIA litigation, the reference product sponsor retained technical experts earlier to test cell culture media used to grow biologic-producing cultured cells. In *Janssen Biotech, Inc. v. Celltrion Healthcare Co., Ltd.*, Janssen sued Celltrion after Celltrion and Hospira had submitted an aBLA seeking permission to market a biosimilar version of Janssen's biological medicine Remicade.[64] One of the asserted patents was a patent that claimed particular compositions of cell culture media used to grow cultured cells that produce the active ingredient in Remicade. Before the commencement of this action, Janssen obtained information about the cell culture media custom made for Celltrion's use in the manufacture of Celltrion's biosimilar. Janssen retained experts who tested this tissue culture media comprising 61 ingredients and alleged that the custom-made media infringed its patent under the doctrine of equivalents.

There are at least two other BPCIA litigations where the reference product sponsor intended to involve or involved technical experts as early as the patent dance. In *AbbVie Inc. & AbbVie Biotechnology Ltd. v. Amgen Inc. & Amgen Manufacturing Ltd.*, AbbVie sued Amgen after Amgen filed its aBLA seeking approval to market a biosimilar of Humira.[65] In its complaint, AbbVie alleged that Amgen refused to enter into a confidentiality agreement with AbbVie, denying access to AbbVie's technical experts to evaluate Amgen's aBLA during the patent dance. In a separate case again involving Humira, *AbbVie Inc. v. Boehringer Ingelheim International GmbH*, AbbVie alleged that Boehringer Ingelheim refused to permit AbbVie's technical experts access to its aBLA.[66] While neither of these refusals resulted in any detriment to the defendants, they demonstrate the use of technical experts, especially with expertise in manufacturing, at an early stage of BPCIA litigation.

B. Damages Experts

Similar to other types of patent cases, two types of damages are available in BPCIA litigation: (1) lost profits, and (2) reasonable royalty. Lost profits are based on an analysis of the market for the parties' products, granting the reference product sponsor the amount of money it would have made had the biosimilar manufacturer never infringed. A reasonable royalty is typically the amount that the parties would have agreed to on the eve of first infringement, presuming that the patent is valid and infringed.

64. No. 1:17-cv-11008-MLV, Dkt. No. 1 (D. Mass. May 31, 2017).
65. No. 1:16-cv-00666-SLR-SRF, Dkt. No. 1 (D. Del. Aug. 4, 2016).
66. No. 1:17-cv-01065-MSG-RL, Dkt. No. 1 (D. Del. Aug. 2, 2017).

Unlike ANDA litigations, where lost profits are not typically sought, BPCIA litigations are more likely to progress to a stage where this is at-risk launch and thus the reference product sponsor can seek lost profits damages. This is because the filing of a patent infringement litigation under 42 U.S.C. § 262(*l*)(6) does not trigger a 30-month stay of FDA approval of the pending aBLA. This is in contrast to ANDA cases, where the filing of an ANDA complaint triggers a 30-month stay of FDA approval of the ANDA.[67] Thus, damages experts can be more important to BPCIA litigations and in particular economic experts who are able to model lost profits. For example, damages experts in BPCIA litigations may need to model how an entry of one or more biosimilars will affect the market share of the reference product sponsor.

To date, 45 biosimilars have been approved and at least 37 are expected to be marketed with only three products approved as interchangeable with the reference biologic in 2023. Generally, biosimilars are priced less than the reference biologics, but not with as much discount as generics. This is partly because while the development time for a generic is from two to three years at a cost of two to three million dollars, this period increases to six to nine years at a cost of 100 to 300 million dollars for a biosimilar. Further, the development of a biologic takes eight to ten years with a cost of about 800 million dollars. As such, biologics and biosimilars are priced higher ranging from small molecules and generics.

Further, due to complexities in reimbursement by Medicare, there are fewer economic incentives to offer biosimilars at reduced prices compared to pricing of generics. Currently, each biosimilar is reimbursed individually under separate codes. Under the current reimbursement scheme, Medicare reimburses each biosimilar at its own average sales price plus 6 percent of the reference biologic's average sales price. Thus, there is no incentive for biosimilar manufacturers to price their products at a significant discount as with lowered prices, the reimbursement amounts are to decrease.

Biosimilar companies respond to this reimbursement scheme by launching their products at lower price points than a generic manufacturer does. For example, when Viatris launched two identical versions of its interchangeable biosimilar for Lantus, a long-acting insulin, it offered two price points. First it offered its branded interchangeable biosimilar, Semglee, at a price of only 5 percent below that of Lantus, and second it offered its unbranded but authorized interchangeable biosimilar at a price of 65 percent lower than that of Lantus. Different payers reacted to this launch in surprising and unpredictable ways: Medicare Part D plans

67. 21 U.S.C. § 355(c)(3)(C), (j)(5)(B)(iii).

continued their preference for Lantus, and Lantus retained 99 percent of the total market. Medicaid plans retained significant use of Lantus but preferred the unbranded, authorized interchangeable biosimilar with a low list price over the branded interchangeable biosimilar product with a high list price. Even then, Lantus retained 89 percent of the total market. And commercial payers adopted the high-priced biosimilar, Semglee, but Lantus still retained 78 percent of the total commercial market almost one year after the biosimilar launched. In a similar move to Viatris, in February 2023, Amgen announced the launch of both a high-list/high-rebate and a low-list/low-rebate version of its first noninterchangeable biosimilar of Humira in early 2023 and it is too soon to tell how the payers will react to these two different price points for Amgen's biosimilar. What is clear is that the projected market share and price analysis of each biosimilar will continue to remain challenging to damages experts in making any accurate predictions about lost profits.

VI. Trial in BPCIA Cases

To date, only four BPCIA litigations have progressed to trial. There have been three bench trials and one jury trial: *Amgen Inc. v. Apotex Inc.*,[68] *Amgen Inc. v. Hospira, Inc.*,[69] *Immunex Corp. v. Sandoz Inc.*,[70] and *Regeneron Pharmaceuticals, Inc. v. Mylan Pharmaceuticals Inc.*[71]

The trial issues and pretrial disputes have not generally been different than traditional patent trials. The timing of the trial vis-à-vis the projected approval of the biosimilar product is, however, a unique consideration for BPCIA litigations. Ensuring the trial occurs significantly before the reference product's regulatory exclusivity under 42 U.S.C. § 262(k)(7) expires may be critical to the availability of an injunction under 35 U.S.C. § 271(e)(4)(D).[72] BPCIA litigants should also consider the extent

68. No. 15-cv-61631-CIV-JIC/BSS (S.D. Fla. 2015) (Neupogen and Neulasta) (bench trial in July 2016).

69. No. 15-839 (RGA) (D. Del. 2015) (Epogen) (jury trial in September 2017).

70. No. 16-1118 (D.N.J. 2016) (Enbrel) (bench trial in September 2019).

71. No. 1:22-cv-00061-TSK (N.D. W. Va. 2022) (Eylea) (bench trial in June 2023).

72. 35 U.S.C. § 271(e)(4)(D) provides:

> (4) For an act of infringement described in paragraph (2) . . . (D) the court shall order a permanent injunction prohibiting any infringement of the patent by the biological product involved in the infringement until a date which is not earlier than the date of the expiration of the patent that has been infringed under paragraph (2)(C), provided the patent is the subject of a final court decision, as defined in section 351(k)(6) of the Public Health Service Act, in an action for infringement of the patent under section 351(*l*)(6) of such Act, and the biological product has not yet been approved because of section 351(k)(7) of such Act.

to which their pre-litigation BPCIA exchanges can be used at the trial. As discussed in this part, in the BPCIA context the biosimilar applicant's pre-litigation statements may be considered party admissions but do not bind the biosimilar applicant from advancing different positions in litigation.[73]

A. Amgen v. Apotex *Biosimilar Neupogen and Neulasta Trial*

In *Amgen v. Apotex*—the first BPCIA trial—the Southern District of Florida held a six-day bench trial from July 11–18, 2016.[74] The trial occurred before approval and launch of Apotex's biosimilar Neupogen and Neulasta products.[75] One patent was at issue at the trial, which related to manufacturing methods.[76] The tried issues were infringement; invalidity based on enablement; and injunctive relief.[77] The Southern District of Florida found no infringement, and did not render an opinion on enablement or injunctive relief.[78] The Federal Circuit affirmed.[79]

At issue before the trial court and the Federal Circuit was the extent to which the pre-litigation BPCIA exchanges can be used during the trial. During the pre-litigation BPCIA exchanges, Apotex identified a filgrastim (the protein of interest) concentration between 0.9–1.4 grams per liter (g/L) in its refold buffer.[80] During the litigation, the district court, adopting Amgen's claim construction, found that the patent claims required a protein concentration of at least about 1.0 g/L.[81] At trial, Apotex presented evidence that the maximum concentration of protein is 0.708 g/L (i.e., less than the protein-of-interest concentration identified in Apotex's BPCIA exchanges and less than the 1.0 g/L protein required by the patent claims).[82] Apotex's fact witness testified that Apotex's BPCIA exchanges were factually inaccurate.[83] The district court ruled for Apotex on this

73. In the ANDA context, multiple district courts have addressed this issue and held that ANDA filers are not limited to the theories raised in their Paragraph IV letters. *See, e.g.*, Bausch Health Ir. Ltd. v. Mylan Pharms. Inc., No. 22-cv-20, 2023 WL 2726432, at *3 (N.D. W. Va. Mar. 30, 2023); Abbott Lab'ys, Inc. v. Apotex Inc., 725 F. Supp. 2d 724, 728 (N.D. Ill. 2010); Takada Chem. Indus., Ltd. v. Mylan Lab'ys, Inc., No. 3-cv-8253, 2005 WL 1457696, at *1 (S.D.N.Y. June 15, 2005).

74. No. 15-61631-CIV, 2016 WL 11783299, at *1 (S.D. Fla. Sept. 6, 2016).

75. *Id.*

76. *Id.*

77. Amgen's Proposed Post-Trial Findings of Fact and Conclusions of Law, Amgen Inc. v. Apotex Inc., No. 15-61631-CIV, Dkt. No. 265-1 (S.D. Fla. Aug. 19, 2016).

78. *Amgen Inc.*, 2016 WL 11783299, at *12.

79. Amgen Inc. v. Apotex Inc., 712 F. App'x 985, 987 (Fed. Cir. 2017).

80. *Id.* at 988.

81. *Id.*

82. *Id.*

83. *Id.*

issue, finding that Amgen had failed to prove by a preponderance of the evidence that Apotex's processes would meet the 1.0 g/L requirement.[84]

On appeal, Amgen argued that the district court erred in disregarding the BPCIA exchanges.[85] The Federal Circuit first stated that the district court "cannot ignore letters sent during the BPCIA's information exchange if properly offered into evidence"—reasoning that the "pre-litigation information exchange is part of the BPCIA's 'carefully calibrated scheme for preparing to adjudicate, and then adjudicating, claims of infringement,'" and that they are "party admissions" "hav[ing] *some* probative weight."[86] However, the Federal Circuit determined that the district court did not err because it "gave the letters their evidentiary due" and that it had "sufficient basis in the evidence" to find that the letters were indeed factually inaccurate.[87] The Federal Circuit noted that Amgen did not dispute that the letters were not binding on Apotex.[88]

Based on the *Amgen v. Apotex* case, BPCIA litigants should not be surprised if their adversaries seek to offer the BPCIA exchanges into evidence at trial—whether they are binding admissions or not. BPCIA dancers should thus take care that the facts presented in their exchanges are clear, precise, and accurate. If an inaccuracy is discovered during litigation, action to correct it should be considered to be taken before the trial. Additionally, BPCIA litigants should consider ways to make the facts presented in their adversary's BPCIA exchanges "binding"—perhaps through corporate deposition testimony or written discovery requests.

B. Amgen v. Hospira *Biosimilar Epogen Trial*

In *Amgen v. Hospira*, the District of Delaware held a five-day jury trial from September 18–22, 2017.[89] The trial occurred before approval of Hospira's biosimilar Epogen product.[90] At trial, Amgen asserted that Hospira's manufacture of its drug substance for its biosimilar infringed claims of two patents.[91] The tried issues were infringement of both patents, invalidity of one patent, Hospira's safe harbor defense, and damages.[92] The jury found each of the asserted claims not proved invalid, decided that the asserted claims of the '349 patent were not infringed, and returned a verdict of

84. *Id.*

85. *Id.* at 989.

86. *Id.* (quoting Sandoz Inc. v. Amgen Inc., 582 U.S. 1, 8 (2017)).

87. *Id.*

88. *Id.*

89. 336 F. Supp. 3d 333, 339 (D. Del. 2018), *aff'd*, 944 F.3d 1327 (Fed. Cir. 2019).

90. Order on Motions in Limine, Amgen Inc. v. Hospira, Inc., No. 1:15-cv-00839-RGA, Dkt. No. 302 (D. Del. Sept. 11, 2017).

91. *Amgen*, 336 F. Supp. 3d at 339.

92. Final Judgment, *Amgen Inc.*, No. 1:15-cv-00839-RGA, Dkt. No. 393.

infringement of all asserted claims of the '298 patent.[93] The jury also found that seven of Hospira's 21 batches of drug substance were entitled to the safe harbor defense, awarding Amgen $70 million in reasonable-royalty damages for Hospira's infringement of the '298 patent with respect to the 14 other batches.[94] The Federal Circuit affirmed the district court's decisions on the parties' post-trial motions.[95]

On appeal, the parties disputed the proper jury instructions for the safe harbor defense as it relates to a manufacturing patent—an issue not resolved by a previous Hatch-Waxman case.[96] At trial, the district court provided the jury with the following instructions:

> You must evaluate each of the accused activities separately to determine whether the Safe Harbor applies. If you find that an accused activity was reasonably related to the development and submission of information to the FDA for the purpose of obtaining FDA approval, then Hospira has proved its Safe Harbor defense as to that activity. If Hospira has proved that the manufacture of a particular batch was reasonably related to developing and submitting information to the FDA in order to obtain FDA approval, Hospira's additional underlying purposes for the manufacture and use of that batch do not remove that batch from the Safe Harbor defense.[97]

Hospira argued that the final sentence of the instructions improperly focused on Hospira's intent for manufacturing batches of its drug substance, and that Hospira "only had to prove that the *use* of the patented invention was reasonably related to submission of information to the FDA, not the *manufacture*."[98] The Federal Circuit disagreed, finding the jury instructions proper.[99] The court reasoned that, because the patented inventions are Amgen's claimed methods of manufacture, the accused activity is Hospira's use of Amgen's claimed methods of manufacture, and therefore the "relevant inquiry" is "not *how* Hospira used each batch it manufactured, but whether each act of manufacture was for uses reasonably related to submitting information to the FDA."[100]

---

93. *Amgen*, 336 F. Supp. 3d at 339.
94. *Id.*
95. Amgen Inc. v. Hospira, Inc., 944 F.3d 1327, 1332 (Fed. Cir. 2019).
96. *Id.* at 1337–38.
97. *Id.* at 1338.
98. *Id.*
99. *Id.*
100. *Id.*

C. Immunex v. Sandoz *Biosimilar Enbrel Trial*

In *Immunex v. Sandoz*, the District of New Jersey held a two-week bench trial from September 11–25, 2019.[101] The trial occurred after FDA approval, in August 2016, of Sandoz's biosimilar version of Enbrel, called Erelzi.[102] But Sandoz had not launched its product prior to trial, as it consented to a preliminary injunction.[103] Prior to trial, Sandoz also stipulated to infringement of both asserted patents.[104] The invalidity of the patents was the only tried issue.[105] The District of New Jersey found the asserted patents not invalid,[106] and the Federal Circuit affirmed.[107]

Notably, Sandoz stipulated to a permanent injunction until the expiration of the asserted patents, and the district court did not order permanent injunction discovery.[108] The court entered final judgment and a permanent injunction pursuant to the parties' stipulation.[109]

D. Regeneron v. Mylan *Biosimilar Eylea Trial*

In *Regeneron v. Mylan*, the Northern District of West Virginia held a two-week bench trial from June 12–23, 2023.[110] The trial occurred before FDA approval of Mylan's biosimilar product.[111] Indeed, *Regeneron v. Mylan* was the first BPCIA case to proceed while the reference product's regulatory exclusivity under 42 U.S.C. § 262(k)(7) remained in place.[112] As a result, the availability of an injunction under 35 U.S.C. § 271(e)(4)(D) was front and center in the parties' dispute over the timing of the trial.

---

101. 395 F. Supp. 3d 366, 374 (D.N.J. 2019), *aff'd*, 964 F.3d 1049 (Fed. Cir. 2020).

102. *Id.* at 375.

103. Consent Preliminary Injunction, Immunex Corp. v. Sandoz Inc., No. 16-1118, Dkt. No. 95 (D.N.J. Aug. 11, 2016); Amended Consent Preliminary Injunction, Immunex Corp. v. Sandoz Inc., No. 16-1118, Dkt. No. 509 (D.N.J. June 7, 2018).

104. *Immunex Corp.*, 395 F. Supp. 3d at 375.

105. *Id.*

106. *Id.*

107. Immunex Corp. v. Sandoz Inc., 964 F.3d 1049, 1053 (Fed. Cir. 2020).

108. Stipulated Permanent Injunction, Immunex Corp. v. Sandoz Inc., No. 16-1118, Dkt. No. 718 (D.N.J. Oct. 8, 2019).

109. Final Judgment and Order of Permanent Injunction, *Immunex Corp.*, No. 16-1118, Dkt. No. 719.

110. Docket Sheet, Regeneron Pharms., Inc. v. Mylan Pharms. Inc., No. 1:22-cv-00061-TSK (N.D. W. Va.).

111. Regeneron's Motion Requesting Expedited Status Conference, *Regeneron Pharms., Inc.*, No. 1:22-cv-00061-TSK, Dkt. No. 7 (N.D. W. Va. Aug. 8, 2022).

112. Plaintiff's Reply in Support of Motion Requesting Expedited Status Conference, *Regeneron Pharms., Inc.*, No. 1:22-cv-00061-TSK, Dkt. No. 41, at 5 (N.D. W. Va. Aug. 23, 2022). 42 U.S.C. § 262(k)(7)(A) provides: "Approval of an application under this subsection may not be made effective by the Secretary until the date that is 12 years after the date on which the reference product was first licensed under subsection (a)."

Regeneron filed its complaint on August 2, 2022.[113] Three days later, Regeneron filed a motion requesting an expedited status conference and "to position this case for trial no later than June 2023, so that Regeneron may avail itself of the relief provided by § 271(e)(4)(D)."[114] Regeneron argued that, without a trial within ten months of its complaint, it could be deprived of an injunction under § 271(e)(4)(D), which provides that "a court 'shall order a permanent injunction' against a proposed biosimilar product upon issuance of 'a final court decision' of patent infringement."[115] According to Regeneron, a "final court decision" "in all likelihood [would] require a decision from the" Federal Circuit, and § 271(e)(4)(D) "requires that at the time of the 'final court decision,' 'the biological product has not yet been approved because of section 351(k)(7).'"[116] Regeneron calculated that it needed a final court decision by May 18, 2024, to avail itself of § 271(e)(4)(D).[117] And thus, according to it, Regeneron needed a trial "no later than June 2023."[118] To prepare the case for a trial in ten months, Regeneron proposed that the case's "initial stage" involve no more than 12 of the 24 asserted patents.[119] Mylan opposed.[120] Mylan argued that a June 2023 trial was not feasible; that Regeneron's concerns about injunctive relief were overstated because it will be free to seek such relief by satisfying the traditional injunction requirements; and that Regeneron's proposal "disrupts the careful balance created by Congress" allowing Regeneron to "hold a substantial number of patents over Mylan's head to assert later."[121]

The Northern District of West Virginia issued a scheduling order setting the trial for June 2023.[122] However, the court ordered Regeneron, within three days, to "identif[y] *6 patents* from *3 patent families* for initial proceedings" and to stipulate that it will not seek injunctive relief on the other 18 patents with respect to Mylan's biosimilar product.[123] The court further ordered that, seven days after the *Markman* order or seven

113. Complaint, *Regeneron Pharms., Inc.*, No. 1:22-cv-00061-TSK, Dkt. No. 1 (N.D. W. Va. Aug. 2, 2022).

114. Regeneron's Motion Requesting Expedited Status Conference, *Regeneron Pharms., Inc.*, No. 1:22-cv-00061-TSK, Dkt. No. 7, at 1 (N.D. W. Va. Aug. 8, 2022).

115. *Id.* at 4.

116. *Id.*

117. *Id.* at 4–5.

118. *Id.* at 5.

119. *Id.* at 6.

120. Mylan Pharmaceuticals Inc.'s Response to Motion Requesting Expedited Status Conference, *Regeneron Pharms., Inc.*, No. 1:22-cv-00061-TSK, Dkt. No. 26 (N.D. W. Va. Aug. 19, 2022).

121. *Id.* at 1–3, 13.

122. Scheduling Order, *Regeneron Pharms., Inc.*, No. 1:22-cv-00061-TSK, Dkt. No. 87 (N.D. W. Va. Oct. 25, 2022).

123. *Id.*

days after the close of fact discovery, whichever is later, Regeneron must narrow the "initial proceedings" to only three patents and 25 claims.[124] Regeneron so narrowed and so stipulated to not seeking injunctive relief on the remaining patents, and the case proceeded to a June 2023 trial as scheduled.[125]

124. *Id.*

125. Regeneron's Stipulation Regarding Case Narrowing and Injunctive Relief, *Regeneron Pharms., Inc.*, No. 1:22-cv-00061-TSK, Dkt. No. 88 (N.D. W. Va. Oct. 28, 2022); Regeneron's Stipulation Regarding Summary Judgment and Case Narrowing, *Regeneron Pharms., Inc.*, No. 1:22-cv-00061-TSK, Dkt. No. 433 (N.D. W. Va. Apr. 27, 2023).

chapter 8

"Second Wave" Infringement Action*

Whereas the first phase of litigation set up by the Biologics Price Competition and Innovation Act (BPCIA) involves an orderly and collaborative "patent dance,"[1] the second phase of litigation is more akin to a melee. As one commentator has put it, "all hell can break loose" at the second phase, which opens up the gauntlet of patent litigation over a forthcoming biosimilar product.[2] Furthermore, while the term "second phase" would suggest that it occurs after the patent dance, that is frequently not the case where the relevant biologic no longer enjoys regulatory exclusivity under the BPCIA, which has been the case in most phase-two litigation to date. As a result, the second phase often occurs in parallel with the first, producing dual-track litigation on the balance of available patents.

This chapter discusses the second phase—or at least second track—of BPCIA litigation in two parts. Part I provides an overview of the statutory and procedural operation of the second phase. Part II discusses strategic consideration behind when to trigger it.

I. Statutory and Procedural Overview

A. The Notice of Commercial Marketing

The second phase of litigation set up by the BPCIA is triggered when the biosimilar applicant provides the product sponsor with "notice of commercial marketing" pursuant to 42 U.S.C. § 262(*l*)(8).[3] The BPCIA does not

*Louis Fogel, Ph.D. and Shaun M. Van Horn, Fish & Richardson P.C.; Jacob Wentzel, Jenner & Block LLP

1. Chapter 7, Section II.A.1; *see also* Chapter 4.

2. *See* Alejandro Menchaca, *The Inner Workings of the BPCIA Patent Dance*, Ctr. for Biosimilars (July 24, 2021), https://www.centerforbiosimilars.com/view/the-inner-workings-of-the-bpcia-patent-dance.

3. Sandoz Inc. v. Amgen Inc., 582 U.S. 1, 9 (2017).

define the term "commercial marketing," but courts consistently equate commercial marketing with market entry.[4]

Under section (*l*)(8)(A),[5] the applicant "shall provide notice to the reference product sponsor not later than 180 days before the date of the first commercial marketing of the biological product licensed under subsection (k)."[6] In *Amgen Inc. v. Apotex Inc.*, one of the few major cases addressing phase-two litigation, the Federal Circuit held that under section (*l*)(8)(A), providing notice of commercial marketing is mandatory even when the biosimilar applicant has already provided the information required under section (*l*)(2)(A) to the reference product sponsor and the parties have begun the patent dance.[7] Noting that "[t]he word 'shall' generally indicates that the directive is mandatory," *Apotex* extended the Federal Circuit's holding in *Amgen Inc. v. Sandoz Inc.* (*Sandoz I*) that section (*l*)(8)(A) is mandatory where the applicant has *not* provided its abbreviated biologics license application (aBLA) pursuant to section (*l*)(2)(A) and has opted out of the patent dance, to situations where the applicant *has* provided its aBLA pursuant to section (*l*)(2)(A), reasoning that section (*l*)(8)(A) "contains no words that make the applicability of its notice rule turn on whether the applicant took the earlier step of giving the (2)(A) notice that begins the § 262(*l*) information-exchange process."[8] The court further held that, given its mandatory nature, compliance with section (*l*)(8)(A) is enforceable by an injunction preventing the applicant from commencing commercial marketing for a period of 180 days after providing notice of commercial marketing.[9]

B. When and How to Provide Notice of Commercial Marketing

Section (*l*)(8)(A) requires the biosimilar applicant to provide notice of commercial marketing "*not later than* 180 days before the date of the first

4. *See, e.g.*, Amgen Inc. v. Sandoz Inc., No. 14-CV-04741-RS, 2015 WL 1264756, at *8 (N.D. Cal. Mar. 19, 2015), *aff'd in part, vacated in part, and remanded*, 794 F.3d 1347 (Fed. Cir. 2015), *rev'd in part, vacated in part, and remanded*, 582 U.S. 1 (2017), *and aff'd*, 877 F.3d 1315 (Fed. Cir. 2017).

5. Common shorthand abbreviations (e.g., "section (*l*)(8)(A)," "(*l*)(8)(A)," etc.) used in this chapter refer to the respective BPCIA statutory sections (e.g., § 262(*l*)(8)(A), etc.).

6. 42 U.S.C. § 262(*l*)(8)(A); *see Sandoz*, 582 U.S. at 10.

7. 827 F.3d 1052, 1060–61 (Fed. Cir. 2016), *cert. denied*, 580 U.S. 1030 (2016). In *Apotex*, Amgen brought an immediate infringement action under section (*l*)(6), then sought a preliminary injunction requiring Apotex to provide notice of commercial marketing under section (*l*)(8) "if and when" it received U.S. Food and Drug Administration (FDA) approval "and to delay marketing for 180 days from that notice." *Id.* at 1059–60.

8. *Id.* at 1059–60; *see* Amgen Inc. v. Sandoz Inc. (*Sandoz I*), 794 F.3d 1347, 1359 (Fed. Cir. 2015), *rev'd in part, vacated in part, and remanded*, 582 U.S. 1 (2017), *and aff'd*, 877 F.3d 1315 (Fed. Cir. 2017).

9. *Apotex*, 827 F.3d at 1055, 1061.

commercial marketing."[10] As this language speaks to a cutoff date, the statute leaves open the question of when the applicant may provide notice of commercial marketing *at the earliest*.

The U.S. Supreme Court largely answered this question in *Sandoz Inc. v. Amgen Inc.*,[11] the only case to date addressing phase-two litigation on which the high court has granted certiorari. In that case, Sandoz had provided notice of commercial marketing just one day after the U.S. Food and Drug Administration (FDA) accepted its biosimilar application for review and nearly eight months before the FDA ultimately approved the drug at issue (a biosimilar filgrastim product under the brand name Zarxio), notifying Amgen that it intended to market the drug immediately upon FDA approval.[12] On appeal, the Federal Circuit concluded that an applicant's biosimilar must already be approved (i.e., licensed) by the FDA before the applicant may provide notice of commercial marketing, such that Sandoz's pre-licensure notice did not comply with section (*l*)(8)(A).[13]

The Supreme Court reversed, holding that "the applicant may provide notice either before or after receiving FDA approval."[14] The Supreme Court's holding rested largely on statutory interpretation: contrary to the Federal Circuit, it concluded that the statutory phrase "'of the biological product licensed under subsection (k)' modifies 'commercial marketing' rather than 'notice,'" such that the biosimilar need not be licensed or approved by the FDA prior to submitting notice, while rejecting Amgen's other statutory and policy reasons for requiring the applicant to first obtain FDA approval.[15] The Supreme Court thus ruled that Sandoz's pre-licensure notice fully complied with section (*l*)(8)(A).[16]

Once a biosimilar applicant has provided notice of a commercial marketing, one court has held that the applicant need not provide new notice

---

10. 42 U.S.C. § 262(*l*)(8)(A) (emphasis added).

11. 582 U.S. 1.

12. *Id.* at 2; *see also Sandoz I*, 794 F.3d at 1353.

13. *Sandoz I*, 794 F.3d at 1357–58.

14. *Sandoz*, 582 U.S. at 19. In so holding, the Supreme Court also vitiated the parties' concession in *Apotex* that Apotex's pre-licensure notice of commercial marketing provided during the parties' immediate infringement action was "of no effect" under section (*l*)(8) based on the Federal Circuit's holding in *Sandoz I*. *See Apotex*, 827 F.3d at 1060.

15. *Sandoz*, 582 U.S. at 19–21.

16. *Id.* at 21. The only case that has addressed whether an applicant may provide notice of commercial marketing before even *submitting* an aBLA for FDA approval answered that question in the negative, but did so on the basis that notice may not be provided until the biosimilar is FDA approved, which is no longer good law after the Supreme Court's decision in *Sandoz*. *See* Sandoz Inc. v. Amgen Inc., No. C-13-2904 MMC, 2013 WL 6000069, at *1–3 (N.D. Cal. Nov. 12, 2013), *aff'd on other grounds*, 773 F.3d 1274 (Fed. Cir. 2014); *see also infra* note 44 and accompanying text.

after supplementing an approved aBLA.[17] In *Genentech, Inc. v. Immunex Rhode Island Corp.*, the district court reasoned "because the FDA can approve a supplement after it has approved . . . the application," the product subject to the original application must be the same product subject to the supplement.[18] As a result, a notice provided prior to supplementing the application for the same product is sufficient notice for marketing the supplemented version of the product.[19] Note that it remains an open question whether new notice of commercial marketing is required when an applicant withdraws an aBLA or the FDA issues a complete response letter (CRL).[20]

In terms of *how* to provide notice of commercial marketing, the BPCIA itself does not provide any relevant guidance. But the case law indicates that biosimilar applicants typically send a letter to the reference product sponsor through counsel. In *Apotex*, for instance, the Federal Circuit recounted that Apotex "sent a letter to Amgen stating that it was thereby providing notice of future commercial marketing pursuant to (8)(A)."[21] Likewise, in *Genentech*, the court related that the applicant had sent the sponsor "a letter captioned '[Applicant's] Notice of Commercial Marketing Under § 262(l)(8)(A),'" which "read[] in relevant part: 'Pursuant to 42 U.S.C. § 262(l)(8)(A), [applicant] hereby provides notice that it will commence commercial marketing of [its biosimilar] no earlier than 180 days from the date of this letter.'"[22]

C. Effect of Providing Notice of Commercial Marketing

Providing notice of commercial marketing under section (*l*)(8)(A) creates two possible types of second-phase litigation: (1) preliminary injunction actions, and (2) declaratory judgment actions.

17. Genentech, Inc. v. Immunex R.I. Corp., 395 F. Supp. 3d 357, 362 (D. Del. 2019), *aff'd*, 964 F.3d 1109 (Fed. Cir. 2020). A supplemental aBLA is referred to as an sBLA. *See, e.g.*, Genentech, Inc. v. Amgen Inc., No. CV 17-1407-CFC, 2019 WL 1349464, at *1 (D. Del. Mar. 26, 2019).

18. 395 F. Supp. 3d at 363–64. Specifically, FDA regulations define a "supplement" as "a request to approve a change in an approved license application." 21 C.F.R. § 600.3(gg) (2024); *see also id.* § 601.12 (requiring an applicant to file a supplement when there is a change to the "product, production process, quality controls, equipment, facilities, responsible personnel, or labeling *established in the approved license application*").

19. *Genentech*, 395 F. Supp. 3d at 365–66.

20. A CRL reflects that that FDA "will not approve the application or abbreviated application in its present form for one or more of the reasons given in [21 C.F.R.] § 314.125 or [21 C.F.R.] § 314.127." 21 C.F.R. § 314.10(a) (2024).

21. Amgen Inc. v. Apotex Inc., 827 F.3d 1052, 1059 (Fed. Cir. 2016).

22. *Genentech*, 395 F. Supp. 3d at 362.

1. The Sponsor May Bring an Action for Preliminary Injunction

First, at any time between receipt of the notice and the date of the first commercial marketing of the relevant biosimilar product, the reference product sponsor "may seek a preliminary injunction prohibiting the [biosimilar] applicant from engaging in the commercial manufacture or sale of [the biosimilar] product until the court decides the issue of patent validity, enforcement, and infringement" pursuant to section (*l*)(8)(B).[23] When the sponsor seeks a preliminary injunction, the parties must "reasonably cooperate to expedite such further discovery as is needed in connection with the preliminary injunction motion."[24]

As the Federal Circuit noted in *Apotex*, "the reference product sponsor may seek a preliminary injunction based on any patent within either of two classes."[25] The first class consists of "any patents that were included on the parties' § 262(*l*)(3) lists but not litigated in the first phase."[26] This includes any patents listed on either the reference product sponsor's initial list under section (*l*)(3)(A) or the applicant's initial list under section (*l*)(3)(B),[27] provided that the patent was excluded from the final list of patents selected for the first phase under section (*l*)(4) or (*l*)(5)(B).[28] As a result, any patents that the applicant manages to keep out of the first phase remain available to the sponsor in the second phase.

The second class of patents available in phase-two litigation "consists of certain patents that were issued to or exclusively licensed by the reference product sponsor after it gave the applicant its (3)(A) list."[29] As to those patents, section (*l*)(7) provides that a reference product sponsor may supplement its (3)(A) list to include any newly issued or licensed patent that it "reasonably believes" could serve as the basis of a claim for patent infringement "if a person not licensed by the reference product sponsor engaged in the making, using, offering to sell, selling, or importing" of the biosimilar.[30] Section (*l*)(7) further provides that such patents "shall be subject to paragraph (8) when the sponsor provides a statement to the applicant pursuant to paragraph (3)(B)" within 30 days of the issuance

---

23. 42 U.S.C. § 262(*l*)(8)(B); *see* Sandoz Inc. v. Amgen Inc., 582 U.S. 1, 11 (2017).
24. 42 U.S.C. § 262(*l*)(8)(C).
25. *Apotex*, 827 F.3d at 1056–57.
26. *Sandoz*, 582 U.S. at 9.
27. 42 U.S.C. § 262(*l*)(8)(B)(i).
28. *Id.* § 262(*l*)(8)(B)(ii); *see also Apotex*, 827 F.3d at 1057 ("The first class . . . consists of patents that appeared on any of the original paragraph (3) lists, minus patents that were the subject of paragraph (6) litigation (by agreement under (4) or by the narrowing process under (5)).").
29. *Apotex*, 827 F.3d at 1057.
30. 42 U.S.C. § 262(*l*)(7).

or licensing of the relevant patent,[31] "which evidently means that patents within [paragraph] (7) are to be treated as falling under [paragraph] (8)(B)."[32]

2. Either Party May Bring an Action for Declaratory Judgment

Second, either the reference product sponsor or the biosimilar applicant may bring an action for declaratory judgment pursuant to section (*l*)(9)(A).[33] In other words, the limitation on seeking a declaratory judgment that applies once the patent dance has begun is lifted—for both parties—on the date when notice of commercial marketing is received.[34] A declaratory judgment is then available with respect to the "infringement, validity, or enforceability of any patent that is described in clauses (i) and (ii) of paragraph (8)(B),"[35] which describe the universe of patents that were included in the parties' section (*l*)(3) lists but not litigated in the first phase.[36] Section (*l*)(9)(A) leaves it unclear whether newly issued or exclusively licensed patents under section (*l*)(7) that are "subject to paragraph (8)" are available in a post-notice declaratory judgment action, and no court has yet decided this issue.

D. Effect of Not *Providing Notice of Commercial Marketing*

In the event that the biosimilar applicant fails to provide notice of commercial marketing pursuant to section (*l*)(8)(A), then pursuant to section (*l*)(9)(B), the reference product sponsor—and not the applicant—may bring an action for a declaratory judgment.[37] In this case, the sponsor may seek a declaratory judgment with respect to the infringement, validity, or enforceability of *any* patent from the sponsor's (3)(A) list, as well as any newly issued or exclusively licensed patents falling under section (*l*)(7).[38] The applicant's failure to comply with section (*l*)(8)(A) thus lifts the declaratory judgment bar as to the sponsor alone, thereby incentivizing the applicant to provide timely notice of commercial marketing.[39]

---

31. *Id.* § 262(*l*)(7)(B).
32. *Apotex*, 827 F.3d at 1057.
33. Sandoz Inc. v. Amgen Inc., 582 U.S. 1, 11 (2017); *see* 42 U.S.C. § 262(*l*)(8)(B)(i)–(ii), (*l*)(9)(A).
34. 42 U.S.C. § 262(*l*)(9)(A); *see* Chapter 7, Section II.B.
35. 42 U.S.C. § 262(*l*)(9)(A).
36. *See id.* § 262(*l*)(8)(B)(i)–(ii).
37. *Id.* § 262(*l*)(9)(B).
38. *Id.*
39. *See* Amgen Inc. v. Apotex Inc., 827 F.3d 1052, 1057 (Fed. Cir. 2016). For a discussion of the scenarios where the sponsor can seek a declaratory judgment under (*l*)(9) based on the applicant's decision to opt out of, or failure to comply with, the patent dance, see Chapter 7, Section II.B.

Of course, this consequence of failing to provide notice of commercial marketing is only meaningful once the applicant has triggered the patent dance by complying with section (*l*)(2)(A).[40] As the Federal Circuit noted in *Sandoz I*, the BPCIA does not specify any consequence for failing—or even contemplate that an applicant might fail—to comply with *both* section (*l*)(8)(A) *and* section (*l*)(2)(A), as Sandoz had done in that case.[41] This observation reinforced the Federal Circuit's conclusion that the notice requirement of section (*l*)(8)(A) is mandatory and enforceable by injunction, which the court demonstrated by enjoining Sandoz from marketing the drug at issue for 180 days from the date on which Sandoz obtained FDA approval.[42]

Furthermore, Federal Circuit precedent holds that providing notice of commercial marketing is mandatory and that failure to do so can result in an injunction preventing the commencement of commercial marketing until 180 days after providing notice.[43] As a result, not providing notice of commercial marketing does not avoid the inevitable, but only delays the onset of a biosimilar's entry on to the market.

II. Strategic Considerations in Timing Phase-Two Litigation

A. Considerations for Bringing a Second-Phase Action

The second phase of BPCIA litigation permits an array of possibilities regarding when to bring an action and by which party. Although there is relatively little case law exploring these possibilities thus far, a few decisions provide notable guidance, particularly with respect to declaratory judgment actions.

Do not file a declaratory judgment action before seeking FDA approval or completing the patent dance. On at least a few occasions, biosimilar companies have sought to bring declaratory judgment actions under section (*l*)(9)(A) before even filing an application with the FDA for the subject biosimilar. In two cases, the courts dismissed the actions for lack of an actual case or controversy, reasoning that without so much as an FDA application on file, any act of infringement (counting artificial

40. *Sandoz I*, 794 F.3d 1347, 1359 (Fed. Cir. 2015).

41. *Id.*

42. *Id.* at 1360.

43. *See Apotex*, 827 F.3d at 1055, 1061; *supra* note 7 and accompanying text.

infringement) was too speculative to create a live dispute.[44] Although these decisions predate the Supreme Court's decision in *Sandoz*, they are consistent with the Supreme Court's holding that an applicant "may provide notice either before or after receiving FDA approval," which implies that the applicant must at least have sought FDA approval.[45]

Going further, two courts have signaled that a phase-two action—or at least an applicant's declaratory judgment action—must await completion of the patent dance. In *Amgen Inc. v. Genentech, Inc.*, the court declined to hear Amgen's declaratory judgment action that was filed after seeking FDA approval, but before exchanging final patent lists with Genentech pursuant to section (*l*)(5).[46] "Rather than proceeding with the final patent exchange procedures set out by the BPCIA for the first phase, Amgen immediately filed [its] lawsuit for declaratory judgment as to all twenty-seven patents on Genentech's § [(3)(A)] list" in order "to remove the cloud of uncertainty flowing from Genentech's inconsistent and changing positions during the BPCIA exchange and negotiations."[47] The parties subsequently completed the patent dance and Genentech filed its "first phase" lawsuit a few weeks later.[48] Noting that "the BPCIA sets out a 'carefully calibrated scheme' for the parties to follow in preparing to litigate these types of disputes," and that the parties' beginning the patent dance "created an expectation that Genentech would soon . . . bring suit against Amgen," the court "decline[d] to hear a case where Amgen effectively attempted to bypass the BPCIA's scheme for negotiations and eventual litigation."[49] In the end, the court stayed Amgen's phase-two action pending a determination by the court in Genentech's phase-one action regarding whether to transfer that action to the court in Amgen's action.[50]

Similarly, in *Celltrion v. Genentech*, the court held that Celltrion's provision of commercial marketing did not "enable it to file these declaratory judgment actions, regardless of its compliance with other portions of the

44. *See* Sandoz Inc. v. Amgen Inc., No. C-13-2904 MMC, 2013 WL 6000069, at *1–3 (N.D. Cal. Nov. 12, 2013); Celltrion Healthcare Co., Ltd. v. Kennedy Tr. for Rheumatology Rsch., No. 14 Civ. 2256(PAC), 2014 WL 6765996, at *2–5 (S.D.N.Y. Dec. 1, 2014).

45. *See* Sandoz Inc. v. Amgen Inc., 582 U.S. 1, 19 (2017).

46. No. CV 17-7349-GW(AGRX), 2018 WL 910198, at *2 (C.D. Cal. Jan. 11, 2018).

47. *Id.*

48. *Id.*

49. *Id.* at *3–4.

50. *Id.* at *5. Transferring a parallel phase-two declaratory judgment by the biosimilar applicant to the venue of the phase-one infringement action by the reference product sponsor has not been uncommon in the small universe of phase-two cases. *See also* Alvotech USA Inc. v. AbbVie Inc., No. 2:21-CV-265-RAJ-DEM, 2021 WL 4942806, at *2 (E.D. Va. Oct. 22, 2021) (ordering that second-filed phase-two suit be transferred to venue of first-filed phase-one suit).

BPCIA."[51] Much as in *Amgen v. Genentech*, Celltrion refused to provide its (5)(A) number or (5)(B) list after engaging in section (*l*)(4) negotiations, and instead filed for a declaratory judgment.[52] Genentech moved to dismiss under Rule 12(b)(6), contending that "Celltrion's failure to perform the BPCIA's 'patent dance' deprives this Court of jurisdiction."[53] The court agreed, concluding that "a Notice of Commercial Marketing only opens the door for an applicant to file a declaratory judgment action if the applicant complies with the rest of the statute" and granting Genentech's motion to dismiss.[54]

Do not wait too long to seek a preliminary injunction. Whereas biosimilar applicants have at times brought declaratory judgment actions too early, on at least one occasion, a reference product sponsor filed for a preliminary injunction too late. In *Genentech, Inc. v. Amgen Inc.* (the parallel phase-one action filed shortly after the *Amgen v. Genentech* case discussed earlier), the court denied Genentech's motion for preliminary injunction due to excessive delay.[55] Genentech had moved for preliminary injunction (as well as a temporary restraining order) four weeks after the relevant biosimilar received FDA approval, but, by that time, 14 months had gone by since Amgen provided notice of commercial marketing, and a year had gone by since Amgen had filed for FDA approval.[56] Genentech had even known the latest date on which FDA approval could come for months in advance, yet still did not file suit until after FDA approval.[57] Reasoning that "[a] patentee's undue delay in seeking a preliminary injunction 'negates the idea of irreparability,'" and that "the 180-day period is designed to prevent" the exact "'race to court for immediate relief to avoid irreparable harm from market entry,'" the court held that "Genentech's undue delay in requesting a preliminary injunction" was "sufficient by itself to deny the motion."[58] In short, once notice of commercial marketing has been given and assuming FDA approval is expected to exist upon expiration of the 180-day wait period, a reference product sponsor is on the clock to seek any preliminary injunctive relief.

---

51. Celltrion v. Genentech, No. 18-CV-00274-JSW, 2018 WL 2448254, at *7 (N.D. Cal. May 9, 2018).

52. *Id.* at *5.

53. *Id.* at *4.

54. *Id.* at *8.

55. No. CV 18-924-CFC, 2019 WL 3290167, at *2–4 (D. Del. July 18, 2019), *aff'd*, 796 F. App'x 726 (Fed. Cir. 2020).

56. *Id.* at *1.

57. *Id.* at *2.

58. *Id.* at *3 (quoting Pfizer, Inc. v. Teva Pharms., USA, Inc., 429 F.3d 1364, 1382 (Fed. Cir. 2005), and Amgen Inc. v. Apotex Inc., 827 F.3d 1052, 1063 (Fed. Cir. 2016), respectively).

B. Considerations for Timing the Notice of Commercial Marketing

Strategic considerations also come into play when a biosimilar applicant decides when to issue notice of commercial marketing. The primary consideration is whether the relevant biologic product remains in the exclusivity period for which the BPCIA provides.[59]

As the court summarized in *Genentech v. Immunex*, the statute provides that "[a] biosimilar manufacturer . . . cannot submit an application to the FDA until four years after 'the reference product was first licensed' by the FDA."[60] Furthermore, "the FDA cannot approve a biosimilar application until 12 years after 'the reference product was first licensed.'"[61] "As a result, the manufacturer of a new biologic enjoys a 12-year period when its biologic may be marketed without competition from biosimilars."[62]

Biologics on the market can thus be divided into two classes: (1) those that were approved more than 12 years ago and no longer enjoy exclusivity from biosimilar competition, and (2) those that were approved less than 12 years ago and retain exclusivity from biosimilar competition. The timing of phase-two litigation tends to vary widely between these two classes of reference products.

1. The BPCIA's Orderly Scheme of Two-Phase Litigation Works Best with New Biologics

Where the reference product remains within the 12-year exclusivity period, it makes sense for biosimilar applicants to complete phase one, litigating only the limited number of patents selected for the patent dance, before proceeding to phase two, where every other patent on the parties' initial list is on the table. If the FDA cannot approve an application until it has been 12 years since the reference biologic was approved, and a product cannot be marketed until it is approved, there is no reason to provide notice of commercial marketing for any biosimilar whose reference product has been licensed for less than approximately 11.5 years (12 years minus 180 days).

Conversely, there may well be reason to file an application for FDA approval while the reference biologic is much newer. While the FDA often approves new aBLAs within six months to a year, some biosimilar products are denied approval on their first submission by issuance of a CRL.[63]

59. *See* Chapter 3.

60. Genentech, Inc. v. Immunex R.I. Corp., 395 F. Supp. 3d 357, 361 (D. Del. 2019), *aff'd*, 964 F.3d 1109 (Fed. Cir. 2020) (quoting 42 U.S.C. § 262(k)(7)(B)).

61. *Id.* (quoting 42 U.S.C. § 262(k)(7)(A)).

62. *Id.* (quoting Sandoz Inc. v. Amgen Inc., 582 U.S. 1, 7 (2017)).

63. *See supra* note 20 and accompanying text.

The time to resubmit for approval and receive FDA consideration of the resubmission typically exceeds a year.[64] Thus, an applicant may want to file early to ensure there is time for approval before the exclusivity period expires. Additionally, a biosimilar applicant may want to reserve enough time to complete phase one (successfully) so that it can enter the market on day one of the post-exclusivity period without the threat of the reference product sponsor's priority patents hanging over the launch.

As a result, the exclusivity period creates a scenario where biosimilar applicants are incentivized to progress through the BPCIA one phase at a time. The statute's two-phase scheme works best—or perhaps only works at all—in this environment, where the cabined scope of litigation arising out of the patent dance can proceed unimpaired by the disorder of phase two's grab bag of litigation possibilities.

Ironically, few BPCIA cases to date have involved a biologic that was still within the exclusivity period. In fact, just one case has done so: *Regeneron Pharmaceuticals, Inc. v. Mylan Pharmaceuticals Inc.*[65] That case has not yielded any significant decisions to date, but publicly accessible filings indicate that Regeneron filed its complaint following the patent dance, asserting 24 patents from the parties' (*l*)(5) lists,[66] and that the parties proceeded to a bench trial in approximately June 2023.[67] While there is no telling when the court may issue its ruling, the parties have substantially completed phase one before proceeding to any phase-two litigation (which has not been filed to date).

Despite the framework contemplated by the statute, it is perhaps not surprising that few biosimilar applicants have filed an aBLA where the reference product remained a long way from the end of the exclusivity period. While doing so allows an applicant to engage in the patent dance unimpaired, it also entails the headache of patent litigation so far in advance of commercial marketing. Ideally, the patent dance is timed to end just before exclusivity expires—a Goldilocks moment of sorts. There's also the reality that the first applicant to file bears the brunt of litigation from the sponsor, while successive filers can ride the coattails and take advantage of any judgment against the sponsor or, if a settlement occurs, obtain license entry dates. It may well be the case that, much as Congress

64. *See* FDANEWS, FDA COMPLETE RESPONSE LETTER ANALYSIS: HOW 51 COMPANIES TURNED FAILURE TO SUCCESS, https://www.fdanews.com/products/ 44634-pdf-edition-fda-complete-response-letter-analysis-how-51-companies-turned-failure-to-success (noting that a CRL delays a product's entry on to the market by 14 months on average).

65. No. 1:22-CV-61 (N.D. W. Va. filed Aug. 2, 2022).

66. *See* Complaint, *Regeneron Pharms., Inc.*, No. 1:22-CV-61, ECF No. 1.

67. For further discussion of the *Regeneron v. Mylan* trial, see Chapter 7, Section VI.D.

wanted biosimilar companies to dance with biologics companies, its patent-list scheme often does not provide enough incentive.

2. In the Case of Old Biologics, Phase-One and Phase-Two Litigation Often Happen Simultaneously

Most phase-two litigation to date has involved older biologics that are outside of the 12-year exclusivity period. In these cases, the incentive structure often produces a scenario where biosimilar applicants provide notice of commercial marketing relatively soon after submitting an aBLA, thereby triggering overlapping phase-one and phase-two litigation.

Recall that, under the Supreme Court's decision in *Sandoz*, a biosimilar applicant may provide notice of commercial marketing "either before or after receiving FDA approval."[68] Sandoz had provided notice of commercial marketing the day after the FDA accepted its application for review because Sandoz wanted to market the drug "immediately upon FDA approval."[69] Especially since the Supreme Court blessed that approach, other biosimilars have often done the same when the reference biologic no longer enjoys exclusivity, such that a biosimilar could be marketed as soon as it receives FDA approval so long as notice of commercial marketing was filed 180 days earlier.[70]

Publicly available data about phase-two cases involving biologics without exclusivity indicate that the biosimilar applicant provided notice of commercial marketing before the date by which the FDA committed to completing its review of the aBLA—referred to as the "PDUFA" date (a reference to the Prescription Drug User Fee Act)—in 15 of 18 cases for which data could be located (see Table 1). And, on average, the applicant beat the PDUFA date by approximately 220 days. In other words, applicants overwhelmingly provided notice far enough in advance to clear the 180-day period under section (*l*)(8)(A) by the time they could expect to receive FDA approval, so as to be ready to enter the market immediately upon approval.[71]

---

68. Sandoz Inc. v. Amgen Inc., 582 U.S. 1, 19 (2017); *see also supra* note 14 and accompanying text.

69. *Sandoz*, 582 U.S. at 2.

70. *See* 42 U.S.C. § 262(*l*)(8)(A).

71. *See Sandoz*, 582 U.S. at 2.

TABLE 1. Cases and PDUFA Dates

Litigation	Before v. After PDUFA Date	# of Days
Janssen Biotech v. Amgen, No. 1:22-CV-1549 (D. Del.)	Before	300
Genentech v. Pfizer, No. 17-1672 (D. Del.)	Before	497
Genentech v. Amgen, No. 18-924 (D. Del.)	Before	13
Genentech v. Samsung Bioepis, No. 18-1363 (D. Del.)	After	N/A
Amgen v. Apotex, No. 15-61631 (S.D. Fla.)	After	N/A
Amgen v. Sandoz, No. 16-2581 (N.D. Cal.)	Before	105
Amgen v. Mylan, No. 17-1235 (W.D. Pa.)	Before	187
Amgen v. Hospira, No. 20-201 (D. Del.)	Before	163
Janssen v. Samsung Bioepis, No. 17-3524 (D.N.J.)	Before	330
Amgen v. Sandoz, No. 14-4741 (N.D. Cal.)	Before	303
Amgen v. Apotex, No. 15-62081 (S.D. Fla.)	Before	240
Amgen v. Kashiv, No. 18-3347 (D.N.J.)	Before	300
Amgen v. Hospira, Nos. 18-1064, 20-561 (D. Del.)	Before	197
Amgen v. Hospira, No. 15-839 (D. Del.)	Before	191
Genentech v. Amgen, Nos. 17-1407, -1471, 19-602 (D. Del.)	After	N/A
Genentech v. Pfizer, No. 19-638 (D. Del.)	Before	159
Genentech v. Samsung Bioepis, No. 20-859 (D. Del.)	Before	173
AbbVie v. Alvotech, Nos. 21-2258, -2899 (N.D. Ill.)	Before	131

Being able to market one's product as soon as FDA approval is received provides a clear incentive to provide notice of commercial marketing early on when the reference biologic has lost exclusivity. Granted, there are also downsides to the trend of providing early notice. Primarily, it requires collapsing the orderly and limited first phase—with respect to which a biosimilar applicant wields substantial control[72]—with the disorderly and unbounded second phase. This means the prospect of litigating not only *every* patent on the parties' (3)(A) lists, as opposed to only the patents on the winnowed (*l*)(5) list, but also litigating on two fronts at once, as has often been true of cases involving biologics outside of exclusivity.[73] Nonetheless, experience thus far has shown that the ability to enter the market as soon as possible is often the driving factor in timing one's notice of commercial marketing.

72. *See* Chapter 7, Section II.A.1.

73. *See, e.g.*, *supra* note 50 and accompanying text.

chapter 9

BPCIA Declaratory Judgment Actions*

The Biologics Price Competition and Innovation Act (BPCIA) puts limitations on when a party can bring a declaratory judgment lawsuit. This chapter explores the different scenarios under which a sponsor and an applicant can bring a declaratory judgment action.

I. Declaratory Judgment Actions by the Sponsor

A. Reasons for a Sponsor to Bring a Declaratory Judgment Action

Generally speaking, there is little need for a sponsor to bring a declaratory judgment action against a BPCIA applicant. As discussed in Chapter 8, the BPCIA requires that the applicant notify the sponsor 180 days before it intends to market the biosimilar.[1] The sponsor can then seek a preliminary injunction to stay approval of the biosimilar until the patent litigation is resolved.[2] This assumes, however, that the parties are involved in patent litigation because they have completed the "patent dance" and a litigation has been filed. But what happens if the applicant refuses to participate or only partially participates in the patent dance? If that happens, the only way for the sponsor to enforce its patents against the applicant before the biosimilar is marketed is by filing a declaratory judgment action against the biosimilar.

*Rebecca J. Cantor, Brooks Kushman P.C.

1. 42 U.S.C. § 262(*l*)(8)(A).
2. *Id.* § 262(*l*)(8)(B).

B. Statutory Basis for and Limitations on Declaratory Judgment Actions under the BPCIA

Under the BPCIA, the filing of a biologics license application (BLA) for a biosimilar constitutes an artificial act of infringement that creates an actual case or controversy sufficient to allow federal courts to hear patent infringement claims.[3] The BPCIA, however, generally limits the parties from bringing declaratory judgment actions based on this artificial act of infringement before a notice of commercial marketing is received, particularly if the applicant and sponsor engage in the patent dance:[4]

> If a subsection (k) applicant provides the application and information required under paragraph (2)(A), neither the reference product sponsor nor the subsection (k) applicant may, prior to the date notice is received under paragraph (8)(A), bring any action under section 2201 of title 28 for a declaration of infringement, validity, or enforceability of any patent that is described in clauses (i) and (ii) of paragraph (8)(B).[5]

If the applicant refuses to participate in the patent dance or fails to disclose all relevant information required by subsection (k), however, the BPCIA does allow for declaratory judgment actions:

> If a subsection (k) applicant fails to complete an action required of the subsection (k) applicant under paragraph (3)(B)(ii), paragraph (5), paragraph (6)(C)(i), paragraph (7), or paragraph (8)(A), the reference product sponsor, but not the subsection (k) applicant, may bring an action under section 2201 of title 28 for a declaration of infringement, validity, or enforceability of any patent included in the list described in paragraph (3)(A), including as provided under paragraph (7).[6]

Similarly, if the applicant fails to inform the sponsor of the application, the sponsor may bring a declaratory judgment action against the applicant:

> If a subsection (k) applicant fails to provide the application and information required under paragraph (2)(A), the reference product sponsor, but not the subsection (k) applicant, may bring an action under section 2201 of title 28 for a declaration of infringement,

3. 35 U.S.C. § 271(e)(2)(C).
4. See Chapter 4 for additional information regarding the patent dance.
5. 42 U.S.C. § 262(*l*)(9)(A).
6. *Id.* § 262(*l*)(9)(B).

validity, or enforceability of any patent that claims the biological product or a use of the biological product.[7]

Notably, these subsections only allow the sponsor—not the applicant—to bring a declaratory judgment action. Thus, an applicant cannot create its own declaratory judgment jurisdiction by failing to disclose the application or other information to the sponsor.

C. Declaratory Judgment Is the Sole Remedy for Failure to Participate in the Patent Dance

As discussed earlier, if an applicant fails to participate in the patent dance, the sponsor is statutorily permitted to bring a declaratory judgment action. But is there any way to force the applicant to participate in the patent dance instead of pursuing declaratory judgment? In 2017, the U.S. Supreme Court took up this question in *Sandoz Inc. v. Amgen Inc.*[8] and unanimously found that the patent dance is optional, and the sponsor cannot force the applicant to participate through an injunction.

The *Sandoz* case arose out of Sandoz Inc.'s application to market a biosimilar version of Amgen's filgrastim product, which was sold under the brand name Neupogen.[9] Sandoz filed its application in May 2014 and the U.S. Food and Drug Administration (FDA) notified Sandoz that the application had been accepted on July 7, 2014.[10] The next day, Sandoz notified Amgen that it had submitted the application to the FDA and that Sandoz intended to market its biosimilar version of filgrastim under the name Zarxio in the first half of 2015.[11] Sandoz subsequently informed Amgen that it did not intend to participate in the patent dance.[12]

On October 14, 2014, Amgen filed a declaratory judgment lawsuit against Sandoz in the Northern District of California.[13] Amgen also claimed that Sandoz "had behaved unlawfully under 42 U.S.C. § 262 by failing to comply with its disclosure and negotiation procedures" and that this failure also gave rise to unfair competition claims under California's Unfair Competition Law, California Business and Professions Code section 17200.[14] Amgen sought, inter alia, an injunction and preliminary injunction forcing Sandoz to participate in the patent dance.[15]

7. *Id.* § 262(*l*)(9)(C).
8. 582 U.S. 1, 14 (2017).
9. *Id.* at 12.
10. *Id.*
11. *Id.*
12. *Id.*
13. Amgen Inc. v. Sandoz Inc., No. 14-cv-04741-RS, 2015 WL 1264756, at *1 (N.D. Cal. Mar. 19, 2015).
14. *Id.*
15. *Id.* at *9.

On March 19, 2015, the district court entered an order dismissing Amgen's claims under the BPCIA and California Business and Professions Code section 17200, and denying Amgen's motion for a preliminary injunction.[16] In particular, the district court found that the patent dance was not mandatory because the statute specifically provided an alternative for the sponsor if the applicant did not participate in the patent dance—namely, filing a declaratory judgment action.[17] As the district court explained:

> Indeed Sandoz's decision not to comply with subsection (*l*) reflects how the statute's overall scheme operates to promote expedient resolution of patent disputes. Compliance with the disclosure process affords an applicant many benefits: it allows the applicant to preview which patents the reference product sponsor believes are valid and infringed, assess related factual and legal support, and exercise some control over which patents are litigated and when. An applicant with a high (or unknown) risk of liability for infringement could benefit considerably from this process: it would be able to undergo the information exchange while protected by the statute's safe harbor from litigation, and if necessary, delay its product launch to protect the investment it made in developing its biosimilar.
>
> On the other hand, subsection (*l*) lays out a process that could take up to 230 days—just to commence patent litigation. An applicant who values expedience over risk mitigation may believe that the disclosure and negotiation process would introduce needless communications and delay. Such an applicant may have good reason to believe that no unexpired relevant patents relate to its biosimilar, and that it is likely to prevail if challenged with an infringement suit. The applicant may, in such an instance, opt to forego its ability to bring certain types of declaratory actions and receive information about potentially relevant patents from the reference product sponsor, and instead commence litigation immediately.[18]

The district court also dismissed the claims under California Business and Professions Code section 17200 because there was "no unlawful or wrongful predicate act to sustain Amgen's claims" since the court found that Sandoz did not violate the BPCIA.[19]

16. *Id.* at *1–2.
17. *Id.* at *6.
18. *Id.* at *6–7.
19. *Id.* at *8.

Amgen subsequently appealed the district court's decision to the U.S. Court of Appeals for the Federal Circuit.[20] The Federal Circuit affirmed finding that if the patent dance was mandatory, it would render 42 U.S.C. § 262(*l*)(9)(C) and 35 U.S.C. § 271(e)(2)(C)(ii) superfluous.[21] The Federal Circuit also relied on 35 U.S.C. § 271(e)(4), which provides that the remedies of 35 U.S.C. § 271(e)(4)(A)–(D) are "the only remedies which may be granted by a court" for the artificial act of infringement of filing a biosimilar application.[22] But an injunction forcing the applicant to comply with the patent dance is not one of the remedies listed in 35 U.S.C. § 271(e)(4)(A)–(D). The Federal Circuit thus reasoned that if the sponsor were allowed get an injunction to force the applicant to participate in the patent dance, it would obviate the limitation on remedies in 35 U.S.C. § 271(e)(4).[23] The Federal Circuit also affirmed the dismissal of Amgen's claim under California Business and Professions Code section 17200 because there was no predicate unlawful act.[24]

Amgen appealed the Federal Circuit's decision to the Supreme Court.[25] The Supreme Court unanimously[26] held that Sandoz did not violate the BPCIA by failing to participate in the patent dance.[27] The Supreme Court found that "[t]he remedy provided by § 262(*l*)(9)(C) excludes all other federal remedies including injunctive relief."[28] The Supreme Court disagreed, however, with the Federal Circuit's reasoning that 35 U.S.C. § 271(e)(4) precluded entry of an injunction.[29] The Supreme Court explained that Sandoz's failure to participate in the patent dance did not implicate 35 U.S.C. § 271(e)(4) because "Sandoz's failure to disclose its application and manufacturing information was not an act of artificial infringement, and thus was not remediable under § 271(e)(4)."[30] Finally, the Supreme Court remanded the case to the Federal Circuit to determine whether "California law would treat noncompliance with § 262(*l*)(2)(A) as 'unlawful'" and, if

20. Amgen Inc. v. Sandoz Inc., 794 F.3d 1347 (Fed. Cir. 2015).

21. *Id.* at 1356.

22. *Id.*

23. *Id.*

24. *Id.* at 1360.

25. Sandoz Inc. v. Amgen Inc., 582 U.S. 1 (2017). The Federal Circuit also reversed part of the district court's decision that was not relevant to whether Sandoz could be forced to participate in the patent dance. *See id.* at 13. Sandoz appealed those issues to the Supreme Court, and Amgen filed a conditional cross-petition for certiorari on the patent dance issues. *Id.*

26. Justice Breyer filed a concurring opinion agreeing with the judgment but noting that if the FDA "determines that a different interpretation would better serve the statute's objectives, it may well have authority to depart from, or to modify, today's interpretation." *Id.* at 22.

27. *Id.* at 14.

28. *Id.* at 16.

29. *Id.* at 14.

30. *Id.*

so, whether the "BPCIA pre-empts any additional remedy available under state law for an applicant's failure to comply with § 262(*l*)(2)(A)."[31]

On remand, the Federal Circuit found "that the BPCIA preempts state law claims predicated on an applicant's failure to comply with § 262(*l*)(2)(A)."[32] Note that this language would seem to apply to any state law that purports to allow injunctive relief based on an applicant's failure to comply with the patent dance, not just California Business and Professions Code section 17200.

In sum, the *Amgen v. Sandoz* case precludes using an injunction to force an applicant to comply with the patent dance either under federal or state law. Thus, the only option a sponsor has in the event an applicant fails to participate in the patent dance is to bring a declaratory judgment action under 42 U.S.C. § 262(*l*)(9)(B) or (C).

II. A BPCIA Applicant's Ability to Bring a Declaratory Judgment Action

The BPCIA provides few opportunities for a BPCIA applicant to bring a declaratory judgment action. In fact, and as described in Section I.B, two of the BPCIA's declaratory judgment provisions specifically exempt an applicant from bringing a declaratory judgment case.[33] Rather, an applicant may only bring a declaratory judgment action after it has provided the sponsor with a notice of commercial marketing.[34] This section explores why and when an applicant can bring a declaratory judgment case.

A. Reasons for an Applicant to Bring a Declaratory Judgment Action

As discussed in Chapter 4, the culmination of the patent dance is a lawsuit that is limited to a certain number of patents.[35] Frequently, however, a sponsor may have many additional patents it claims covers the reference product. An applicant therefore may want to file a declaratory judgment action to obtain clarity on the unasserted patents before it begins marketing its biosimilar. Additionally, the patent dance takes time; approximately six and a half months for the dance itself plus another 30 days before the sponsor has to file a lawsuit.[36] An applicant may want to bring

31. *Id.* at 19.
32. Amgen Inc. v. Sandoz Inc., 877 F.3d 1315, 1327 (Fed. Cir. 2017).
33. 42 U.S.C. § 262(*l*)(9)(B), (C).
34. *Id.* § 262(*l*)(9)(A).
35. *Id.* § 262(*l*)(4)–(5).
36. *Id.* § 262(*l*)(3)–(6).

a declaratory judgment suit soon after its application is filed in an attempt to avoid the delay that is implicit in the patent dance.

B. Statutory Basis for a Declaratory Judgment Action by the Applicant

As mentioned, the BPCIA provisions that allow a sponsor to bring a declaratory judgment action generally prevent an applicant from bringing a declaratory judgment action. The one exception to this is once an applicant has provided the sponsor with a notice of commercial marketing.[37] As the Supreme Court explained, after the notice of commercial marketing is provided "*either* party may sue for declaratory judgment."[38]

C. Relevant Cases

There have been relatively few cases in which an applicant has sought to bring a declaratory judgment action against sponsors. These cases generally fall into two categories: (1) cases that were filed by an applicant before that applicant had filed an application for the biosimilar with the FDA, and (2) cases that were filed after the applicant both filed its application with the FDA and provided the sponsor with a notice of marking. As will be seen, these cases indicate that it is almost impossible for an applicant to bring a declaratory judgment action against a sponsor.

1. Cases Filed before a Biosimilar Application Has Been Filed

Sandoz Inc. v. Amgen Inc.[39] Amgen was the sponsor of Enbrel, a human tumor necrosis factor receptor known as etanercept, which Amgen averred was covered by two patents.[40] In 2013, Sandoz was "conducting clinical trials to test" a biosimilar that contained etanercept and intended to apply for a biosimilar license upon completion of the clinical trials.[41] Sandoz filed a lawsuit while these clinical trials were pending (and before filing an application with the FDA) seeking a declaration that its biosimilar did not infringe the two patents identified by Amgen and that the patents were invalid and unenforceable.[42] Amgen moved to dismiss the lawsuit for "lack[] of statutory authority to consider a patent dispute involving a biosimilar product until after such time as an application for FDA approval

---

37. *Id.* § 262(*l*)(9)(A).
38. Sandoz Inc. v. Amgen Inc., 582 U.S. 1, 11 (2017) (citing 42 U.S.C. § 262(*l*)(9)(A)).
39. No. C-13-2904 MMC, 2013 WL 6000069 (N.D. Cal. Nov. 12, 2013).
40. *Id.* at *1.
41. *Id.*
42. *Id.*

of the biosimilar has been filed" and because no cognizable case or controversy existed between the parties.[43]

The court dismissed the case.[44] The court stated that while the declaratory judgment act does allow the court to decide certain declaratory judgment cases if there is an actual controversy between the parties, the court's discretion to hear such cases is subject to certain limitations set forth in, inter alia, 42 U.S.C. § 262.[45] The court went on to find that under 42 U.S.C. § 262 "neither a reference product sponsor [] nor an applicant [] may file a lawsuit until they have engaged in a series of statutorily-mandated exchanges of information."[46] The court went on to state that Sandoz had not, and indeed could not, comply with these obligations because it had not filed an application with the FDA.[47] Sandoz attempted to argue that 42 U.S.C. § 262(*l*)(8)(A) allowed it to bring a declaratory judgment suit upon a notice of commercial marketing.[48] The court found, however, that this was irrelevant, as Sandoz did not and could not provide a notice of commercial marketing because it did not have FDA approval for its biosimilar and even if Sandoz had filed a notice of commercial marketing, Sandoz still could not bring a declaratory judgment lawsuit until it complied with all of its obligations under 42 U.S.C. § 262(*l*).[49]

Finally, the court noted that there was no immediate threat to Sandoz.[50] Amgen had never threatened Sandoz with a lawsuit over Sandoz's proposed biosimilar. Rather, Sandoz merely relied on a public statement by Amgen that Enbrel was covered by the two patents at issue.[51] Moreover, the court found Sandoz's intent to file a future application insufficient to create a case or controversy.[52]

Sandoz appealed, and the Federal Circuit affirmed the district court's decision.[53] In particular, the Federal Circuit stated:

> Amgen has not suggested that anything Sandoz is currently doing exposes it to infringement liability, and there is no dispute that Sandoz cannot engage in the only liability-exposing conduct at issue without FDA approval of an application precisely defining

43. *Id.*
44. *Id.* at *3.
45. *Id.* at *1.
46. *Id.* at *2.
47. *Id.*
48. *Id.*
49. *Id.*
50. *Id.*
51. *Id.*
52. *Id.* at *3.
53. Sandoz Inc. v. Amgen Inc., 773 F.3d 1274 (Fed. Cir. 2014).

> the products it may market. Sandoz has not even filed such an application.[54]

The Federal Circuit also noted that it was not a certainty that Sandoz would be able to file an application given that the clinical trials were ongoing.[55] In particular, the Federal Circuit noted:

> Any dispute about patent infringement is at present subject to significant uncertainties—concerning whether it will actually arise and if so what specific issues will require decision. Sandoz's Phase III trial may fail in material ways. If so, perhaps Sandoz will not file for approval, thereby eliminating altogether the patent dispute it has asked the district court to adjudicate. Perhaps, if the trial materially fails, i.e., uncovers significant problems, Sandoz will instead modify its proposed product and ultimately file for FDA approval of the modified product. At a minimum, that scenario could alter the content of any patent dispute: notably, infringement of the specific claims of the specific patents—which cover, e.g., particular proteins, pharmaceutical compositions, polynucleotides, and methods—could present different questions depending on the precise product. In fact, modifying the product now being tested might even eliminate a genuine patent dispute.[56]

The Federal Circuit did not address in detail whether an applicant needs to complete the exchanges of 42 U.S.C. § 262(*l*) before bringing a declaratory judgment action.

Celltrion Healthcare Co., Ltd. v. Kennedy Trust for Rheumatology Research.[57] Kennedy was the owner of patents related to Remicade, a biologic used in the treatment of several diseases such as Crohn's disease and rheumatoid arthritis.[58] Celltrion developed a biosimilar of Remicade called Remsima and gained approval in 47 countries.[59] In 2013, Celltrion began the process of seeking FDA approval for Remsima in the United States.[60] In 2014, Celltrion filed a judgment lawsuit against Kennedy seeking a declaration that three of Kennedy's patents were invalid.[61] At the time Celltrion filed the lawsuit, it had not yet filed an application to

54. *Id.* at 1279.
55. *Id.* at 1280.
56. *Id.*
57. No. 14 Civ. 2256, 2014 WL 6765996 (S.D.N.Y. Dec. 1, 2014).
58. *Id.* at *1.
59. *Id.*
60. *Id.*
61. *Id.*

market its biosimilar with the FDA.[62] Kennedy moved to dismiss the claim for lack of subject matter jurisdiction.[63]

The court dismissed the case finding there was no actual controversy because "Celltrion is simply too far from receiving FDA approval of Remsima for the exercise of declaratory judgment jurisdiction to be proper."[64] Moreover, the court found that Kennedy had "not expressed a clear intent to pursue infringement claims against Celltrion."[65] The court went on to say, however, that even if there was an actual controversy the court would still decline to hear this case in light of the BPCIA framework, stating "Celltrion's attempts to skirt the BPCIA's dispute resolution mechanisms while reaping the benefits of its approval process is improper."[66]

2. Cases Filed after the Applicant Provides the Sponsor with a Notice of Commercial Marketing

Amgen Inc. v Genentech, Inc.[67] Amgen filed an application with the FDA for approval to market a biosimilar to Genentech's Avastin. The parties began the patent dance, but before it was completed Amgen provided Genentech with a notice of commercial marketing.[68] Amgen subsequently filed a lawsuit seeking a declaration that all 27 patents Genentech identified during the patent dance were invalid.[69] Within 24 hours of the lawsuit being filed, Genentech filed a separate lawsuit in the U.S. District Court for the District of Delaware alleging that Amgen's biosimilar infringed the 27 identified patents.[70]

Amgen argued that it had the right to bring a declaratory judgment action under 42 U.S.C. § 262(*l*)(9)(A) because it had provided a notice of commercial marketing.[71] The court rejected this argument, stating that 42 U.S.C. § 262(*l*)(9)(A) only allows an applicant to bring a declaratory judgment lawsuit for patents that were not asserted in a first litigation by the sponsor.[72] In coming to this conclusion, the court noted that in the Supreme Court *Sandoz* case, the Court stated that "[t]he second phase [of BPCIA litigation] is triggered by the applicant's notice of commercial

62. *Id.*
63. *Id.*
64. *Id.* at *3.
65. *Id.* at *4.
66. *Id.*
67. Tentative ruling: No. CV 17-7349, 2018 WL 910198 (C.D. Cal. Feb. 2, 2018). Order adopting ruling: 2018 WL 718418 (C.D. Cal. Feb. 2, 2018).
68. *Amgen Inc.*, 2018 WL 910198, at *2.
69. *Id.*
70. *Id.*
71. *Id.* at *3.
72. *Id.*

marketing and involves *any patents that were not included in the parties' [42 U.S.C. § 262(l)(3)] lists but not litigated in the first phase.*"[73]

Celltrion, Inc. v. Genentech, Inc.[74] Genentech was the sponsor for Herceptin.[75] On May 30, 2017, Celltrion applied for FDA approval to market a biosimilar of Herceptin called Herzuma.[76] The parties subsequently began the patent dance, and Genentech listed 40 patents it believed Celltrion infringed.[77] Genentech then proposed that the parties agree to litigate fewer than all of the 40 patents.[78] Celltrion, on the other hand, wanted to litigate all of the patents Genentech had disclosed.[79] On January 11, 2018, Celltrion served a notice of commercial marketing on Genentech.[80]

Shortly thereafter, Celltrion also filed an application to market a biosimilar version of Genentech's Rituxan, which Celltrion intended to market under the name Truxima.[81] Again, Genentech disclosed 40 patents and Celltrion wished to litigate all of them.[82] On January 11, 2018, Celltrion provided Genentech with a notice of commercial marketing of Truxima.[83] That same day, Celltrion instituted two lawsuits against Genentech; one seeking a declaration that Herzuma would not infringe the patents Genentech listed and one seeking a declaration that Truxima would not infringe the patents Genentech listed.[84] At the time Celltrion filed these lawsuits, the parties were still engaged in the patent dance.[85] Genentech filed motions to dismiss both cases for lack of subject matter jurisdiction and failure to state a claim, and the motions were decided together.[86]

The court held that Celltrion failed to state a claim for relief because it "did not complete its obligations under [42 U.S.C. § 262(*l*)(5)]."[87] In coming to this conclusion, the court relied solely on 42 U.S.C. § 262(*l*)(9)(B).[88] Celltrion argued "that because a notice of commercial marketing lifts the ban on declaratory judgment actions described in [42 U.S.C. § 262(*l*)(9)(A)], a notice of commercial marketing should also lift [42 U.S.C. § 262(*l*)(9)(B)'s

73. *Id.* at *4 (citing Sandoz Inc. v. Amgen Inc., 582 U.S. 1, 10 (2017)).
74. No. 18-cv-00274, 2018 WL 2448254 (N.D. Cal. May 9, 2018).
75. *Id.* at *3.
76. *Id.*
77. *Id.*
78. *Id.*
79. *Id.*
80. *Id.*
81. *Id.*
82. *Id.*
83. *Id.*
84. *Id.*
85. *Id.*
86. *Id.* at *4.
87. *Id.* at *5.
88. *Id.*

and (C)'s] prohibitions."[89] The court rejected this, stating that while a notice of commercial marketing removed the bar set forth under 42 U.S.C. § 262(*l*)(9)(A), it had no effect on the other bars set forth in 42 U.S.C. § 262(*l*)(9).[90] The court thus granted the motion to dismiss. While Celltrion appealed, it voluntarily withdrew the appeal before the Federal Circuit had a chance to rule.[91]

As shown in all of the foregoing cases, it is difficult for an applicant to bring a declaratory judgment action unless that applicant has strictly complied with all of the requirements of the patent dance. Once the patent dance has been completed, however, it is likely that the sponsor will already have sued the applicant for patent infringement, which would likely limit the usefulness of a declaratory judgment action.

D. Counterclaims

The BPCIA's restrictions on bringing declaratory judgment actions do not apply to invalidity or inequitable conduct counterclaims an applicant brings in response to an infringement lawsuit brought by the sponsor under the BPCIA. In *Genentech, Inc. v. Amgen Inc.*,[92] Genentech sued Amgen for patent infringement based on Amgen's application to market a biosimilar of Genentech's Avastin product. In response, Amgen brought 29 declaratory judgment counterclaims alleging that the patents-in-suit and two other patents were invalid and/or unenforceable.[93] Genentech moved to dismiss these counterclaims on the basis that Amgen did not provide the information required by 42 U.S.C. § 262(*l*)(2)(A) and was therefore barred from bringing a declaratory judgment action under 42 U.S.C. § 262(*l*)(9)(C).[94] Amgen disputed that it was deficient in any of its disclosures under the BPCIA.[95] The court denied Genentech's motion without resolving the factual disputes between the parties, stating:

> I need not resolve the parties' factual disputes or decide whether Amgen complied with its [42 U.S.C. § 262(*l*)(2)(A)] obligations, because the filing of counterclaims does not constitute "bringing an action" and, therefore, is not barred by [42 U.S.C. § 262(*l*)(9)(C)]. . . . Accordingly, Amgen's counterclaims are not barred by [42 U.S.C. § 262(*l*)(9)(C)].[96]

89. *Id.* at *7.
90. *Id.*
91. Celltrion, Inc. v. Genentech, Inc., Nos. 2018-2160, -2161, 2018 WL 7046651, at *1 (Fed. Cir. Nov. 30, 2018).
92. No. 17-1407-CFC, 2020 WL 636439, at *1 (D. Del. Feb. 11, 2020).
93. *Id.*
94. *Id.* at *4.
95. *Id.*
96. *Id.*

chapter 10

Post-Issuance Review and Reexamination of Patents*

I. Post-Grant Review and Biosimilar Challenges

Since their creation in the America Invents Act (AIA), inter partes review (IPR) and post-grant review (PGR) proceedings have become a strategic consideration for companies concerned about patent infringement. In the biosimilar space, the use of IPRs and PGRs has become a central pillar of any biosimilar applicant strategy. Post-issuance proceedings are often attractive ways to challenge patents because, among other things, the burden of proof is generally lower than the clear and convincing standard required for district court litigation. Many biosimilar companies have used IPRs to challenge later-expiring patents directed to methods of therapeutic use, formulations, and drug product devices. If and when to file an IPR on a patent covering a branded biologic product is a significant consideration for biosimilar applicants. For the reference product sponsor of the branded biologic product, preparing for offensive PGR proceedings well in advance of the expiry of the 12-year exclusivity for a product is of critical importance. In addition, a reference product sponsor may need to make decisions about filing reissue or reexamination proceedings should the Patent Trial and Appeal Board (PTAB) invalidate the claims of the patent in a PGR proceeding, as well as whether to seek amendment of claims during an IPR proceeding. The strategic considerations relating to PGR proceedings are of paramount importance to all parties preparing for patent challenges arising from biosimilars.

---

*Nicholas Mitrokostas and Shaobo Zhu, A&O Shearman, Boston; Mena Gaballah, A&O Shearman, New York.

II. Current State of Post-Grant Challenges Impacting Biosimilar Products

According to the U.S. Patent and Trademark Office (USPTO), approximately 2 percent of all AIA petitions are directed to challenging biologic patents.[1] The USPTO also reports:

- PGR petitions are used more often to challenge biologic patents, as compared to "Orange Book"-listed patents.
- The institution rate for biologic patents (approximately 59 percent) is lower than the institution rate for Orange Book-listed patents (approximately 62 percent).
- Orange Book-listed patents have had a greater percentage of claims upheld in a final written decision (FWD) as compared to biologics patents.[2]

In addition, the number of PGR challenges to biologics patents have largely been relatively steady, albeit reducing since 2017, as shown in Figure 1.

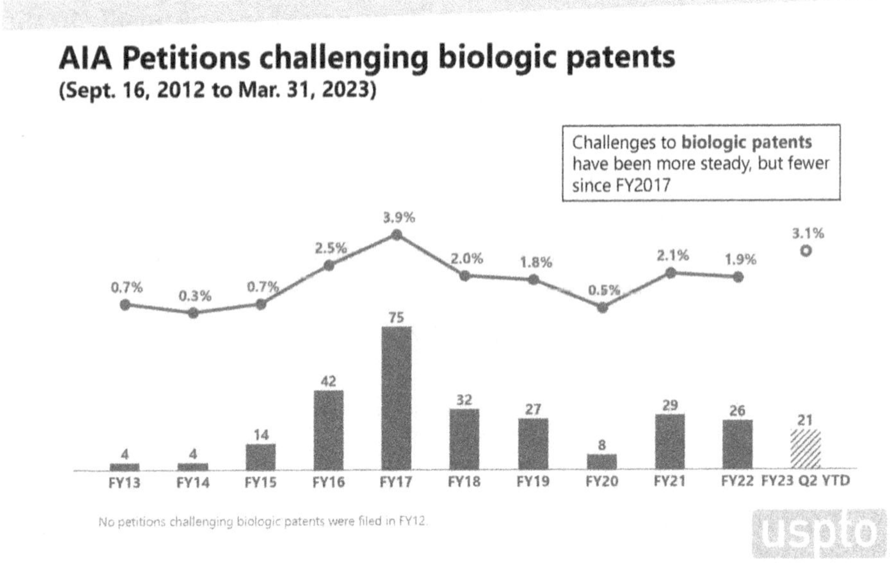

FIGURE 1. AIA Petitions Challenging Biologic Patents

The USPTO's data also shows that while nearly all of the claims in a biologics patent are challenged in an IPR or PGR petition, institution is granted in a little more than 50 percent of petitions filed, and approximately 57 percent of instituted claims are found unpatentable. In short,

1. USPTO, PTAB Orange Book Patent/Biologic Patent Study: FY23 Q2 Update (2023), https://www.uspto.gov/sites/default/files/documents/orange_book_biologics_study_update_thru_march__2023_.pdf.

2. *Id.*

approximately 25 percent of biologics patent claims challenged in an IPR or PGR are found to be unpatentable (see Figure 2).[3]

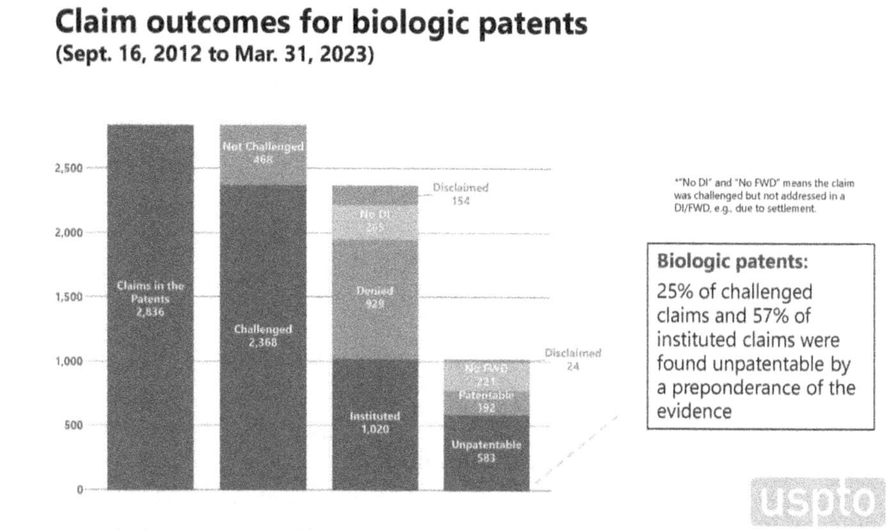

FIGURE 2. Claim Outcomes for Biologics Patents

While the institution rate for biologics patents challenged in PGR varies year by year, the institution rate for biologics patents is not materially different from other technologies (see Figures 3 and 4).[4]

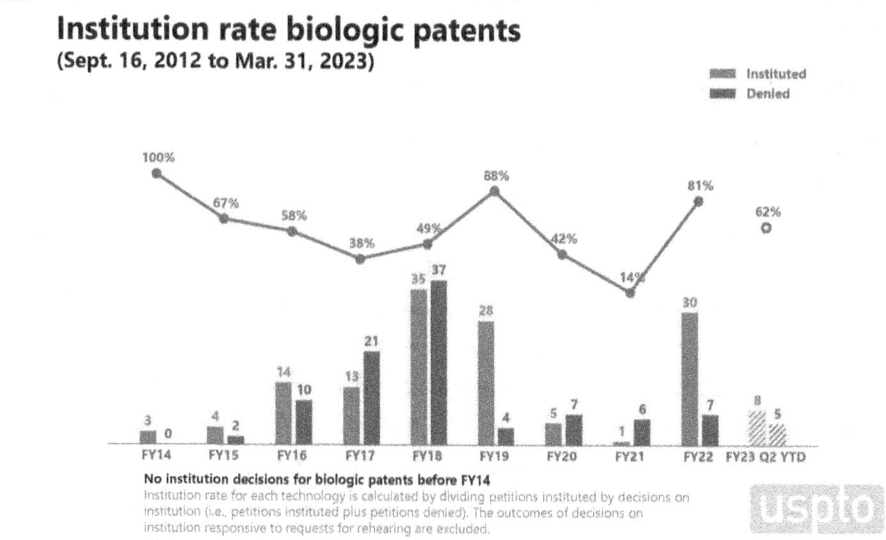

FIGURE 3. Institution Rate for Biologic Patents

3. *Id.*
4. *Id.*

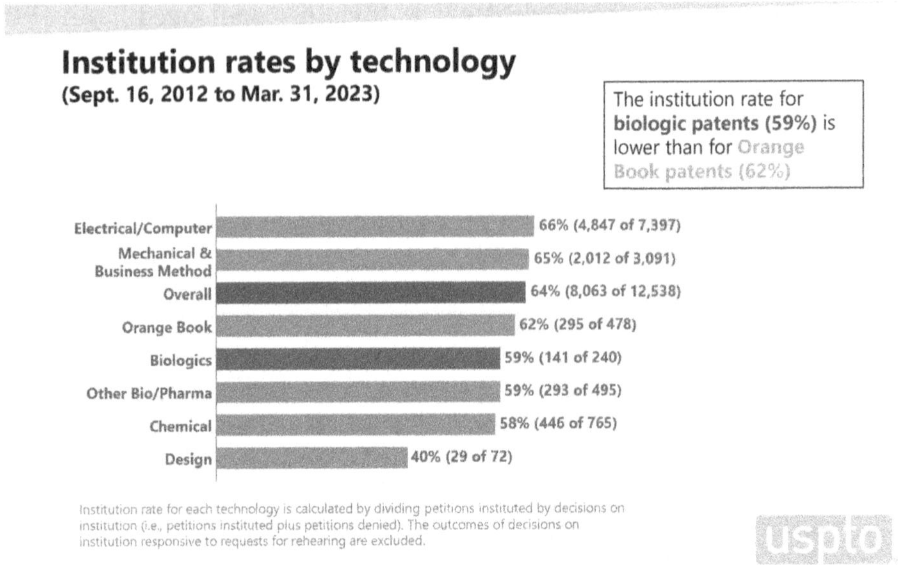

FIGURE 4. Institution Rates by Technology

For all of these reasons, it is not surprising that biosimilar applicants consider PGR proceedings as an important vehicle in their overall biosimilar strategy.

III. Strategic Considerations for Biosimilar Applicants and Reference Product Sponsors

A. Strategic Considerations for Biosimilar Applicants

1. Which Patents and Claims Should Be Challenged in PGR Proceedings?

For most biosimilar applicants, the filing of an IPR or PGR is not a question of *if* but *what* to challenge. One of the first strategic considerations for a biosimilar applicant is assessing and identifying the patents to challenge in post-issuance proceedings in view of its overall biosimilar strategy. Identifying relevant patents is not as straightforward in the biosimilar context as it is in the small-molecule context. Unlike the Orange Book, the "Purple Book" only lists patents that a reference product sponsor has already identified to biosimilar applicants as part of the "patent dance."[5] Therefore, for products that have not been the subject of the "patent dance"

5. 42 U.S.C. § 262(k)(9) (requiring the reference product sponsor, within 30 days of providing a list of patents under subsections (*l*)(3)(A) or (*l*)(7), to provide that list to the U.S. Food and Drug Administration).

previously, a biosimilar applicant may need to separately conduct searches to identify potentially relevant patents. This patent landscape analysis is typically expansive, intending to capture the entire scope of what could potentially pose a challenge from a freedom to operate perspective.

Once potentially relevant patents have been identified, a biosimilar applicant may need to assess such patents to determine which ones to challenge in post-issuance proceedings. A biosimilar applicant may consider factors including the strength of potential invalidity grounds, potential to design around the patent, the competitive landscape for other potential biosimilar applicants, the expiration of the patent, and the scope of the patent portfolio covering the reference product. These factors may also inform the decision regarding which specific claims within a patent to challenge.

For example, strong invalidity grounds may support a decision to challenge patents in post-issuance proceedings. In contrast, a strong noninfringement position based on a design-around or carve-out may favor forgoing post-issuance proceedings, especially if the biosimilar applicant has reason to believe that such noninfringement position is unavailable to competitors. Additionally, a biosimilar applicant may choose to wait out the expiration of a patent rather than challenge it such as in the case of, for example, a composition of matter patent for which there is no noninfringement defense. In practice, the decision to challenge a patent would require balancing all of these factors.

2. What Type of Proceeding Should Be Used?

Another early consideration for a biosimilar applicant challenging patents in post-issuance proceedings is determining which type of proceeding to pursue. Generally, IPR, PGR, and *ex parte* reexamination may be available. Biosimilar applicants may consider estoppel, relative strength of potential grounds, timing, and cost when deciding which type of proceeding to use.

As discussed in more detail later, the permitted grounds, eligibility for filing, window for filing, and scope of estoppel arising from post-issuance proceedings are different depending on the proceeding. Thus, the biosimilar applicant may need to weigh the strategic considerations for each.

For example, patents may be challenged in PGRs under a wide variety of grounds, including 35 U.S.C. §§ 101, 102, 103, and 112, while grounds in IPRs are limited to those under §§ 102 and 103 based on patents and publications. On the other hand, as discussed in detail later, the scope of PGR estoppel is broader than the scope of IPR estoppel. Thus, a biosimilar applicant may need to weigh the relative strength of the IPR-ineligible grounds vis-à-vis the IPR-eligible grounds against the scope of estoppel.

Additionally, to the extent a biosimilar applicant wishes to challenge patents in a PGR, it must closely monitor the prosecution and issuance of potentially relevant patents because PGR is generally only available to no later than nine months after patent issuance or issuance of reissue.

Ex parte reexamination is another avenue for challenging issued patents. Filing fees for ex parte reexaminations are lower than that of PGRs and IPRs,[6] and due to the ex parte nature of the proceeding, attorney fees are often also lower compared to that of PGRs and IPRs. However, because the ex parte reexamination requestor is only permitted limited involvement in the proceeding after the initial request, reexaminations may not be preferable for a party that wishes to be involved in the proceeding. Additionally, unlike IPRs, double patenting may be a ground for challenge in ex parte reexaminations.[7] A biosimilar applicant considering this approach may need to weigh the cost, speed, and available grounds for ex parte reexaminations against the limited control it may have in the proceeding.

3. When Should Patents Be Challenged?

Another early strategic decision for biosimilar applicants wishing to challenge patents through post-issuance proceedings is the matter of timing. The timing question can be complex and may need to take into consideration the biosimilar applicant's regulatory and development strategy. This is because the timing considerations may need to account for standing implications. Although there is no standing requirement for filing IPRs and PGRs, a biosimilar applicant must demonstrate that it has standing in federal courts on appeal. A biosimilar applicant must have an abbreviated biologics license application (aBLA) filed with the U.S. Food and Drug Administration (FDA) to have standing to appeal an unfavorable decision.[8]

For example, IPR proceedings typically take no longer than 18 months to arrive at a FWD, and a party has 63 days to file a notice of appeal. This means that a biosimilar applicant should attempt to time its IPR so that it will have an aBLA filed by the time of the likely deadline for appealing an adverse IPR decision. An IPR petitioner should also keep in mind that

6. *USPTO Fee Schedule*, USPTO, https://www.uspto.gov/learning-and-resources/fees-and-payment/uspto-fee-schedule (last revised Jan. 17, 2024).

7. *See In re* Lonardo, 119 F.3d 960 (Fed. Cir. 1997); *see also In re* Cellect, LLC, No. 2022-1293 (Fed. Cir. Aug. 28, 2023).

8. Sandoz Inc. v. Amgen Inc., 773 F.3d 1274 (Fed. Cir. 2014) (finding no case or controversy where Sandoz had filed a declaratory judgment action seeking to invalidate patents before it had even filed an aBLA); *see also* Celltrion Healthcare Co., Ltd. v. Kennedy Tr. for Rheumatology Rsch., No. 14 Civ. 2256(PAC), 2014 WL 6765996 (S.D.N.Y. Dec. 1, 2014).

there are ways for the patent owner to expedite the IPR proceeding, such as by waiving the patent owner's preliminary response.[9]

4. Estoppel

Estoppel is another strategic consideration to take into account for post-issuance proceedings. In the case of post-issuance proceedings, both collateral estoppel and statutory estoppel under 35 U.S.C. §§ 315 and 325 are relevant.

With respect to collateral estoppel:

> The party seeking to invoke collateral estoppel must show: (1) the issue is identical to one decided in the first action; (2) the issue was actually litigated in the first action; (3) resolution of the issue was essential to a final judgment in the first action; and (4) [the party against whom collateral estoppel is being asserted] had a full and fair opportunity to litigate the issue in the first action.[10]

Of note, in the IPR context, collateral estoppel may attach for unadjudicated patent claims that used slightly different language to describe substantially the same invention as adjudicated patent claims if the differences between the adjudicated and the unadjudicated claims do not materially alter the question of invalidity.[11]

Statutory provisions under 35 U.S.C. §§ 315(e) and 325(e) set forth the scope of estoppel in the IPR and PGR contexts, respectively. These similar provisions preclude a petition or real party in interest from asserting in a civil action, International Trade Commission (ITC) section 337 proceeding, or proceeding before the USPTO any invalidity ground that the petitioner raised or reasonably could have raised during the IPR or PGR. Estoppel under these provisions applies upon issuance of a FWD in these types of actions.[12] Additionally, estoppel only applies to the claims that were challenged in an IPR or PGR, and, therefore, a biosimilar applicant should take careful consideration in deciding whether to challenge all or some claims of a patent.

In the IPR estoppel context, courts have held that grounds that a petitioner "reasonably could have raised" include any grounds that "a skilled searcher conducting a diligent search reasonably could have been expected

9. 37 C.F.R. § 42.107 (2023).
10. Google LLC v. Hammond Dev. Int'l, Inc., 54 F.4th 1377, 1381 (Fed. Cir. 2022).
11. *Id.*
12. 35 U.S.C. §§ 315(e), 325(e).

to discover."[13] There are open questions as to whether non-patent/non-publication prior art relating to the patent or publication prior art asserted as ground is also precluded under IPR estoppel.[14] Thus, a biosimilar applicant challenging a patent should carefully consider which grounds to include in its petition.

The scope of PGR estoppel is an issue that has not been widely addressed. The question is whether a petitioner would be estopped from later raising any of the eligible invalidity grounds available for PGR (i.e., grounds under §§ 101, 102, 103, 112, etc.), and therefore must raise all invalidity grounds in the PGR. Although § 325(e) may be read to encompass such a broad scope of estoppel, there have been few decisions addressing this issue.

B. Strategic Considerations for Reference Product Sponsors

1. Amending Claims

A patent owner may wish to amend or obtain new claims for a patent in response to validity challenges. As discussed earlier, there are multiple ways to amend claims post-issuance: reissue, reexamination, and motions to amend (MTAs) the claims during an IPR proceeding.[15] Such amendments typically cannot broaden the issued claims and must satisfy the requirements of 35 U.S.C. § 112; however, a patent owner may broaden claims in a reissue if a broadening reissue request is filed within two years of issuance of the original patent, and the original patent contains support for the embodiment sought.[16]

Furthermore, patent owners should take into consideration that potential infringers may be shielded from new or modified claims under intervening rights.[17] Therefore, patent owners should assess how such claim amendments may impact any prior damages.

---

13. *See* Ironburg Inventions Ltd. v. Valve Corp., 64 F.4th 1274, 1297 (Fed. Cir. 2023); *see also* SiOnyx, LLC v. Hamamatsu Photonics K.K., 330 F. Supp. 3d 574, 602 (D. Mass. 2018); *see also* Clearlamp, LLC v. LKQ Corp., No. 12 C 2533, 2016 WL 4734389, at *8 (N.D. Ill. Mar. 18, 2016). The initial burden to show what a skilled searcher reasonably could have been expected to discover lies with the party asserting estoppel.

14. Chemours Co. FC, LLC v. Daikin Indus., Ltd., No. CV 17-1612 (MN), 2022 WL 2643517, at *2 (D. Del. July 8, 2022); Wasica Fin. GmbH v. Schrader Int'l, Inc., 432 F. Supp. 3d 448, 454 (D. Del. 2020); Bos. Sci. Corp. v. Cook Grp. Inc., No. 117CV03448JRSMJD, 2023 WL 1452172, at *2 (S.D. Ind. Jan. 31, 2023).

15. On March 15, 2019, the USPTO initiated an MTA for the pilot program that allows patent owners to receive preliminary guidance from the PTAB on the merits of an MTA and an opportunity for a patent owner to file a revised MTA. The USPTO has since extended the program to September 16, 2024. 87 Fed. Reg. 60,134 (Oct. 4, 2022).

16. *See* 35 U.S.C. § 305; *id.* § 251(d).

17. *See id.* § 252; *see also id.* §§ 307(b), 316(b).

One important consideration for patent owners considering a potential MTA strategy is the selection of counsel for an IPR proceeding. A prosecution bar typically will prohibit litigation counsel receiving confidential information from a litigation defendant from participating in patent prosecution, including potentially claim amendments made during an IPR proceeding. Patent owners should consider whether separate counsel either within the same firm, if permitted, or at different firms is needed for an IPR proceeding during co-pending litigation when there is a reasonable possibility that the patent owner may amend the challenged claims during the IPR proceeding.

One recent development in claim amendment procedures during an IPR proceeding is the use of preliminary guidance for an MTA. In 2019, the USPTO instituted a Motion to Amend Pilot Program that permits patent owners to request preliminary guidance from the PTAB panel on proposed amended claims. Following receipt of preliminary guidance, the patent owner, at its option, may proceed with its original MTA, may submit a revised MTA with a different set of proposed claims, or may withdraw the MTA entirely. According to a March 2023 USPTO study, since 2019, of the "2,832 trials that were instituted during the MTA pilot program, 9% (264) of instituted trials included a MTA" and, "of the 264 instituted trials with an MTA, 88% (232) included a request for preliminary guidance."[18] According to the study, 72 percent (168) of the 232 trials with an MTA requesting preliminary guidance filed either a patent owner reply (41) or a revised MTA (127).[19] Finally, the study found that "24% of final determinations had at least one proposed substitute claim granted entry, as opposed to 14% of final determinations prior to the MTA pilot program."[20] The USPTO recently announced its intention to adopt the practice permanently through rulemaking.[21]

18. USPTO, PATENT TRIAL AND APPEAL BOARD MOTION TO AMEND (MTA) STUDY: INSTALLMENT 8 (2023), https://www.uspto.gov/sites/default/files/documents/mta_installment_8_.pdf.
19. *Id.*
20. *Id.*
21. *Id.*

C. *Considerations for Both Reference Product Sponsors and Biosimilar Applicants*

1. Claim Construction

Claim construction can often implicate strategy considerations for both the patent owner and patent challenger.[22] For example, a patentee's disclaimer during an IPR can bind the patentee to a narrower claim interpretation in a subsequent proceeding.[23] Similarly, a patent challenger may need to consider ways to use claim construction strategically to establish a record that might be beneficial for other issues such as infringement or non-prior art grounds for invalidity.

2. Experts

One consideration that both biosimilar applicants and reference product sponsors may face includes the use of experts. Both parties may consider whether to rely on the same expert or experts in the post-issuance proceeding as they would in district court litigation. Benefits to using the same experts may include efficiency and consistency of opinions; however, parties may need to take care in developing these experts' opinions to avoid creating inconsistent positions with respect to certain issues. For example, factual issues underlying novelty or obviousness may be at odds with those underlying other issues, such as enablement or written description.

---

22. On October 11, 2018, the USPTO issued rules changing the patent claim construction standard used by the PTAB in AIA proceedings from the "broadest reasonable interpretation" standard to the "*Phillips*" claim construction standard used by the federal courts and ITC. 83 Fed. Reg. 51,340 (Oct. 11, 2018).

23. Aylus Networks, Inc. v. Apple Inc., 856 F.3d 1353 (Fed. Cir. 2017).

IV. Biosimilar Challenges: Case Studies

Molecule	Parties	IPR Nos.	Patents	Key Points
Eylea (aflibercept)	Mylan (patent challenger) Regeneron (patent owner)	IPR2021-00880 (IPR2022-00257 and IPR2022-00301 joined)	9,669,069 Use of a vascular endothelial growth factor (VEGF) antagonist to treat angiogenic eye disorders (method of use (MOU))	• Method-of-treatment patent with 12 claims • Independent claim 1: A method for treating an angiogenic eye disorder in a patient, said method comprising sequentially administering to the patient a single initial dose of a VEGF antagonist, followed by one or more secondary doses of the VEGF antagonist, followed by one or more tertiary doses of the VEGF antagonist; wherein each secondary dose is administered 2 to 4 weeks after the immediately preceding dose; and wherein each tertiary dose is administered on an as-needed/pro re nata (PRN) basis, based on visual and/or anatomical outcomes as assessed by a physician or other qualified medical professional; wherein the VEGF antagonist is a receptor-based chimeric molecule comprising (1) a VEGFR1 component comprising amino acids 27–129 of SEQ ID NO:2; (2) a VEGFR2 component comprising amino acids 130–231 of SEQ ID NO:2; and (3) a multimerization component comprising amino acids 232–457 of SEQ ID NO:2 • Mylan asserted 5 grounds of invalidity (3 anticipation, 1 anticipation and/or obviousness, 1 obviousness) • FWD • Finding anticipation on grounds I and IV of all challenged claims (FWD at 68) • Finding that, because all challenged claims were anticipated on grounds I and IV, PTAB did not address remaining grounds (FWD at 72–73)

Molecule	Parties	IPR Nos.	Patents	Key Points
		IPR2021-00881 (IPR2022-00258 and IPR2022-00298 joined)	9,254,338 Use of a VEGF antagonist to treat angiogenic eye disorders (MOU)	• Method-of-treatment patent with 26 claims • Independent claim 1: A method for treating an angiogenic eye disorder in a patient, said method comprising sequentially administering to the patient a single initial dose of a VEGF antagonist, followed by one or more secondary doses of the VEGF antagonist, followed by one or more tertiary doses of the VEGF antagonist; wherein each secondary dose is administered 2 to 4 weeks after the immediately preceding dose; and wherein each tertiary dose is administered at least 8 weeks after the immediately preceding dose; wherein the VEGF antagonist is a VEGF receptor-based chimeric molecule comprising (1) a VEGFR1 component comprising amino acids 27–129 of SEQ ID NO:2; (2) a VEGFR2 component comprising amino acids 130–231 of SEQ ID NO:2; and (3) a multimerization component comprising amino acids 232–457 of SEQ ID NO:2 • Mylan asserted 6 grounds of invalidity (5 anticipation, 1 obviousness) • FWD • Finding anticipation on ground I of all challenged claims (FWD at 45) • Finding that, because all challenged claims were anticipated on ground I, board did not address remaining grounds (FWD at 46)

Molecule	Parties	IPR Nos.	Patents	Key Points
		IPR2022-01225	10,130,681 Use of a VEGF antagonist to treat angiogenic eye disorders (MOU)	• Method-of-treatment patent with 26 claims • Independent claim 1: A method for treating an angiogenic eye disorder in a patient, said method comprising sequentially administering to the patient a single initial dose of a VEGF antagonist, followed by one or more secondary doses of the VEGF antagonist, followed by one or more tertiary doses of the VEGF antagonist; wherein each secondary dose is administered 2 to 4 weeks after the immediately preceding dose; and wherein each tertiary dose is administered at least 8 weeks after the immediately preceding dose; wherein the VEGF antagonist is a VEGF receptor-based chimeric molecule comprising (1) a VEGFR1 component comprising amino acids 27–129 of SEQ ID NO:2; (2) a VEGFR2 component comprising amino acids 130–231 of SEQ ID NO:2; and (3) a multimerization component comprising amino acids 232–457 of SEQ ID NO:2; wherein exclusion criteria for the patient include all of: (1) active intraocular inflammation; (2) active ocular or periocular infection; (3) any ocular or periocular infection within the last 2 weeks prior to treatment • Mylan asserted 6 grounds of invalidity (3 anticipation, 3 obviousness) • FWD • Finding anticipation on ground I of all challenged claims (FWD at 61) • Finding that, because all challenged claims were anticipated on ground I, board did not address remaining grounds (FWD at 61)

Molecule	Parties	IPR Nos.	Patents	Key Points
		IPR2022-01226	10,888,601 Use of a VEGF antagonist to treat angiogenic eye disorders (MOU)	• Method-of-treatment patent with 47 claims • Independent claim 1: A method for treating age-related macular degeneration in a patient in need thereof, comprising intravitreally administering, to said patient, an effective amount of aflibercept, which is 2 milligrams (mg) approximately every 4 weeks for the first 3 months, followed by 2 mg approximately once every 8 weeks or once every 2 months • Mylan asserted 7 grounds of invalidity (4 anticipation, 3 obviousness) • FWD • Finding anticipation on ground I of all challenged claims (FWD at 91–92) • Finding that, because all challenged claims were anticipated on ground I, board did not address remaining grounds (FWD at 91–92)
		IPR2023-00099	10,857,205 Use of a VEGF antagonist to treat angiogenic eye disorders (MOU)	• Method-of-treatment patent with 3 claims • Independent claim 1: A method for treating macular edema following retinal vein occlusion in a human subject comprising administering 2 mg aflibercept to the subject by intravitreal injection once every 4 weeks • Mylan asserted 7 grounds of invalidity (3 anticipation, 4 obviousness) • Institution decision • Denied in view of patent owner filing statutory disclaimer, disclaiming all challenged claims (decision at 5)

Molecule	Parties	IPR Nos.	Patents	Key Points
Eylea (aflibercept)	Celltrion (patent challenger) Regeneron (patent owner)	IPR2022-00257 This IPR was joined with IPR2021-00880 and IPR2022- 00301	9,669,069 Use of a VEGF antagonist to treat angiogenic eye disorders (MOU)	See IPR2021-00880
		IPR2022-00258 This IPR was joined with IPR2021-00881 and IPR2022- 00298	9,254,338 Use of a VEGF antagonist to treat angiogenic eye disorders (MOU)	See IPR2021-00881
		IPR2023-00462	10,464,992 VEGF antagonist formulations suitable for intravitreal administration (formulation)	• Formulation patent with 18 claims • Independent claim 1: A vial comprising a VEGF antagonist, an organic co-solvent, a buffer, and a stabilizing agent, wherein the VEGF antagonist is a fusion protein produced in a Chinese hamster ovary (CHO) cell, the fusion protein comprising an immunoglobin-like (Ig) domain 2 of a first VEGF receptor and Ig domain 3 of a second VEGF receptor, and a multimerizing component; and wherein at least 98% of the VEGF antagonist is present in native conformation following storage at 5°C for 2 months as measured by size-exclusion chromatography • Celltrion asserted 2 grounds for invalidity (1 anticipation, 1 obviousness) • Adverse judgment after institution • Board held that patent owner's disclaimer of all claims of the '992 patent would be treated as adverse judgment with respect to all claims (adverse judgment at 2)

Molecule	Parties	IPR Nos.	Patents	Key Points
		IPR2023-00533	10,888,601 Use of a VEGF antagonist to treat angiogenic eye disorders (MOU)	• MOU patent with 47 claims • Independent claim 1: A method for treating age-related macular degeneration in a patient in need thereof, comprising intravitreally administering, to said patient, an effective amount of aflibercept, which is 2 mg approximately every 4 weeks for the first 3 months, followed by 2 mg approximately once every 8 weeks or once every 2 months • Celltrion asserted 7 grounds for invalidity (4 anticipation, 3 obviousness) • FWD • Finding anticipation on ground I of all challenged claims (FWD at 91–92) • Finding that, because all challenged claims were anticipated on ground I, board did not address remaining grounds (FWD at 91–92)

Molecule	Parties	IPR Nos.	Patents	Key Points
		IPR2023-00532	10,130,681 Use of a VEGF antagonist to treat angiogenic eye disorders (MOU)	• Method-of-treatment patent with 26 claims • Independent claim 1: A method for treating an angiogenic eye disorder in a patient, said method comprising sequentially administering to the patient a single initial dose of a VEGF antagonist, followed by one or more secondary doses of the VEGF antagonist, followed by one or more tertiary doses of the VEGF antagonist; wherein each secondary dose is administered 2 to 4 weeks after the immediately preceding dose; and wherein each tertiary dose is administered at least 8 weeks after the immediately preceding dose; wherein the VEGF antagonist is a VEGF receptor-based chimeric molecule comprising (1) a VEGFR1 component comprising amino acids 27–129 of SEQ ID NO:2; (2) a VEGFR2 component comprising amino acids 130–231 of SEQ ID NO:2; and (3) a multimerization component comprising amino acids 232–457 of SEQ ID NO:2; wherein exclusion criteria for the patient includes all of: (1) active intraocular inflammation; (2) active ocular or periocular infection; (3) any ocular or periocular infection within the last 2 weeks prior to treatment • Celltrion asserted 6 grounds for invalidity (3 anticipation, 3 obviousness) • FWD • Finding anticipation on ground I of all challenged claims (FWD at 61) • Finding that, because all challenged claims were anticipated on ground I, board did not address remaining grounds (FWD at 61)

Molecule	Parties	IPR Nos.	Patents	Key Points
		IPR2023-00620	10,406,226 Method of manufacturing VEGF antagonist fusion proteins (MOU)	• Method-of-manufacturing patent with 4 claims • Independent claim 1: A method of manufacturing a VEGF antagonist fusion protein, said method comprising (a) expressing said VEGF antagonist fusion protein in a CHO cell comprising a polynucleotide encoding the VEGF antagonist fusion protein, which comprises amino acids 27–457 of SEQ ID NO:2 wherein said fusion protein binds VEGF; and (b) purifying said VEGF antagonist fusion proteins; wherein at least 90% of the weight of the purified fusion protein is not present as an aggregate • Celltrion asserted 3 grounds for invalidity (obviousness) • Institution decision denied due to disclaimer of all challenged claims

Molecule	Parties	IPR Nos.	Patents	Key Points
		PGR2021- 00117	10,857,231 Formulations of VEG antagonist fusion proteins and method of manufacturing them (formulation and method)	• Formulation patent and method-of-manufacturing patent with 114 claims • Independent claim 1: A formulation comprising 10–50 milligrams per milliliter (mg/ml) of a VEGF antagonist fusion protein comprising amino acids 27–457 of SEQ ID NO:4, a buffer comprising histidine, an organic co-solvent comprising polysorbate, and a stabilizing agent comprising a sugar, an amino acid, or both, wherein said VEGF antagonist fusion protein exhibits less than about 3% degradation after 15 months of storage at 5°C • Independent claim 33: A method of manufacturing a liquid formulation, said method comprising combining a VEGF antagonist fusion protein that comprises amino acids 27–457 of SEQ ID NO:4 with a buffer comprising histidine, an organic co-solvent comprising polysorbate, and a stabilizing agent comprising a sugar, an amino acid, or both; wherein the concentration of said VEGF antagonist fusion protein is 10–50 mg/ml in said liquid formulation; and wherein said VEGF antagonist fusion protein exhibits less than about 3% degradation after 15 months of storage at 5°C • Celltrion asserted 4 grounds for invalidity (1 written description, 1 enablement, 1 indefiniteness, 1 obviousness) • Institution decision denied due to disclaimer of all challenged claims

Molecule	Parties	IPR Nos.	Patents	Key Points
Eylea (aflibercept)	Apotex (patent challenger) Regeneron (patent owner)	IPR2022-00298	9,254,338 Use of a VEGF antagonist to treat angiogenic eye disorders (MOU)	• Method-of-treatment patent with 26 claims • Independent claim 1: A method for treating an angiogenic eye disorder in a patient, said method comprising sequentially administering to the patient a single initial dose of a VEGF antagonist, followed by one or more secondary doses of the VEGF antagonist, followed by one or more tertiary doses of the VEGF antagonist; wherein each secondary dose is administered 2 to 4 weeks after the immediately preceding dose; and wherein each tertiary dose is administered at least 8 weeks after the immediately preceding dose; wherein the VEGF antagonist is a VEGF receptor-based chimeric molecule comprising (1) a VEGFR1 component comprising amino acids 27–129 of SEQ ID NO:2; (2) a VEGFR2 component comprising amino acids 130–231 of SEQ ID NO:2; and (3) a multimerization component comprising amino acids 232–457 of SEQ ID NO:2 • Apotex asserted 6 grounds for invalidity (5 anticipation, 1 obviousness) • FWD finding all challenged claims unpatentable
		IPR2022-00301 This IPR was joined with IPR2021-00880 and IPR2022- 00257	9,669,069 Use of a VEGF antagonist to treat angiogenic eye disorders (MOU)	See IPR2021-00880

Molecule	Parties	IPR Nos.	Patents	Key Points
		IPR2022-01524	11,253,572 Use of a VEGF antagonist to treat angiogenic eye disorders (MOU)	• Method-of-treatment patent with 30 claims • Independent claim 1: A method of treating an angiogenic eye disorder in a patient in need thereof comprising sequentially administering to the patient by intravitreal injection a single initial dose of 2 mg of aflibercept, followed by one or more secondary doses of 2 mg of aflibercept, followed by one or more tertiary doses of 2 mg of aflibercept; wherein each secondary dose is administered approximately 4 weeks following the immediately preceding dose; and wherein each tertiary dose is administered approximately 8 weeks following the immediately preceding dose; wherein the patient achieves a gain in visual acuity within 52 weeks following the initial dose • Apotex asserted 5 grounds for invalidity (4 anticipation, 1 obviousness) • Institution decision denied

Molecule	Parties	IPR Nos.	Patents	Key Points
Eylea (aflibercept)	Samsung Bioepsis Co. (patent challenger) Regeneron (patent owner)	IPR2023-00442	10,130,681 Use of a VEGF antagonist to treat angiogenic eye disorders (MOU)	• Method-of-treatment patent with 26 claims • Independent claim 1: A method for treating an angiogenic eye disorder in a patient, said method comprising sequentially administering to the patient a single initial dose of a VEGF antagonist, followed by one or more secondary doses of the VEGF antagonist, followed by one or more tertiary doses of the VEGF antagonist; wherein each secondary dose is administered 2 to 4 weeks after the immediately preceding dose; and wherein each tertiary dose is administered at least 8 weeks after the immediately preceding dose; wherein the VEGF antagonist is a VEGF receptor-based chimeric molecule comprising (1) a VEGFR1 component comprising amino acids 27–129 of SEQ ID NO:2; (2) a VEGFR2 component comprising amino acids 130–231 of SEQ ID NO:2; and (3) a multimerization component comprising amino acids 232–457 of SEQ ID NO:2; wherein exclusion criteria for the patient include all of: (1) active intraocular inflammation; (2) active ocular or periocular infection; (3) any ocular or periocular infection within the last 2 weeks prior to treatment • Petitioner asserted 1 ground for invalidity (obviousness) • Institution decision granted

Molecule	Parties	IPR Nos.	Patents	Key Points
		IPR2023-00566	10,888,601 Use of a VEGF antagonist to treat angiogenic eye disorders (MOU)	• Method-of-treatment patent with 47 claims • Independent claim 1: A method for treating age-related macular degeneration in a patient in need thereof, comprising intravitreally administering, to said patient, an effective amount of aflibercept, which is 2 mg approximately every 4 weeks for the first 3 months, followed by 2 mg approximately once every 8 weeks or once every 2 months. • Petitioner asserted 7 grounds for invalidity (4 anticipation, 3 obviousness) • FWD • Finding anticipation on ground I of all challenged claims (FWD at 91–92) • Finding that, because all challenged claims were anticipated on ground I, board did not address remaining grounds (FWD at 91–92)
		IPR2023-00739	10,888,601 Use of a VEGF antagonist to treat angiogenic eye disorders (MOU)	• Method-of-treatment patent with 47 claims • Independent claim 1: A method for treating age-related macular degeneration in a patient in need thereof, comprising intravitreally administering, to said patient, an effective amount of aflibercept, which is 2 mg approximately every 4 weeks for the first 3 months, followed by 2 mg approximately once every 8 weeks or once every 2 months • Petitioner asserted 6 grounds for invalidity (1 anticipation and/or obviousness, 5 obviousness)

Molecule	Parties	IPR Nos.	Patents	Key Points
		IPR2023-00884	11,253,572 Use of a VEGF antagonist to treat angiogenic eye disorders (MOU)	• Method-of-treatment patent with 30 claims • Independent claim 1: A method of treating an angiogenic eye disorder in a patient in need thereof comprising sequentially administering to the patient by intravitreal injection a single initial dose of 2 mg of aflibercept, followed by one or more secondary doses of 2 mg of aflibercept, followed by one or more tertiary doses of 2 mg of aflibercept; wherein each secondary dose is administered approximately 4 weeks following the immediately preceding dose; and wherein each tertiary dose is administered approximately 8 weeks following the immediately preceding dose; wherein the patient achieves a gain in visual acuity within 52 weeks following the initial dose • Petitioner asserted 11 grounds for invalidity (5 anticipation, 6 obviousness) • Institution decision granted

Molecule	Parties	IPR Nos.	Patents	Key Points
		IPR2023-01312	10,464,992 VEGF antagonist formulations suitable for intravitreal administration (formulation)	• Formulation patent with 18 claims • Independent claim 1: A vial comprising a VEGF antagonist, an organic co-solvent, a buffer, and a stabilizing agent, wherein the VEGF antagonist is a fusion protein produced in a CHO cell, the fusion protein comprising an Ig domain 2 of a first VEGF receptor and Ig domain 3 of a second VEGF receptor, and a multimerizing component; and wherein at least 98% of the VEGF antagonist is present in native conformation following storage at 5°C for 2 months as measured by size-exclusion chromatography • Petitioner asserted 2 grounds for invalidity (1 anticipation, 1 obviousness) • Adverse judgment after institution • Board held that patent owner's disclaimer of all claims of the '992 patent would be treated as adverse judgment with respect to all claims (adverse judgment at 2)
Eylea (aflibercept)	Chengdu Kanghong Biotechnology Co. (patent challenger) Regeneron (patent owner)	IPR2021-00402	10,464,992 VEGF antagonist formulations suitable for intravitreal administration (formulation)	• Formulation patent with 18 claims • Independent claim 1: A vial comprising a VEGF antagonist, an organic co-solvent, a buffer, and a stabilizing agent, wherein the VEGF antagonist is a fusion protein produced in a CHO cell, the fusion protein comprising an Ig domain 2 of a first VEGF receptor and Ig domain 3 of a second VEGF receptor, and a multimerizing component; and wherein at least 98% of the VEGF antagonist is present in native conformation following storage at 5°C for 2 months as measured by size-exclusion chromatography • Chengdu asserted 3 grounds for invalidity (1 anticipation, 2 obviousness) • Chengdu filed a motion to dismiss the petition and to terminate the proceeding, which was granted

Molecule	Parties	IPR Nos.	Patents	Key Points
		PGR2021- 00035	10,828,345 Use of a VEGF antagonist to treat angiogenic eye disorders (MOU)	• Method-of-treatment patent with 11 claims • Independent claim 1: A method for treating an angiogenic eye disorder in a patient, said method comprising sequentially administering to the patient a single initial dose of a VEGF antagonist, followed by one or more secondary doses of the VEGF antagonist, followed by one or more tertiary doses of the VEGF antagonist; wherein each secondary dose is administered 4 weeks after the immediately preceding dose; and wherein each tertiary dose is administered 12 weeks after the immediately preceding dose; wherein the VEGF antagonist is a receptor-based chimeric molecule comprising an Ig domain 2 of a first VEGF receptor, which is FLT1 and Ig domain 3 of a second VEGF receptor, which is FLK1, and a multimerizing component • Chengdu asserted 3 grounds for invalidity (1 anticipation, 1 obviousness, 1 written description) • Chengdu filed a motion to dismiss the petition and to terminate the proceeding, which was granted

Molecule	Parties	IPR Nos.	Patents	Key Points
Humira (adalimumab)	Sandoz Inc. (patent challenger) AbbVie (patent owner)	IPR2018-00156	9,187,559 Multiple-variable dose regimen for treating idiopathic inflammatory bowel disease (MOU)	• Method-of-treatment patent with 30 claims • Independent claim 1: A multiple-variable dose method for treating idiopathic inflammatory bowel disease in a human subject in need thereof, comprising subcutaneously administering to the human subject: a first dose of 160 mg of adalimumab administered to the human subject within a day; and a second dose of 80 mg of adalimumab administered to the human subject within a day, wherein the second dose is administered 2 weeks following administration of the first dose • Sandoz asserted 1 ground for invalidity (obviousness) • Institution decision denied
		IPR2018-00002	9,512,216 Use of tumor necrosis factor alpha (TNFα) inhibitor (MOU)	• Method-of-treatment patent with 16 claims • Independent claim 1: A method for treating moderate to severe chronic plaque psoriasis, comprising subcutaneously administering to an adult patient having moderate to severe chronic plaque psoriasis an initial dose of 80 mg of adalimumab, followed by 40 mg of adalimumab every other week starting 1 week after said first dosing, wherein the patient achieves at least Psoriasis Area and Severity Index (PASI) 75 response at week 12 of the treatment • Sandoz asserted 1 ground for invalidity (obviousness) • Institution decision denied • Sandoz appealed decision

Molecule	Parties	IPR Nos.	Patents	Key Points
		IPR2017-02106	9,067,992 Use of TNFα inhibitor for treatment of psoriatic arthritis (MOU)	• Method-of-treatment patent with 9 claims • Independent claim 1: A method of treatment of moderate to severe active psoriatic arthritis in adult patients, wherein each said patient has ≥3 swollen and ≥3 tender joints prior to the treatment and has failed nonsteroidal anti-inflammatory drug (NSAID) therapy, comprising subcutaneously administering to each said patient 40 mg of adalimumab every other week, wherein 23% of said patients achieve 70% reduction in American College of Rheumatology (ACR) score at week 24 of the treatment • Sandoz asserted 3 grounds for invalidity (1 anticipation, 2 obviousness) • Institution decision granted • Case settled prior to FWD
		IPR2017-02105	9,090,689 Use of TNFα inhibitor for treatment of psoriasis (MOU)	• Method-of-treatment patent with 21 claims • Independent claim 1: A method of administering adalimumab for treatment of moderate to severe chronic plaque psoriasis, comprising filling adalimumab into vessels and subcutaneously administering 40 mg of said adalimumab to a patient having moderate to severe chronic plaque psoriasis every other week • Sandoz asserted 2 grounds for invalidity (obviousness) • Institution decision granted • Case settled prior to FWD

Molecule	Parties	IPR Nos.	Patents	Key Points
		IPR2017-01988	8,974,790 Methods of administering anti-TNFα antibodies (MOU)	• Method-of-treatment patent with 6 claims • Independent claim 1: A method for treating ulcerative colitis in a human subject, comprising administering subcutaneously to a human subject having ulcerative colitis a total body dose of 40 mg of a human anti-TNFα antibody once every 13–15 days for a time period sufficient to treat the ulcerative colitis, wherein the anti-TNFα antibody comprises an IgG1 heavy chain constant region; a variable light (VL) chain region comprising a complementarity-determining region (CDR)1 having the amino acid sequence of SEQ ID NO:7, a CDR2 having the amino acid sequence of SEQ ID NO:5, and a CDR3 having the amino acid sequence of SEQ ID NO:3; and a variable heavy (VH) chain region comprising a CDR1 having the amino acid sequence of SEQ ID NO:8, a CDR2 having the amino acid sequence of SEQ ID NO:6, and a CDR3 having the amino acid sequence of SEQ ID NO:4 • Sandoz asserted 2 grounds for invalidity (obviousness) • Institution decision denied

Molecule	Parties	IPR Nos.	Patents	Key Points
		IPR2017-01987	8,911,737 Methods of administering anti-TNFα antibodies (MOU)	• Method-of-treatment patent with 6 claims • Independent claim 1: A method for treating Crohn's disease in a human subject, comprising administering subcutaneously to a human subject having Crohn's disease a total body dose of 40 mg of a human anti-TNFα antibody once every 13–15 days for a time period sufficient to treat Crohn's disease, wherein the anti-TNFα antibody comprises an IgG1 heavy chain constant region; a VL chain region comprising a CDR1 having the amino acid sequence of SEQ ID NO:7, a CDR2 having the amino acid sequence of SEQ ID NO:5, a CDR3 having the amino acid sequence of SEQ ID NO:3; a VH chain region comprising a CDR1 having the amino acid sequence of SEQ ID NO:8, a CDR2 having the amino acid sequence of SEQ ID NO:6, and a CDR3 having the amino acid sequence of SEQ ID NO:4 • Sandoz asserted 2 grounds for invalidity (obviousness) • Institution decision denied
		IPR2017-01824	9,512,216 Use of a TNFα inhibitor (MOU)	• Method-of-treatment patent with 16 claims • Independent claim 1: A method for treating moderate to severe chronic plaque psoriasis, comprising subcutaneously administering to an adult patient having moderate to severe chronic plaque psoriasis an initial dose of 80 mg of adalimumab, followed by 40 mg of adalimumab every other week starting 1 week after said first dosing, wherein the patient achieves at least PASI 75 response at week 12 of the treatment • Sandoz asserted 1 ground for invalidity (obviousness) • Institution decision denied; rehearing denied • Sandoz appealed

Molecule	Parties	IPR Nos.	Patents	Key Points
		IPR2017-01823	8,802,100 Formulation of human antibodies for treating TNFα-associated disorders (formulation)	• Formulation patent with 29 claims • Independent claim 1: A stable liquid aqueous pharmaceutical formulation comprising (a) a human IgG1 anti-human TNFα antibody, or an antigen-binding portion thereof, at a concentration of 45–150 mg/ml, (b) a polyol, (c) a polysorbate at a concentration of 0.1–10 mg/ml, and (d) a buffer system having a pH of 4.5–7.0, wherein the antibody comprises the light chain variable region (LCVR) and the heavy chain variable region (HCVR) of D2E7. • Sandoz asserted 1 ground for invalidity (obviousness) • Institution decision denied
Humira (adalimumab)	Coherus BioSciences (patent challenger) AbbVie (patent owner)	IPR2017-01009	9,085,619 Anti-TNF antibody formulations (formulation)	• Formulation patent with 30 claims • Independent claim 1: An aqueous pharmaceutical formulation consisting essentially of: (a) an anti- TNFα antibody comprising an LCVR having a CDR3 domain comprising the amino acid sequence of SEQ ID NO:3, a CDR2 domain comprising the amino acid sequence of SEQ ID NO:5, and a CDR1 domain comprising the amino acid sequence of SEQ ID NO:7, and an HCVR having a CDR3 domain comprising the amino acid sequence of SEQ ID NO:4, a CDR2 domain comprising the amino acid sequence of SEQ ID NO:6, and a CDR1 domain comprising the amino acid sequence of SEQ ID NO:8, wherein the concentration of the antibody is 50–200 mg/ml; and (b) water • Coherus asserted 1 ground for invalidity (obviousness) • Institution decision denied

Molecule	Parties	IPR Nos.	Patents	Key Points
		IPR2017-01008	9,085,619 Anti-TNF antibody formulations (formulation)	• Formulation patent with 30 claims • Independent claim 1: An aqueous pharmaceutical formulation consisting essentially of: (a) an anti- TNFα antibody comprising an LCVR having a CDR3 domain comprising the amino acid sequence of SEQ ID NO:3, a CDR2 domain comprising the amino acid sequence of SEQ ID NO:5, and a CDR1 domain comprising the amino acid sequence of SEQ ID NO:7, and an HCVR having a CDR3 domain comprising the amino acid sequence of SEQ ID NO:4, a CDR2 domain comprising the amino acid sequence of SEQ ID NO:6, and a CDR1 domain comprising the amino acid sequence of SEQ ID NO:8, wherein the concentration of the antibody is 50–200 mg/ml; and (b) water • Coherus asserted 2 grounds for invalidity (obviousness) • Institution decision denied
		IPR2017-00827	9,085,619 Anti-TNF antibody formulations (formulation)	• Formulation patent with 30 claims • Independent claim 1: An aqueous pharmaceutical formulation consisting essentially of: (a) an anti- TNFα antibody comprising an LCVR having a CDR3 domain comprising the amino acid sequence of SEQ ID NO:3, a CDR2 domain comprising the amino acid sequence of SEQ ID NO:5, and a CDR1 domain comprising the amino acid sequence of SEQ ID NO:7, and an HCVR having a CDR3 domain comprising the amino acid sequence of SEQ ID NO:4, a CDR2 domain comprising the amino acid sequence of SEQ ID NO:6, and a CDR1 domain comprising the amino acid sequence of SEQ ID NO:8, wherein the concentration of the antibody is 50–200 mg/ml; and (b) water • Coherus asserted 2 grounds for invalidity (obviousness) • Board dismissed the proceeding per petitioner's request in order to proceed with IPR2017-01008 and IPR2017-01009, which replace IPR2017-00826 and IPR2017-00827

Molecule	Parties	IPR Nos.	Patents	Key Points
		IPR2017-00826	9,085,619 Anti-TNF antibody formulations (formulation)	• Formulation patent with 30 claims • Independent claim 1: An aqueous pharmaceutical formulation consisting essentially of: (a) an anti- TNFα antibody comprising an LCVR having a CDR3 domain comprising the amino acid sequence of SEQ ID NO:3, a CDR2 domain comprising the amino acid sequence of SEQ ID NO:5, and a CDR1 domain comprising the amino acid sequence of SEQ ID NO:7, and an HCVR having a CDR3 domain comprising the amino acid sequence of SEQ ID NO:4, a CDR2 domain comprising the amino acid sequence of SEQ ID NO:6, and a CDR1 domain comprising the amino acid sequence of SEQ ID NO:8, wherein the concentration of the antibody is 50–200 mg/ml; and (b) water • Coherus asserted 1 ground for invalidity (obviousness) • Board dismissed the proceeding per petitioner's request in order to proceed with IPR2017-01008 and IPR2017-01009, which replace IPR2017-00826 and IPR2017-00827
		IPR2017-00823	9,085,619 Anti-TNF antibody formulations (formulation)	• Formulation patent with 30 claims • Independent claim 1: An aqueous pharmaceutical formulation consisting essentially of: (a) an anti- TNFα antibody comprising an LCVR having a CDR3 domain comprising the amino acid sequence of SEQ ID NO:3, a CDR2 domain comprising the amino acid sequence of SEQ ID NO:5, and a CDR1 domain comprising the amino acid sequence of SEQ ID NO:7, and an HCVR having a CDR3 domain comprising the amino acid sequence of SEQ ID NO:4, a CDR2 domain comprising the amino acid sequence of SEQ ID NO:6, and a CDR1 domain comprising the amino acid sequence of SEQ ID NO:8, wherein the concentration of the antibody is 50–200 mg/ml; and (b) water • Coherus asserted 1 ground for invalidity (anticipation) • Institution decision denied

Molecule	Parties	IPR Nos.	Patents	Key Points
		IPR2017-00822	9,085,619 Anti-TNF antibody formulations (formulation)	• Formulation patent with 30 claims • Independent claim 1: An aqueous pharmaceutical formulation consisting essentially of: (a) an anti- TNFα antibody comprising an LCVR having a CDR3 domain comprising the amino acid sequence of SEQ ID NO:3, a CDR2 domain comprising the amino acid sequence of SEQ ID NO:5, and a CDR1 domain comprising the amino acid sequence of SEQ ID NO:7, and an HCVR having a CDR3 domain comprising the amino acid sequence of SEQ ID NO:4, a CDR2 domain comprising the amino acid sequence of SEQ ID NO:6, and a CDR1 domain comprising the amino acid sequence of SEQ ID NO:8, wherein the concentration of the antibody is 50–200 mg/ml; and (b) water • Coherus asserted 2 grounds for invalidity (1 anticipation, 1 obviousness) • Institution decision denied
		IPR2016-01018	9,114,166 Formulation of human antibodies for treating TNFα-associated disorders (formulation)	• Formulation patent with 30 claims • Independent claim 1: A stable liquid aqueous pharmaceutical formulation comprising a human anti-human TNFα IgG1 antibody at a concentration of 50 mg/ml, wherein the antibody comprises the LCVR and the HCVR of D2E7, and a buffer system; wherein the formulation is isotonic, suitable for single-use subcutaneous injection, and has a pH of 4.0–8.0 • Coherus asserted 1 ground for invalidity (obviousness) • Institution decision denied • Request for rehearing denied

Molecule	Parties	IPR Nos.	Patents	Key Points
		IPR2016-00189	9,073,987 Methods of administering anti-TNFα antibodies (MOU)	• Method of treatment patent with 2 claims • Independent claim 1: A method of reducing signs and symptoms in a patient with moderately to severely active rheumatoid arthritis, comprising administering to said patient a total body dose of 40 mg of a human anti-TNFα antibody, wherein the dose is administered subcutaneously from a 40 mg dosage unit form once every 13–15 days, and wherein the anti-TNFα antibody comprises an IgG1 heavy chain constant region; a VL chain region comprising a CDR1 having the amino acid sequence of SEQ ID NO:7, a CDR2 having the amino acid sequence of SEQ ID NO:5, and a CDR3 having the amino acid sequence of SEQ ID NO:3; and a VH chain region comprising a CDR1 having the amino acid sequence of SEQ ID NO:8, a CDR2 having the amino acid sequence of SEQ ID NO:6 and a CDR3 having the amino acid sequence of SEQ ID NO:4 • Coherus asserted 1 ground for invalidity (obviousness) • Institution decision granted • FWD finding all challenged claims unpatentable • AbbVie appealed

Molecule	Parties	IPR Nos.	Patents	Key Points
		IPR2016-00188	9,017,680 Methods of administering anti-TNFα antibodies (MOU)	• Method-of-treatment patent with 4 claims • Independent claim 1: A method of reducing signs and symptoms in a patient with moderately to severely active rheumatoid arthritis, comprising administering to said patient, in combination with methotrexate, a human anti-TNFα antibody, wherein the human anti-TNFα antibody is administered subcutaneously in a total body dose of 40 mg once every 13–15 days, and wherein the anti-TNFα antibody comprises an IgG1 heavy chain constant region; a VL chain region comprising a CDR1 having the amino acid sequence of SEQ ID NO:7, a CDR2 having the amino acid sequence of SEQ ID NO:5, and a CDR3 having the amino acid sequence of SEQ ID NO:3; and a VH chain region comprising a CDR1 having the amino acid sequence of SEQ ID NO:8, a CDR2 having the amino acid sequence of SEQ ID NO:6, and a CDR3 having the amino acid sequence of SEQ ID NO:4 • Coherus asserted 1 ground for invalidity (obviousness) • Institution decision granted • FWD finding all challenged claims unpatentable • AbbVie appealed

Molecule	Parties	IPR Nos.	Patents	Key Points
		IPR2016-00172	8,889,135 Methods of administering anti-TNFα antibodies (MOU)	• Method-of-treatment patent with 5 claims • Independent claim 1: A method for treating rheumatoid arthritis in a human subject, comprising administering subcutaneously to a human subject having rheumatoid arthritis a total body dose of 40 mg of a human anti-TNFα antibody once every 13–15 days for a time period sufficient to treat the rheumatoid arthritis, wherein the anti-TNFα antibody comprises an IgG1 heavy chain constant region; a VL chain region comprising a CDR1 having the amino acid sequence of SEQ ID NO:7, a CDR2 having the amino acid sequence of SEQ ID NO:5, and a CDR3 having the amino acid sequence of SEQ ID NO:3; and a VH chain region comprising a CDR1 having the amino acid sequence of SEQ ID NO:8, a CDR2 having the amino acid sequence of SEQ ID NO:6, and a CDR3 having the amino acid sequence of SEQ ID NO:4 • Coherus asserted 1 ground for invalidity (obviousness) • Institution decision granted • FWD finding all challenged claims unpatentable • AbbVie appealed

Molecule	Parties	IPR Nos.	Patents	Key Points
Humira (adalimumab)	Boehringer Ingelheim (patent challenger) AbbVie (patent owner)	IPR2016-00408	8,889,135 Methods of administering anti-TNFα antibodies (MOU)	• Method-of-treatment patent with 5 claims • Independent claim 1: A method for treating rheumatoid arthritis in a human subject, comprising administering subcutaneously to a human subject having rheumatoid arthritis a total body dose of 40 mg of a human anti-TNFα antibody once every 13–15 days for a time period sufficient to treat the rheumatoid arthritis, wherein the anti-TNFα antibody comprises an IgG1 heavy chain constant region; a VL chain region comprising a CDR1 having the amino acid sequence of SEQ ID NO:7, a CDR2 having the amino acid sequence of SEQ ID NO:5, and a CDR3 having the amino acid sequence of SEQ ID NO:3; and a VH chain region comprising a CDR1 having the amino acid sequence of SEQ ID NO:8, a CDR2 having the amino acid sequence of SEQ ID NO:6, and a CDR3 having the amino acid sequence of SEQ ID NO:4 • Boehringer asserted 1 ground of invalidity (obviousness) • FWD finding all challenged claims unpatentable • Appeal filed by AbbVie
		IPR2016-00409	8,889,135 Methods of administering anti-TNFα antibodies (MOU)	Same as above

Molecule	Parties	IPR Nos.	Patents	Key Points
Humira (adalimumab)	Amgen (patent challenger) AbbVie (patent owner)	IPR2015-01514	8,916,157 Formulation of human antibodies for treating TNFα-associated disorders (formulation)	• Formulation patent with 30 claims • Independent claim 1: A stable liquid aqueous pharmaceutical formulation comprising (a) a human IgG1 anti-human TNFα antibody, or an antigen-binding portion thereof, at a concentration of 20–150 mg/ml, (b) a tonicity agent, (c) a surfactant, and (d) a buffer system having a pH of 4.0–8.0, wherein the antibody comprises the LCVR and the HCVR of D2E7 • Amgen asserted 2 grounds of invalidity (obviousness) • Institution decision • Denying institution finding that Amgen had not persuaded the board that the skilled artisan would have had a reasonable expectation of success in applying the formulations commercially available and found in the prior art to the claimed formulation or that the skilled artisan would have had a reasonable likelihood of success in combining prior art references (decision at 16, 19, 23)

Molecule	Parties	IPR Nos.	Patents	Key Points
		IPR2015-01517	8,916,158 Formulation of human antibodies for treating TNFα-associated disorders (formulation)	• Formulation patent with 30 claims • Independent claim 1: A stable liquid aqueous pharmaceutical formulation comprising (a) a human IgG1 anti-human TNFα antibody, or an antigen-binding portion thereof, at a concentration of 20–150 mg/ml, (b) a polyol, (c) a surfactant, and (d) a buffer system having a pH of 4–8, wherein the antibody comprises the LCVR and the HCVR of D2E7 • Amgen asserted 2 grounds of invalidity (obviousness) • Institution decision • Denying institution finding that Amgen had persuaded the board that the skilled artisan would have had a reasonable expectation of success in applying the formulations commercially available and found in the prior art to the claimed formulation or that the skilled artisan would have had a reasonable likelihood of success in combining prior art references (decision at 17, 20–21, 25–26)

chapter 11

Antitrust Litigation and Product Liability Considerations*

I. Antitrust Actions

A. Antitrust Actions Generally

Antitrust law, whether applied to the pharmaceutical industry or elsewhere, is intended to preserve competition by promoting innovation, fostering price competition, and enhancing consumer welfare. The pharmaceutical industry, though, has become a centerpiece of antitrust scrutiny, largely because there are public and private concerns about rising costs of health care and prices of prescription medicines. For instance, antitrust investigations have been initiated and lawsuits have been filed against pharmaceutical industry-players by the U.S. Department of Justice (DOJ), the Federal Trade Commission (FTC), state attorneys general, drug wholesalers, retail pharmacy chains, insurance companies, union welfare plans, consumers, and competing drug manufacturers, among others.

The type and degree of scrutiny for the pharmaceutical industry has turned on a wide variety of conduct. Some scrutinized conduct is not unique to the pharmaceutical industry, such as allegations of price-fixing among follow-on competitors.[1] Other scrutinized conduct, by contrast, focuses on unique features of the pharmaceutical industry and likely would not arise in any other context. One such uniquely scrutinized feature of the pharmaceutical industry has been referred to as "product hopping," whereby

---

*Daryl L. Wiesen, Alexandra D. Valenti, Alison Siedor, and Eric Levi, Goodwin Procter LLP.

1. *See* Press Release, U.S. Attorney's Office, Eastern District of Pennsylvania, Heritage Pharmaceuticals Pays Over $7 Million to Resolve Civil False Claims Act Allegations (May 31, 2019), https://www.justice.gov/usao-edpa/pr/heritage-pharmaceuticals-pays-over-7-million-resolve-civil-false-claims-act-allegations.

brand companies in the Hatch-Waxman space are alleged to thwart the operation of AB-rated generic substitution under state drug selection laws by undertaking the effort to switch the market to new, patented variants of old drugs.[2] Another uniquely scrutinized feature of the pharmaceutical industry is mergers that routinely require divestitures of products or other remedies to maintain competition.

Scholars, lawyers, and industry professionals alike have reason to believe that this same intensity of antitrust scrutiny will apply to biologic and biosimilar products; indeed, such has already been the case.[3] As an indicator and guidepost for what is likely to come, the U.S. Food and Drug Administration (FDA) and FTC released a joint statement in February 2020 describing "key steps the agencies will take to address false or misleading promotion about biosimilars within their respective authorities and deter anti-competitive behavior in this space."[4] The discussion to follow provides a brief overview of antitrust theories applied to the pharmaceutical industry, and how these theories are likely to apply to the biologics and biosimilars industries moving forward.

B. Sham Litigation and Walker Process *Fraud*

The premise of a sham litigation claim is that the party who initiated or continued to press a lawsuit is leveraging the lawsuit's statutorily prescribed pendency provisions themselves, rather than the merits of the lawsuit or sought-after outcome, as an anticompetitive weapon. In the Hatch-Waxman context, such claims often allege that a brand company has filed or is maintaining a patent infringement lawsuit it knows to be meritless, simply to reap the benefits from an automatic 30-month stay of an abbreviated new drug application's (ANDA's) approval; such benefit

2. *E.g.*, New York *ex rel.* Schneiderman v. Actavis PLC, 787 F.3d 638 (2d Cir. 2015); *see also In re* Suboxone (Buprenorphine Hydrochloride & Naloxone) Antitrust Litig., 421 F. Supp. 3d 12, 40 (E.D. Pa. 2019).

3. *See, e.g., In re* Actos End-Payor Antitrust Litig., 417 F. Supp. 3d 352 (S.D.N.Y. 2019), *motion to certify appeal granted*, No. 13-cv-9244 (RA), 2020 WL 433710 (S.D.N.Y. Jan. 28, 2020); Biocad JSC v. F. Hoffmann-La Roche, 942 F.3d 88 (2d Cir. 2019); *In re* Remicade Antitrust Litig., No. 17-cv-04326 (E.D. Pa. Mar. 15, 2023) (consolidated).

4. News Release, FDA, FDA and FTC Announce New Efforts to Further Deter Anti-Competitive Business Practices, Support Competitive Market for Biological Products to Help Americans (Feb. 3, 2020), https://www.fda.gov/news-events/press-announcements/fda-and-ftc-announce-new-efforts-further-deter-anti-competitive-business-practices-support. The statement identifies four joint goals to help in this effort: (1) FDA and FTC will coordinate to promote greater competition in biologic markets; (2) FDA and FTC will work together to deter behavior that impedes access to samples needed for the development of biologics, including biosimilars; (3) FDA and FTC intend to take appropriate action against false or misleading communications about biologics, including biosimilars, within their respective authorities; and (4) FTC will review patent settlement agreements involving biologics, including biosimilars, for antitrust violations.

includes the postponement of generic entry.[5] That said, sham litigation claims are also pursued outside the Hatch-Waxman context. The absence of a 30-month stay analog in the Biologics Price Competition and Innovation Act (BPCIA) context does not itself preclude biosimilar applicants or others from being able to assert sham litigation claims; their high burden of proof and low likelihood of success are more likely deterrents.

Why do antitrust plaintiffs pursuing claims of sham litigation face high burdens? As an initial matter, a patentee's act of filing a lawsuit to enforce its patent rights is a form of petitioning. Under the First Amendment and *Noerr-Pennington* doctrine, that act of petitioning is immune from antitrust challenge, unless an exception applies.[6] Proof that the lawsuit is a sham is an established exception and lifts *Noerr-Pennington* immunity.[7] To clear the First Amendment hurdle, proving the sham exception, the antitrust plaintiff must establish that both (1) the lawsuit against it was "objectively baseless," demonstrating that no reasonable litigant could have expected to prevail on the merits, and (2) the lawsuit was "subjectively intended to interfere directly with a competitor's business" through the litigation process itself.[8] Once the antitrust plaintiff clears that hurdle, it must still prove all remaining elements of a traditional antitrust claim, including market power and harm to competition.

To date, sham litigation claims in the pharmaceutical industry have been brought as counterclaims in patent litigation, as part of freestanding antitrust claims filed by consumers, and in government enforcement actions.[9] As one example, the FTC won a sham litigation case against a brand drug company based on the argument that patent lawsuits against two generic competitors were objectively baseless because prosecution history estoppel prevented the brand company from asserting the theory of infringement on which its cases relied.[10] In another matter, a biosimilar applicant alleged that a patent litigation brought by the reference drug company was a sham, but the claim was voluntarily dismissed before trial.[11]

---

5. *E.g.*, *In re* Wellbutrin XL Antitrust Litig. Indirect Purchaser Class, 868 F.3d 132, 147 (3d Cir. Aug. 9, 2017), *judgment entered*, No. 15-cv-2875, 2017 WL 3529114 (3d Cir. 2017); Rochester Drug Coop., Inc. v. Braintree Lab'ys, 712 F. Supp. 2d 308, 311 (D. Del. 2010).

6. E. R.R. Presidents Conf. v. Noerr Motor Freight, Inc., 365 U.S. 127 (1961); United Mine Workers of Am. v. Pennington, 381 U.S. 657 (1965).

7. Pro. Real Est. Invs., Inc. v. Columbia Pictures Indus., Inc., 508 U.S. 49 (1993).

8. *Id.* at 60–61; FTC v. AbbVie Inc., 329 F. Supp. 3d 98, 117 (E.D. Pa. 2018).

9. *See, e.g.*, Otsuka Pharm. Co., Ltd. v. Torrent Pharms. Ltd., Inc., 118 F. Supp. 3d 646 (D.N.J. 2015); *Wellbutrin XL Antitrust Litig. Indirect Purchaser Class*, 868 F.3d 132; *AbbVie*, 329 F. Supp. 3d 98.

10. *AbbVie*, 329 F. Supp. 3d. at 125–27.

11. Amgen Inc. v. Apotex Inc., No. 15-cv-61631-CIV-JIC/BSS, (S.D. Fla. Aug. 6, 2015), ECF Nos. 35, 180.

Closely related to sham litigation is the *Walker Process* doctrine, which addresses situations in which a patentee seeks to enforce a patent that was procured by fraud.[12] To make out a *Walker Process* claim, an antitrust plaintiff must show that the patent at issue would not have issued but-for intentional fraud, and that the party asserting the patent(s) knows of the fraud.[13] If proven, *Walker Process* fraud strips the patentee of *Noerr-Pennington* immunity, and the antitrust plaintiff can assert that the filing and prosecution of the case was an antitrust violation.[14] As with sham litigation, an antitrust plaintiff that proves the elements of *Walker Process* still must satisfy the remaining elements of an antitrust claim.[15]

Although the *Walker Process* theory has yet to be fully tested in the biologics arena, *In re Remicade Antitrust Litigation* demonstrates that there is no reason to believe antitrust-targeted scrutiny would not surface in the biosimilars context in appropriate circumstances.[16] In *In re Remicade Antitrust Litigation*, plaintiffs asserted both sham litigation and *Walker Process* claims in an antitrust action brought by consumers challenging the legality of patent infringement claims pursued by a reference product sponsor (RPS) against a biosimilar applicant. The court rejected both claims on a motion to dismiss, yet, notably, it raised no question about whether the doctrines would apply.

C. "Patent Thickets"

In addition to the well-established doctrines of sham litigation and *Walker Process* fraud, the newer concept of a so-called "patent thicket" has attracted considerable attention in the biosimilar space. The notion of a patent thicket is not well defined but rests on the premise that a company has obtained multiple, overlapping, seemingly unnecessary yet shield-like patents for the purpose of deterring or delaying competitive entry. As some may say, the best offense is a great defense.

The premise is that, at some point, such conduct becomes improper. The concept has arisen in the context of Humira, a biologic product alleged to be protected by more than 100 patents filed in the U.S. Patent and Trademark Office (USPTO). In one patent infringement action involving a biosimilar to Humira, the biosimilar manufacturer premised an unclean hands defense on allegations that AbbVie, the RPS for Humira, had acted

12. Walker Process Equip., Inc. v. Food Mach. & Chem. Corp., 382 U.S. 172 (1965); *In re* Lipitor Antitrust Litig., 868 F.3d 231 (3d Cir. 2017), *cert. denied*, 138 S. Ct. 983 (2018), *and cert. denied*, 138 S. Ct. 984 (2018).

13. Abbott Lab'ys v. Teva Pharms. USA, Inc., 432 F. Supp. 2d 408, 432 (D. Del. 2006).

14. Nobelpharma AB v. Implant Innovations, Inc., 141 F.3d 1059, 1068 (Fed. Cir. 1998).

15. *Lipitor Antitrust Litig.*, 868 F.3d at 266.

16. 345 F. Supp. 3d 566, 581–82 (E.D. Pa. 2018).

improperly in erecting a patent thicket to safeguard its product.[17] In the Humira patent litigation, while the court allowed certain discovery on the patent-thicket allegations to proceed as part of an unclean hands defense, it noted:

> Whether the creation of a "patent thicket" can amount to a cognizable defense to a claim of patent infringement, such as unclean hands, and where the boundary line between licit and illicit conduct might be, is not clear. The simple act of applying for, and receiving a patent, standing alone, can hardly be the basis for patent invalidation.[18]

Various consumer groups have piggybacked on these theories and filed follow-on antitrust litigation making similar allegations, asserting that Humira's alleged patent thicket has improperly delayed entry of biosimilar products in the United States. For instance, in *In re Humira Antitrust Litigation*, plaintiffs alleged that AbbVie improperly exercised monopoly power over the market for adalimumab, both by amassing and enforcing a large patent estate (a patent thicket) and by settling patent litigations with biosimilar manufacturers such that earlier entry in the European market was a "bargaining chip" for delayed entry in the United States. Plaintiffs alleged that these practices amount to a scheme to violate federal and state antitrust laws. But the district court ruled and Seventh Circuit affirmed that these allegations, even if true, would not amount to an antitrust violation.[19] At most, AbbVie had exploited advantages conferred on it through lawful petitioning practices—obtaining patents from the USPTO, defending the validity of those patents before the Patent Trial and Appeal Board, and asserting its patents against biosimilar manufacturers in BPCIA litigation. The district court found that to the extent these practices have kept prices high for Humira, existing antitrust

17. AbbVie Inc. v. Boehringer Ingelheim Int'l GmbH, No. 17-cv-01065-MSG-RL, 2019 WL 1571666, at *3 (D. Del. Apr. 11, 2019) (noting that "the unclean hands defense alleges that AbbVie created a 'patent thicket' of 'overlapping and non-inventive patents for the purpose of . . . delaying competition'").

18. AbbVie Inc. v. Boehringer Ingelheim Int'l GmbH, No. 17-cv-01065-MSG-RL (D. Del. June 4, 2018), ECF No. 112. This case was dismissed following a settlement prior to any further substantive ruling on the viability of the unclean hands defense. AbbVie Inc. v. Boehringer Ingelheim Int'l GmbH, No. 17-cv-01065-MSG-RL (D. Del. May 15, 2019), ECF No. 506. Plaintiffs alleged that AbbVie "applied for, obtained, and asserted patents to gain the power it needed to elbow its competitors . . . out of the Humira market in the United States (in violation of § 2 of the Sherman Act)," and "created a thicket of intellectual property protection so dense that it prevented would-be challengers from entering the market with cheaper biosimilar alternatives." *In re* Humira (Adalimumab) Antitrust Litig., No. 19-cv-1873 (N.D. Ill. Mar. 18, 2019), ECF No. 170, at 1, 4; *see also* Mayor & City Council of Balt. v. AbbVie Inc., 42 F.4th 709, 711–14 (7th Cir. 2022).

19. *See generally* ECF No. 170; *AbbVie Inc.*, 42 F.4th 709.

doctrine does not prohibit it.[20] The Seventh Circuit agreed with the district court that AbbVie's petitioning was largely protected by the *Noerr-Pennington* doctrine because, "unless its petitions—its patent applications, patent dance exchanges, and the lawsuits that followed—were objectively baseless," plaintiffs' theory of antitrust injury was too speculative.[21] The district court noted, for example, AbbVie's 53.4 percent success rate in converting patent applications into patents and that its success rate during inter partes review proceedings was even higher, such that "allegations about AbbVie's petitioning of the USPTO are not plausible acts of sham petitioning."[22] The district court concluded that "the vast majority of the alleged scheme is immunized from antitrust scrutiny, and what's left are a few sharp elbows thrown at sophisticated competitors participating in regulated patent and biologic-drug regimes."[23] Thereafter, the Seventh Circuit affirmed that applying for, obtaining, and "invoking [a large number of patents] against the biosimilars," without more, is a "protected activity" and is not anticompetitive conduct in violation of the Sherman Antitrust Act.[24]

Legislation regarding patent thickets has been proposed in Congress and continues to draw policymakers' attention.[25]

D. Patent Settlement Agreements

The reach of antitrust violations and scrutinized activity further extends to patent litigation settlement agreements. Patent settlement agreements are a representation of a plaintiff's and defendant's business- and litigation-driven decision-making process when settling a dispute. These scrutinized activities are themselves the basis for challenges to the settlement agreement.

One example of scrutinized activity is dubbed the "reverse payment" or "pay for delay" doctrine. The gist of this doctrine is that the brand company

20. *Humira (Adalimumab) Antitrust Litig.*, ECF No. 170, at 2.

21. *Id.* at 24. *See AbbVie Inc.*, 42 F.4th at 713 ("AbbVie's patent applications cannot be called baseless" under the *Walker Process* doctrine where "the 132 patents issued").

22. *Humira (Adalimumab) Antitrust Litig.*, ECF No. 170, at 25–26.

23. *Id.* at 31. *In re Humira* was appealed to the U.S. Court of Appeals for the Seventh Circuit on July 30, 2020. Mayor & City Council of Balt. v. AbbVie Inc., No. 20-2402 (7th Cir. July 30, 2020), ECF No. 1. The Seventh Circuit heard oral arguments on February 25, 2021, during which the judges focused part of their questioning on the impact if there was even one valid patent claim among the 132 patents. Circuit Judge Frank H. Easterbrook showed the most skepticism that appellants would be able to show that each and every one of the 132 patents was invalid, stating the likelihood "is astoundingly small." The Seventh Circuit affirmed the district court's decision on August 1, 2022. *AbbVie Inc.*, 42 F.4th at 713.

24. *See AbbVie Inc.*, 42 F.4th at 712 ("The patent laws do not set a cap on the number of patents any one person can hold—in general, or pertaining to a single subject.").

25. *E.g.*, Biologic Patent Transparency Act, S. 659, 116th Cong. (2019).

pays the generic company to "wait"—accordingly, the generic company accepts a later market entry date in exchange for some other economic benefit from the brand company (i.e., some fiscal incentive in the form of money or contractual agreement(s)). Consequently, the fiscal incentive provides the generic company with a more favorable scenario than what could or would otherwise have been available. The fiscal consequence of such payment or agreement is offset (and indirectly funded) by the brand drug company's enhanced monopoly over profits. The fiscal consequence for both parties is lowered or offset as a result of the brand drug company's postponement of generic entry. Such activity benefits the settling parties yet harms the consuming public. Consumers are harmed because they are denied earlier access to lower cost generic alternatives. Ultimately, these theories arose in the context of small-molecule, brand-generic settlements. And the degree to which large-molecule (i.e., biologic, biosimilar, and/or interchangeable) settlements will be implicated has yet to play out.

More specifically, before 2013, the substantial majority of these types of antitrust challenges routinely failed under a scope-of-the-patent test.[26] Under such a test, it was per se non-anticompetitive behavior where the settlement agreement permitted generic entry prior to expiration of the patent(s) at issue. As a matter of law, generic entry prior to patent expiration could not evidence anticompetitive behavior, regardless of whether the agreement included a reverse payment, because the agreement did not prevent competition beyond the potential exclusionary scope of the patent. In other words, the purportedly exclusionary behavior was framed as a result of the patent, instead of the settlement agreement.

Then, in 2013, and more specifically in *FTC v. Actavis*, the U.S. Supreme Court reshaped the proper application of the antitrust standard to reverse-payment challenges.[27] The action commenced with the FTC filing a lawsuit that challenged several settlement agreements involving generic versions of Androgel, which allegedly contained improper reverse payments. Pursuant to the scope-of-the-patent test, the district court dismissed the case, and the Eleventh Circuit affirmed. Once the matter progressed to the Supreme Court, FTC argued that any agreement containing a reverse-payment scheme should be construed as presumptively unlawful, regardless of whether it allowed generic entry prior to patent expiry. Unsurprisingly, industry defendants argued the Supreme Court

26. *E.g.*, *In re* Tamoxifen Citrate Antitrust Litig., 466 F.3d 187 (2d Cir. 2006), *rejected by In re* K-Dur Antitrust Litig., 686 F.3d 197 (3d Cir. 2012), *and abrogated by* FTC v. Actavis, Inc., 570 U.S. 136 (2013); *In re* Ciprofloxacin Hydrochloride Antitrust Litig., 544 F.3d 1323 (Fed. Cir. 2008), *rejected by K-Dur Antitrust Litig.*, 686 F.3d 197, *and abrogated by Actavis, Inc.*, 570 U.S. 136.

27. 570 U.S. 136.

should reaffirm the scope-of-the-patent test. Instead, the Court rejected both positions and adopted a middle ground: the Court found reverse payments "unusual," internalized the consuming public's concern, and stated that "there is reason for concern that settlements taking this form tend to have significant adverse effects on competition."[28] However, the Court recognized that there may be benefits and justifications for reverse payments, which include the promotion of settlement, a well-established goal of the law.[29] The Court held that the possibility of anticompetitive effects justifies reversing the lower court's dismissal because "these anticompetitive consequences will at least sometimes prove unjustified."[30] Ultimately, the Court reversed the grant of a motion to dismiss and allowed the case to continue. Notably though, the Court maintained its position that there should *not* be a presumption of unlawfulness or anticompetitive effect, holding that in a reverse-payment case, "the FTC [or a private plaintiff] must prove its case as in other rule-of-reason cases."[31]

Following the post-*Actavis* line of cases, courts have denied motions to dismiss cases regarding alleged reverse-payment patent settlements, including:

- Agreements under which the generic company is paid to provide goods or services to the brand (including on products other than the one at issue in the settlement), such as co-promotion agreements or back-up supply agreements[32]
- Agreements by the brand company not to market an authorized generic version of its product during the generic first filer's 180-day exclusivity period[33]
- Situations in which the parties settle cases involving two drugs at the same time, one of which resolves a damages claim by the brand against the generic on one product allegedly for less than it is worth, as a form of alleged compensation for delayed entry on the second product[34]

---

28. *Id.* at 147–48.
29. *Id.* at 156.
30. *Id.*
31. *Id.* at 159.
32. *E.g.*, *In re* Niaspan Antitrust Litig., 42 F. Supp. 3d 735 (E.D. Pa. 2014); *In re* Aggrenox Antitrust Litig., 94 F. Supp. 3d 224 (D. Conn. 2015).
33. *E.g.*, King Drug Co. of Florence, Inc. v. Smithkline Beecham Corp., 791 F.3d 388, 404 (3d Cir. 2015); *In re* Loestrin 24 Fe Antitrust Litig., 261 F. Supp. 3d 307, 332–33 (D.R.I. 2017).
34. *E.g.*, *In re* Nexium (Esomeprazole) Antitrust Litig., 842 F.3d 34, 44–45 (1st Cir. 2016); *In* re Lipitor Antitrust Litig., 868 F.3d 231, 253 (3d Cir. 2017), *cert. denied*, 138 S. Ct. 983 (2018), *and cert. denied*, 138 S. Ct. 984 (2018).

Further expanding the scope of scrutinized conduct and agreements, as applied to reverse-payment schemes, several cases have addressed "accelerator" or "contingent launch" provisions, which allow a generic company to launch its products earlier than a default entry date if certain events occur; such events include a launch by competing generics or an authorized generic, and a final court decision that could lead a first filer to forfeit its 180-day exclusivity if it does not begin marketing its product within 75 days thereafter. Still, most courts have held that such provisions are non-actionable reverse payments; notably though, one court denied a motion to dismiss a complaint where issues of fact remained as to whether the alleged reverse payments were larger than necessary to compensate the generic company for its litigation expenses (among other issues).[35]

To date, courts have yet to examine the scenario where a biosimilar applicant and RPS enter into a settlement containing a large and unexplained reverse payment. And in such a scenario, particularly involving the pharmaceutical industry, there is no reason why the principles of *Actavis* and the reverse-payment doctrine would not apply. However, reverse payments themselves may be a unique feature in the small-molecule context: reverse payments arguably arose as a result of the unique regulatory and economic features of competition under Hatch-Waxman and state drug substitution laws. State drug substitution laws include automatic AB-rated substitution of generic products for prescriptions written for the brand. And under Hatch-Waxman, the presence of the 180-day exclusivity period arguably allows a brand company to pay off the first filer to "park" its exclusivity and thereby delay not just its own entry, but the entry of all other later ANDA filers. To the extent that those or comparable features do not exist in the biosimilar space, the incentives for parties to enter into reverse-payment agreements may be reduced or nonexistent such that these agreements simply do not play out.

Nevertheless, plaintiffs will continue to explore footholds that permit scrutiny of settlement agreements for antitrust violations. One such case involved biosimilars of Humira.[36] The Humira-related complaints allege that several biosimilar applicants settled with AbbVie, the RPS, in agreements that allowed biosimilar entry in the European Union (EU) years earlier than in the United States. According to the complaints, earnings that the biosimilar applicants would receive from EU entry amount to a reverse

35. *E.g.*, *In re* Actos End Payor Antitrust Litig., No. 13-cv-9244 (RA), 2015 WL 5610752, at *15–16 (S.D.N.Y. Sept. 22, 2015), *aff'd in part, vacated in part*, 848 F.3d 89 (2d Cir. 2017); Sergeants Benevolent Ass'n Health & Welfare Fund v. Acta Vis, PLC, Nos. 15-cv-6549 (CM), 15-cv-7488 (CM), 2016 WL 4992690, at *14–15 (S.D.N.Y. Sept. 13, 2016).

36. *In re* Humira (Adalimumab) Antitrust Litig., No. 19-cv-1873 (N.D. Ill. Mar. 18, 2019).

payment that delayed U.S. entry. On June 8, 2020, in a memorandum opinion and order,[37] Judge Shah of the Northern District of Illinois Eastern Division granted AbbVie's motion to dismiss plaintiffs' complaint, ruling that "even when considered broadly and together for their potential to restrain trade—[the plaintiffs' allegations] fall short of alleging the kind of competitive harm remedied by antitrust law."[38] The court refused to treat the settlements as market allocations that violate the antitrust law per se, and also refused to apply the "quick look" doctrine, because the effect of the agreements is not facially anticompetitive. Instead, the court held, assuming the agreements contained reverse payments, the traditional rule-of-reason analysis would apply. Ultimately, the question of which standard to apply proved beside the point because the court held that the agreements did not contain reverse payments that could be challenged under the Supreme Court's decision in *FTC v. Actavis*, and, thus, there was no basis for challenging them at all. The court reasoned:

> [The] transfer of value, as large as it was, did not have the hallmarks of an unjustified and otherwise inexplicable payment because the package either increased competition or preserved an anticompetitive status quo. . . . The effect of the payment was to increase, not restrain competition by bringing competitors into the market when patents otherwise prohibited the competition.[39]

As a nod to a well-established underpinning of the law, the court went on to state that "[t]here is also a broader reason to uphold these agreements under antitrust review: encouraging patent litigants to settle worldwide patent disputes."[40]

On August 1, 2022, the Seventh Circuit affirmed dismissal of plaintiffs' complaint, agreeing that the complaint failed to state an antitrust violation under section 1 of the Sherman Antitrust Act.[41] The Seventh Circuit found that the plaintiffs' argument

> boil[ed] down to a contention that, by leaving money on the table in Europe, AbbVie effectively paid the potential entrants for

37. *Humira (Adalimumab) Antitrust Litig.*, ECF No. 170.

38. *Id.* at 18.

39. *Id.* at 46.

40. *Id.*

41. Mayor & City Council of Balt. v. AbbVie Inc., 42 F.4th 709 (7th Cir. 2022). AbbVie's settlement agreements with biosimilar manufacturers provided an October 2018 market entry date for Europe and a 2023 entry date in the United States. *Id.* at 714 ("If this is a cartel (AbbVie and its potential competitors carving up the market, 100% in AbbVie's favor, from 2017 through 2022), then all settlements of patent cases violate the Sherman Act, yet the Supreme Court has said repeatedly that normal settlements of patent litigation are lawful.").

delay in the United States. This is a use of the economic concept of opportunity cost, which treats a foregone earning opportunity (fewer years of monopoly profit in Europe) as equivalent to a payment out of pocket.[42]

However, the Seventh Circuit held that the Supreme Court had already "considered, and rejected, the argument that an opportunity cost is the same thing as a reverse-payment settlement."[43] Therefore, the Seventh Circuit rejected the idea that the "traditional" deal structure—allowing earlier entry in Europe, purportedly in exchange for later entry in the United States—is a reverse payment in violation of the Sherman Act.[44]

These issues have drawn attention from Congress, such as in 2021 when legislation was proposed to prevent reverse-payment settlements.[45] The president then articulated in an Executive Order an instruction to the FTC to issue rules that ban so-called "pay for delay" agreements.[46] Moving forward, with approvals of interchangeables and an uptick in the biosimilars market, these issues will likely continue to draw the attention of policymakers.[47]

To facilitate antitrust scrutiny of settlement agreements in the pharmaceutical industry, since 2003, the Medicare Modernization Act (MMA) has required that certain agreements between brand and generic drug companies, or between two or more generic drug companies, must be filed with FTC and the DOJ. The coverage of the MMA originally was limited to agreements pertaining to ANDAs with Paragraph IV certifications under Hatch-Waxman. In 2018, Congress amended the MMA to extend its coverage to biosimilars.

Under the MMA, certain agreements between biosimilar applicants and the RPS must be filed.[48] The filing requirement is triggered in those circumstances if the agreement concerns any of the time periods referred to in section 351(k)(6) that apply to the biosimilar product or the manufacturing, marketing, or sale of the biosimilar product.[49] For instance, an agreement must be filed if it pertains to

42. *Id.* at 715.

43. *Id.* at 716.

44. *Id.* at 715. "In each [settlement,] AbbVie agreed to entry before the last patents expired and didn't pay anyone to delay entry. As the district judge saw things, 0 + 0 = 0. We see this the same way." *Id.*

45. Preserve Access to Affordable Generics and Biosimilars Act, S. 1428, 117th Cong. (2021).

46. Exec. Order No. 14,036, 86 Fed. Reg. 36,987 (July 9, 2021).

47. *See Biosimilars in the United States 2023–2027*, IQVIA (Jan. 31, 2023), https://www.iqvia.com/insights/the-iqvia-institute/reports/biosimilars-in-the-united-states-2023-2027.

48. 21 U.S.C.A. § 355 note (section 1112(a)(1)).

49. *Id.* (section 1112(b)(2)).

- the manufacturing, marketing, or sale of the reference product;
- the manufacturing, marketing, or sale of the biosimilar; or
- any of the time periods referred to in section 351(k)(6) that apply to the biosimilar.[50]

Certain agreements between two or more biosimilar applicants for the same reference product also must be filed.[51]

Filing requirements extend beyond the specific agreement that falls into one of the categories described above. Parties must also file certain "other agreements." This category, too, expanded in 2018. "Other agreements" that need to be filed fall into two categories.

1. The first one is based on content: other agreements between the parties that are contingent on, or related to, the agreement that is subject to the statute must be filed, even if the other agreement itself would not otherwise meet the filing requirement.
2. The second category of "other agreements" is based on timing: other agreements between the parties that are entered into within 30 days of the agreement that is subject to the statute must be filed, whether related or not.[52]

To the extent such agreements have not been reduced to writing, the parties must prepare and file a written description sufficient to disclose its terms.[53] Filings required by the MMA must be filed no later than ten business days after the agreements are executed.[54] Failure to file may result in civil penalties.[55]

Materials submitted under the MMA are exempt from disclosure under 5 U.S.C.A. § 552.[56] Filing does not trigger any waiting period. The filing is for notice purposes only, and the filing parties may hear nothing from the agencies in response thereto. That said, the FTC has initiated certain enforcement actions on the basis of information it received under the MMA. The FTC also periodically publishes reports describing information it receives under the MMA (with company- and product-identifying information removed).[57]

---

50. *Id.* (section 1112(a)(2)).
51. *Id.* (section 1112(b)(1)).
52. *Id.* (section 1112(c)(2)).
53. *Id.* (section 1112(c)(3)).
54. *Id.* (section 1113).
55. *Id.* (section 1115).
56. *Id.* (section 1114).
57. *See, e.g.*, *Pharmaceutical Agreement Filings*, FTC, https://www.ftc.gov/advice-guidance/competition-guidance/industry-guidance/competition-health-care-marketplace/pharmaceutical-agreement-filings (last visited Feb. 15, 2024).

E. Exclusionary Contracting and Rebating Strategies

Another area of emerging antitrust scrutiny involving biosimilar products concerns exclusionary contracting strategies. Antitrust law has long recognized that, in certain circumstances, exclusive contracts and bundled rebate agreements are potentially anticompetitive, which necessarily implicates the pharmaceutical industry.[58]

In one case, a biosimilar applicant, Pfizer, filed an antitrust lawsuit against the RPS, Johnson & Johnson, challenging its contracting policies. The biosimilar applicant alleged that the reason its infliximab biosimilar product achieved minimal sales after approval, despite its lower price, is that the RPS entered into exclusive dealing contracts and bundled rebate agreements with payers and providers. The biosimilar applicant further alleged that the effect of those contracts was to block access to its biosimilar product, even though it allegedly was a less expensive alternative. The court denied a motion to dismiss and allowed the case to proceed to discovery.[59] As Judge Joyner stated:

> J&J's efforts to foreclose Pfizer from the market, as Pfizer has alleged, have led to increased prices for consumers and limited competitive options for end payers, providers, and patients. Pfizer provides detailed allegations regarding J&J's exclusionary terms with many of the nation's largest insurers, the incentive structure that forces end payers and providers into accepting those terms, Pfizer's efforts to compete, including its guarantees that Inflectra would cost less than Remicade, and showed how market participants on many levels are injured from J&J's ability to sell Remicade without having to compete with Inflectra and other biosimilars.[60]

Discovery in the indirect-purchaser antitrust class action was consolidated with discovery in the antitrust action brought by Pfizer, and in the midst of fact discovery, the parties entered into a confidential settlement agreement.[61] Thereafter, the parties in the indirect-purchaser antitrust class

---

58. *E.g.*, SmithKline Corp. v. Eli Lilly & Co., 575 F.2d 1056 (3d Cir. 1978) (affirming antitrust liability for bundled rebate strategy in pharmaceuticals).

59. Pfizer Inc. v. Johnson & Johnson, 333 F. Supp. 3d 494 (E.D. Pa. 2018) (citing 15 U.S.C.A. § 6a); *see also In re* Remicade Antitrust Litig., 345 F. Supp. 3d 566 (E.D. Pa. 2018). *But see* Shire US, Inc. v. Allergan, Inc., 375 F. Supp. 3d 538 (D.N.J. 2019) (dismissing complaint alleging use of exclusive contracts and anticompetitive bundling to exclude competing product from Medicare Part D prescription plans).

60. *Pfizer*, 333 F. Supp. 3d at 502.

61. Pfizer Inc. v. Johnson & Johnson, No. 2:17-cv-04180 (E.D. Pa. July 20, 2021), ECF No. 167 (stipulating to dismissal with prejudice pursuant to Federal Rule of Civil Procedure 41(a)(1)(A)(ii)).

action stipulated to a settlement wherein defendants were to deposit $25 million into a settlement fund.[62] And in March 2023, the court granted plaintiffs' motion for final approval of settlement, plan of allocation and distribution, award of attorneys' fees and expenses, and service awards, which, among other things, awarded class counsel $7 million in attorneys' fees and $2.3 million in expenses.[63]

In another case, Regeneron filed antitrust claims challenging Amgen's contracting policies for Repatha® (evolocumab). Regeneron alleged actual and attempted monopolization of the relevant market through "unlawful, anticompetitive bundling" and "below-cost pricing" in violation of section 2 of the Sherman Act, and unreasonable restraint of trade in violation of section 1 of the Sherman Act, among other counts.[64] Regeneron contended that the scheme forces third-party payers to "jettison" Regeneron's competing product, Praluent® (alirocumab), "in favor of" Repatha® by conditioning significant rebates on Amgen's "unrelated mega-products."[65] Further, Regeneron contended that Amgen's "bundled rebate scheme further excludes competition" by pricing Amgen's biologic below its costs such that the applicant "cannot make a financially viable case for [its biosimilar]."[66] Together, according to Regeneron, the scheme "coerce[s] intermediaries who cover and pay the majority of the costs of these drugs into eliminating competition in the much smaller PCSK9i market."[67] Regeneron contended the scheme, in conjunction with significant barriers to entry that are unique to the PCSK9i market and the biosimilar market-at-large, harm competition.[68] More recently, Judge Andrews adopted Magistrate Judge Hall's report and recommendation,[69] denying Amgen's Federal Rule of Civil Procedure 12(b)(6) motion to dismiss Regeneron's antitrust claims.[70] The litigation, filed in June 2022, remains pending.

Given the nature of competition between biologics and biosimilars, which often will not involve automatic substitution and instead will require companies to compete for coverage and prescriptions, courts and policymakers are likely to grapple with these exclusionary and rebating strategies moving forward.

62. *In re* Remicade Antitrust Litig., ECF No. 177 (E.D. Pa. Aug. 2, 2022).
63. *In re* Remicade Antitrust Litig., ECF Nos. 226, 227 (E.D. Pa. Mar. 15, 2023).
64. Regeneron Pharms., Inc. v. Amgen Inc., No. 1:22-cv-00697-RGA-JLH (D. Del. May 27, 2022), ECF No. 1.
65. *Id.* at 2, 6.
66. *Id.* at 9.
67. *Id.* at 6.
68. *Id.* at 32–67.
69. *Amgen Inc.*, ECF No. 49 (D. Del. Feb. 10, 2023).
70. *Amgen Inc.*, ECF No. 62 (D. Del. Mar. 21, 2023).

II. Product Liability Claims against Biosimilars

A. Failure to Warn Claims: Preemption and the Learned Intermediary Doctrine

In product liability litigation, failure to warn claims arise from the principle that a manufacturer or seller must provide adequate warnings regarding the dangers associated with the use, or foreseeable misuse, of its products.[71] To establish a failure to warn claim, a plaintiff must usually show that (1) the manufacturer had a duty to warn of a known or foreseeable risk; (2) the manufacturer breached that duty; and (3) the manufacturer's breach caused injury to the plaintiff.

For small-molecule generic drug products approved pursuant to the Hatch-Waxman Act, federal law preempts failure to warn claims, because federal law requires that the generic product label be "the same as the labeling approved for the [brand-name] drug."[72] Since it would be impossible for the generic drug manufacturer to comply with both the federal requirement of sameness and the state tort law standards requiring additional or different warnings, this federal law preempts any failure to warn claims arising under state law.[73]

Unlike small-molecule generic drugs, however, the label of a biosimilar may differ to a certain extent from the reference product label and still comply with federal law. In July 2018, the FDA released a final guidance titled "Labeling for Biosimilar Products." In the guidance, the FDA recommends that biosimilar product labeling incorporate relevant data and information from the reference product labeling, but notes that some differences

---

71. Failure to warn claims are widely recognized. *See, e.g.*, Gurley By & Through Gurley v. Am. Honda Motor Co., Inc., 505 So. 2d 358 (Ala. 1987); Aguayo v. Crompton & Knowles Corp., 183 Cal. App. 3d 1032 (Cal. Ct. App. 1986); Evridge v. Am. Honda Motor Co., 685 S.W.2d 632 (Tenn. 1985); Billiar v. Minn. Mining & Mfg. Co., 623 F.2d 240 (2d Cir. 1980); Nolan v. Dillon, 276 A.2d 36 (Md. 1971); Kozlowski v. John E. Smith's Sons Co., 275 N.W.2d 915 (Wis. 1979); Libbey-Owens Ford Glass Co. v. L & M Paper Co., 205 N.W.2d 523 (Neb. 1973).

72. *See* 21 U.S.C.A. § 355(j)(2)(A)(v); PLIVA, Inc. v. Mensing, 564 U.S. 604 (2011).

73. Guarino v. Wyeth LLC, 823 F. Supp. 2d 1289 (M.D. Fla. 2011), *aff'd*, 719 F.3d 1245 (11th Cir. 2013) (granting generic defendant's motion to dismiss based on *Mensing* because "Plaintiff's claims are, on their face, premised on allegedly inadequate warnings"); Morris v. Wyeth, Inc., No. 09-CV-854, 2011 WL 4973839 (W.D. La. Oct. 19, 2011), *aff'd*, 713 F.3d 774 (5th Cir. 2013); Strayhorn v. Wyeth Pharms., Inc., 887 F. Supp. 2d 799 (W.D. Tenn. 2012), *aff'd*, 737 F.3d 378 (6th Cir. 2013); Chatman v. Pfizer, Inc., 960 F. Supp. 2d 641 (S.D. Miss. 2013), *modified*, No. 11-cv-0069, 2014 WL 4546042 (S.D. Miss. Sept. 11, 2014); Lashley v. Pfizer, Inc., 750 F.3d 470 (5th Cir. 2014); Bowman v. Wyeth, LLC, No. 10-1946 (JNE/SER), 2012 WL 684116 (D. Minn. Mar. 2, 2012).

between the two may be appropriate.[74] For example, "biosimilar product labeling may include information specific to the biosimilar product that is necessary to inform safe and effective use of the [biosimilar] product, including administration, preparation, storage, or safety information."[75]

The guidance further advises:

> [R]elevant data and information from the reference product labeling that should be incorporated into the biosimilar product labeling will depend on whether the applicant is seeking licensure for all conditions of use (e.g., indication(s), dosing regimen(s)) or fewer than all conditions of use of the reference product for the biosimilar product.[76]

In sections of the biosimilar product labeling that are based on the reference product labeling, the text should be similar to the corresponding text in the reference product labeling, but "need not be identical to the reference product labeling."[77] The biosimilar product labeling "should reflect currently available information necessary for the safe and effective use of the biosimilar product."[78]

For warnings and precautions on biosimilar labels, when the risk warned of applies to both the biosimilar product and the reference product, the biosimilar label should use the core name[79] of the reference product to indicate that the risk or other safety information applies to both the biosimilar and the reference product.[80] When the risk or safety information applies only to the biosimilar, the label should indicate this by using the biosimilar's proper name (the core name, followed by the approved suffix), or by using the biosimilar's proprietary name.[81] For example, when

---

74. FDA, Labeling for Biosimilar Products: Guidance for Industry (2018), 2018 WL 3727910, at *5 [hereinafter Labeling Guidance] ("Certain differences between the biosimilar and reference product labeling may be appropriate. . . . [B]iosimilar product labeling may include information specific to the biosimilar product that is necessary to inform safe and effective use of the product, including administration, preparation, storage, or safety information."); *see also* Goodwin Procter LLP, Guide to Biosimilars Litigation and Regulation in the U.S. § 9:2 (Nov. 2022 ed.).

75. Labeling Guidance, *supra* note 74, at *4.

76. *Id.* at * 2.

77. *Id.* at *4.

78. *Id.* ("Text based on the reference product labeling need not be identical to the reference product labeling and should reflect currently available information necessary for the safe and effective use of the biosimilar product.").

79. Biosimilars follow a specified naming guidance. "Core names" are shared among the reference biologic product and any related biosimilar products, and indicate relatedness between products. "Proper names" include a distinguishing suffix of four lowercase letters attached to the core name. For example, "adalimumab" is a core name, and "adalimumab-adaz" is a proper name.

80. Labeling Guidance, *supra* note 74, at *5–7.

81. *Id.*

warning of a risk that applies to all adalimumab products (both reference product and biosimilar products), the biosimilar label should warn that certain adverse events were associated with "adalimumab products."[82] When warning of a risk that applies only to the biosimilar, the label should warn that certain adverse events were associated with "adalimumab-[xxxx]," or should use the biosimilar's proprietary name.[83]

When new information becomes available that causes information in labeling to be inaccurate, false, or misleading, the biosimilar applicant must take steps to change the content of its product labeling. Under 21 C.F.R. § 601.12, a biosimilar manufacturer must submit to the FDA a supplement for any change in the package insert, package label, or container label to reflect newly acquired information intended to add or strengthen an instruction about dosage and administration that is intended to increase the safety of the use of the product. Under 21 C.F.R. § 601.12, a manufacturer can even distribute the drug with the updated labeling before FDA approval of the updated labeling, so long as the changes are made in order to:

- Add or strengthen a contraindication, warning, precaution, or adverse reaction for which the evidence of a causal association satisfies the standard for inclusion in the labeling
- Add or strengthen a statement about abuse, dependence, psychological effect, or overdosage
- Add or strengthen an instruction about dosage and administration that is intended to increase the safety of the use of the product
- Delete false, misleading, or unsupported indications for use or claims for effectiveness

If the proposed changes are to any of the other labeling requirements set forth in 21 C.F.R. § 201.57(a) (which details the information that must appear in all prescription drug labeling), the biosimilar manufacturer must wait for FDA approval before distributing the updated labeling. In situations where the biosimilar manufacturer must wait for FDA approval after submitting a supplement regarding labeling changes, impossibility preemption may apply.[84]

82. *Id.*

83. *Id.*

84. *See* PLIVA, Inc. v. Mensing, 564 U.S. 604, 620–24 (2011) (holding that federal drug regulations that prevented manufacturers from independently changing generic drugs' safety labels preempted state-law failure to warn claims); *see also* Mutual Pharm. Co., Inc. v. Bartlett, 570 U.S. 472, 492 (2013) (holding that state-law design defect claims that place a duty on manufacturers to render a drug safer by either altering its composition or altering its labeling are in conflict with federal laws that prohibit manufacturers from unilaterally altering drug composition or labeling).

Because the requirements for labeling small-molecule generic drugs under the Hatch-Waxman scheme differ from the labeling requirements for biosimilars, it is unclear whether the federal preemption that applies to failure to warn claims against generic small-molecule manufacturers will equally apply to biosimilar manufacturers. For example, if the FDA permits biosimilar manufacturers to change their labels unilaterally in response to post-marketing reports, without involving the FDA, federal law may not preempt state tort law claims with respect to the adequacy of warnings.[85] Moreover, if a biosimilar's label merely recites information about the reference biologic product and does not include specific information pertaining to additional risks that a manufacturer may be aware of that are specific to the biosimilar product, a court may find the biosimilar's label fails to provide a warning that is adequate. Conversely, plaintiffs might even claim that the biosimilar label mirrored the biologic reference product label *too* much, since a biosimilar does not have the exact same chemical makeup as the biologic reference product. In other words, the approach that the FDA takes to biosimilar labeling, whether as a whole or with respect to a particular product, may have an impact on the extent to which failure to warn claims are preempted.

In most jurisdictions, a drug manufacturer of a prescription pharmaceutical product can fulfill its duty to warn by providing adequate warnings to a prescribing health care provider. This "learned intermediary" doctrine shields manufacturers of prescription drugs from failure to warn claims when they have adequately warned health care providers of a drug's adverse effects.[86]

In the small-molecule context, the learned intermediary doctrine has been held to apply to drug manufacturers even when a pharmacist substitutes a generic for the prescribed branded drug.[87] In certain instances, there may even be grounds for dismissal of the claims as to the generic drug if the prescriber reviewed the warnings on only the branded drug's labeling.[88]

Nearly all states have implemented legislation allowing for a pharmacist to substitute an interchangeable biosimilar for a prescribed biologic

85. *Compare Mensing*, 564 U.S. at 620–24, *with* Wyeth v. Levine, 555 U.S. 555, 569–71 (2009) (holding that preemption did not bar claims when there is no evidence that the FDA would prohibit a label change, and it was thus not impossible for the drug manufacturer to satisfy both federal regulatory and state tort duties); *see also* Felix v. Hoffmann-LaRoche, Inc., 540 So. 2d 102, 105 (Fla. 1989) (examining text of package insert and explaining that the adequacy of a prescription drug warning "become[s] a question of law where the warning is accurate, clear, and unambiguous").

86. Restatement (Third) of Torts: Prod. Liab. § 6 (Am. L. Inst. 1998).

87. *See, e.g.*, Fullington v. Pfizer, Inc., 720 F.3d 739, 747 (8th Cir. 2013).

88. *See, e.g.*, Brinkley v. Pfizer, Inc., 772 F.3d 1133, 1138–39 (8th Cir. 2014).

reference product.[89] In instances where a pharmacy makes this substitution, courts may likewise apply the learned intermediary doctrine to limit or dismiss claims as to biosimilars manufacturers. However, where a biosimilar label differs from the reference product, it is unclear whether courts will also dismiss claims where the prescribing physician has reviewed only the biologic reference product's labeling.

B. Manufacturing Defect Claims

Manufacturing defect claims arise from an alleged deviation from the intended design of a product. A departure from the manufacturer's own design specification for that product is said to be a deviation from its "intended design."[90] In the drug manufacturing context, a manufacturing defect could include, for example, contamination of a product during manufacturing, or exceeding specified impurity or excipient levels in a product.

One potential issue in the biosimilar field is the complexity of biosimilar and biologic products. Variability in their manufacture could potentially lead to a greater risk of variability within the product. The

89. *See, e.g.*, Ala. Code § 34-23-8.1 (West 2020); Cal. Bus. & Prof. Code § 4073.5 (West 2020); Fla. Stat. Ann. § 465.0252 (West 2020); Ga. Comp. R. & Regs. 480-51-02 (West 2020); Haw. Rev. Stat. Ann. § 328-92 (West 2019); Idaho Admin. Code r. 27.01.01.404 (West 2019); 201 Ky. Admin. Regs. 2:116 (West 2020); Mass. Gen. Laws Ann. ch. 112, § 12EE (West 2020); Miss. Code Ann. § 73-21-117 (West 2020); N.H. Rev. Stat. Ann. § 318:47-dd (West 2020); N.J. Admin. Code § 13:39-7.23 (West 2020); N.D. Cent. Code Ann. § 19-02.1-14.3 (West 2020); Or. Admin. R. 855-041-1105 (West 2020); 22 Tex. Admin. Code § 309.3 (West 2020); Va. Code Ann. § 54.1-3408.04 (West 2019).

90. *See, e.g.*, Barker v. Lull Eng'g Co., 573 P.2d 443 (Cal. 1978) ("a defective product is one that differs from the manufacturer's intended result or from other ostensibly identical units of the same product line"); Banks v. ICI Ams., Inc., 450 S.E.2d 671, 673 (Ga. 1994) (in a manufacturing defect case "it is assumed that the design of the product is safe and had the product been manufactured in accordance with the design it would have been safe for consumer use"); La. Rev. Stat. Ann. § 9:2800.55 (West 1988) ("product deviated in a material way from the manufacturer's or designer's specifications or performance standards for the product or from otherwise identical products manufactured by the same manufacturer"); Singleton v. Int'l Harvester Co., 685 F.2d 112, 115 (4th Cir. 1981) (applying Maryland law) ("In manufacturing defect cases, the plaintiff proves that the product is defective by simply showing that it does not conform to the manufacturer's specifications."); Back v. Wickes Corp., 378 N.E.2d 964, 968–69 (Mass. 1978) (describing design defect as deviation from the manufacturer's design standard); Prentis v. Yale Mfg. Co., 365 N.W.2d 176, 182 (Mich. 1984) ("In the case of a 'manufacturing defect,' the product may be evaluated against the manufacturer's own production standards, as manifested by that manufacturer's other like products."); Miss. Code Ann. § 11-1-63 (1993) (product "deviated in a material way from the manufacturer's or designer's specifications or from otherwise identical units manufactured to the same manufacturing specifications"); Rix v. Gen. Motors Corp., 723 P.2d 195, 200 (Mont. 1986) (product is "flawed or defective because it was not constructed correctly by the manufacturer"; product does not conform to its intended design); Thibault v. Sears, Roebuck & Co., 395 A.2d 843, 846 (N.H. 1978) ("defect is an accidental variation caused by a mistake in the manufacturing process; that is, where the product does not 'conform to the great majority of products manufactured in accordance with that design'").

regulations applicable to vaccines and biosimilars require that an application for a license "spells out the manufacturing method that must be followed and the directions and warnings that must accompany the product."[91] Although the Supreme Court has not yet opined on this provision in a biosimilar or biologic context, in the vaccine context, it commented that deviation from the manufacturing method spelled out in the license is "objective evidence" of a manufacturing defect.[92] But there is an intrinsic risk of variation within the biosimilar product because biosimilars, unlike conventional pharmaceuticals, are composed of large molecules derived from natural processes rather than small-molecule chemical substances with known structures. Courts may require a plaintiff to demonstrate that a variation falls outside the scope of normal biosimilar variability, and that the deviation was responsible for the alleged injury. Conversely, courts may conclude that small variations among batches of a biosimilar product are sufficient to constitute "defects" within the spirit of the law governing manufacturing defect claims.[93]

C. Product Design Defect Claims

Design defects are alleged flaws in the design of the product, rendering a product unreasonably dangerous.[94] Unlike a manufacturing defect, a design defect applies not just to single products (or batches) deviating from the norm, but to *every* product manufactured according to the allegedly

---

91. Bruesewitz v. Wyeth LLC, 562 U.S. 223, 237 (2011).

92. In *Wyeth*, the Supreme Court held that plaintiff's design defect claims were expressly preempted by federal statute; the Court also discussed manufacturing defects, noting:

> *Deviations from the license thus provide objective evidence of manufacturing defects or inadequate warnings.* Further objective evidence comes from the FDA's regulations . . . that pervasively regulate the manufacturing process, down to the requirements for plumbing and ventilation systems at each manufacturing facility. Material noncompliance with any one of them, or with any other the FDA regulation, could cost the manufacturer its regulatory-compliance defense.

562 U.S. at 237 (emphasis added).

93. *See In re* MDL 2700 Genentech Herceptin (Trastuzumab) Mktg. & Sales Prac. Litig., 960 F.3d 1210 (10th Cir. 2020) (holding that state-law claims did not conflict with FDA's regulations regarding "reasonable variations" in biological packaging, and that defendant drug manufacturer failed to meet its burden to prove that it could not have changed the drug concentration statements on its product labeling).

94. *See* Restatement (Third) of Torts: Prod. Liab. § 2 (Am. L. Inst. 1998) ("Whereas a manufacturing defect consists of a product unit's failure to meet the manufacturer's design specifications, a product asserted to have a defective design meets the manufacturer's design specifications but raises the question whether the specifications themselves create unreasonable risks.").

defective design.[95] A plaintiff must typically show that a "reasonable alternative design" existed for the product.[96]

For generic drugs, the FDA requires a new drug applicant to file an ANDA containing data showing that it is bioequivalent to the branded drug.[97] A generic drug is considered bioequivalent if there is no "significant difference" in the time it takes for the generic drug's active ingredient to become available when administered at the same dose under similar conditions, compared with the time it takes for the branded drug.[98] For this reason, state-law claims that seek to hold a manufacturer of a generic drug liable for failing to alter the composition of the generic drug are subject to impossibility preemption.[99]

42 U.S.C.A. § 262(i)(2) regulates similarity between biosimilars and biologics. A biosimilar is "highly similar" to the biologic product "notwithstanding minor differences in inactive components" and it must have "no clinically meaningful differences" in terms of safety, purity, and potency.[100] Biosimilarity is established by (1) analytical "fingerprint" studies proving "high similarity"; (2) animal studies (including toxicity studies); and/or (3) at least one clinical study sufficient to demonstrate safety, purity, and potency for at least one condition of use for which the reference product is approved.[101] Under biosimilar regulations, a biosimilar cannot have any "clinically meaningful differences" from its reference product.[102] It is possible that if the statutory term "clinically meaningful difference" is treated the same as "bioequivalence" for generic drugs, impossibility preemption may apply to biosimilar product design defect claims in the same way that it applies to generic small-molecule design defect claims.

In a case where design defect was alleged against a biologic manufacturer, the court held that if the biologic at issue was incapable of being

---

95. *Id.*

96. *See id.* ("[T]he test is whether a reasonable alternative design would, at reasonable cost, have reduced the foreseeable risks of harm posed by the product and, if so, whether the omission of the alternative design by the seller or a predecessor in the distributive chain rendered the product not reasonably safe.").

97. *See* 21 C.F.R. § 314.94(a)(7) (2023).

98. *See id.* § 314.3.

99. *See* Mutual Pharm. Co., Inc. v. Bartlett, 570 U.S. 472, 492 (2013) (holding that state-law design defect claims that place a duty on manufacturers to render a generic drug safer by either altering its composition or altering its labeling are in conflict with federal laws that prohibit generic drug manufacturers from unilaterally altering drug composition or labeling).

100. 42 U.S.C.A. § 262(i)(2).

101. *Id.* § 262(k)(2).

102. *Id.* § 262(i)(2)(B).

reformulated, *Bartlett*[103] would bar any design defect claim based on an alleged failure to redesign the biologic.[104] The court further held that, even if the biologic was capable of being reformulated, it was likely that any claim that the design should have been changed before seeking FDA approval would also be preempted.[105]

For biosimilar design defect litigation, it is possible that courts may consider the reference biologic product to be evidence of a "reasonable alternative design" for the purposes of a negligent design defect claim. Conversely, courts may decide that since a biosimilar has "no clinically meaningful differences" from the reference biologic,[106] there is no difference for purposes of a "reasonable alternative design." Plaintiffs might be required to demonstrate that the biosimilar varied from the biologic in a "meaningful" way; however, this may implicate preemption by federal law and FDA regulations. Like the biologic reference product, and like generic small-molecule drugs, biosimilar products are required to receive FDA approval for proposed changes to the manufacturing process (or design) of a drug product. Meanwhile, state-law design defect claims necessarily allege that a drug manufacturer should change its manufacturing process in order to comply with tort standards. Because a drug manufacturer cannot change its manufacturing process without FDA approval, courts have found that design defect claims as to small-molecule products are

103. *Bartlett*, 570 U.S. at 492 (holding that state-law design defect claims that place a duty on manufacturers to render a drug "safer" by either altering its composition or altering its labeling are in conflict with federal laws that prohibit manufacturers from unilaterally altering drug composition or labeling, and are therefore preempted by federal law).

104. Small v. Amgen, Inc., No. 2:12-cv-476-FtM-29MRM, 2016 WL 7228863, at *4 (M.D. Fla. Sept. 28, 2016) (explaining that "*Bartlett* found that when a drug is 'chemically incapable' of being redesigned, it is impossible for a drug manufacturer to make the drug safer and thus state-law design-defect claims are preempted").

105. *Id.*

106. *See* 42 U.S.C.A. § 262(i)(2)(B).

preempted by federal law.[107] The same preemption theory may apply to claims involving alleged design defects in a biologic reference product.[108]

D. Field Preemption and Primary Jurisdiction

In addition to impossibility preemption, other theories may also be applied to block state-law product liability claims relating to biosimilars. As one example, field preemption could apply to bar state-law product liability claims against biosimilars. Field preemption occurs when states attempt to regulate a field where a pervasive scheme of federal regulation already exists.[109] More specifically, courts may find that Congress did not intend for the states to interfere with the pervasive federal regulatory scheme

107. *See Bartlett*, 570 U.S. at 492.

108. For example, in *In re Genentech, Inc.*, 367 F. Supp. 3d 1274 (N.D. Okla. 2019), the court held that the plaintiffs' labeling claims conflicted with federal law, which allowed a range of "reasonable variations" for solid drugs sold in vials. The court also held that plaintiffs' claims that defendant could comply with plaintiffs' state-law-based demands by changing either the manufacturing process of the biologic or the labeling of the biologic failed as a matter of law under the doctrine of impossibility preemption, because these changes required FDA approval. Citing *Jones v. Rath Packing Co.*, 430 U.S. 519 (1977), and distinguishing *Wyeth v. Levine*, 555 U.S. 555 (2009), the court held that "Plaintiffs' labeling claims conflict with federal law, which permits reasonable variations for solid drugs sold in vials. . . . [T]he regulatory scheme expressly allows a range of 'reasonable variations' for solid drugs sold in vials, and Plaintiffs' state-law claims conflict with these regulations." *Genentech*, 367 F. Supp. 3d at 1288–89. In granting the motion for summary judgment, the district court also held that plaintiffs' claims that defendant could comply with plaintiffs' state-law-based demands by changing either the manufacturing process or the labeling of Herceptin failed as a matter of law under the doctrine of impossibility preemption, because these changes required FDA approval. *Id.* On appeal, however, the Tenth Circuit reversed summary judgment, finding that because

> the product labels of the vials of Herceptin that were sold to plaintiffs all stated that the vials contained 440 mg of trastuzumab, [the federal regulations] effectively required those vials to all contain at least 440 mg of trastuzumab. Therefore, the federal regulatory standard is precisely the same as the state law standards sought to be imposed by plaintiff. Consequently, the doctrine of obstacle pre-emption does not bar plaintiffs' claims.

In re MDL 2700 Genentech Herceptin (Trastuzumab) Mktg. & Sales Prac. Litig., 960 F.3d 1210, 1224 (10th Cir. 2020). The Tenth Circuit likewise rejected the manufacturer's impossibility preemption arguments, because the manufacturer failed to establish that complying with the target range of trastuzumab per vial would have resulted in a "major change" under 21 C.F.R. § 601.12(b) that would require FDA preapproval. *Id.* at 1239.

109. Pennsylvania v. Nelson, 350 U.S. 497, 502–04 (1956) (holding that if "the scheme of federal regulation [is] so pervasive as to make reasonable the inference that Congress left no room for the States to supplement it, state law is preempted regardless of whether it purports to supplement the federal law").

pertaining to biosimilars under the BPCIA, warranting application of field preemption.[110]

As an alternative example, courts may apply the primary jurisdiction doctrine. The primary jurisdiction doctrine "is concerned with 'promoting proper relationships between the courts and administrative agencies charged with particular regulatory duties.'"[111] Courts would stay proceedings, deferring issues to a federal agency, where state-law claims involve issues specifically within that agency's ambit and expertise. Relevant factors for such an inquiry include (1) whether the question at issue is within the conventional experience of judges or whether it involves technical or policy considerations within the agency's particular field of expertise; (2) whether the question at issue is particularly within the agency's discretion; (3) whether there exists a substantial danger of inconsistent rulings; and (4) whether a prior application to the agency has been made.[112] Together, field preemption and the primary jurisdiction doctrine provide viable strategies to combat state-law product liability claims.

110. *But see* Levine v. Am. Home Prods., Inc., No. 670-12-01 Wncv, 2003 WL 25648135 (Vt. Super. Ct. Dec. 23, 2003) (rejecting defendant drug manufacturer's field preemption argument that the FDA's regulatory activity is so extensive with regard to the content of drug labels that state tort law actions asserting failure to warn claims effectively are preempted as a matter of law). Defendant did not advance its rejected field preemption argument on appeal to the Supreme Court. *See Wyeth*, 555 U.S. at 560.

111. Ellis v. Tribune Television Co., 443 F.3d 71, 81 (2d Cir. 2006) (quoting United States v. W. Pac. R.R. Co., 352 U.S. 59, 63 (1956)).

112. *Id.* at 82–83.

Part III

chapter 12

Product Case Studies (Humira®, Neupogen®/ Neulasta®, and Herceptin®)*

When deciding product development strategy with respect to biosimilars, facing down a patent thicket may seem daunting at best, insurmountable at worst. Yet, the reality is that those worth the investment are likely those that will involve a patent dance, oftentimes with a large number of patents.

With that in mind, this chapter digs into four well-known and publicized biosimilar product case studies: AbbVie's Humira® (adalimumab), Amgen's Neupogen® (filgrastim)/Neulasta® (pegfilgrastim), and Genentech's Herceptin® (trastuzumab).

I. Humira®

A. Biologic Overview and Background

The biologics license for Humira® (adalimumab) was approved on December 31, 2002, by the U.S. Food and Drug Administration (FDA).[1] The original and sole indication for Humira® was for "reducing signs and symptoms and inhibiting the progression of structural damage in adult patients with moderately to severely active rheumatoid arthritis who have had an inadequate response to one or more disease-modifying anti-rheumatic drugs (DMARDs)."[2]

---

*Deepro R. Mukerjee and Lance A. Soderstrom, Katten Muchin Rosenman LLP, New York; and Jillian M. Schurr and Matthew M. Holub, Katten Muchin Rosenman LLP, Chicago.

1. *AbbVie Inc. Humira® (Adalimumab) Package Insert*, FDA, https://www.accessdata.fda.gov/drugsatfda_docs/label/2002/adalabb123102LB.htm (last updated Jan. 27, 2023).

2. AbbVie Inc. Humira® (Adalimumab) Label (2004), https://www.accessdata.fda.gov/drugsatfda_docs/label/2004/125057_0016lbl.pdf.

The indications were subsequently amended to include "inducing major clinical response" and "improving physical function" in adults with moderately to severely active rheumatoid arthritis; for active arthritis in patients with psoriatic arthritis;[3] reducing signs and symptoms in patients with active ankylosing spondylitis;[4] reducing signs and symptoms and maintaining clinical remission in adult patients with moderately to severely active Crohn's disease;[5] treatment of adult patients with moderate to severe chronic plaque psoriasis;[6] juvenile idiopathic arthritis;[7] ulcerative colitis;[8] pediatric Crohn's disease;[9] hidradenitis suppurativa;[10] and uveitis.[11]

The exhaustive list of initial and follow-on indications provides a glimmer into what AbbVie's (and Abbott's before it[12]) patent strategy was with respect to Humira®. As phrased in a 2019 complaint alleging antitrust violations, the Humira® patents "served their purpose: creating a minefield of [intellectual property] so extensive that competitors would have to engage in costly and time-consuming litigation over dozens upon dozens of patents before they could launch competing products."[13] But such a minefield did not thwart a large amount of challengers under the Biologics Price Competition and Innovation Act (BPCIA). A number of companies engaged in the patent dance with AbbVie while others settled without having to tango.

---

3. AbbVie Inc. Humira® (Adalimumab) Label (2005), https://www.accessdata.fda.gov/drugsatfda_docs/label/2005/125057s0045,0046lbl.pdf.

4. *Id.*

5. AbbVie Inc. Humira® (Adalimumab) Label (2007), https://www.accessdata.fda.gov/drugsatfda_docs/label/2007/125057s060LBL.pdf.

6. AbbVie Inc. Humira® (Adalimumab) Label (2008), https://www.accessdata.fda.gov/drugsatfda_docs/label/2008/125057s114lbl.pdf.

7. AbbVie Inc. Humira® (Adalimumab) Label (2009), https://www.accessdata.fda.gov/drugsatfda_docs/label/2009/125057s196lbl.pdf.

8. AbbVie Inc. Humira® (Adalimumab) Label (2014), https://www.accessdata.fda.gov/drugsatfda_docs/label/2014/125057s368lbl.pdf.

9. AbbVie Inc. Humira® (Adalimumab) Label (2016), https://www.accessdata.fda.gov/drugsatfda_docs/label/2016/125057s400lbl.pdf.

10. *Id.*

11. *Id.*

12. AbbVie split from Abbott in 2013, where AbbVie became a new independent biopharmaceutical company. Press Release, Abbott, Abbott Completes Separation of Research-Based Pharmaceuticals Business (Jan. 2, 2023), https://www.prnewswire.com/news-releases/abbott-completes-separation-of-research-based-pharmaceuticals-business-185406542.html.

13. Amended Complaint ¶ 4, *In re* Humira (Adalimumab) Antitr. Litig., No. 1:19-cv-01873, Doc. No. 109 (N.D. Ill. Aug. 9, 2019). This antitrust action on behalf of indirect purchasers of Humira® was dismissed without prejudice as the court held that "what plaintiffs describe is not an antitrust violation. AbbVie has exploited advantages conferred on it through lawful practices and to the extent this has kept the prices high for Humira, existing antitrust doctrine does not prohibit it." Opinion and Order at 2, *In re* Humira (Adalimumab) Antitr. Litig., No. 1:19-cv-01873, Doc. No. 170 (N.D. Ill. June 8, 2020).

The willingness of biosimilar companies to challenge AbbVie's patent thicket should not obscure the amount of investment and legal defense that AbbVie engaged in to protect its Humira® intellectual property. As shown in a 2015 investor presentation, the initial composition of matter patent for Humira® expired on December 31, 2016.[14]

While the initial composition of matter patent (U.S. Patent No. 6,090,382) may have expired only three years after AbbVie split with Abbott, AbbVie continued to file and receive patents for new indications, formulations, manufacturing process(es), and diagnostics/devices.[15] One of those new formulations was the citrate-free, high-concentration version of Humira® that promised lower pain compared to the original marketed formulation that was launched in 2018.[16] That formulation was also subject to challenges under the BPCIA and subsequent biosimilar competition, as outlined later in the chapter.

B. Litigation and Settlement History

1. Patent Dances

a. AbbVie v. Amgen, Case No. 16-666 (D. Del.)

Amgen was the first to file an abbreviated biologics license application (aBLA) for Humira® on November 25, 2015.[17] The parties began the patent dance in 2016, shortly before the FDA's approval of Amgen's Amjevita in September 2016.[18] Initially, Amgen provided its aBLA to AbbVie and did not agree to allow AbbVie to expand the individuals who could review its aBLA beyond the one person allowed by the statute[19]—a move that AbbVie took issue with. In its 3A list,[20] AbbVie identified 61 patents and five allowed patent applications out of the more than 100 patents in its Humira® portfolio.[21] AbbVie supplemented its 3A list three times to list the then-issued patents from the five patent applications previously

---

14. Richard Gonzalez, AbbVie, AbbVie Long-Term Strategy 14 (2015), https://investors.abbvie.com/static-files/af79eef2-5901-4b62-9354-982d2d95404e.

15. *See* Mayor & City Council of Balt. v. AbbVie Inc., 42 F.4th 709, 711 (7th Cir. 2022) ("The basic U.S. patent for Humira, No. 6,090,382, expired at the end of 2016, but AbbVie, its owner, obtained 132 additional patents related to the medicine, for details such as manufacturing or administering the drug. The last of these expires in 2034.").

16. *See* Gonzalez, *supra* note 14, at 14–17.

17. Complaint ¶ 36, AbbVie Inc. v. Amgen Inc., No. 16-cv-666 (D. Del. Aug. 4, 2016).

18. Press Release, FDA, FDA Approves Amjevita, a Biosimilar to Humira (Sept. 23, 2016), https://www.fda.gov/news-events/press-announcements/fda-approves-amjevita-biosimilar-humira.

19. Complaint ¶ 38, *AbbVie Inc.*, No. 16-cv-666.

20. AbbVie's list pursuant to 42 U.S.C. § 262(*l*)(3)(A).

21. Complaint ¶ 39, *AbbVie Inc.*, No. 16-cv-666.

listed.[22] AbbVie later identified 60 patents total in its 3C statement,[23] removing six that it was no longer pursuing and adding a newly issued patent, bringing the total to 61 patents.[24]

Pursuant to the statute, the parties began discussing how many of the patents they believed should be litigated. AbbVie's initial position was that *all* patents should be included in the suit to "further[] the interests in judicial economy, by avoiding two waves of litigation."[25] Amgen's proposal was far fewer, listing six patents it would agree to be sued on and making the maximum number pursuant to the BPCIA to be 12 (six patents from each side).[26] AbbVie ultimately initiated suit with ten patents at issue, given the overlap of two patents on the parties' lists.[27]

During litigation the parties underwent contentious discovery, complete with discovery disputes, protective order disputes, and contention exchanges. Just over a year from initiating litigation, on September 28, 2017, the parties submitted a stipulation of dismissal following a settlement agreement.[28] The settlement agreement granted Amgen a nonexclusive license, which would begin on January 31, 2023, in the United States and on October 16, 2018, in most countries in the European Union.[29] In turn, Amgen would pay royalties to AbbVie as specified under the confidential agreement and acknowledged the validity of AbbVie's intellectual property related to Humira®.[30]

b. AbbVie v. Boehringer Ingelheim, Case No. 17-1065 (D. Del.)

Amgen was the first to file an aBLA for Humira®, but Boehringer Ingelheim was close behind and submitted its aBLA for its Cyltezo® product

---

22. *Id.* ¶ 40.

23. Provided pursuant to 42 U.S.C. § 262(*l*)(3)(C).

24. Complaint ¶ 42–44, *AbbVie Inc.*, No. 16-cv-666.

25. *Id.* ¶ 46.

26. *Id.*; 42 U.S.C. § 262(*l*)(5)(B)(ii)(I).

27. Complaint ¶ 47, *AbbVie Inc.*, No. 16-cv-666.

28. Stipulation of Dismissal, AbbVie v. Amgen, No. 16-666 (D. Del. Sept. 28, 2017), ECF No. 113; Press Release, AbbVie, AbbVie Announces Global Resolution of Humira® (Adalimumab) Patent Disputes with Amgen (Sept. 28, 2017), https://news.abbvie.com/2017-09-28-AbbVie-Announces-Global-Resolution-of-HUMIRA-R-adalimumab-Patent-Disputes-with-Amgen.

29. Press Release, AbbVie, *supra* note 28. The agreement also disclosed that the license would cover various other countries on other dates for which AbbVie has intellectual property.

30. *Id.*

in 2016.[31] Cyltezo® was initially approved by the FDA in 2017[32] as a biosimilar but was granted interchangeable status in 2021.[33] Cyltezo® was the first and only interchangeable biosimilar, until recently. It is now joined by Pfizer's Abrilada™ and Alvotech/Teva's Simlandi®.[34] Following the FDA's approval of Boehringer's aBLA in January 2017, the parties began the patent dance.[35] In March 2017, AbbVie provided Boehringer with its 3A list identifying 72 patents.[36] AbbVie took the same position it did with Amgen and proposed that the parties litigate all of the identified patents.[37] Not surprisingly, Boehringer took a similar approach to Amgen and agreed to be sued on only five patents.[38] Pursuant to 42 U.S.C. § 262(*l*)(5) the parties exchanged their lists of five patents, two of which overlapped, and resulted in a total of eight patents at issue in the litigation.[39]

The litigation began in August 2017 and continued through May 2019. During the pendency of the litigation, the parties engaged in a significant amount of written discovery, depositions, subpoenas, protective orders, and discovery motions. Boehringer took the litigation as an opportunity to allege AbbVie's patent thicket was created in order to delay competition and in doing so, filed motions to compel the production of previous litigation documents and settlements.[40] The parties stipulated to dismissal of

31. Complaint ¶ 49, AbbVie Inc. v. Boehringer Ingelheim Int'l GmbH, No. 17-cv-01065, Doc. No. 1 (D. Del. Aug. 2, 2017).

32. Press Release, Boehringer Ingelheim, Boehringer Ingelheim Pharmaceuticals, Inc. Receives FDA Approval for Cyltezo™ (Adalimumab-adbm), a Biosimilar to Humira®, for the Treatment of Multiple Chronic Inflammatory Diseases (Aug. 29, 2017), https://www.boehringer-ingelheim.com/us/press-release/boehringer-ingelheim-pharmaceuticals-inc-receives-fda-approval-cyltezo-adalimumab.

33. *Id.* Boehringer Ingelheim announced that the FDA approval of its supplemental biologics license application (sBLA) for Cyltezo® was supported by positive data from its Phase III randomized VOLTAIRE-X clinical trial. *See id.*

34. *Purple Book Database of Licensed Biological Products: Humira*, FDA, https://purplebooksearch.fda.gov/results?query=adalimumab&title=Humira (last visited Mar. 4, 2024); *see also* Press Release, Pfizer, FDA Grants Interchangeable Designation to Pfizer's Biosimilar ABRILADA™ (Oct. 5, 2023), https://www.pfizer.com/news/announcements/fda-grants-interchangeable-designation-pfizers-biosimilar-abriladatm; Press Release, Teva, Alvotech and Teva Announce U.S. Approval of SIMLANDI® (Adalimumab-ryvk) Injection, the First Interchangeable High-Concentration, Citrate-Free Biosimilar to Humira® (Feb. 24, 2024), https://www.tevapharm.com/news-and-media/latest-news/alvotech-and-teva-announce-u.s.-approval-of-simlandi-adalimumab-ryvk-injection-the-first-interchangea/.

35. Complaint ¶¶ 52–54, AbbVie Inc. v. Boehringer Ingelheim Int'l GmbH, No. 17-1065, Doc. No. 1 (D. Del. Aug. 2, 2017).

36. *Id.* ¶ 54.

37. *Id.* ¶ 59.

38. *Id.*

39. *Id.* ¶ 60.

40. Answer ¶ 21, AbbVie Inc. v. Boehringer Ingelheim Int'l GmbH, No. 17-065, Doc. No. 20 (D. Del. Sept. 11, 2017); *see also id.* Doc. No. 472 (granting defendants' motion to compel the production of Amgen's 3B and 3C statements, as well as certain settlement agreements entered into by the plaintiffs with third parties).

the litigation after reaching a settlement agreement. AbbVie announced that in resolving the litigation, the terms of the settlement would grant Boehringer a nonexclusive license to its Humira®-related intellectual property in the United States, which would allow Boehringer to launch Cyltezo® beginning on July 1, 2023.[41] Just as with the settlement agreement with Amgen, the settlement agreement with Boehringer requires royalties to be paid and Boehringer to acknowledge the validity as well as the enforceability[42] of the licensed patents.

c. AbbVie v. Sandoz, Case No. 18-cv-12668 (D.N.J.)

Sandoz's aBLA for Humira® was accepted by the FDA in January 2018.[43] In its 3C statement, AbbVie identified 84 patents.[44] In response, Sandoz responded that it would only agree to be sued on a single patent.[45] That resulted in only two patents being at issue in the litigation. Following the initiation of the litigation on August 10, 2018, the parties engaged in discussions and came to an agreement for the dismissal of the action in October 2018. Under the terms of the settlement agreement, Sandoz was granted a nonexclusive license beginning on September 30, 2023, in the United States and the agreement did not include any acceleration clause.[46] The terms also required Sandoz to pay royalties and to acknowledge the validity of the licensed patents.[47] Sandoz's biosimilar Hyrimoz® was approved by the FDA on October 31, 2018.[48]

While the district court litigation was short-lived, resulting in a dismissal before Sandoz filed its answer, the parties had engaged in litigation in a separate forum. Prior to litigation in the district court, Sandoz had filed at least six inter partes review (IPR) petitions at the Patent Trial and

41. Press Release, AbbVie, AbbVie Resolves HUMIRA® (Adalimumab) U.S. Patent Litigation with Boehringer Ingelheim (May 14, 2019), https://news.abbvie.com/2019-05-14-AbbVie-Resolves-HUMIRA-R-adalimumab-U-S-Patent-Litigation-with-Boehringer-Ingelheim.

42. The difference in language between the Amgen agreement press release and the Boehringer press release is likely related to the fact that Boehringer put forth an unclean hands defense alleging unenforceability. *See, e.g.*, Memorandum and Order, AbbVie Inc. v. Boehringer Ingelheim Int'l GmbH, No. 17-065, Doc. No. 112 (D. Del. June 4, 2018).

43. Complaint ¶ 66, AbbVie Inc. v. Sandoz Inc., No. 18-12668, Doc. No. 1 (D.N.J. Aug. 10, 2018).

44. *Id.* ¶ 71.

45. *Id.* ¶ 72.

46. Press Release, AbbVie, AbbVie Announces Global Resolution of HUMIRA® (Adalimumab) Patent Disputes with Sandoz (Oct. 11, 2018), https://news.abbvie.com/2018-10-11-AbbVie-Announces-Global-Resolution-of-HUMIRA-R-adalimumab-Patent-Disputes-with-Sandoz.

47. *Id.*

48. Press Release, Sandoz, Sandoz Receives US FDA Approval for Biosimilar Hyrimoz™ (Adalimumab-adaz) (Oct. 31, 2028), https://www.us.sandoz.com/news/media-releases/sandoz-receives-us-fda-approval-biosimilar-hyrimoz-adalimumab-adaz/.

Appeal Board (PTAB) where institution was denied.[49] While AbbVie was successful defending against the majority of the IPRs brought by Sandoz and others, at least some of its patents were invalidated in front of the PTAB.[50]

d. AbbVie v. Alvotech, Case Nos. 21-cv-22558, 21-cv-02899 (N.D. Ill.)

In 2020, Alvotech submitted its aBLA for its proposed Humira® biosimilar, AVT02, for review and announced on November 19, 2020, that the FDA had accepted it.[51] The parties began the patent dance in November 2020 followed by AbbVie providing its 3C statement in March 2021, which included allegations with respect to 62 patents.[52] Alvotech proposed that only four of the 62 patents be a part of the litigation.[53] As such, the initial litigation between the parties went forward with only those four patents.[54] Yet, the case did not progress as others did. AbbVie initiated litigation against Alvotech in the Northern District of Illinois[55] and in response, Alvotech filed a declaratory judgment action on the same patents in the Eastern District of Virginia.[56] But litigation did not stop there. Under the BPCIA, there are two contemplated waves of litigation, one pursuant to the exchanges between the parties under 42 U.S.C. § 262(*l*)(3) and the second that is triggered by the applicant providing its notice of commercial marketing.[57] On the same day it filed suit in the Eastern District of Virginia, Alvotech provided its notice of commercial marketing under 42 U.S.C. § 262(*l*)(8)(4). As a result, AbbVie filed a second suit in the Northern District of Illinois on May 28, 2021.[58]

---

49. Complaint ¶ 3 n.1, AbbVie Inc. v. Sandoz Inc., No. 18-12668, Doc. No. 1 (D.N.J. Aug. 10, 2018) (collecting cases).

50. In three IPRs brought by Coherus BioSciences Inc., the PTAB issued three final written decisions finding claims 1–5 of U.S. Patent No. 8,889,135, claims 1–4 of U.S. Patent No. 9,017,680, and claims 1 and 2 of U.S. Patent No. 9,073,987 unpatentable. *See* Christopher J. Betti & Maria E. Doukas, *Humira Patents Invalidated in Inter Partes Reviews*, Morgan Lewis (June 14, 2017), https://www.morganlewis.com/pubs/2017/06/humira-patents-invalidated-in-inter-partes-reviews.

51. Press Release, Alvotech, U.S. FDA and EMA Have Accepted Regulatory Submissions for AVT02-Alvotech (Nov. 19, 2020), https://www.alvotech.com/newsroom/alvotech-announces-that-the-u.s.-fda-and-ema-have-accepted.

52. Complaint ¶¶ 45–48, AbbVie Inc. v. Alvotech hf., No. 1:21-cv-02258, Doc. No. 1 (N.D. Ill. Apr. 27, 2021).

53. *Id.* ¶ 49.

54. *Id.* ¶ 61.

55. *See generally id.*

56. Alvotech USA Inc. v. AbbVie Inc., No. 21-cv-00265 (E.D. Va. May 11, 2021); *see also* Skylar Jeremias, *Alvotech Heats Up Patent Dispute Conflict by Suing AbbVie Over Humira Biosimilar*, AJMC (May 11, 2021), https://www.ajmc.com/view/alvotech-heats-up-patent-dispute-conflict-by-suing-abbvie-over-humira-biosimilar.

57. *See* 42 U.S.C. § 262(*l*)(8)–(9).

58. AbbVie Inc. v. Alvotech hf., No. 1:21-cv-02899 (N.D. Ill. May 28, 2021).

Just under a year from the initiation of the first litigation, AbbVie and Alvotech reached a settlement with respect to AVT02.[59] Under the terms of the agreement, AbbVie granted Alvotech a nonexclusive license to its Humira-related patents in the United States beginning on July 1, 2023. Like others, Alvotech would pay royalties to AbbVie and acknowledge the validity and enforceability of the licensed patents.[60] As outlined later, Alvotech and Teva announced in late February 2024 that AVT02, now known and marketed as Simlandi®, was approved by the FDA as an interchangeable biosimilar for Humira®.[61]

2. Biosimilar without the Patent Dance

a. Samsung Bioepis

Prior to even submitting its aBLA, Samsung Bioepis reached resolution with AbbVie regarding "its proposed biosimilar adalimumab product" on April 5, 2018.[62] The agreement provided Samsung Bioepis with a nonexclusive license, which would begin on June 30, 2023, in the United States and October 16, 2018, in most countries in the European Union. Included within the press release was a statement regarding AbbVie's settlement with Amgen: "On September 28, 2017, AbbVie announced a global resolution with Amgen to enter the U.S. market on January 31, 2023. Samsung Bioepis' U.S. license date will not be accelerated upon Amgen's entry."[63]

As part of the resolution, all litigation pending between the parties, including Samsung Bioepis's European partner (Biogen) were to be dismissed. Samsung Bioepis was the second to settle with AbbVie following Amgen. Samsung Bioepis's biosimilar Hadlima® low-concentration formulation was approved by the FDA in July 2019 and the high-concentration citrate-free approved in August 2022.[64]

---

59. Press Release, AbbVie, AbbVie Resolves HUMIRA® (Adalimumab) U.S. Litigation with Alvotech (Mar. 8, 2022), https://news.abbvie.com/2022-03-08-AbbVie-Resolves-HUMIRA-R-adalimumab-U-S-Litigation-with-Alvotech.

60. *Id.*

61. *See* Press Release, Teva, *supra* note 34.

62. Press Release, AbbVie, AbbVie Announces Global Resolution of HUMIRA® (Adalimumab) Patent Disputes with Samsung Bioepis (Apr. 5, 2018), https://news.abbvie.com/index.php?s=2429&item=123539.

63. *Id.*

64. Press Release, Organon, Samsung Bioepis and Organon Announce FDA Approval of Citrate-Free High-Concentration HUMIRA® Biosimilar HADLIMA® (Adalimumab-bwwd) (Aug. 17, 2022), https://www.organon.com/news/samsung-bioepis-and-organon-announce-fda-approval-of-citrate-free-high-concentration-humira-biosimilar-hadlima-adalimumab-bwwd/.

b. Mylan

On July 17, 2018, AbbVie announced resolution with Mylan following its submission of its aBLA for Hulio, its biosimilar to Humira®.[65] Like the settlements before it, Mylan was granted a nonexclusive license that would begin on July 31, 2023, in the United States and would not be accelerated by Amgen's or Samsung Bioepis's entry. As with others, Mylan will pay royalties to AbbVie and acknowledged the validity of the licensed patents.[66] Hulio was approved by the FDA on July 6, 2020.[67]

c. Fresenius Kabi

On October 18, 2018, AbbVie announced resolution of all intellectual property-related litigation with Fresenius Kabi.[68] Under the terms of the agreement, the terms of the nonexclusive license would begin on September 30, 2023, in the United States and upon approval from the European Medicines Agency for the European Union.[69] Fresenius Kabi subsequently received FDA approval of its biosimilar, Idacio®, on December 14, 2022.[70] Idacio® was originally launched in 2019 outside of the United States and is a citrate-free biosimilar to Humira®.

d. Momenta

On November 6, 2018, AbbVie announced that it had entered patent license agreements with Momenta over its proposed biosimilar for Humira®, noting that the license would begin on November 20, 2023, and "will not be accelerated by the entry of companies who have already taken a license" (i.e., Amgen, Samsung Bioepis, Mylan, Fresenius, Sandoz).[71] However, in October 2018, Momenta announced that it would exit the biosimilar drug

---

65. Press Release, AbbVie, AbbVie Announces HUMIRA® (Adalimumab) Patent License with Mylan (July 17, 2018), https://news.abbvie.com/2018-07-17-AbbVie-Announces-HUMIRA-R-adalimumab-Patent-License-with-Mylan.

66. *Id.*

67. *FDA Approves Mylan's Biosimilar of HUMIRA (Adalimumab)*, BIG MOLECULE WATCH (July 7, 2020), https://www.bigmoleculewatch.com/2020/07/07/fda-approves-mylans-biosimilar-of-humira-adalimumab/.

68. Press Release, AbbVie, AbbVie Announces Global Resolution of HUMIRA® (Adalimumab) Patent Disputes with Fresenius Kabi (Oct. 18, 2018), https://news.abbvie.com/2018-10-18-AbbVie-Announces-Global-Resolution-of-HUMIRA-R-adalimumab-Patent-Disputes-with-Fresenius-Kabi.

69. *Id.*

70. *Fresenius Kabi Receives U.S. FDA Approval for Biosimilar Idacio® (Adalimumab)*, FRESENIUS KABI AG (Dec. 14, 2022), https://www.fresenius-kabi.com/news/fresenius-kabi-receives-fda-approval-for-biosimilar-Idacio.

71. Press Release, AbbVie, AbbVie Announces HUMIRA® (Adalimumab) Global Patent License with Momenta (Nov. 6, 2018), https://news.abbvie.com/2018-11-06-AbbVie-Announces-HUMIRA-R-adalimumab-Global-Patent-License-with-Momenta.

development space and direct resources instead to its novel pipeline.[72] In doing so, Momenta terminated its development on its Humira® biosimilar, noting the litigation and patent agreement landscape that AbbVie had created.[73]

e. Pfizer

On November 30, 2018, Pfizer announced that it had entered into licensing agreements with AbbVie for its biosimilar of Humira®.[74] Under the terms of the agreement, Pfizer would be able to launch its product in the United States on November 20, 2023.[75] The FDA approved Pfizer's biosimilar, Abrilada®, in November 2019.[76]

f. Celltrion

In April 2022, Celltrion announced that it reached a "patent agreement" with AbbVie that allowed it to enter the U.S. Humira® biosimilar market with its product Yuflyma in July 2023.[77] Yuflyma is a high-concentration formulation of adalimumab where Celltrion has also received approval in at least the European Union, Korea, and Canada.

g. Coherus BioSciences

On January 25, 2019, Coherus BioSciences announced that it had resolved all disputes with AbbVie related to its proposed Humira® biosimilar.[78] Coherus was granted a license date of December 15, 2023, under the agreement.[79] Coherus announced that at that time it was currently preparing its aBLA (CHS-1420) for submission to the FDA with an anticipated filing in late 2019.[80]

---

72. Jessica Merrill, *Momenta Is Exiting Biosimilars: Is That a Bellwether for Biosimilar Sentiment?*, Scrip Citeline (Oct. 2, 2018), https://scrip.citeline.com/SC123934/Momenta-Is-Exiting-Biosimilars-Is-That-A-Bellwether-For-Biosimilar-Sentiment.

73. *Id.*

74. Press Release, Pfizer, Pfizer Reaches a Global Agreement with AbbVie (Nov. 30, 2018), https://www.pfizer.com/news/press-release/press-release-detail/pfizer_reaches_a_global_agreement_with_abbvie.

75. *Id.*

76. Press Release, Pfizer, FDA Approves Pfizer's Biosimilar, ABRILADA™ (Adalimumab-afzb) for Multiple Inflammatory Conditions (Nov. 18, 2019), https://www.pfizer.com/news/press-release/press-release-detail/fda_approves_pfizer_s_biosimilar_abrilada_adalimumab_afzb_for_multiple_inflammatory_conditions.

77. Lee Han-soo, *Celltrion to Start Marketing Humira Biosimilar in US from July 2023*, Korea Biomed. Rev. (Apr. 27, 2022), https://www.koreabiomed.com/news/articleView.html?idxno=13584.

78. Press Release, Coherus BioSciences, Coherus BioSciences Announces Global Settlement with AbbVie Securing Rights to Commercialize Its Adalimumab Biosimilar Candidate, CHS-1420 (Jan. 25, 2019), https://investors.coherus.com/news-releases/news-release-details/coherus-biosciences-announces-global-settlement-abbvie-securing.

79. *Id.*

80. *Id.*

While the parties may not have engaged in the patent dance with each other, they took on each other in a more recent litigation duel. In the summer of 2023, Mark Cuban's discount drug company, Mark Cuban Cost Plus Drug Co., announced that it planned to sell Coherus's biosimilar of Humira®, branded as Yusimry and set to launch in July 2023.[81] Normally that announcement would be noncontroversial. However, Cuban announced that the price of Yusimry would be substantially lower than the brand. Indeed, it would be only $569.27 for a carton of two autoinjectors compared to the $6,922 charged by AbbVie monthly.[82]

In response to this announcement, AbbVie sent a letter to Coherus asserting that by entering into the agreement with Cuban, it would be a breach of the parties' licensing agreements.[83] Coherus revealed this in a June 6 Securities and Exchange Commission filing.[84] In response, Coherus filed a temporary restraining order in a Delaware court, which was met with AbbVie filing a request for a preliminary injunction.[85] Shortly thereafter, on June 15, 2023, Coherus announced that it had agreed to retract a restraining order against AbbVie as they continue to discuss the terms of launching Coherus's biosimilar.[86] Coherus ultimately launched its biosimilar on July 3, 2023.[87]

C. Biosimilar Impact on AbbVie's Humira® Revenue

AbbVie announced its second quarter 2023 financial results in July 2023, reporting a global Humira® net revenue of $4.012 billion.[88] It reported that the net revenue was a "decrease[] of 25.2 percent on a reported basis, or 24.8 percent on an operational basis."[89] With respect to the net revenue for the United States, AbbVie reported Humira® to be $3.452 billion, a decrease of 26 percent.[90]

---

81. Kevin Dunleavy, *Coherus Breached Humira Patent Settlement by Striking Deal with Mark Cuban's Drug Firm, AbbVie Contends*, Fierce Pharma (June 15, 2023), https://www.fiercepharma.com/pharma/coherus-breached-humira-patent-settlement-striking-deal-mark-cubans-drug-firm-abbvie.

82. *Id.*

83. *Id.*

84. *Id.*

85. *Id.*

86. *Coherus Resolves Part of Dispute with AbbVie over Humira Biosimilar*, Reuters (June 15, 2023), https://www.reuters.com/business/healthcare-pharmaceuticals/abbvie-coherus-agree-resolve-dispute-over-humira-biosimilar-2023-06-15/.

87. *Coherus BioSciences Launches Biosimilar Version of AbbVie's Blockbuster Humira*, Reuters (July 3, 2023), https://www.reuters.com/business/healthcare-pharmaceuticals/coherus-biosciences-launches-biosimilar-version-abbvies-blockbuster-humira-2023-07-03/.

88. Press Release, AbbVie, AbbVie Reports Second-Quarter 2023 Financial Results (July 27, 2023), https://investors.abbvie.com/static-files/4e2baf8c-1b83-4167-8afc-eb468995afab.

89. *Id.* at 2.

90. *Id.*

The benefit of having exclusivity without biosimilar entry can be gleaned from the vast sales of Humira® prior to the entry of the first biosimilar. However, what is important for clients when negotiating into settlements for their biosimilar is to consider the benefit for having a portion of biosimilar exclusivity. Amgen was able to enter the market in January 2023 with its biosimilar Amjevita®. The company announced that sales for Amjevita® in the first quarter were $51 million during its six months of exclusivity competing only with AbbVie's Humira®.[91] After that exclusivity ended and other biosimilars were able to enter the market, Amgen's reported Amjevita® sales for the second quarter dropped down to $19 million, a 63 percent drop from the first quarter.[92]

D. Current Biosimilar Landscape

As of today, the FDA's "Purple Book" lists three interchangeables (Cyltezo (Boehringer Ingelheim), Abrilada (Pfizer), Simlandi (Alvotech/Teva)) and seven biosimilars (Amjevita (Amgen); Hadlima (Samsung Bioepis); Hulio (Mylan); Hyrimoz (Sandoz); Idacio (Fresenius); Yuflyma (Celltrion); and Yusimry (Coherus BioSciences)).[93] Amgen's Amjevita, the first biosimilar for Humira® approved by the FDA, launched on January 31, 2023.[94] Table 1 includes those biosimilars for which AbbVie has granted nonexclusive licenses, which were discussed earlier, regardless of current FDA approval.

TABLE 1. Biosimilars for Which AbbVie Has Granted Nonexclusive Licenses

Company	Biosimilar	Entry/License Date
Amgen	Amjevita®	January 31, 2023[95]
Boehringer Ingelheim	Cyltezo®	July 1, 2023[96]
Alvotech	AVT02 (Simlandi®)	February 23, 2024[97]

---

91. Kevin Dunleavy, *Amgen's Hyped Humira Biosimilar Fritters Away Its Exclusivity Advantage*, Fierce Pharma (Aug. 4, 2023), https://www.fiercepharma.com/pharma/amgens-hyped-humira-knockoff-fritters-away-its-exclusivity-advantage.

92. *Id.*

93. *Purple Book Database of Licensed Biological Products: Humira*, *supra* note 34.

94. Press Release, Amgen, Amjevita™ (Adalimumab-atto), First Biosimilar to Humira®, Now Available in the United States (Jan. 31, 2023), https://www.amgen.com/newsroom/press-releases/2023/01/amjevita-adalimumabatto-first-biosimilar-to-humira-now-available-in-the-united-states.

95. *Id.*

96. Press Release, Boehringer Ingelheim, Cyltezo®, First and Only FDA-Approved Interchangeable Biosimilar to Humira®, Now Commercially Available in the U.S. (July 1, 2023), https://www.boehringer-ingelheim.com/us/press-releases/interchangeable-biosimilar-now-available-us.

97. As outlined earlier, Alvotech was given a license date of July 1, 2023, in the United States, but was not approved by the FDA until February 23, 2024.

Company	Biosimilar	Entry/License Date
Sandoz	Hyrimoz®	September 30, 2023 July 1, 2023 (citrate-free)[98]
Pfizer	Abrilada®	November 20, 2023[99]
Samsung Bioepis	Hadlima®	July 1, 2023[100]
Biocon[101] (Mylan)	Hulio®	July 3, 2023[102]
Fresenius Kabi	Idacio®	July 3, 2023[103]
Celltrion	Yuflyma®	July 2023[104]
Coherus BioSciences	Yusimry®	December 15, 2023 (license) July 3, 2023 (launch)[105]

Alvotech, in partnership with Teva Pharmaceuticals, has faced repeated hurdles at the FDA in gaining approval.[106] On June 30, 2023, Alvotech announced that it is likely that a reinspection of its manufacturing facility would be required to gain FDA approval and anticipates that it would occur following its resubmission for AVT02. Alvotech resubmitted its biologics license application (BLA) seeking interchangeable designation

98. Press Release, Novartis, Sandoz to Launch Hyrimoz® (Adalimumab-adaz) High-Concentration Formulation, Marking Sandoz Entrance into US Immunology Space (July 1, 2023), https://www.novartis.com/news/media-releases/sandoz-launch-hyrimoz-adalimumab-adaz-high-concentration-formulation-marking-sandoz-entrance-us-immunology-space.

99. Coherus Settles with AbbVie, and Sues Amgen, over Adalimumab Biosimilars (Updated), Big Molecule Watch (Mar. 18, 2019), https://www.bigmoleculewatch.com/2019/03/18/coherus-settles-with-abbvie-and-sues-amgen-over-adalimumab-biosimilars/.

100. Press Release, Organon, Organon & Samsung Bioepis Announce US Launch of HUMIRA Biosimilar HADLIMA™ (Adalimumab-bwwd) in Multiple Presentations Consistent with Originator (July 1, 2023), https://www.organon.com/news/organon-samsung-bioepis-announce-us-launch-of-humira-biosimilar-hadlima-adalimumab-bwwd-in-multiple-presentations-consistent-with-originator/.

101. Biocon Biologics acquired Mylan's (Viatris's) global biosimilars business in 2022. Press Release, Biocon, Biocon Biologics Completes Acquisition of Viatris' Global Biosimilars Business (Nov. 29, 2022), https://www.biocon.com/biocon-biologics-completes-acquisition-of-viatris-global-biosimilars-business/.

102. Press Release, Biocon, after Five Years of Successful Experience Internationally, Biocon Biologics' Hulio® Biosimilar to Humira®, Now Available in the United States (July 3, 2023), https://www.biocon.com/after-five-years-of-successful-experience-internationally-biocon-biologics-hulio-biosimilar-to-humira-now-available-in-the-united-states/.

103. Press Release, Fresenius Kabi, Fresenius Kabi Launches Its Biosimilar Adalimumab Idacio in the U.S. (July 3, 2023), https://www.fresenius.com/node/6630.

104. *Celltrion Launches Biosimilar of AbbVie's Blockbuster Drug Humira in US*, Reuters (July 5, 2013), https://www.reuters.com/business/healthcare-pharmaceuticals/celltrion-launches-biosimilar-abbvies-blockbuster-drug-humira-us-2023-07-05/.

105. *Coherus BioSciences Launches Biosimilar Version of AbbVie's Blockbuster Humira*, *supra* note 87.

106. *New Blow for Alvotech and Teva's Humira Biosimilar*, Pharma letter (June 30, 2023), https://www.thepharmaletter.com/article/new-blow-for-alvotech-and-teva-s-humira-biosimilar/.

in August 2023.[107] Alvotech and Teva announced on February 23, 2024, that AVT02, now known and marketed as Simlandi®, was approved by the FDA with interchangeable status.[108]

The Humira® biosimilar market is still developing, with only a small amount of time with multiple biosimilars on the market at the time of this publication. As such, it is arguably worth following the financial benefit to these companies in the United States as the market becomes more saturated with biosimilars.

II. Herceptin®

A. Biologic Overview and Background

Herceptin (trastuzumab) was originally approved on September 25, 1998, under BLA No. 103792 to applicant Genentech, Inc.[109] Its original indication is reproduced below:

> HERCEPTIN as a single agent is indicated for the treatment of patients with metastatic breast cancer whose tumors overexpress the HER2 protein and who have received one or more chemotherapy regimens for their metastatic disease. HERCEPTIN in combination with paclitaxel is indicated for treatment of patients with metastatic breast cancer whose tumors overexpress the HER2 protein and who have not received chemotherapy for their metastatic disease. HERCEPTIN should only be used in patients whose tumors have HER2 protein overexpression.

After its original approval, Herceptin went through multiple indication changes. Currently, Herceptin is indicated for:

> [A]djuvant treatment of HER2 overexpressing node positive or node negative (ER/PR negative or with one high risk feature . . .) breast cancer
>
> - as part of a treatment regimen consisting of doxorubicin, cyclophosphamide, and either paclitaxel or docetaxel

---

107. Tristan Manalac, *Alvotech Tries Again for FDA Interchangeable Designation for Humira Biosimilar*, BioSpace (Sept. 1, 2023), https://www.biospace.com/article/alvotech-tries-again-for-interchangeability-designation-for-humira-biosimilar/; *Event Details: Q2 2023 Earnings*, Alvotech, https://investors.alvotech.com/events/event-details/q2-2023-earnings (last visited Feb. 14, 2024).

108. Press Release, Teva, *supra* note 34.

109. Herceptin Label (1998), https://www.accessdata.fda.gov/drugsatfda_docs/label/1998/trasgen092598lb.pdf.

- as part of a treatment regimen with docetaxel and carboplatin
- as a single agent following multi-modality anthracycline based therapy.[110]

Genentech describes Herceptin as containing "a genetically engineered antibody, trastuzumab, which works by attaching to receptors that in large amounts lead to certain cancers, like breast cancer. By attaching to these receptors, trastuzumab stops the cancer cells from growing and dividing."[111] Based on clinical testing provided by Genentech to FDA, Herceptin is approved for use in treating breast cancer and gastric cancer.[112] Genentech has stated that it is one of the top selling medicines in the United States.[113]

As of the date of this publication, FDA's Purple Book lists five patents provided by Genentech to FDA. However, and as discussed more fully later, Genentech has alleged that it could reasonably assert as few as seven and as many as 40 patents in its 3A lists served during the patent dance with biosimilar sponsors.

B. Litigation and Dispute History

1. Genentech v. Pfizer, Case No. 17-1672 (D. Del.)

FDA accepted Pfizer's aBLA No. 761081 for review on August 21, 2017.[114] Shortly thereafter, the parties began, but never completed, the patent dance.[115] On November 17, 2017, Pfizer notified Genentech pursuant to 42. U.S.C. § 262(*l*)(3)(A) that it intended to commence commercial marketing of its aBLA product in the United States.[116] The very same day, Genentech filed suit alleging infringement of 40 patents.

After about a year of litigation, the parties filed a stipulation and (proposed) order of dismissal that the court entered on December 4, 2018.[117] The parties explained in the stipulation that they had entered into a

110. Herceptin, Highlights of Prescribing Information (2018), https://www.accessdata.fda.gov/drugsatfda_docs/label/2018/103792s5345lbl.pdf.
111. Genentech v. Tanvex, No. 22-809, Dkt. No. 1, ¶ 42 (S.D. Cal. June 2, 2022).
112. *Id.*
113. *Id.*
114. Complaint ¶¶ 19, 20, Genentech v. Pfizer, No. 17-1672 (D. Del. Nov. 17, 2017).
115. *Id.* ¶¶ 19–25.
116. *Id.* ¶ 26.
117. *Id.* Dkt. No. 15, Joint Status Report (Feb. 12, 2018).

settlement agreement. FDA approved Pfizer's biosimilar Trazimera on March 11, 2019, which Pfizer currently markets.[118]

2. Genentech v. Celltrion, Case Nos. 18-095, 18-1025 (D. Del.)

On July 31, 2017, Celltrion announced that FDA had accepted its aBLA for review.[119] The next day, Genentech sent a letter to Celltrion's outside counsel requesting a copy of the aBLA along with certain manufacturing information.[120] In its complaint for infringement, Genentech alleged that Celltrion did not provide that manufacturing information, and that it therefore reiterated to Celltrion that it needed the information to evaluate whether the proposed product infringed specific patents.[121] Celltrion allegedly refused to produce the manufacturing information, but, nevertheless, Genentech provided its 3A list, which included 40 operative patents.[122]

Celltrion responded with a detailed statement concerning noninfringement and invalidity, which Genentech alleged was deficient for numerous reasons.[123] Even still, Genentech responded and proposed that the parties litigate 18 of the originally listed 40 patents.[124] Celltrion replied that it wished to litigate all 40 of the patents listed in Genentech's 3A list and, on the very same day, it filed for declaratory judgment of noninfringement, invalidity, and/or unenforceability in the Northern District of California.[125] The next day, Genentech filed an infringement action against Celltrion in the District of Delaware.[126] The Northern District of California action was dismissed in May 2018 when the court held that an applicant cannot file an action for declaratory judgment if it had not completed all steps of the patent dance.[127] Thereafter, the parties continued litigating the patents in the Delaware actions.

Genentech and Celltrion settled the dispute in December 2018, and the court dismissed the remaining actions shortly thereafter.[128] FDA approved

---

118. Center for Drug Evaluation and Research, Approval Package for Application Number 761081Orig1S000, at 1 (2019), https://www.accessdata.fda.gov/drugsatfda_docs/nda/2019/761081Orig1s000Approv.pdf.

119. Complaint ¶ 30, Genentech v. Celltrion, No. 18-095 (D. Del. Jan. 12, 2018).

120. *Id.* ¶ 31.

121. *Id.* ¶ 32.

122. *Id.*

123. *Id.* ¶ 33.

124. *Id.*

125. *Id.* ¶ 35 (citing Celltrion v. Genentech, No. 18-cv-274 (N.D. Cal. filed Jan. 11, 2018)).

126. *Id.*

127. *Id.* Dkt. No. 78 (granting motion to dismiss).

128. *Id.* Dkt. No. 100.

Celltrion's biosimilar Herzuma on December 14, 2018, which it currently markets in the United States.[129]

3. Genentech v. Amgen, Case No. 18-924 (D. Del.)

In July 2017, Amgen announced that it had submitted an aBLA for a biosimilar version of Herceptin.[130] Although Amgen provided its aBLA and certain manufacturing information to Genentech, Genentech alleged that the disclosures were deficient.[131] Nevertheless, Genentech provided a 3A list containing 36 patents and the parties continued to engage in the patent dance through May 2018.[132] They eventually agreed to litigate 37 patents, and Genentech filed suit against Amgen on June 21, 2018. The litigation lasted for almost two years until the court dismissed the action in view of the parties' settlement in July 2020.[133] Prior to resolution of the dispute, FDA approved Amgen's biosimilar Kanjinti in June 2019.[134] Kanjinti was the first biosimilar for Herceptin approved by FDA, and it is currently marketed by Amgen.

4. Genentech v. Samsung Bioepis, Case No. 18-1363 (D. Del.)

In December 2017, Samsung Bioepis announced that it had submitted, and FDA accepted for review, an aBLA for a biosimilar version of Herceptin.[135] In its complaint for patent infringement, Genentech alleged that Samsung Bioepis failed to properly engage in the patent dance.[136] Regardless, Genentech provided Samsung Bioepis with a list of patents that it believed could be reasonably asserted in a patent infringement action.[137] The parties engaged in multiple back-and-forth correspondence, and eventually agreed to litigate 21 patents.[138] Genentech filed suit on September 4, 2018.

---

129. Center for Drug Evaluation and Research, Approval Package for Application Number 761091Orig1s000, at 1 (2018), https://www.accessdata.fda.gov/drugsatfda_docs/nda/2018/761091Orig1s000Approv.pdf.

130. Complaint ¶ 19, Genentech v. Amgen, No. 18-924, Dkt. No. 10 (redacted complaint) (D. Del. June 21, 2018).

131. *Id.* ¶¶ 21–23.

132. *Id.* ¶¶ 24–33.

133. Stipulation and Dismissal, *Genentech*, No. 18-924, Dkt. No. 555 (D. Del. July 7, 2020).

134. Center for Drug Evaluation and Research, Approval Letter for BLA 761073, at 1 (June 13, 2019), https://www.accessdata.fda.gov/drugsatfda_docs/appletter/2019/761073Orig1s000ltr.pdf.

135. Complaint ¶ 19, Genentech v. Samsung Bioepis, No. 18-1363 (D. Del. Sept. 4, 2018).

136. *Id.* ¶¶ 20–25.

137. *Id.* ¶ 28.

138. *Id.* ¶¶ 28–32.

The parties settled the dispute in June 2019 and the case was dismissed in July 2019.[139] Prior to resolution of the dispute, FDA approved Samsung Bioepis's biosimilar Ontruzant on January 18, 2019.[140] Samsung Bioepis currently markets Ontruzant.

5. Genentech v. Tanvex, Case No. 22-809 (S.D. Cal.)

On October 4, 2021, Tanvex announced that FDA accepted its aBLA for review.[141] Despite its allegations that Tanvex did not properly comply with the patent dance exchanges under the BPCIA, Genentech provided Tanvex with a 3A list that contained seven patents.[142] The parties continued with their patent dance exchanges, eventually agreeing to litigate three patents.[143] On June 2, 2022, Genentech brought suit against Tanvex.

In January 2023, the parties notified the court that they had settled the dispute.[144] Subsequently, in February 2023, the court dismissed the case.[145] As of the date of this publication, Tanvex does not currently have FDA approval to market its proposed biosimilar of Herceptin.

6. Mylan and Biocon

In March 2017, Mylan announced that it had reached a settlement agreement that granted it a license to market its Herceptin biosimilar in the United States.[146] Prior to the announcement, Mylan and its partner Biocon Ltd. had submitted an aBLA for the biosimilar. As part of the settlement, Mylan agreed to withdraw certain IPR challenges on patents allegedly covering Herceptin.[147] On December 1, 2017, FDA approved the biosimilar Ogivri, which is now marketed by Biocon Biologics Inc.[148]

---

139. Stipulation and Dismissal, Genentech v. Samsung Bioepis, No. 18-1363, Dkt. No. 160 (D. Del. July 1, 2019).

140. Center for Drug Evaluation and Research, Approval Package for Application Number 761100Orig1s000, at 1 (2019), https://www.accessdata.fda.gov/drugsatfda_docs/nda/2019/761100Orig1s000Approv.pdf.

141. Complaint ¶ 53, Genentech v. Tanvex, No. 22-809 (S.D. Cal. June 2, 2022).

142. *Id.* ¶¶ 54–57.

143. *Id.* ¶¶ 58–61.

144. *Genentech*, No. 22-809, Dkt. No. 55.

145. *Id.* Dkt. No. 60.

146. *See* Ned Pagliarulo, *Mylan Clears Way for Biosimilar Herceptin Launch in US*, Biopharma Dive (Mar. 13, 2017), https://www.biopharmadive.com/news/mylan-herceptin-roche-license-settlement-trastuzumab/437963/.

147. *See Mylan Obtains Global License to Trastuzumab in IPR Settlement*, Big Molecule Watch (Mar. 13, 2017), https://www.bigmoleculewatch.com/2017/03/13/mylan-obtains-global-license-to-trastuzumab-in-ipr-settlement/.

148. *See* Center for Drug Evaluation and Research, Approval Package for Application Number 761074Orig1s000, at 1 (2017), https://www.accessdata.fda.gov/drugsatfda_docs/nda/2017/761074Orig1s000Approv.pdf.

C. Current Biosimilar Landscape

As of the date of this publication, FDA's Purple Book lists five biosimilars that cite to Herceptin as a reference product.[149] Those products, along with their market entry dates, are listed in Table 2.

TABLE 2. Herceptin Biosimilars

Company	Biosimilar	Entry Date
Amgen Inc.	Kanjinti	July 2019[150]
Biocon Biologics Inc.	Ogivri	December 2019[151]
Pfizer Ireland Pharmaceuticals	Trazimera	February 2020[152]
Celltrion, Inc.	Herzuma	March 2020[153]
Samsung Bioepis Co., Ltd.	Ontruzant	April 2020[154]

D. Market Impact of Herceptin Biosimilars

As described in the previous sections, there are currently five biosimilars for Herceptin, providing physicians and patients with six overall choices for trastuzumab. These options have provided researchers with an interesting case study on the impact of pricing and market share due to biosimilar entrants. One such group of researchers at the University of Southern California (USC) Leonard D. Schaeffer Center for Health Policy and Economics performed an analysis of the trastuzumab market and published their findings in 2023, four years after the first biosimilar entrant.[155]

---

149. *See Purple Book Database of Licensed Biological Products: Simple Search Results for: Herceptin*, FDA, https://purplebooksearch.fda.gov/results?query=trastuzumab&title=Herceptin (last visited Feb. 14, 2024).

150. Press Release, Amgen, Amgen and Allergan's MVASI™ (Bevacizumab-awwb) and KANJINTI™ (Trastuzumab-anns) Now Available in the United States (July 18, 2019), https://www.amgen.com/newsroom/press-releases/2019/07/amgen-and-allergans-mvasi-bevacizumabawwb-and-kanjinti-trastuzumabanns-now-available-in-the-united-states.

151. News Release, Mylan, Mylan and Biocon Launch Trastuzumab Biosimilar, Ogivri™ (Trastuzumab-dkst), in the U.S. (Dec. 2, 2019), https://investor.mylan.com/news-releases/news-release-details/mylan-and-biocon-launch-trastuzumab-biosimilar-ogivritm.

152. *Pfizer Launches Trastuzumab Biosimilar*, Ctr. For Biosimilars (Feb. 20, 2020), https://www.centerforbiosimilars.com/view/pfizer-launches-trastuzumab-biosimilar.

153. Tony Hagen, *Teva, Celltrion Launch Fourth Trastuzumab Biosimilar*, Ctr. for Biosimilars (Mar. 16, 2020), https://www.centerforbiosimilars.com/view/teva-celltrion-launch-fourth-trastuzumab-biosimilar.

154. News Release, Merck, Merck Announces US Launch of ONTRUZANT® (Trastuzumab-dttb), a Biosimilar of Herceptin® (Trastuzumab) (Apr. 15, 2020), https://www.merck.com/news/merck-announces-us-launch-of-ontruzant-trastuzumab-dttb-a-biosimilar-of-herceptin-trastuzumab/.

155. News Release, USC, Biosimilars Drug Market Isn't Broken After All, USC Schaeffer Study Finds (June 6, 2023), https://www.eurekalert.org/news-releases/991617.

One of the co-authors of the study, Alice Chen, associate professor and vice dean for research at the USC Sol Price School of Public Policy and senior fellow at the USC Schaeffer Center, put it succinctly:

> In just three years, the trastuzumab market displayed important hallmarks of competition: doctors could choose among six products; new entrants rapidly captured market share from the originator; and prices steadily declined on all six options. Prices of some versions declined by more than half, and the originator lost half of the market.[156]

The USC researchers made several findings with respect to Herceptin and its biosimilars. As of the second quarter of 2022, the average sales price for the biosimilars ranged from 28 percent to 58 percent of Herceptin's first quarter 2019 (pre-biosimilar entry) average sales price. Additionally, Herceptin's average sales price fell 21 percent. With respect to the timing of market entry, Kanjinti (the first biosimilar entrant) acquired what was deemed a "first-mover advantage" over the later launched biosimilars. With this advantage, it was and is able to maintain a higher market share versus the later launchers.[157] As additional biosimilars are approved and launched—including potentially a biosimilar from Tanvex—it will no doubt continue to be interesting to study the impact on the trastuzumab market.

III. Neupogen®/Neulasta®

A. Biologic Overview and Background

Neupogen (filgrastim) was originally approved in February 1991 under BLA No. 103353 to applicant Amgen, Inc.[158] Over the years, it has gone through multiple label revisions and supplemental approvals.[159] Neupogen is a leukocyte growth factor currently indicated to:

> Decrease the incidence of infection, as manifested by febrile neutropenia, in patients with nonmyeloid malignancies receiving myelosuppressive anti-cancer drugs associated with a significant incidence of severe neutropenia with fever . . . . Reduce the

156. *Id.*
157. *Id.*
158. *Drugs@FDA: FDA-Approved Drugs—Biologic License Application (BLA): 103353*, FDA, https://www.accessdata.fda.gov/scripts/cder/daf/index.cfm?event=overview.process&ApplNo=103353 (last visited Feb. 14, 2024).
159. *Id.*

> time to neutrophil recovery and the duration of fever, following induction or consolidation chemotherapy treatment of patients with acute myeloid leukemia (AML) . . . . Reduce the duration of neutropenia and neutropenia-related clinical sequelae, e.g., febrile neutropenia, in patients with nonmyeloid malignancies undergoing myeloablative chemotherapy followed by bone marrow transplantation (BMT). . . . Mobilize autologous hematopoietic progenitor cells into the peripheral blood for collection by leukapheresis. . . . Reduce the incidence and duration of sequelae of severe neutropenia (e.g., fever, infections, oropharyngeal ulcers) in symptomatic patients with congenital neutropenia, cyclic neutropenia, or idiopathic neutropenia . . . . Increase survival in patients acutely exposed to myelosuppressive doses of radiation (Hematopoietic Syndrome of Acute Radiation Syndrome).[160]

Neulasta (pegfilgrastim) was originally approved in January 2002 under BLA No. 125031 to applicant Amgen, Inc.[161] Similar to Neupogen, Neulasta has gone through multiple label revisions in the decades since its approval.[162] Neulasta is a leukocyte growth factor currently indicated to:

> Decrease the incidence of infection, as manifested by febrile neutropenia, in patients with non-myeloid malignancies receiving myelosuppressive anti-cancer drugs associated with a clinically significant incidence of febrile neutropenia. . . . Increase survival in patients acutely exposed to myelosuppressive doses of radiation (Hematopoietic Subsyndrome of Acute Radiation Syndrome).[163]

As of the date of this publication, FDA's Purple Book lists a single patent for Neulasta and no patents for Neupogen.[164] As discussed more fully in the following section, however, Amgen has asserted multiple patents against multiple defendants related to biosimilars for Neulasta and Neupogen.

---

160. Amgen, Neupogen Label 1 (2023), https://www.accessdata.fda.gov/drugsatfda_docs/label/2023/103353s5198lbl.pdf.

161. Letter from Jay P. Siegel, Director, Office of Therapeutics Research and Review, Center for Biologics Evaluation and Research, FDA, to Jeffrey N. Fellows, Director, Regulatory Affairs, Amgen (Jan. 31, 2002), https://www.accessdata.fda.gov/drugsatfda_docs/appletter/2002/pegfamg013102L.htm.

162. *Drugs@FDA: FDA-Approved Drugs—Biologic License Application (BLA): 125031*, FDA, https://www.accessdata.fda.gov/scripts/cder/daf/index.cfm?event=overview.process&ApplNo=125031 (last visited Feb. 14, 2024).

163. Amgen, Neulasta Label 1 (2021), https://www.accessdata.fda.gov/drugsatfda_docs/label/2021/125031s203lbl.pdf.

164. *Purple Book Database of Licensed Biological Products—Patent List*, FDA, https://purplebooksearch.fda.gov/patent-list (last updated Jan. 29, 2024).

B. Litigation History

1. Amgen v. Sandoz, Case Nos. 14-4741, 16-2581 (N.D. Cal.)

Amgen commenced these litigations in 2014 for Sandoz's filgrastim biosimilar and in 2017 for Sandoz's pegfilgrastim biosimilar. In the filgrastim litigation, Amgen alleged that Sandoz failed to comply with the disclosures required by the BPCIA (that is, the patent dance).[165] In a letter to Amgen, Sandoz explained that it simply opted not to engage in the dance.[166] Although Amgen objected, the U.S. Supreme Court ultimately held that the patent dance is not mandatory.[167] Eventually, the district court granted summary judgment of noninfringement in Sandoz's favor in both the filgrastim and pegfilgrastim litigations.[168] Amgen appealed, but the Federal Circuit affirmed the order of the district court.[169]

2. Amgen v. Apotex, Case Nos. 15-62081, 15-61631 (S.D. Fla.)

Amgen filed suit in 2015 against Apotex for both Apotex's filgrastim biosimilar and pegfilgrastim biosimilar. The parties went through the patent dance for both biosimilars, with the pegfilgrastim dance beginning at the end of 2014[170] and the filgrastim dance beginning March 2015.[171] As a result of these dances, Amgen alleged infringement of two patents in the pegfilgrastim litigation and two patents in the filgrastim litigation.[172] In both proceedings, Amgen alleged infringement of U.S. Patent No. 8,952,138 (the '138 patent). Eventually the proceedings were consolidated and the '138 patent remained the only asserted patent.

The court held a bench trial in July 2016 and found that "Amgen has not met its burden to prove that Apotex's process for refolding Filgrastim and Pegfilgrastim infringe, either literally or under the doctrine of equivalents,

165. Complaint ¶ 64, Amgen v. Sandoz, Nos. 14-4741 (N.D. Cal. Oct. 24, 2024), 16-2581 (N.D. Cal. May 12, 2016) (consolidated).

166. Complaint ¶¶ 67–69, *Amgen*, No. 14-4741.

167. Sandoz Inc. v. Amgen Inc., 137 S. Ct. 1664 (2017).

168. *See* Order Granting Summary Judgment at 11, *Amgen*, No. 14-4741, Dkt. No. 346 (N.D. Cal. Dec. 19, 2017).

169. Opinion at 3, Amgen Inc. v. Sandoz Inc., No. 18-1551 (Fed. Cir. May 8, 2019).

170. Complaint ¶ 12, Amgen Inc. v. Apotex Inc., No. 15-cv-61631 (S.D. Fla. Aug. 6, 2015) [hereinafter Neulasta Complaint].

171. Complaint ¶ 12, Amgen Inc. v. Apotex Inc., No. 15-cv-62081 (S.D. Fla. Oct. 2, 2015) [hereinafter Neupogen Complaint].

172. Neulasta Complaint, *supra* note 170, ¶¶ 49–51; Neupogen Complaint, *supra* note 171, ¶ 47.

each limitation of the '138 Patent."[173] Amgen appealed, and the Federal Circuit affirmed the district court's judgment of noninfringement.[174]

3. Amgen Inc. v. Coherus BioSciences Inc., Case No. 17-546 (D. Del.)

Amgen filed suit against Coherus in 2017 related to its biosimilar for Neulasta. After engaging in the patent dance, the parties agreed that a single patent should be included in the litigation.[175] Coherus filed a motion to dismiss the complaint, arguing that Amgen was barred from arguing infringement under the doctrine of equivalents due to prosecution history estoppel and the disclosure-dedication doctrine.[176] The magistrate judge agreed with Coherus and issued a report and recommendation to dismiss the case with prejudice. The district court judge agreed and adopted the report and recommendation. Amgen appealed, and the Federal Circuit affirmed the district court judgment.[177]

4. Amgen v. Mylan, Case No. 17-1235 (W.D. Pa.)

Also in 2017, Amgen filed suit against Mylan related to its biosimilar for Neulasta. After the parties engaged in the patent dance—which Amgen alleged was inadequate due to the nature of Mylan's disclosures—Amgen filed suit alleging infringement of two patents.[178] Following a claim construction order from the court and a decision from the Federal Circuit affirming noninfringement by another party on a related patent, the parties entered a stipulation that Mylan does not infringe the asserted claims of the asserted patent.[179] Specifically, the parties stipulated that "under the reasoning of the Federal Circuit's decision as to the [patent related to the asserted patent], Mylan's accused process does not meet the claim limitation . . . and thus Mylan does not infringe any of the asserted claims off the [asserted patent]."[180]

---

173. Findings of Fact and Conclusions of Law at 2, Amgen Inc. v. Apotex Inc., Dkt. No. 267 (S.D. Fla. Sept. 6, 2016).

174. Opinion at 3, 15, Amgen Inc. v. Apotex Inc., No. 2017-1010 (Fed. Cir. Nov. 13, 2017).

175. Complaint ¶ 161, Amgen Inc. v. Coherus BioScis. Inc., No. 17-546 (D. Del. May 10, 2017).

176. Motion to Dismiss, *Amgen Inc.*, No. 17-546, Dkt. No. 9 (*see also* Dkt. No. 15, redacted opening brief).

177. Opinion, Amgen Inc. v. Coherus BioScis. Inc., No. 2018-1993 (Fed. Cir. July 29, 2019).

178. Complaint ¶¶ 64, 68, 69, Amgen v. Mylan, No. 17-1235 (W.D. Pa. Sept. 22, 2017).

179. *Amgen*, No. 17-1235, Dkt. No. 283, at 2–3.

180. *Id.*

5. Litigations Ending in Stipulations of Dismissal

Over the past few years, Amgen has filed multiple lawsuits across the country against multiple applicants for biosimilars of filgrastim and pegfilgrastim. Many of these cases ended in voluntary dismissals. The cases listed below progressed through various stages of litigation (as noted), though the common factor among them all is that they each ended in a stipulation of dismissal.

- *Amgen v. Hospira & Pfizer*, Case No. 18-1064 (D. Del.). Stipulated dismissal ordered in September 2021.[181] Of the cases listed in this subsection, this particular matter went the furthest in litigation, having gone through pretrial proceedings.
- *Amgen v. Hospira & Pfizer*, Case No. 20-201 (D. Del.). Stipulated dismissal ordered in March 2022 (order dated March 21, 2022). This matter went through briefing for summary judgment of non-infringement just prior to dismissal.
- *Amgen Inc. v. Apotex*, Case No. 18-61828 (S.D. Fla.). This matter was dismissed in November 2019, after the court denied a motion for dismissal and the parties continued through early litigation.[182]
- *Amgen v. Adello*, Case No. 18-3347 (D.N.J.). This matter was dismissed after going through the contentions phase of litigation.[183]
- *Amgen v. Tanvex*, Case No. 19-1374 (S.D. Cal.). This matter was dismissed after going through the early case management stage.[184]

C. Current Biosimilar Landscape

As of the date of this publication, FDA's Purple Book lists six biosimilars that cite to Neulasta as a reference product and three that cite to Neupogen as a reference product. Those products, along with their market entry dates, are listed in Table 3.

---

181. Stipulated/Agreed—Motion to Dismiss, Amgen v. Hospira & Pfizer, No. 18-1604 (D. Del. Sept. 8, 2021).

182. *See* Order Approving Stipulation of Dismissal, Amgen Inc. v. Apotex, No. 18-61828, Dkt. No. 120 (S.D. Fla. Nov. 15, 2019).

183. Amgen v. Adello, No. 18-3347, Dkt. No. 161 (D.N.J.).

184. Amgen v. Tanvex, No. 19-1374, Dkt. No. 44 (S.D. Cal.).

TABLE 3. Neulasta/Neupogen Biosimilars

Company	Biosimilar	Entry Date
Amneal/Kashiv	Fylnetra (pegfilgrastim-pbbk)	May 2023[185]
Mylan/Biocon	Fulphila (pegfilgrastim-jmdb)	July 2018[186]
Coherus	Udenyca (pegfilgrastim-cbqv)	January 2019[187]
Sandoz	Ziextenzo (pegfilgrastim-bmez)	November 2019[188]
Pfizer	Nyvepria (pegfilgrastim-apgf)	Late 2020/Early 2021[189]
Fresenius Kabi	Stimufend (pegfilgrastim-fpgk)	February 2023[190]
Sandoz	Zarxio (filgrastim-sndz)	September 2015[191]
Pfizer	Nivestym (filgrastim-aafi)	October 2018[192]
Amneal/Kashiv	Releuko (filgrastim-ayow)	November 2022

D. Market Impact of Neulasta/Neupogen Biosimilars

As discussed with respect to Herceptin, biosimilar entry into the marketplace provides an interesting study on competition in the biologics marketplace. In 2021, researchers at Harvard University, Harvard Medical

185. Press Release, Amneal Pharmaceuticals, Inc., Amneal Launches Third Biosimilar with FYLNETRA™ (Pegfilgrastim-pbbk) in the United States (May 16, 2023), https://www.businesswire.com/news/home/20230516005033/en/Amneal-Launches-Third-Biosimilar-with-FYLNETRA%E2%84%A2-pegfilgrastim-pbbk-in-the-United-States.

186. *Biocon: "Mylan Has Launched" Fulphila™ (Pegfilgrastim-jmdb) Biosimilar in the U.S.*, Big Molecule Watch (July 26, 2018), https://www.bigmoleculewatch.com/2018/07/26/biocon-mylan-has-launched-fulphila-pegfilgrastim-jmdb-biosimilar-in-the-u-s/.

187. *Coherus Confirms That It Has Launched Its Pegfilgrastim Biosimilar, Udencya*, Ctr. For Biosimilars (Jan. 4, 2019), https://www.centerforbiosimilars.com/view/coherus-confirms-that-it-has-launched-its-pegfilgrastim-biosimilar-udenyca.

188. Kelly Davio, *Novartis Confirms It Has Launched Biosimilar Pegfilgrastim, Ziextenzo, in the United States*, Ctr. For Biosimilars (Nov. 15, 2019), https://www.centerforbiosimilars.com/view/novartis-confirms-it-has-launched-biosimilar-pegfilgrastim-ziextenzo-in-the-united-states.

189. Tony Hagen, *FDA Approves Pfizer Pegfilgrastim Biosimilar Nyvepria*, Ctr. for Biosimilars (June 11, 2020), https://www.centerforbiosimilars.com/view/fda-approves-pfizer-pegfilgrastim-biosimilar-nyvepria.

190. Press Release, Fresenius Kabi, Fresenius Kabi Launches Biosimilar Stimufend® (Pegfilgrastim-fpgk) in the U.S. (Feb. 16, 2023), https://www.fresenius-kabi.com/news/fresenius-kabi-launches-biosimilar-stimufend-in-the-us.

191. Press Release, Novartis, Sandoz Launches Zarxio™ (Filgrastim-sndz), the First Biosimilar in the United States (Sept. 3, 2015), https://www.novartis.com/news/media-releases/sandoz-launches-zarxiotm-filgrastim-sndz-first-biosimilar-united-states.

192. Kelly Davio, *Pfizer Launches Biosimilar Filgrastim, Nivestym, at a Substantial Discount*, Ctr. For Biosimilars (Oct. 3, 2018), https://www.centerforbiosimilars.com/view/pfizer-launches-biosimilar-filgrastim-nivestym-at-a-substantial-discount.

School, and the Brookings Institute released a study that assessed the impact of filgrastim and pegfilgrastim biosimilar entry.[193] At the time of that 2021 publication, there were six total biosimilars for Neulasta and Neupogen combined as compared to the nine total available as of the date of this publication. Additionally, the researchers combined data from five other biosimilar entrants to arrive at their conclusions.

With respect to pricing, the researchers concluded the following:

> [A]t this early stage of market development, competitive forces yield important price reductions as the number of competitors increase, albeit weaker than what has been found for small molecules. Our estimates indicate that weighted average price ratios after biosimilar entry fall by an average of between 4% and 10% points per biosimilar entrant.[194]

While the average price does tend to decrease, the authors interestingly found that there are two basic patterns of response from originators that will require additional study as the biosimilar marketplace expands. The first response is that originators drop their prices as biosimilars enter, allowing them to retain a large portion of the market. The second response is that the originator does not offer price reductions, and the lower pricing is achieved through customers shifting to biosimilars. Although hesitant to draw any strong conclusions from this observation, the authors conclude that "one possibility is that such price responses by the originator may create the opportunity to exercise market power in the future if biosimilar entrants do not find the market profitable."[195] Despite the cautious nature of the authors' conclusions, one thing is for certain: the market impact of biosimilars to Neulasta, Neupogen, and other biologics is certainly something to keep an eye on.

---

193. Richard G. Frank et al., *Biosimilar Competition: Early Learning*, 31 HEALTH ECON. 647 (2022).

194. *Id.* at 658.

195. *Id.*

chapter 13

Reference Product Sponsor Counseling and Strategies*

I. Pre-Litigation Counseling and Strategies

A. Introduction

Under the Biologics Price Competition and Innovation Act (BPCIA), for parties relying upon the reference product's (RP's) safety and efficacy testing, a biosimilar application may be filed four years after the original approval of the RP, but will not be approved until 12 years after the approval of the RP.[1] This timeframe (up to eight years) provides the parties with a period in which they may resolve any patent infringement issues, through the information exchange known as the "patent dance" and any ensuing litigation.[2] As the patent dance begins with the disclosure of the abbreviated biologics license application (aBLA) to the reference product sponsor (RPS) by the biosimilar applicant, the RPS must be ready to immediately "dance" at that time and, therefore, should conduct pre-litigation due diligence in preparation for a potential biosimilar challenge.[3] The due diligence investigation will serve several purposes, including (1) locating and collecting key documents, facts, and witnesses; (2) identifying the patents to be asserted in litigation or defended in post-grant proceedings and assessing their strength; and (3) exploring areas to expand the existing patent portfolio, and strengthen the product's exclusivity. The end product of this due diligence exercise should be a comprehensive memorandum that will serve as a repository of all pertinent facts and documents as well as legal analyses for consultation in the future should a

*Lisa M. Ferri and Richard J. McCormick, Mayer Brown LLP.

1. 42 U.S.C. § 262(k)(7)(A)–(B).

2. *Id.* § 262(*l*).

3. Specifically, within 60 days of receiving a copy of the aBLA, the RPS must provide the applicant with a list of potentially infringed patents (*id.* § 262(*l*)(3)(A)(i)).

biosimilar challenge arise (i.e., a "break glass in case of emergency" master memo). Vetting patent litigation strategies prior to initiation of the patent dance is of the utmost importance and is addressed in the following sections in more detail.

B. Timeline for Preparation: When Should an RPS Begin Due Diligence?

In creating a pre-litigation due diligence timeline, an RPS should begin by looking to the expiry of the four-year data exclusivity—the earliest date a biosimilar manufacturer can file an aBLA—as that is the initial trigger for a potential patent dance (should the U.S. Food and Drug Administration (FDA) accept the application).[4] While a cautious approach may counsel that preparation should begin prior to data expiry (i.e., upon FDA approval of the RP), experience, economics, market uncertainty, and other factors may render that approach impractical.[5] In determining when due diligence preparation should begin, an RPS can prepare a model to assess the potential timeline for challenges by considering the following factors:

1. Present and forecasted sales of the RP[6]
2. Indications and potential for label expansion of the RP
3. Third-party competitors with approved or pipeline products
4. Discovery of new mechanisms of action to the target
5. Patent expiration dates (before or after market exclusivity)

While due diligence can begin as early as post-new drug application (NDA) approval, or as late as the mid-marketing exclusivity period—the key is that an RPS should not be caught flat-footed. In preparing a timeline, an RPS should monitor the activities of biosimilar developers, including (1) press releases announcing biosimilar pipelines and planned clinical trials; (2) registrations of clinical trials with the FDA comparing a biosimilar to a biologic (clinicaltrials.gov); and (3) requests made to the RPS for biologic samples (to be used in clinical trials).

An additional reason for early preparation is the possibility that a biosimilar manufacturer will file a post-grant proceeding in order to clear a path through the patent landscape prior to commencing the patent dance

---

4. *See id.* § 262(*l*). To date, however, the patent dance has not been initiated by an applicant immediately upon expiry of the four-year period following licensure of the RPS.

5. Available data shows that aBLAs are typically filed approximately ten years after data exclusivity expires. For example, Lucentis was approved in June 2006, but the first aBLA was not filed until September 2020 (Byooviz biosimilar application); for Eylea, which was approved November 2011, the first aBLA was submitted October 2021; and for Actemra, which was first approved in January 2010, the first aBLA was submitted June 2022.

6. For instance, a large-selling product may garner more interest and potential competition.

and to possibly facilitate early settlement.[7] The timing for the filing of an inter partes review (IPR) or post-grant review (PGR) is set by statute but otherwise can be brought at any time and is not subject to the regulatory exclusivity periods.[8] There are, however, standing issues that may arise for a biosimilar manufacturer if a petition is filed too early in the development period, or a biosimilar otherwise cannot show injury at the time of appeal.[9] A review of post-grant filings shows that, to date, the bulk of challenges have been brought well into the exclusivity period—however, that is changing with the more recent waves of biologic products.[10] As the post-grant process provides biosimilars with an expedited, economical proceeding with a lower burden of proof, there is strong incentive for filing—and an RPS should not be caught unprepared with a short timeline to respond.[11] From the RPS standpoint, the potential of a favorable final written decision that will provide broad estoppel in any future litigation, or a successful blocking of institution that may color any subsequent invalidity challenge, provides more than enough incentive to undertake early due diligence.[12]

7. Examples include PGR2022-00037 filed against Boehringer Ingelheim by Sandoz relating to risankizumab (Skyrizi); IPR2021-00880 filed against Regeneron by Mylan relating to aflibercept (Eylea); IPR2019-00739 filed against Alexion by Amgen relating to eculizumab (Soliris); and IPR 2021-01024 filed against Chugai Seiyaku Kabushiki Kaisha by Fresenius Kabi USA relating to tocilizumab (Actemra).

8. Post-grant proceedings are directed to patents without regard to any particular biologic product and, therefore, do not identify an RP. As per statute, however, a PGR petition must be filed within the first nine months following patent grant (37 C.F.R. § 42.202) and an IPR petition may be filed any time after the nine-month mark following patent grant (37 C.F.R. § 42.102).

9. To appeal a final written decision to the U.S. Federal Circuit Court of Appeals, a petitioner must establish that it has Article III standing both at the time the appeal is filed and throughout the duration of the appeal. *See* Momenta Pharms., Inc. v. Bristol-Myers Squibb, 915 F.3d 764 (Fed. Cir. 2019) (Federal Circuit denied standing to the petitioner of a failed IPR, because as of appeal date, it did not have an approved biosimilar or one in development); *see also* ModernaTX, Inc. v. Arbutus Biopharma Corp., 18 F.4th 1352 (Fed. Cir. 2021).

10. For example, Sandoz's PGR against Boehringer Ingelheim's U.S. Patent No. 11,078,265 relating to Skyrizi was filed (May 5, 2022) within three years of approval (April 23, 2019).

11. According to the U.S. Patent and Trademark Office (USPTO), the institution rates for biologics is 59 percent and the percentage of final written decisions in which all claims are found patentable is 6 percent; 25 percent of challenged claims and 57 percent of instituted claims were found unpatentable (Sept. 16, 2021–to Mar. 31, 2023). USPTO, PTAB Orange Book Patent/Biologic Patent Study: FY23 Q2 Update (2023), https://www.uspto.gov/sites/default/files/documents/orange_book_biologics_study_update_thru_march__2023_.pdf.

12. Estoppel prevents the petitioner from maintaining a validity challenge at the USPTO, in district court, or before the International Trade Commission based on a ground that the petitioner "raised or reasonably could have raised" during the IPR (35 U.S.C. § 315(e)). *See* Cal. Inst. of Tech. v. Broadcom Ltd., 25 F.4th 976 (Fed. Cir. 2022).

C. Assembling a Pre-Litigation Legal Team

It is important to assemble a team composed of members from the RPS's internal product team and in-house counsel along with outside counsel. This team will spearhead the identification, collection, and analysis of the relevant information during due diligence, and will eventually become the litigation support and trial team. Under the BPCIA, the aBLA materials and any associated manufacturing information provided to the RPS as part of the patent dance are subject to confidentiality provisions and a prosecution bar.[13] For this reason, it is important to designate a responsible in-house counsel that does not engage in patent prosecution of the RP early on, so that confidentiality issues do not hamper a quick mobilization and response once the patent dance is triggered. As the owner of patents exclusively licensed to the RPS (with patent assertion rights) must also agree to confidentiality before gaining access to the biosimilar applicant's materials, the RPS should contact the licensors during the due diligence period in order to make arrangements for future assertion in any litigation and for confidential future access to the aBLA.[14] In assembling a team, the RPS should confer with consultants and consider engaging expert witnesses necessary to a post-grant proceeding or trial (e.g., infringement, validity, commercial success).

D. Fact Investigation and Preliminary Witness Interviews

While the patent information exchanges of the patent dance are certainly consequential, as the first stage of the biosimilar challenge, a pre-litigation due diligence must also prepare for any potential litigations (first and second wave). During due diligence, the RPS should identify facts, documents, and witnesses that will support the invention story, the drug product's success, and the validity of the inventions. In order to gather all necessary facts, counsel should interface across research, clinical, regulatory, commercial, and legal departments. For the invention story, inventors should be identified and located (contact information for those inventors no longer at the company should be maintained). Preliminary discussions with the inventors and product developers are helpful to issue spot as the patent assessment is developed. Clinical trial partners and investigators should be interviewed, as they will have important information necessary to the invention story and to any validity investigation, and they are also a good source for expert witnesses from the industry and academia.

---

13. RPS in-house and outside counsel who "do not engage formally or informally, in patent prosecution relevant or related to the reference product." 42 U.S.C. § 262(*l*)(1)(B)(ii)(I). Therefore, while prosecution expertise may be helpful to the preparation, the team of lawyers should not be those with responsibility for prosecuting the RP patents.

14. *Id.* § 262(*l*)(1)(B)(iii).

Once an RPS receives notice of an aBLA, the company should consult counsel and the corporate document retention policy and consider instituting an internal litigation hold. An important aspect of compiling the key pre-litigation preparation documents is to identify custodians and other sources with relevant documents. Documents necessary to a pre-litigation assessment include research and development memoranda, lab notebooks, regulatory filings (investigational new drug (IND), biologics license application (BLA)), licenses, and collaboration agreements that may implicate additional areas for further investigation for patent portfolio identification.

E. Preparing for the Patent Dance: Identifying and Assessing the Patents to Be Asserted

The most important undertaking of the pre-litigation due diligence is the review of the RPS's patent portfolios to determine the patents to be asserted during the patent dance (i.e., the "3A list").[15] By failing to identify a patent through the 3A list, the RPS forfeits the right to enforce the patent in litigation. To that end, the RPS must thoroughly investigate and identify all patents potentially assertable against a biosimilar, including:

1. Product-related patents (e.g., compositions, methods of treatment, formulations, diagnostics, packaging, and delivery devices)
2. Platform patents (e.g., manufacturing, processes, purification, expression systems, cell lines, host cells, devices)

An analysis of the scope of these patents must be undertaken in order to assess what patents will likely be infringed by a biosimilar, as this list will form the basis of a "Purple Book" listing.[16] The list should also include expiration dates including any patent term extensions (PTEs) or adjustments. The next step is to assess the strength of these patents in the face of an invalidity or enforceability challenge. With this information, counsel should prepare a "loss of exclusivity" or "LOE" assessment to apprise business decision-makers of the exclusivity landscape. The RPS will expect, at a minimum, to have no competition until 12 years after approval (the marketing exclusivity period). The composition of matter (COM) patents are the next line of defense, and are usually the strongest patents, but typically add only a few years of exclusivity after marketing exclusivity expires. After that, formulation, method of treatment, process or

15. *Id.* § 271(e)(6)(C).

16. The Purple Book is a searchable, online database that contains information about biological products, including the FDA exclusivity expiration dates and patent information as required by the Biological Product Patent Transparency Act of the Consolidated Appropriations Act of 2021. *Purple Book Database of Licensed Biological Products*, FDA, https://purplebooksearch.fda.gov/ (last updated Jan. 29, 2024).

manufacturing, diagnostics, and device patents can offer many additional years of exclusivity beyond the COM patent(s).

The due diligence analysis of the patent portfolio should include an assessment of validity (i.e., 35 U.S.C. §§ 101, 102, 103, and 112) and enforceability as well as a prioritization of the patents, taking into consideration the substance, expiry dates, and the like. This prioritized list will assist in devising an overall strategy to defend the portfolio, and the arguments supporting the validity and infringement of the patents will form the basis for the RPS's counter-detailed statement to be provided in the patent dance.[17] For instance, it is important to pressure test the COM patents, as they are key to an RPS's defense of its market. The COM patents cannot easily be designed around by the biosimilar applicant, but some modifications to amino acid sequence may be possible.[18] The formulation patents form the second line of defense. These patents typically add additional years to the LOE timeline. For the formulation patents, it is important to look for potential obviousness issues by reviewing the disclosures in prior art COM patent specifications. Another issue for formulation patents is "design-arounds," as many of the approved biosimilars have made formulation changes[19] while still remaining within the FDA guidelines of "similarity."[20] Also, an RPS should anticipate biosimilar

17. 42 U.S.C. § 262(*l*)(3)(C).

18. "Minor modifications" to the amino acid sequence may be acceptable, and carefully crafted patent claims could capture any such inconsequential variants. *See* FDA, Draft Guidance for Industry: Development of Therapeutic Protein Biosimilars: Comparative Analytical Assessment and Other Quality-Related Considerations 11 (2019) ("It is expected that the expression construct for a proposed product will encode the same primary amino acid sequence as its reference product. However, minor modifications, such as N- or C-terminal truncations (e.g., the heterogeneity of C-terminal lysine of a monoclonal antibody) that are not expected to change the product performance, may be justified and should be explained by the sponsor.").

19. A review of available data shows that 18 (out of 41) approved biosimilars have meaningfully different formulations than the 11 corresponding RPs. For example, biosimilars to Genentech's Avastin (bevacizumab) made a number of substitutions to the excipient list including substituting a,a-trehalose dihydrate (60 milligrams (mg)), polysorbate 20 (0.4 mg), sodium phosphate dibasic, anhydrous (1.2 mg), and sodium phosphate monobasic, monohydrate (5.8 mg) with edetate disodium dihydrate (0.05 mg), polysorbate 80 (0.2 mg), succinic acid (2.36 mg), and sucrose (85 mg). Biosimilars with modified formulations that received approval include Enbrel, Epogen, Herceptin, Humira, Neulasta, Neupogen, Remicade, and Rituxan biosimilars.

20. Deviations from the formula of the RP are permitted in certain circumstances. FDA, Guidance for Industry: Questions and Answers on Biosimilar Development and the BPCI Act 5 (2021) ("Differences between the formulation of a proposed biosimilar product and the reference product may be acceptable. A 351(k) application must contain information demonstrating that the biological product is highly similar to the reference product notwithstanding minor differences in clinically inactive components. In addition, an applicant would need to demonstrate that there are no clinically meaningful differences between the biological product and the reference product in terms of safety, purity, and potency.").

manufacturers' potential design-arounds for buffers, sugars, stabilizers, pH, and so on, and have claims to cover these alternate formulations. The next line of defense is method-of-treatment patents, which also may add additional years to an RPS's exclusivity, but such patents are also subject to obviousness issues that may be created by the disclosures in prior art COM patent specifications. Some issues to identify that are particularly relevant include (1) genus/species; (2) prior art disclosures in a COM disclosing the treatment of a disease state generally; (3) later method-of-treatment claims covering approved indications to a subset of the relevant disease state;[21] and (4) prior art in the form of posted protocols on clinical-trial.gov describing rationales.[22] As there may likely be obviousness-type double patenting across the patent families, the RPS can use mitigation strategies (e.g., terminal disclaimers), particularly where there are patent term adjustments (PTAs), in view of *In re Cellect.*[23] Also, the RPS can strategize in selecting the patents designated for PTEs. While the default is usually COM, if an RPS is confident in the strength of another patent (on both infringement and validity), opportunities exist to extend LOE even further by adding PTE to, for example, method-of-treatment or method-of-manufacturing patents.[24] If adding PTE to a COM patent, an RPS should consider selecting an amino acid sequence patent (instead of nucleic acid sequence) to avoid potential for design-around.

By anticipating certain strategic moves on the part of biosimilar manufacturers, an RPS may be in a position to mitigate the risk of certain outcomes. For instance, a biosimilar manufacturer may seek to avoid induced infringement with a label carve-out while still expecting some incidental

---

21. *See, e.g.*, Aventis Pharms., Inc. v. Barr Lab'ys, Inc., 411 F. Supp. 2d 490 (D.N.J. 2006), *aff'd per curiam*, 208 F. App'x 842 (Fed. Cir. 2006) (prior art method of treating allergic patients (as a general patient population) with an antihistamine inherently anticipates claimed method of treating allergic patients suffering from impaired liver function (as a specific patient subpopulation) with an antihistamine).

22. Clinical trial-related publications, such as the listing on clinicaltrials.gov, press releases, conference presentations, or scientific papers, may qualify as a printed publication (35 U.S.C. § 102(a)). *See* Sanofi v. Glenmark, 204 F. Supp. 3d 665 (D. Del. 2016).

23. 81 F.4th 1216 (Fed. Cir. 2023) (invalidity under obviousness-type double patenting (ODP) is determined *after* PTA is applied to a patent's normal expiration date, rendering it a later-expiring patent for purposes of ODP); *see also* Scott A. McMurry & Ryan T. Babcock, *Does PTAB's* Ex Parte Cellect *Decision Endanger Biopharmaceutical Patent Terms?*, Mayer Brown (Apr. 20, 2022), https://www.mayerbrown.com/en/perspectives-events/publications/2022/04/does-us-ptabs-ex-parte-cellect-decision-endanger-valuable-patent-terms-of-biopharmaceuticals.

24. 35 U.S.C. § 156(a) (PTE may be added to a patent "which claims a product, a method of using a product, or a method of manufacturing a product." Recent examples of such PTEs to patents other than COM are U.S. Patent Nos. 9,586,978 (method of treatment), 9,580,461 (method of manufacture), and 9,572,856 (method of treatment).

off-label prescribing of its product (and erosion of RP market share).[25] The RPS may be in a position to mitigate the risk of certain of these outcomes—for instance, the RPS can incorporate data into its label for first primary indication (not carved out by biosimilar) to establish evidence of "encouragement" to doctors to prescribe for a carved out indication.[26]

F. *Are There Exclusivity or Marketing Strategies Available to Strengthen Exclusivity of the RP?*

During the due diligence phase, an RPS may also explore regulatory strategies to strengthen the exclusivity period of the RP, including:

- **Pediatric exclusivity**. Under the Best Pharmaceuticals for Children Act, if pediatric studies are conducted pursuant to a written request from FDA, sponsors can earn a six-month extension of the 12-year "reference product exclusivity."
- **Additional product presentations and/or devices**. Biosimilars have to match the reference biologic product in strength (which includes total drug content as well as concentration), so an additional product presentation such as a high-concentration version should be explored.
- **Combination uses**. Providing a combination product or even co-packaged kit could be beneficial to exclusivity. For example, while there are approved biosimilars for Rituxan (rituximab), there are no approved biosimilars for Rituxan Hycela (rituximab and hyaluronidase).

G. *Master Memo: A Comprehensive Compendium of the Due Diligence Assessment*

The final product of the diligence investigation, including all information, custodians, witnesses, patents, and other documents, should be identified and collected in a comprehensive memorandum (Master Memo) so that the team(s) given responsibility for defending against the challenge can quickly identify as well as update the materials. This Master Memo identifies:

25. A review of available data shows that 21 (out of 41) approved biosimilars have skinny labels compared to the 11 corresponding RPs, but typically only one or two indications are carved out, while most others remain in the label. For example, biosimilar Byooviz to Lucentis carved out two indications, (1) diabetic retinopathy, and (2) myopic choroidal neovascularization, from their label, while for Neulasta, most biosimilars carved out one indication, for hematopoietic subsyndrome of acute radiation syndrome.

26. GlaxoSmithKline LLC v. Teva Pharms. USA, Inc., 7 F.4th 1320 (2021) (cert. denied); Sanofi v. Watson Lab'ys Inc., 875 F.3d 636 (Fed. Cir. 2017).

1. Inventors and individuals with knowledge regarding patents, products, and so on
2. Patent analyses, portfolio expansion opportunities, and associated spreadsheet (with titles, inventors, expiry dates, etc.)
3. Licenses and collaboration agreements spreadsheet
4. Documents (e.g., notebooks, regulatory, manufacturing, etc.)
5. Expert witnesses

As part of the Master Memo, the RPS should create a spreadsheet documenting the location of relevant documents and update the document periodically as custodians change and/or new relevant documents are created.

II. Litigation Counseling and Strategies

A. Introduction

It has become a truth universally acknowledged that the BPCIA's patent dance largely favors biosimilar applicants over RPSs. The biosimilar applicant directs much of how resolution of infringement proceeds, first and foremost in its ability to forgo the dance in its entirety by refusing to participate in it. To the extent that it participates at all in the dance, the biosimilar applicant also has "substantial control" over the scope of the patents asserted in the first-wave litigation—in both the number of patents to be litigated and the identity of at least half of them—as well as the timing of the second-wave litigation, where the remaining patents on the RPS's 3A list can be asserted.[27] Participation in the patent dance also provides the aBLA applicant with a comprehensive understanding of the RPS's relevant patent portfolio in the form of the sponsor's 3A list of patents. And because the applicant has the option to receive the list without having to participate further by providing its detailed statement of invalidity and noninfringement contentions, applicants can gain important insights into the scope of assertable patents without having to prematurely reveal their substantive defensive arguments to the sponsor.

It is against this backdrop that the RPS must operate, seeking counseling and planning their strategies going forward to offset as much as possible the advantages that biosimilar applicants have in the process from the outset. Trends in how biosimilar applicants have navigated the patent dance and the ensuing litigations since passage of the BPCIA, and the associated significant body of case law, are instructive to RPSs in crafting a set of best practices for biosimilar litigations.

27. Sandoz Inc. v. Amgen Inc., 137 S. Ct. 1664, 1666, 1671–72 (2017).

B. The Patent Dance and Litigation Landscape 14 Years after Enactment of the BPCIA

In May 2024, when this book went to press, the BPCIA had just passed the 14-year anniversary of its enactment. Since that enactment, the FDA has approved 46 biosimilars[28] (seven of which achieved interchangeable status) under the BPCIA's regulatory pathway, 35 U.S.C. § 351(k); these approved biosimilars correspond to 14 different RPs.[29] For 23 of these approved biosimilars there were associated district court patent infringement litigations that proceeded under the BPCIA framework and that have all now reached final disposition.[30] (The remaining 23 approved biosimilars did not have associated district court litigations.[31]) In addition, there were associated district court infringement litigations (also all now fully disposed) related to nine biosimilar applications that have to date not received approval from the FDA.[32] Moreover, there are currently nine pending district court litigations regarding unapproved biosimilar applications corresponding to five different RPs.[33]

In all, the BPCIA has generated litigations in connection with 41 separate biosimilar applications—many of which have involved multiple complaints filed by the RPS and declaratory judgment lawsuits filed by the biosimilar applicant. There is therefore now a robust set of patent dance and litigation outcomes and related data from which RPSs can draw to anticipate how aBLA applicants may capitalize on the BPCIA framework and use it to their advantage. This experience is informative for RPSs—even if it only helps to establish reasonable expectations, and how to manage them—and provides RPSs with tools to craft reciprocal strategies around the patent dance and district court litigations in order to optimize

28. *See Biosimilar Product Information*, FDA, https://www.fda.gov/drugs/biosimilars/biosimilar-product-information (last updated Dec. 8, 2023).

29. These RPs are Actemra, Avastin, Enbrel, Epogen, Herceptin, Humira, Lantus, Lucentis, Neulasta, Neupogen, Remicade, Rituxan, Stelara, and Tysabri. There was also a second Lantus biosimilar approved, but this was through the Federal Food, Drug, and Cosmetic Act § 505(b)(2) application regulatory pathway and did not implicate the BPCIA.

30. There are 11 RPs corresponding to these 23 litigations: Actemra, Avastin, Enbrel, Epogen, Herceptin, Humira, Neulasta, Neupogen, Remicade, Rituxan, and Stelara. There were no BPCIA litigations involving Lantus or Lucentis. However, the FDA's Purple Book listing of patents for Lucentis is evidence that there was a patent dance (and identification of a list of 3A patents) associated with at least one of the Lucentis biosimilar applications that did not result in a district court litigation but was resolved before suit was filed.

31. The large majority of these 23 biosimilars were approved well after the launches of earlier approved biosimilars that were involved in litigations, where the RPS either settled with the earlier aBLA applicant or voluntarily dismissed the lawsuit, or where the patents were found invalid or not infringed.

32. The corresponding RPs for these nine biosimilar applications were Avastin, Herceptin, Humira, Neulasta, Neupogen, Rituxan, and Stelara.

33. These RPs are Eylea, Prolia/Xgeva, Rituxan, Soliris, and Tysabri.

outcomes consistent with their business needs. Many of the counseling tips and strategies discussed in the following sections proceed from a synthesis of this patent dance and litigation data and focus on key decision points RPSs will face during the process.

C. Biosimilar Applicant Declaratory Judgment Lawsuits of Invalidity and Noninfringement before the aBLA Is Filed with FDA Are Unlikely but Still Possible

The BPCIA sets out when a biosimilar applicant may and may not file a declaratory judgment action for invalidity or noninfringement on sponsor patents after FDA has accepted the aBLA for review and once the patent dance has begun. (An overview of the jurisprudence concerning post-aBLA-filing declaratory judgment lawsuits by biosimilar applicants is discussed in Section II.E.) However, there are no provisions in the BPCIA governing such actions before the applicant files the aBLA with FDA. In such instances, the "case or controversy" requirement of Article III controls: do the "facts alleged, under all the circumstances, show that there is a substantial controversy, between parties having adverse legal interests, of sufficient immediacy and reality to warrant the issuance of a declaratory judgment?"[34] In the two cases that have come to bar on this issue so far, the answer has been "No."

In *Sandoz Inc. v. Amgen Inc.*, Sandoz sought declaratory judgment relief on the invalidity, unenforceability, and noninfringement of sponsor Amgen's patents covering Enbrel on the same day it began Phase III trials of its biosimilar product.[35] Under the "all the circumstances" standard, the Federal Circuit assessed "immediacy" by considering "how far in the future the potential infringement is, whether the passage of time might eliminate or change any dispute, and how much if any harm the potential infringer is experiencing, at the time of suit, that an adjudication might redress" and "reality" by examining "any uncertainties about whether the plaintiff will take an action that will expose it to potential infringement liability and, if so, exactly what action."[36] On the facts before it, but "[w]ithout adopting a categorical rule," the court concluded that Sandoz did not meet the requirements of immediacy and reality.[37] The filing of the aBLA was still at least several years away when Sandoz sued Amgen, and longer still until FDA approval, which itself was potentially subject to numerous and significant contingencies.[38] In the final analysis, "the events

34. MedImmune, Inc. v. Genentech, Inc., 549 U.S. 118, 127 (2007).
35. 773 F.3d 1274, 1276 (Fed. Cir. 2014).
36. *Id.* at 1278.
37. *Id.* at 1279.
38. *Id.* at 1279–80.

exposing Sandoz to infringement liability 'may not occur as anticipated, or indeed may not occur at all.'"[39] The Federal Circuit did not pass on the district court's alternate ground for dismissing Sandoz's suit: that the BPCIA itself precludes a declaratory judgment where the applicant has not followed the BPCIA's patent-related procedures (i.e., compliance with the patent dance obligations under § 262(*l*)(2)–(6)).[40] Because Sandoz had not yet filed its aBLA, there was necessarily no compliance with, or even ability to undertake, the statutory dance requirements.[41]

In *Celltrion Healthcare Co., Ltd. v. Kennedy Trust for Rheumatology Research*, the district court reached a similar conclusion on the question of whether a case or controversy existed:

> Celltrion is simply too far from receiving FDA approval of [its biosimilar] for the exercise of declaratory judgment jurisdiction to be proper. . . . Although [the steps that would have to occur for there to even be the potential for patent infringement] are not wholly speculative or unlikely, they demonstrate that any opinion of the Court on the present claims would be largely based on the disfavored "hypothetical state of facts."[42]

Furthermore, the patent owner had "not expressed a clear intent to pursue infringement claims against Celltrion"—even where there was earlier litigious conduct on the same patents against other companies but no "concrete claim of a specific right" against Celltrion prior to its suit.[43] Finally, like the district court in *Sandoz v. Amgen*, discussed earlier, the court also held that the BPCIA statutory scheme did not permit applicants to seek declaratory judgment relief before aBLA filing.[44]

RPSs therefore should not expect to see declaratory judgment lawsuits from biosimilar applicants that are years out from aBLA filing, especially where the sponsors have not engaged in particularized saber-rattling

---

39. *Id.* at 1281 (quoting Texas v. United States, 523 U.S. 296, 300 (1998)).

40. *Id.* at 1277; *see also* Sandoz Inc. v. Amgen Inc., No. C-13-2904 MMC, 2013 WL 600069, at *1–2 (N.D. Cal. Nov. 12, 2013) ("Specifically, with limited exceptions not applicable here, neither a reference product sponsor, such as Amgen, nor an applicant, such as Sandoz, may file a lawsuit unless and until they have engaged in a series of statutorily-mandated exchanges of information.").

41. *Sandoz Inc.*, 2013 WL 600069, at *1–2 ("Here, Sandoz does not contend, and cannot contend, it has complied with its obligations under §§ 262(l)(2)–(6), because, as it concedes in its complaint and opposition, it has not, to date, filed an application with the FDA.").

42. Celltrion Healthcare Co., Ltd. v. Kennedy Tr. for Rheumatology Rsch., No. 14 Civ. 2256(PAC), 2014 WL 6765996, at *3 (S.D.N.Y. Dec. 1, 2014).

43. *Id.* at *4.

44. *Id.* at *5 ("The BPCIA purposefully keys its dispute resolution procedures to the occurrence of certain events on the path to FDA approval. Celltrion has failed to show why this carefully crafted and well-timed procedure should be avoided here.").

toward the applicant. But the risk of such an action may be heightened in instances where aBLA filing is imminent—even if still contingent on FDA acceptance for review and subsequent approval—and there are other indicia supporting the immediacy of a dispute (e.g., applicant's successful Phase III clinical trials, and multiple prior biosimilar approvals for the same RP) and the reality of the parties having adverse legal interests (e.g., where the patent owner has communicated staked-out concrete infringement claims against the applicant). However, even where the "case or controversy" requirement may be otherwise satisfied, whether the BPCIA framework itself implicitly rules out any such pre-aBLA-filing declaratory judgment lawsuits, as the district courts in *Sandoz v. Amgen* and *Celltrion v. Kennedy Trust* have held, is still an open question at the Federal Circuit.

D. Shall We Dance? Even If the Dance Proceeds beyond First Position, RPSs Should Not Count on Completing All of the Steps

Once the aBLA is filed with and accepted by the FDA, the BPCIA framework, including the steps of the patent dance, is implicated—at least potentially, insofar as the "carefully calibrated scheme" intended to streamline the dispute resolution process against infringing biosimilars was effectively rendered optional by the U.S. Supreme Court when it ruled that biosimilar applicants could opt out of the patent dance at its inception and could not be enjoined from doing so.[45] Because biosimilar applicants need not dance—in whole or in part—with the RPS, there are various inflection points in the dance where biosimilar applicants may uncouple from it, leaving the RPS with various forks in the road and associated decision-making on how to proceed.

1. No aBLA, No Dice, No Dance: When the Biosimilar Applicant Refuses to Participate in the Information Exchange from the Start

First, the biosimilar applicant may choose to not enter the dance at all. Of the 41 biosimilar applications filed to date that have resulted in litigation, this has happened nine times. In five cases, the applicant sent a letter to the RPS indicating that they would not provide the aBLA or participate in the dance; in the other four cases, the sponsor learned of the aBLA filing through the applicant's press releases or the FDA website's disclosure of approval of the aBLA. When the biosimilar applicant fails to provide the aBLA, § 262(*l*)(9)(A) authorizes the RPS to bring an immediate action for

45. Sandoz Inc. v. Amgen Inc., 137 S. Ct. 1664, 1674 (2017).

a declaration of infringement, validity, or enforceability "of any patent that claims the biological product or a use of the biological product."[46]

In all nine of the cases, the RPSs filed such a suit against the applicants. In one case, the applicant had voluntarily provided access to the RPS of its aBLA for 60 days, after which the RPS asserted 24 patents; in the other eight cases, the sponsors asserted in their original complaints between one to 39 patents. The patents asserted included COM, method of treatment, expression and manufacturing, purification, and apparatus patents. Sponsors pleaded their initial allegations of infringement "on information and belief," noting their inability to provide a more detailed infringement analysis where applicants did not provide the aBLA, particularly where they did not have access to the applicant's purification and manufacturing schemes for purposes of comparison to the patent claim limitations. In three of the cases, the applicant subsequently provided the aBLA, but not as part of the formal dance process. Sponsors filed amended complaints in these cases, either increasing the number of patents or removing patents based on the information in the aBLAs.

Although sitting out the dance entirely is an infrequent strategic choice by applicants, sponsors cannot assume that they will receive the aBLA and have access to sufficient technical information to make a pre-filing determination of infringement across the full range of their pertinent patent portfolios. There are no apparent strong trends in the nine cases that indicate particular circumstances where an applicant is more likely than not to refrain from the dance. None of the six RPs had remaining regulatory exclusivity when the aBLAs were filed.[47] And although the number of patents ultimately asserted is largely weighted towards the lower end—between two to six—the types of patents asserted across the cases are fairly evenly distributed.

So what is an RPS to do when an applicant refuses to dance at the outset and the sponsor has no access to the aBLA from which it can determine infringement of the patents it has identified during its due diligence? There is no real choice but to file a declaratory judgment suit as authorized by 42 U.S.C. § 262(*l*)(9)(A) for the act of infringement described in 35 U.S.C. § 271(e)(2)(c)(ii). As to what patents should be asserted in the

46. Although the language of the statute appears to exclude the assertion of process or manufacturing patents under this pathway, the corresponding section of the Patent Statute, 35 U.S.C. § 271(e)(2)(c)(ii), makes it clear that any patent that could be identified in the sponsor's 3A list may be asserted. *See also* Amgen Inc. v. Sandoz Inc., 794 F.3d 1347, 1356 n.3 (Fed. Cir. 2015), *aff'd*, 137 S. Ct. 1664 (2017).

47. Most of the RPs were so-called "legacy" biosimilars, approved 12 or more years before the BPCIA was passed, and whose retroactive 12-year regulatory exclusivity had therefore been long expired when the biosimilar applicants filed their aBLAs.

suit, even without the aBLA the sponsor can likely allege with a good degree of confidence infringement of any composition-of-matter patents, as these would be difficult to design around (particularly claims to amino acid sequences) while still remaining "highly similar" to the RP.[48] Method-of-treatment patents covering the RP's approved indications are the next line of reasonably assertable patents—particularly insofar as biosimilar applicants have only rarely sought approval of skinny-labeled indications that could potentially avoid infringement of carved out major indications.[49] Infringement of formulation patents covering the RP may also be alleged, especially as fewer than half of the approved biosimilars have materially different (potentially noninfringing) formulations compared to the RP.[50]

As for the other types of patents that sponsors may have in their portfolio arsenal, including process patents (manufacturing and purification), the lack of access to the applicant's aBLA will deprive the sponsor of information necessary to demonstrate infringement. For these patents, the best practice for sponsors is to allege infringement "on information and belief," based on any publicly available information regarding the biosimilar pertinent to infringement, while referencing the applicant's withholding of the aBLA. This should be sufficient to satisfy Rule 11's requirements that allegations be made "to the best of the person's knowledge, information, and belief, formed after an inquiry reasonable under the circumstances," while permitting those that "will likely have evidentiary support after a reasonable opportunity for further investigation or discovery."[51]

2. Once the Dance Is Initiated, Most Applicants Complete It, but Many Exit before the First-Wave Lawsuit Is Filed

Of the 32 instances where the dance was initiated, 21 resulted in first-wave infringement actions being filed either through the negotiation process (§ 262(*l*)(4)(A)) or the exchange of patent lists (§ 262(*l*)(4)(B)).[52] In the remaining 11 instances, the applicants exited at various points in the process: five after receipt of the sponsor's 3A list, two after receipt of the sponsor's counter-detailed statement of infringement and validity, and four before the negotiation process could be completed.

At each stage of the dance, particularly where the applicant may opt to leave, there are decisions to make, opportunities for counseling, and

48. *See supra* note 18.

49. *See supra* note 25.

50. *See supra* notes 19–20.

51. *See* Amgen Inc. v. Hospira, Inc., 866 F.3d 1355, 1362 (Fed. Cir. 2017) ("Thus, if a sponsor forms a belief based on an inquiry limited by an applicant's withholding of information, the sponsor has still satisfied Rule 11.").

52. Of these 20 litigations, 15 were the result of a negotiated and agreed-upon list of patents to be asserted, while five were the result of an exchange of patent lists.

strategies to implement. Discussed in the following subsections are several pivotal points in the dance that implicate important choices that sponsors must make in continuing the dance or exiting to litigation.

a. RPSs Should Assume That the Biosimilar Applicant Will Not Disclose Additional Manufacturing Information beyond the aBLA

Even applicants that provide the aBLA and intend to continue the exchange of information for at least part of the dance may subsequently choose not to disclose to the sponsor the second set of materials identified in § 262(*l*)(2)(A), namely, "such other information that describes the process or processes used to manufacture the biological product that is the subject of such application."[53] Information regarding the processes related to the biosimilar product (beyond what is in the aBLA) may be crucial to determining infringement of the sponsor's manufacturing and purification patents. Given that more than half of the patents asserted in BPCIA litigations are directed to manufacturing and purification processes,[54] they represent a substantial portion of a sponsor's assertable portfolio available to potentially forestall competition.

Despite the importance of these patents to sponsors, or perhaps because of it, biosimilar applicants have largely refused to produce process information in addition to the aBLA. In nearly all of the 32 instances where the applicant provided the aBLA, it did not also disclose any additional process-related documentation. The sponsor has two sometimes overlapping options at this juncture. First, § 262(*l*)(2)(A) authorizes the filing of an immediate declaratory judgment action for failing to comply with § 262(*l*)(2)(A) with respect to process information (separate and apart from the aBLA). Second, the sponsor can continue the dance, identify its 3A list of patents, and request (or be given) the information later in the dance (e.g., with the applicant's detailed statement supporting noninfringement) or seek it further downstream during the discovery process.[55]

---

53. The full text makes it clear that both the aBLA and manufacturing information are required if the applicant wishes to comply with § 262(*l*)(2)(A):

> [N]ot later than 20 days after the Secretary notifies the subsection (k) applicant that the application has been accepted for review, the subsection (k) applicant (A) shall provide to the reference product sponsor a copy of the application submitted to the Secretary under subsection (k), *and* such other information that describes the process or processes used to manufacture the biological product that is the subject of such application.

(Emphasis added.)

54. Chorong Song, *How Non-Product-Specific Manufacturing Patents Block Biosimilars*, 71 DUKE L.J. 1923, 1937–39 (2022) (data through May 2021).

55. In one case, the RPS filed a declaratory judgment action after the applicant initially refused to provide the process information beyond what was present in the aBLA. The parties nevertheless continued the dance and agreed upon a negotiated set of patents for a first-wave litigation, which was the subject of an amended complaint by the RPS.

In either instance, the sponsor must still make the determination as to which patents to identify in either the declaratory judgment action or its 3A list and any associated first-wave litigation that follows. The considerations here are similar to those discussed earlier where the applicant does not provide an aBLA. Even in the absence of complete process information from the applicant against which the sponsor's manufacturing and purification patents may be compared for infringement purposes, the Federal Circuit has held that a sponsor should identify all patents in their 3A list that it "believes . . . *could* reasonably be asserted."[56] The BPCIA "provides no sanction for holding or asserting a mistaken belief in good faith" in connection with a sponsor's 3A list; moreover, once a patent is listed, the applicant's detailed statement addressing infringement would "inform whether 'a claim of patent infringement . . . could' or could not 'reasonably be asserted.'"[57] And if the applicant does not provide a detailed statement of noninfringement, "the sponsor would have a reasonable basis for asserting a claim of patent infringement."[58]

Moreover, to the extent that, once a lawsuit is instituted, an applicant continues to withhold information concerning its processes from which infringement may be demonstrated, sponsors have recourse to 35 U.S.C. § 295. That statute provides a presumption of infringement of a process patent (with the burden placed on the accused infringer to establish otherwise) if "a substantial likelihood exists that the product was made by the patented process" and "plaintiff has made a reasonable effort to determine the process actually used in the production of the product and was unable to so determine." The Federal Circuit has approved of the use of this statutory presumption in biosimilar litigations.[59] The burden on sponsors of establishing a "substantial likelihood of infringement" is "less than . . . proving successfully at a trial by a fair preponderance of the evidence that a product in question was in fact made by the patented process but would be more than a slight possibility that the product was so made."[60]

56. *Amgen Inc.*, 866 F.3d at 1362 (quoting § 262(*l*)(3)(A)).

57. *Id.*

58. *Id.*; *see also supra* note 51 (discussing Rule 11's requirement for patent assertions).

59. Amgen Inc. v. Sandoz Inc., 794 F.3d 1347, 1356 n.4 (Fed. Cir. 2015) ("[W]e note the existence of a rebuttable presumption in actions alleging infringement of a process patent under 35 U.S.C. § 271(g) relating to importation of products made abroad by a patented process."). Although on its face the statutory language applies to both foreign and domestic manufacturing, the legislative history appears to limit the presumption to products manufactured overseas and imported into the United States. *See* Senate Judiciary Committee, Report on the Process Patents Amendments Act of 1989, S. Rep. No. 100-83, at 45 (1987) ("The rebuttable presumption would be inapplicable if the defendant has used the process in the United States . . . . In these circumstances, the discovery provisions of the Federal Rules of Civil Procedure and the equitable powers of Federal courts should be sufficient to allow the plaintiff to ascertain what process was employed.").

60. LG Display Co., Ltd. v. AU Optronics Corp., 709 F. Supp. 2d 311, 335 (D. Del. 2010).

Sponsors "need only present evidence that would support a reasonable conclusion that the imported product was made by the patented process."[61] A sponsor's "reasonable effort to determine the process" may include its "discovery efforts and consider whether [it] followed all of the avenues of discovery likely to uncover the defendant's process, including written discovery requests, facility inspections, first-hand observation of the process, independent testing of process samples, the use of experts, and depositions of the defendant's officials."[62] In addition, although the issue has not been addressed in any biosimilar litigation to date, sponsors may also point to efforts during the patent dance to uncover the biosimilar applicant's manufacturing and purification information.

b. List It or Lose It? The Consequences May Be Catastrophic if a Sponsor Fails to List a Patent That It Later Wishes to Assert in a Litigation

A sponsor is precluded from litigating any patent not on its § 262(*l*)(3)(A) list. The scope of that preclusion is set out, albeit ambiguously, in 35 U.S.C. § 271(e)(6)(C): "The owner of a patent that should have been included in the [3A list] . . . but was not timely included in such list, may not bring an action *under this section* for infringement of the patent with respect to the biological product." (Emphasis added.) So what are the consequences if a sponsor fails to identify an assertable patent in its 3A list with respect to a biosimilar applicant but later wishes to sue on that patent against the same applicant? One reading of the statute is that "under this section" means "under § 271(e)," which would still permit an action for actual infringement under § 271(a) upon commercial sale and marketing of the biosimilar. But another reading is that "under this section" means "under § 271" generally—essentially a forfeiture of *all* rights to sue on the patent, at least with respect to the same biosimilar applicant.

There is no case law definitively construing § 271(e)(6)(C) and the scope of the forfeiture. There is Federal Circuit dicta in *Amgen v. Apotex* suggesting a broad waiver of rights: if a patent that the sponsor "should have included on its (3)(A) list . . . 'was not timely included,' then the owner of that patent may not sue for infringement *under 35 U.S.C. § 271* with respect to the biological product at issue."[63] Similarly, in *Genentech, Inc. v. Amgen Inc.*, in ruling on Amgen's motion to transfer the instant Delaware litigation to California where Amgen had filed an earlier declaratory judgment action, the district court referenced Genentech's argument that "under the BPCIA, if Genentech fails to list a patent, it could be barred

61. *Id.*
62. *Id.*
63. 827 F.3d 1052, 1058 (Fed. Cir. 2016) (emphasis added).

permanently from asserting that patent against Amgen's biosimilar."[64] The district court denied Amgen's motion, based in part on the court's acceptance of Genentech's proposition as true: because Genentech "filed their immediate patent infringement action without including those additional patents, it appears that those missing patents cannot lead to an actual controversy."[65]

Given the continuing uncertainty as to the scope of the forfeiture, sponsors should take a liberal approach to selecting patents for the 3A list, consistent with the parameters discussed in Section II.D.1. If later steps in the dance reveal that some of those patents were improvidently included on the list, they may be withheld from assertion in a later-filed litigation. Sponsors should note, however, that while the BPCIA does not limit the number of patents that can be asserted, biosimilar applicants may assert an unclean hands defense by arguing that the sponsor has created and asserted an improper "patent thicket."[66]

c. The Applicant's Detailed Statement and Sponsor's Counter-Detailed Statement

When the applicant provides its detailed statement of noninfringement, invalidity, and unenforceability (§ 262(*l*)(3)(B)), the sponsor should not expect this to be the last, inalterable word on the subject. Applicants may, and are likely to, expand on arguments in the detailed statement and add new ones as the litigation progresses, and the RPS will be hard-pressed to be able to limit applicants to the exact arguments in the detailed statement. For example, in *Genentech, Inc. v. Amgen Inc.*, the district court denied Genentech's motion to dismiss the invalidity arguments in Amgen's counterclaims to the extent they were not disclosed in the patent dance.[67] The court reasoned that the Supreme Court's decision in *Sandoz* foreclosed Genentech's position: filing a declaratory judgment lawsuit under § 262(*l*)(9)(B)

> is the exclusive federal remedy available to the reference product sponsor to address an applicant's failure to comply with [the detailed statement requirements of] § 262(*l*)(3)(B)(ii). . . . Nothing in § 262(*l*)(9)(B) or in any other provision of the BPCIA limits the defenses an applicant can assert in such an action [and] the fact

64. No. 17-1407, 2018 WL 503253, at *6 (D. Del. Jan. 22, 2018).

65. *Id.*

66. In *AbbVie Inc. v. Boehringer Ingelheim International GmbH*, No. 17-cv-01065-MSG-RL, 2018 WL 2604825 (D. Del. June 4, 2018), AbbVie asserted 74 patents covering Humira against Boehringer Ingelheim, which asserted an "unclean hands" defense, alleging that AbbVie engaged in a pattern of pursuing numerous overlapping and non-inventive patents for the purpose of developing a "patent thicket," using the patenting process itself as a means to seek to delay competition.

67. No. 17-cv-1407, 2020 WL 636439 (D. Del. Feb. 11, 2020).

> that Congress did not expressly limit an applicant's defenses in a declaratory judgment action brought pursuant to § 262(*l*)(9)(B) "provides strong evidence that Congress did not intend" to limit those defenses.[68]

On the other hand, the applicant has no similar remedy concerning the sponsor's own "counter" detailed statement (of infringement, validity, and enforceability) under § 262(*l*)(3)(C). While this subject has been scarcely litigated, it is a best practice for an RPS to address each of the applicant's contentions of noninfringement, invalidity, or unenforceability with at least as much detail as the applicant provided, and on a claim-by-claim basis.

Relatedly, an applicant's substantive comments made to a sponsor during the patent dance, even those rising to "party admissions," may be later modified or disavowed by the applicant. In *Amgen v. Apotex*, Apotex sent Amgen several "pre-litigation" letters arguing noninfringement of a particular Amgen patent.[69] Amgen later tried to rely on these patent dance disclosures to prove infringement, but Apotex's expert testified that the disclosures were factually inaccurate and that the biosimilar fell outside of Amgen's patent claims.[70] The Federal Circuit affirmed the district court's crediting of the expert's testimony and holding that Apotex did not infringe.[71] Although Apotex's patent dance disclosures were "party admissions and therefore have *some* probative weight," they were "not sufficiently probative to outweigh other evidence presented at trial indicating that the information in the letters was inaccurate."[72]

d. Selecting Patents to Assert in First- and Second-Wave Litigations: Applicants Hold the Cards, but Sponsors Can Make Strategic Patent-Staging Decisions to Optimize Successful Outcomes

Whether the sponsor and applicant reach the good faith negotiation phase of the dance and either agree upon a set of patents to litigate under § 262(*l*)(4)(A) or, failing that, engage in the exchange contemplated by § 262(*l*)(5), the sponsor will need to decide how to divide the assertable patents in its 3A list between the first- and second-wave litigations. Much of the control over the scope of patents litigated in the first wave is in the hands of the applicant, but, at a minimum, even if the parties do not reach agreement, § 262(*l*)(5)(B)(ii)(II) allocates to the sponsor the ability to identify at least one patent to assert in the first wave. However, the more

---

68. *Id.* (quoting Sandoz Inc. v. Amgen Inc., 137 S. Ct. 1664, 1675 (2017)).
69. 712 F. App'x 985, 988 (Fed. Cir. 2017).
70. *Id.*
71. *Id.*
72. *Id.* at 989.

likely scenario under the § 262(*l*)(5) schema is that at least two patents will be litigated in the first wave.[73] Whatever number of patents the applicant wishes to identify for a first-wave lawsuit—three, four, or more—the sponsor should expect that at most, and at best, only half of them will be exclusive to the sponsor (where there is no overlap with the applicant's selection) and will represent the sponsor's own prioritized selection of patents to be volleyed in advance of a second-wave litigation.

The sponsor's strategic choices to apportion patents across the two waves of litigation should be based on multiple litigation-specific factors and guided by the sponsor's ultimate business goals. Sponsors should first identify the strongest patents on its 3A list. Here, "strength" should be assessed from the standpoint both of the patent's ability to withstand noninfringement and invalidity challenges (e.g., composition-of-matter and method-of-treatment patents are usually the strongest in this regard) and the patent's expiration date (with those that expire the latest beyond the 12-year exclusivity period being, all other things equal, stronger than those that expire earlier). The challenge for the sponsor is that typically the strongest patents based on the first criterion—such as core composition-of-matter patents—are often those that expire the earliest, typically only a few years after regulatory exclusivity is over. On the other hand, manufacturing patents may be the latest-expiring ones, but proving infringement of them may be more challenging.

However the manner in which the sponsor identifies its strongest patents, they should be split across the two waves. Strong patents in the first wave will set the tone for the dispute and create a first barrier of protection against biosimilar competition, while strategically reserving the remaining strong patents for the second wave will discourage at-risk launches. Moreover, reserving some strong patents for the second wave will preserve them against any substantive (infringement or validity) challenges that would occur in a first-wave litigation, thereby placing them in a better position to support likelihood-of-success arguments in connection with any motion by the RPS for a preliminary injunction to prevent an at-risk launch.

The RPS must also decide when to litigate platform and research tool patents. These may be broad enough to cover any biosimilar variant or manufacturing process irrespective of the RP and may be considered strong in their own right. But if these patents are royalty-bearing on other, third-party products not at issue in the litigation, the sponsor will

---

73. This assumes that the applicant notifies the sponsor that it wishes to litigate one patent (under § 262(*l*)(5)(A)) and that the one patent identified by the applicant and the sponsor under § 262(*l*)(5)(B)(i) is not the same patent.

not want to risk invalidation earlier than necessary. Finally, despite an RPS's best-laid plans to prioritize its patents for each of the two phases of litigation, a degree of being forewarned to be forearmed is warranted. Some patents that the sponsor might rather litigate in the second wave will possibly be identified by the applicant for a first-wave lawsuit, and the RPS should be ready to proceed on enforcing and defending those patents sooner than expected.

E. Biosimilar Applicant Declaratory Judgment Lawsuits Filed during the Dance Have Been Dismissed, but None So Far Have Been Reviewed by the Federal Circuit

Applicants are expressly prohibited from filing offensive declaratory judgment actions if they fail to comply with the disclosure requirements of the BPCIA—for example, by not providing the aBLA, detailed statement, notice of commercial marketing, and so on.[74] Nevertheless, in an attempt to avoid the full dance and exit the process without otherwise running afoul of the BPCIA requirements leading up to the first-wave litigation, applicants have tried to file such actions mid-dance immediately after providing the 180-day notice of commercial marketing. To date these actions have been dismissed at the district court level, and no appeals have been taken.

In *Amgen Inc. v. Genentech*, Amgen began the dance by providing its aBLA and proceeded until the patent negotiation process of § 262(*l*)(4)(A), but then, before completing the final negotiation steps, gave notice of commercial marketing and filed a declaratory judgment action on all patents listed on Genentech's 3A list.[75] Amgen alleged that it was forced to file suit "to remove the cloud of uncertainty flowing from Genentech's inconsistent and changing positions during the BPCIA exchange and negotiations,"[76] arguing that "it was entitled to bring suit after providing its notice of commercial marketing . . . even though it had not completed the rest of the BPCIA's patent list exchange steps."[77] The district court dismissed the lawsuit, declining to exercise declaratory judgment jurisdiction under its discretion. The district court relied on language in the Supreme Court's decision in *Sandoz v. Amgen*, stating that "[t]he second phase is triggered by the applicant's notice of commercial marketing and involves *any patents that were included in the parties' § 262(l)(3) lists but not litigated in the first phase*."[78] In the view of the district court, the Supreme Court thus

74. 42 U.S.C. § 262(*l*)(9)(B), (C).

75. No. 17-7349-GW, 2018 WL 910198, at *2 (C.D. Cal. Jan. 11, 2018).

76. *Id.*

77. *Id.* at *3.

78. *Id.* at *4 (quoting Sandoz Inc. v. Amgen Inc., 137 S. Ct. 1664, 1671 (2017)) (emphasis added by district court).

> expressed an expectation that the parties finish the exchanges and negotiations contemplated by the BPCIA, allow the product sponsor the first opportunity to file suit on those first-phase patents, and only then allow either party to file suit on any remaining patents after the applicant has brought its notice of commercial marketing.[79]

The district court concluded that "[a]llowing an applicant to side-step the BPCIA's exchange and negotiation requirements and bring suit on any patent simply by filing its notice of commercial marketing would effectively vitiate the BPCIA's provisions."[80]

In *Celltrion v. Genentech*, the parties began the dance, but after they exchanged detailed statements, Celltrion provided notice of commercial marketing, exited the dance, and sued Genentech for a declaratory judgment.[81] The district court dismissed the complaint, rejecting Celltrion's contention "that because a notice of commercial marketing lifts the ban on declaratory judgment actions described in Section (*l*)(9)(A), a notice of commercial marketing should also lift Sections (*l*)(9)(B) and (C)'s prohibitions."[82] The court reasoned that

> serving a notice of commercial marketing lifts the prohibition imposed by Section (*l*)(9)(A)—and Section (*l*)(9)(A) alone. . . . In other words, a notice of commercial marketing only opens the door for an applicant to file a declaratory judgment action if the applicant complies with the rest of the statute. A notice of commercial marketing is no *carte blanche*, and Celltrion points to no authority that offers a contradictory interpretation."[83]

RPSs can therefore expect not to see similar declaratory judgment actions, although they have not yet been foreclosed by the Federal Circuit and applicants may continue to present test cases for appellate review. Moreover, it remains an open question whether an applicant with a filed and FDA-accepted aBLA that does not intend to participate at all in the dance may provide notice of commercial marketing followed by a declaratory judgment action, as such a sequence of events does not implicate the adjudicated facts in *Amgen Inc. v. Genentech* and *Celltrion v. Genentech*.

79. *Id.*
80. *Id.*
81. No. 18-cv-00274, 2018 WL 2448254, at *3 (N.D. Cal. May 9, 2018).
82. *Id.* at *7.
83. *Id.* at *7–8.

chapter 14

BLA Applicant Counseling and Strategies*

I. Pre-Litigation: aBLA Preparation and Pre-Litigation Strategy

Developing a biosimilar product under the Biologics Price Competition and Innovation Act (BPCIA) tends to be a much more involved process than developing a small-molecule pharmaceutical under the Hatch-Waxman Act. The timelines from product selection to filing an abbreviated biologics license application (aBLA) are longer, there is increased complexity of the product itself, and the clinical pathways are more involved. It is also important to counsel biosimilar clients at every step along the way if possible. Developing the most solid intellectual property (IP) strategy requires input from counsel as early as product selection through product development and pre-litigation strategy implementation.

A. Product Selection

Ideally, IP counseling should begin at the biosimilar product selection phase. Most companies pursuing biosimilar opportunities select and bring products into the development timeline using a multidisciplinary team or committee to evaluate potential candidates. The purpose of these teams is to analyze information concerning candidates to determine the financial opportunity, internal development and manufacturing capabilities, the regulatory pathway, the need for third-party involvement, and the timing of entry into the pipeline. The teams usually comprise individuals from a wide array of departments within the organization including portfolio

---

*Joanna Fuller, Shannon Lentz, Laura Lydigsen, and Debbie Yellin of Crowell & Moring LLP; Kent Walker, retired, formerly of Crowell & Moring.

management, sales and marketing, research and development (R&D), regulatory, manufacturing, and legal.

The legal function is primarily represented by IP counsel. Counsel's role is to assess the patent portfolio of the reference product sponsor (RPS) to determine, at a high level, the key blocking patents and the later-expiring follow-on patents, and to present an initial strategy for each. Counseling at this stage of the biosimilar life cycle includes preliminary decisions on which patents will not be challenged, which patents may require invalidity as a defense and which patents may be able to use noninfringement as a defense (i.e., designed around based on the development approach chosen). Preliminary decisions concerning possible opposition at the U.S. Patent and Trademark Office (USPTO) such as inter partes review (IPR) or post-grant review (PGR) may also be made at this point. Strategic considerations related to USPTO proceedings will be discussed in more detail later in this chapter.

Counseling in the product selection phase usually requires conducting a search for innovator patents that could reasonably be found to protect some aspect of the RPS. It is also advisable to characterize each of the patents into categories based on what they claim.

One important category is compound patents that protect the antibody or protein of concern or the underlying sequence of the drug substance or its genetic material. These types of patents should be examined in detail to make an initial assessment on whether invalidity or noninfringement defenses are viable versus waiting for expiry prior to commercial marketing. All categories of patents other than the compound patents may be considered "secondary" patents.

A second category consists of patents protecting characteristics of the finished product such as formulation of the product or dosage form of the product. Patents covering processes used in the manufacture of the product constitute a third category. These two categories—formulation and process patents—will typically be patents that lend themselves to a potential noninfringement defense, but conferring with the selection team is necessary to determine the viability of any changes that might be necessary to set up a noninfringement argument. R&D and regulatory input is of primary importance here because the proposed changes may or may not be feasible or allowed by regulatory requirements.

A fourth category of patents will likely be patents claiming various methods of use for the RPS. It is important to counsel the product selection team on the RPS labeling concerning indications that are covered by patents in their portfolio. A colorable noninfringement argument can often be set up by omitting or "carving out" certain indications in the label. However, counsel may need to consider looking into invalidity if certain of these indications need to remain in the biosimilar label based on feedback from the team. As discussed more thoroughly later, there are multiple factors to consider in developing a biosimilar label including whether and when interchangeability will be sought.

Once a biosimilar candidate is selected for development, timing for entry into the active development pipeline will be sought. Often, these selection decisions are made many years in advance of the targeted market entry of the product. One of the many considerations for establishing a development date will usually be based on the expiration of certain key patents that will not be challenged by the biosimilar applicant. This is akin to the situation in Hatch-Waxman where an applicant submits to the U.S. Food and Drug Administration (FDA) a certification pursuant to 21 U.S.C. § 355(j)(2)(A)(vii)(III) (Paragraph III certification) indicating that it does not intend to launch its product until after expiration of the certified patents.[1] In this situation, the proposed market entry date will usually drive the timing to begin active development. The start date for development or kickoff may be back-calculated by subtracting the estimated length of development through filing BPCIA patent issues from the anticipated launch date. Once the project is kicked off, counsel will then begin working with the team on the next phase of developing IP strategy, specifically product development.

B. Product Development

Now that a biosimilar candidate has entered active development, one of the first priorities will be counseling the R&D and regulatory teams on potential opportunities to design around the claims of the secondary patents identified in the search for innovator patents. At this point, the team will be able to take a much deeper and more granular dive into aspects such as formulation design, process development, and proposed labeling.

Counseling on product and process specifications in order to create a noninfringement position usually requires ongoing communication between technical personnel and counsel. There will usually be quite a bit of back and forth between counsel and the client as the feasibility of proposed legal advice is assessed in relation to the development of the product. It is always advisable to keep these communications as targeted as possible, only involving counsel and essential personnel concerned with that aspect of development. Keeping the communication focused sets up a strong argument for attorney-client privilege that may be useful down

1. *See* 21 U.S.C. § 355(j)(2)(A)(viii)(III) (describing "a certification, in the opinion of the applicant and to the best of his knowledge, with respect to each patent . . . of the date on which such patent will expire").

the road. Additionally, it is advisable to keep all written documentation of the experimentation involved in attempting any design-around efforts documented separately and marked as privileged attorney work product to protect them if litigation ensues later. Parties should be mindful that when marking documents as work product, it is advisable to also generate a litigation hold.[2]

As development proceeds, it will become clear which aspects of the product can be altered to create a noninfringement position and which will not be amenable to change. As the IP picture becomes clear, counsel can reassess and recategorize the relevant patents and begin to investigate invalidity defenses for patents covering any product attributes that may not be changed in a sufficient manner for noninfringement.

C. Pre-Litigation

As filing of the aBLA application nears, counsel should have a concrete strategy in place concerning each of the patents in the innovator portfolio. In the months leading up to filing the aBLA and beyond counsel should be firming the contentions that will be incorporated into its detailed statement pursuant to 42 U.S.C. § 262(*l*)(3)(B) (3(B) statement),[3] if the applicant chooses to engage in the "patent dance."[4] It is advisable that counsel have the defense to anticipated RPS's patents in near final condition before aBLA filing because, once the patent dance begins, deadlines are short; the aBLA filer must provide its application and any other relevant information to the RPS within 20 days of acceptance of its aBLA by the FDA.[5] As of 2023, it typically takes about two months for the FDA to issue an acceptance letter to the aBLA applicant after the application has been

2. *E.g.*, Sanofi-Aventis Deutschland GmbH v. Glenmark Pharms. Inc., No. 07-5855, 2010 WL 2652412, at *5 (D.N.J. July 1, 2010) ("Defendants' argument that the duty to impose a 'litigation hold' did not arise until mid-2007 upon the filing of the Paragraph IV certification is also misguided, especially where Defendants' claim privilege with respect to documents from 2006."), *aff'd*, 748 F.3d 1354, 1362 (Fed. Cir. 2014); Medeva Pharma Suisse A.G. v. Roxane Lab'ys, Inc., No. 07-5165, 2011 WL 310697, at *15 (D.N.J. Jan. 28, 2011) ("[T]he court cannot fathom why Roxane failed to institute a litigation hold prior to July 2007 when it clearly anticipated litigation and had a duty to preserve information at least as early as February 2002, when it knew it would be filing a Paragraph IV Certification, and perhaps as far back as July 31, 2001 if its privilege log claiming work product protection over a document with that date is to be credited.").

3. 42 U.S.C. § 262(*l*)(3)(B) requires that within 60 days of receipt of the list of patents provided by the RPS under 42 U.S.C. § 262(*l*)(3)(A), the biosimilar applicant provides its own list of potential patents for resolution and its defenses to the patents identified on the RPS's list.

4. Participation in the disclosures contemplated by the so-called "patent dance" of 42 U.S.C. § 262(*l*) is not mandatory. *See generally* Amgen Inc. v. Sandoz Inc., 794 F.3d 1347 (Fed. Cir. 2015).

5. 42 U.S.C. § 262(*l*)(2).

filed. Once the acceptance letter is issued it is a good practice to have as much work as possible done on the defenses so that any last-minute work may be focused on unanticipated patents identified in the RPS's list of patents pursuant to 42 U.S.C. § 262(*l*)(3)(A), also called a "3(A) list."

The pre-litigation phase may also be a good time to establish a strategy on the timing for providing notice of commercial marketing to the RPS. The applicable statute is 42 U.S.C. § 262(*l*)(8)(A), which states that an applicant "shall provide notice to the RPS not later than 180 days before the date of the first commercial marketing of the biological product licensed under subsection (k) [i.e., the biosimilar in question]." Upon receiving such notice, the sponsor may bring a declaratory judgment action based on any remaining patents not yet litigated.

The U.S. Supreme Court clarified the particulars of when a biosimilar applicant may provide notice of commercial marketing in its 2017 decision in *Sandoz Inc. v. Amgen Inc.*[6] The Court held the BPCIA allows for commercial notice of a "biosimilar product" to be effective if given prior to approval by the FDA and that declaratory judgment was the only relief available as a remedy despite Amgen's arguments that notice of commercial marketing was only proper after a biosimilar applicant has received approval from the FDA. The decision also held that a biosimilar need not disclose its application under § 262(*l*)(2)(A) if it chose.

The decision created a new range of strategy options for a biosimilar applicant to consider as it approaches the filing date for its aBLA. Counsel will need to consider whether or not to engage in the patent dance and when to give notice of marketing. In *Sandoz*, the applicant decided not to disclose its aBLA to the RPS and notified of its intent to begin commercial marketing when it received acceptance of its aBLA by the FDA, which started the clock on the 180-day waiting period set by the statute. This is one viable option today, but there are others. For instance, an aBLA applicant may choose to notify the RPS at some point during the patent dance or early in first-wave litigation. This early notice might prompt second-wave litigation earlier in the timeline and allow the aBLA applicant to seek resolution on all patents sooner rather than later. Alternatively, an aBLA applicant that chooses to pursue settlement aggressively may want to wait on providing notice until all of the RPS patents are accounted for with certainty (e.g., in a settlement agreement) before notifying of commercial marketing. Regardless of the approach, it is important to counsel a biosimilar applicant in advance of filing its aBLA with the FDA of the potential strategies at the filer's disposal.

---

6. 582 U.S. 1 (2017).

1. Labeling Considerations

Labeling choices by aBLA applicants can have a major impact on patent strategy. A full label can make for a much more onerous patent strategy that relies on invalidity positions, but may be necessary when seeking therapeutic equivalence. Seeking approval for a biosimilar with less than all the RPS's indications may give rise to a noninfringement position, but the current state of labeling case law arising from Hatch-Waxman litigation may make that noninfringement position somewhat risky.[7]

Under FDA regulations, all prescription drug labeling must provide adequate information to enable health care providers to "use a drug safely and for the purposes for which it is intended."[8] To this end, the approved prescribing information summarizes the essential scientific information needed by health care providers for the safe and effective use of a drug.[9]

Many of the same labeling regulations applicable to small molecules also govern biosimilars. Like labeling for recently approved new drug applications, 21 C.F.R. § 201.56(c)(1) requires biosimilar product labeling to meet the requirements of the physician labeling rule (PLR) as described in 21 C.F.R. § 201.56(d) and § 201.57.[10] This requirement must be met for biosimilars regardless of the format of the reference product labeling. The relevant data and information from the reference product labeling that should be incorporated into the biosimilar product labeling will depend on several factors. However, it is usually the case that biosimilar product labeling will be similar to the corresponding text in the reference product labeling. Like generic drug labeling, biosimilar labeling does not need to be identical to the reference product labeling and certain differences are acceptable. Certain differences such as brand name, product presentation, and instructions for use, among others, may differ between a reference product and a biosimilar product. Additionally, a biosimilar sponsor may choose to seek approval for less than all of the indications for use in a

---

7. GlaxoSmithKline LLC v. Teva Pharms. USA, Inc., 7 F.4th 1320, 1340 (Fed. Cir. 2021) (holding Teva liable for more than $240 million in damages despite FDA-approved carve-out of patented indication for carvedilol); AstraZeneca LP v. Apotex, Inc., 633 F.3d 1042, 1047, 1060–61 (Fed. Cir. 2010) (affirming grant of preliminary injunction against Apotex where it had modified its label so that it "contain[ed] no explicit mention of once-daily administration" as claimed by AstraZeneca's patent).

8. 21 C.F.R. § 201.5 (2024).

9. *See id.* §§ 201.100, 201.56(a)(1).

10. *See* Requirements on Content and Format of Labeling for Human Prescription Drug and Biological Products, 71 Fed. Reg. 3,922, 3,922–97 (Jan. 24, 2006). This rule is commonly referred to as the PLR. FDA, GUIDANCE FOR INDUSTRY: LABELING FOR HUMAN PRESCRIPTION DRUG AND BIOLOGICAL PRODUCTS—IMPLEMENTING THE PLR CONTENT AND FORMAT REQUIREMENTS 1 n.1 (2013), https://www.fda.gov/media/71836/download.

reference product by carving certain indications out of its labeling as discussed in more detail in the following section.

Finally, a biosimilar labeling will differ from the RPS's labeling because it will have a unique four-letter suffix added to the nonproprietary core name of the reference product. The distinguishing suffix must be devoid of any meaning and will be composed of four letters attached by a hyphen to the core name of the innovator product.[11] For example, HUMIRA® (adalimumab), which was approved prior to the 2017 guidance and is not identified by a four-letter suffix, has four biosimilars currently available. Hyrimoz® (adalimumab-adaz), Idacio® (adalimumab-aacf), Yuflyma® (adalimumab-aaty), and Yusimry® (adalimumab-aqvh) were all approved post-FDA guidance and bear unique four-letter suffixes. The FDA instituted the naming convention to facilitate pharmacovigilance for originator biological products and biosimilar products containing related drug substances when other means to track a specific dispensed product are not readily accessible and to also facilitate accurate identification of these biological products by health care practitioners and patients. The distinguishing suffixes also reduce inadvertent substitution of any such products that have not been determined to be interchangeable.

a. Carve-Outs

The Hatch-Waxman Act explicitly provides that an applicant can seek approval for only some of the uses for which the reference product is approved,[12] thereby allowing applicants for abbreviated new drug applications (ANDAs) to "carve out" certain conditions of use (e.g., approved indications or dosing regimens) from its labeling and avoid providing notice to RPSs on the method-of-use patents covering those indications. However, the BPCIA does not contain similar language specifically allowing these labeling changes for biosimilar products. This left many questions for early biosimilar applicants wishing to file an aBLA with a label containing less than all the RPS's indications in its proposed label. Applicants were left with questions that could only be addressed by trial and error or via direct communication with the FDA. The results applicants obtained from their proposed carve-outs varied by product and the particular facts of the data contained in their applications.

---

11. *See* FDA, Guidance for Industry: Nonproprietary Naming of Biological Products (2017).

12. 21 U.S.C. § 355(j)(2)(A)(viii) (providing alternative to certifications under Paragraphs I–IV "if with respect to the listed drug referred to in clause (i) information was filed under subsection (b) or (c) for a method of use patent which does not claim a use for which the applicant is seeking approval under this subsection," the ANDA applicant can instead provide "a statement that the method of use patent does not claim such a use").

Then in 2018, the FDA previewed the Biosimilars Action Plan (BAP),[13] a guidance intended to "provide additional clarity to biosimilar applicants who seek approval for fewer than all conditions of use for which the reference product is licensed because, for example, one of the licensed conditions of use of the reference product is protected by a patent," signaling to industry that FDA intended to permit carve-outs in biosimilar labeling. In February 2020, the guidance finally arrived.

The new guidance, "Biosimilars and Interchangeable Biosimilars: Licensure for Fewer Than All Conditions of Use for Which the Reference Product Has Been Licensed," explicitly lays out the FDA's thinking that carve-outs are allowed for biosimilars. The guidance explains the situations where approval of fewer than all conditions of use for which the reference product is licensed may occur when a condition of use is protected by a patent or regulatory exclusivity. Therefore, the FDA can license the biosimilar for any indications or conditions of use that are not protected by the relevant exclusivities or patents. As with any aBLA, sponsors seeking to carve out an indication must submit draft labeling including all information from the reference product labeling to support the conditions of use that are sought.

FDA considers the information to be omitted and makes determinations on whether it represents essential scientific information needed for safe use of the product; if it is, FDA will not permit the carve-out. The process for omitting label information is different between ANDAs and aBLAs. The guidance states that "FDA does not expect an applicant to submit a justification for the applicant's decision not to seek licensure of a biosimilar for all of the reference product's licensed conditions of use,"[14]

---

13. Dr. Scott Gottlieb, then commissioner of the FDA, laid out the BAP in remarks made at the Brookings Institution on July 18, 2018. Statement, FDA, Remarks from FDA Commissioner Scott Gottlieb, M.D., as Prepared for Delivery at the Brookings Institution on the Release of the FDA's Biosimilars Action Plan (July 18, 2018), https://www.fda.gov/news-events/press-announcements/remarks-fda-commissioner-scott-gottlieb-md-prepared-delivery-brookings-institution-release-fdas.The BAP applied many of the lessons learned from FDA experience with generic drugs to accelerate biosimilar competition with four key strategies: improving the efficiency of biosimilar product development and approval; maximizing scientific and regulatory clarity for the biosimilar product developers; developing effective communications to improve understanding of biosimilars among patients, providers, and payers; and supporting market competition by reducing gaming of FDA requirements or other attempts to unfairly delay market competition to follow-on products. FDA, Biosimilars Action Plan: Balancing Innovation and Competition 5–9 (2018), https://www.fda.gov/media/114574/download?attachment. One early piece of the plan included industry guidance on labeling carve-outs. FDA, Guidance for Industry: Labeling for Biosimilar Products 5 (2018), https://www.fda.gov/media/96894/download.

14. FDA, Draft Guidance for Industry: Biosimilars and Interchangeable Biosimilars: Licensure for Fewer Than All Conditions of Use for Which the Reference Product Has Been Licensed 6 (2020), https://www.fda.gov/media/134932/download.

unlike a carve-out in an ANDA, which requires a section viii statement to be filed when a filer submits a draft label that has been carved out.[15] However, FDA will accept "information that is intended to inform FDA's review of the draft labeling," such as justification of why certain clinical trial information can be carved out without raising safety or efficacy issues.[16]

Conversely, the guidance also sets out the process for adding indications back into a biosimilar label. This situation can arise for aBLA holders for various reasons, such as market conditions, seeking therapeutic equivalence, or removal of patent barriers. An aBLA holder must submit a supplement to the aBLA containing all data and information needed to support licensure of the biosimilar with that condition of use. FDA stated in the guidance that it expects to review and act on aBLA supplements seeking licensure for additional conditions of use within six months.[17] Though the Biosimilar User Fee Act Goals Letter gives the agency ten months to do so, FDA believed it can surpass this goal, assuming the supplement did not raise novel review issues.

Per the guidance, carve-outs for exclusivity purposes will not be approved by the FDA until expiration of the applicable exclusivity, but carve-outs for patent reasons may be approved as long as the FDA determines all other requirements for licensure have been met. The guidance advises that aBLA applicants may request the FDA act on a supplement prior to a certain date as long as the date occurs prior to the goal date established at the time of supplement filing. However, the FDA will not postpone action after the goal date. If the applicant requests a date beyond the applicable goal date, FDA will not honor the request.

The supplement procedure has the potential to impact ongoing patent litigation under the BPCIA. Since the Public Health Service (PHS) Act provides that the submission of an aBLA is an artificial act of infringement, submission of a supplement adding a patented condition of use can likewise give rise to an act of infringement. The RPS might not know about the supplement in the absence of the patent dance or litigation. Therefore, it is possible that an RPS may not know of the existence of an application or supplement to add a condition until FDA announces its approval. At that point, the RPS can immediately sue for infringement—even if there are only a few days left before patent expiration. Therefore, the exact date of approval of a supplement adding a carved-out condition of use could have a critical effect on infringement litigation. Obviously, this is highly

15. 21 U.S.C. § 355(j)(2)(A)(viii).
16. *See* FDA, Draft Guidance for Industry, *supra* note 14, at 6.
17. *Id.* at 7.

dependent on timing of the supplement and the extent to which the aBLA filer and RPS have engaged concerning the aBLA.

b. Impacts of Interchangeability

The BPCIA amends the PHS Act and other statutes to create an abbreviated licensure pathway in section 351(k) of the PHS Act for biological products shown to be interchangeable with an FDA-licensed biological reference product. The provisions related to interchangeability are codified at 42 U.S.C. § 261(k)(4), which is also commonly referred to as section 351(k)(4) of the PHS Act. A therapeutically equivalent biosimilar is a biological product for which the FDA has determined licensure based on standards for interchangeability set forth in the statute.[18] Therapeutically equivalent or interchangeable biosimilar products are both biosimilar to an FDA-approved reference product and can be expected to produce the same clinical result in patients as the reference product.[19]

Additionally, for a biosimilar product that is administered more than once to an individual, the risk in terms of safety or efficacy of alternating or switching between the biosimilar product and the reference product will not be greater than the risk of using the reference product without alternating or switching.[20]

A therapeutically equivalent biosimilar product may be substituted without the intervention of the health care professional who prescribed the reference product, much the way generic drugs are routinely substituted for brand-name drugs. This most commonly occurs at the pharmacy level and is subject to state pharmacy laws that may vary by jurisdiction.

To date, there are only two interchangeable biosimilar products approved by the FDA. Although the statutory framework for interchangeable biosimilars has been unchanged since the BPCIA was signed into law in 2009, the first approval for an interchangeable biosimilar was not granted until July 2021. Semglee® (insulin glargine-yfgn) was approved as biosimilar to Lantus® in June 2020 and then approved as interchangeable

---

18. 42 U.S.C. § 262(k)(4). Of note, all biosimilar medicines approved in the European Union are automatically considered interchangeable with their reference product or with an equivalent biosimilar. *See* European Medicines Agency & Heads of Medicines Agencies, Statement on the Scientific Rationale Supporting Interchangeability of Biosimilar Medicines in the EU (Apr. 21, 2023).
19. 42 U.S.C. § 262(k)(4)(A).
20. *Id.* § 262(k)(4)(B).

a little more than a year later.[21] The FDA then approved Cyltezo® (adalimumab-adbm) as interchangeable with Humira® in October 2021 after originally approving Cyltezo® as a biosimilar to Humira in 2017.[22]

The financial implications of automatic pharmacy-level substitution to biosimilar applicants cannot be overstated. The ability to gain market share for a biosimilar product while reducing the administrative and operational costs associated with marketing a biosimilar can potentially sway profitability on those products in favor of the biosimilar manufacturer significantly, and, in theory, potentially bring down the costs of interchangeable alternatives to reference biologics as well.

It is, therefore, important that biosimilar applicants carefully consider the regulatory requirements for interchangeability at an early stage in the development of their biosimilar products. While the codified language concerning interchangeability is somewhat sparse and vague, the FDA has issued guidance and draft guidance surrounding the more technical regulatory questions concerning the appropriate biological and clinical pathways to establish interchangeability.[23] In particular, the FDA's 2019 guidance points out product-dependent factors that may impact the type of data needed to support interchangeability, including, for example, the

---

21. Letter from Patrick Archdeacon, Associate Director for Therapeutics, Center for Drug Evaluation and Research, to S. Wayne Talton, Head of Global Regulatory Affairs, Mylan Pharmaceuticals Inc., re: BLA Approval 761201 (July 28, 2021), https://www.accessdata.fda.gov/drugsatfda_docs/nda/2021/761201Orig1s000Approv.pdf; News Release, Mylan, Mylan and Biocon Announce U.S. FDA Approval of Semglee™ (Insulin Glargine Injection) (June 11, 2020), https://investor.mylan.com/news-releases/news-release-details/mylan-and-biocon-announce-us-fda-approval-semgleetm-insulin; Letter from Patrick Archdeacon, Associate Director for Therapeutics, Center for Drug Evaluation and Research, to S. Wayne Talton, Head of Global Regulatory Affairs, Mylan Pharmaceuticals Inc., re: NDA Approval 210605 (June 11, 2020), https://www.accessdata.fda.gov/drugsatfda_docs/appletter/2020/210605Orig1s000ltr.pdf.

22. Letter from Badrul A. Chowdhury, Director, Division of Pulmonary, Allergy, and Rheumatology Products, Center for Drug Evaluation and Research, to Christopher Dougherty, Senior Associate Director, Regulatory Affairs Biosimilars, Boehringer Ingelheim Pharmaceuticals, Inc., re: BLA Approval 761058 (Aug. 25, 2017), https://www.accessdata.fda.gov/drugsatfda_docs/appletter/2017/761058Orig1s000ltr.pdf; Letter from Nikolay P. Nikolov, Director, Division of Rheumatology and Transplant Medicine, Center for Drug Evaluation and Research, to Christopher Dougherty, Director of Regulatory Affairs, Boehringer Ingelheim, re: Supplement Approval Fulfillment of Postmarketing Requirement BLA 761058/S008 (Oct. 15, 2021), https://www.accessdata.fda.gov/drugsatfda_docs/appletter/2021/761058Orig1s008ltr.pdf.

23. In May 2019 the FDA issued Considerations in Demonstrating Interchangeability with a Reference Product as a guidance and issued Biosimilarity and Interchangeability: Additional Q&As on Biosimilar Development and the BPCIA Act as a draft guidance in November 2020. Both the guidance and the draft guidance contain nonbinding recommendations only. Considerations in Demonstrating Interchangeability with a Reference Product; Guidance for Industry; Availability, 84 Fed. Reg. 21,342 (May 10, 2019); Biosimilarity and Interchangeability: Additional Q&As on Biosimilar Development and the BPCIA Act, 85 Fed. Reg. 74,345 (Nov. 16, 2020).

product complexity, the extent of comparative and functional characterization, and the product-specific immunogenicity risk. The guidance notes that the determination of interchangeability will be made on a case-by-case basis considering the totality of the factors and data supporting interchangeability. The guidance goes on to list considerations for switching studies and discusses potential post-marketing data recommendations. The guidance provides a question and answer (Q&A) section with answers to practical questions on submitting a 351(k) biologics license application (BLA) for review of interchangeability. Notably, the FDA recommends that applicants requesting licensure for a proposed interchangeable product seek licensure for all the reference product's licensed conditions of use when possible. This can have a significant impact on developing the patent strategy, as discussed in more detail below in Section I.C.2.a. The FDA expects that all applications for interchangeable products will include data to support that the biosimilar produces the same clinical result as the reference product "in *all* of the reference product's licensed conditions of use."[24]

While the interchangeable biosimilar applicant can still carve out a condition of use, the expectation is that all data demonstrating that the product is interchangeable for that condition of use is submitted with the initial interchangeable application rather than in a supplement. This too raises questions of infringement. Again, because the PHS Act provides that the submission of a BLA is an artificial act of infringement, if there is a patent protecting a condition of use and an interchangeable application is submitted with the intent to carve out that condition of use, the act of submission is enough to allege patent infringement. Therefore, FDA's requirement that interchangeable applications include all data for all conditions of use, even those intended to be carved out, may inherently require an interchangeable applicant to infringe patents for conditions of use that will be carved out. In a way, this requirement actually encourages applicants not to seek approval as an interchangeable product until all patents have expired. In other words, because FDA's requirement leaves interchangeable applicants vulnerable to patent infringement allegations—even if the interchangeable applicant is carving-out a condition of use—one might expect that aBLA applicants would be hesitant to seek interchangeable status until all conditions of use can be included in the label.

A detailed discussion of the FDA recommendations concerning interchangeability is beyond the scope of this chapter, but when counseling biosimilar clients, a competent practitioner should have at least a high-level familiarity with the FDA's positions to inform those clients on the general

24. U.S. Food & Drug Admin., Considerations in Demonstrating Interchangeability with a Reference Product: Guidance for Industry 3 (2019).

requirements and FDA recommendations involved in gaining approval for interchangeable products.

2. Exclusivities under 42 U.S.C. § 262(k)(7)

Biologics and biosimilars may be afforded various types of non-patent, regulatory exclusivity that should be considered by biosimilar applicants when making plans to develop a new biosimilar.

a. Reference Product Exclusivity Period

Reference product exclusivity is established by 42 U.S.C. § 262(k)(7),[25] which provides in part:

> **(A) Effective date of biosimilar application approval.** Approval of an application under this subsection may not be made effective by the Secretary until the date that is 12 years after the date on which the reference product was first licensed under subsection (a).
>
> **(B) Filing period.** An application under this subsection may not be submitted to the Secretary until the date that is 4 years after the date on which the reference product was first licensed under subsection (a).

The straightforward language of the statute establishes that licensure of an application for a biosimilar or interchangeable product under § 262(k) (also known as a 351(k) application) may not be made effective by FDA until the date that is 12 years after the date on which the reference product referred to in the 262(k) application was first licensed under 42 U.S.C. § 262(a). The statute also makes clear that an application for interchangeability may not be submitted to FDA for review until four years after the date of first licensure of the reference product. This time that an application for interchangeability may not be licensed (or submitted for review) is known as the reference product exclusivity period.

Under the above-referenced statutory provisions, exclusivity for the reference product is described in terms of a prohibition on acceptance or approval of an application for a biosimilar or interchangeable product for a period of time starting from the date of first licensure of the reference product. Approval of an application for interchangeability may not be made effective until 12 years after the date of first licensure of the reference

25. 42 U.S.C. § 262(k)(7). Section 262(k)(7) of the BPCIA is also often referred to as "section 351(k) of the PHS Act." Like the Hatch-Waxman Act, which is often referred to by the original numbering of the act rather than by its subsequent section numbering once codified in the U.S. Code, it is also not uncommon to reference the original numbering of the PHS Act rather than the codified version.

product excluding the date of licensure of supplements and certain other applications. An application for an interchangeable biosimilar or biological product cannot be submitted for review until four years after the date on which the reference product was first licensed under 42 U.S.C. § 262(a).

b. Pediatric Exclusivity

As provided by 42 U.S.C. § 262(m), an additional six-month period of exclusivity (in which a biosimilar or interchangeable biological product cannot be licensed or accepted for review) will attach to the 12- and four-year periods, granted to the reference product, respectively, if the sponsor conducts pediatric studies that meet the requirements for pediatric exclusivity pursuant to section 505A of the Federal Food, Drug, and Cosmetic (FD&C) Act.

c. Orphan Drug Exclusivity

Furthermore, a biological product seeking licensure as biosimilar to or interchangeable with a reference product, where the reference product is indicated for a rare disease or condition and granted seven years of "orphan drug exclusivity" under section 527(a) of the FD&C Act, may not be licensed by FDA for the protected orphan indication until after the expiration of the seven-year orphan drug exclusivity period or the 12-year reference product exclusivity period granted under 42 U.S.C. § 262(k)(7), whichever is later.[26]

d. Exclusions

The reference product exclusivity period does not apply to every BLA. Section 351(k)(7) further provides:

> **(C) First licensure**. Subparagraphs (A) and (B) shall not apply to a license for or approval of—
>
> > **(i)** a supplement for the biological product that is the reference product; or
> >
> > **(ii)** a subsequent application filed by the same sponsor or manufacturer of the biological product that is the reference product (or a licensor, predecessor in interest, or other related entity) for—
> >
> > > **(I)** a change (not including a modification to the structure of the biological product) that results in a new indication, route of administration, dosing schedule, dosage form, delivery system, delivery device, or strength; or

26. 21 U.S.C. § 360cc.

(II) a modification to the structure of the biological product that does not result in a change in safety, purity, or potency.

A decision under 351(k)(7)(C) regarding the date of first licensure of a reference product submitted under 351(a) is, in effect, a decision on eligibility for reference product exclusivity and the date on which exclusivity begins to run. Section 351(k)(7) of the PHS Act describes reference product exclusivity as the period of time in which a 351(k) sponsor is not permitted to submit and FDA is not permitted to license a 351(k) application that references a reference product.

Not every licensure of a biological product under 351(a) is considered a "first licensure" that gives rise to its own exclusivity period. Under the terms of 351(k)(7), the dates of licensure of applications for certain changes to previously licensed biological products from the same or certain related sponsors are explicitly not considered the dates of first licensure for purposes of giving rise to a period of reference product exclusivity. Notably, an RPS will generally have superior information about changes to previously licensed products and corporate relationships to other sponsors that are relevant to a determination of the date of first licensure under 351(k)(7)(C).

A biological product submitted for licensure under section 351(a) of the PHS Act (a 351(a) application) may be eligible for a period of exclusivity that commences on the date of its licensure unless its date of licensure is not considered a date of first licensure because it falls within an exclusion under 351(k)(7)(C) such as a change made via supplement to indication, route of administration, dosing schedule, dosage form, delivery system, delivery device, strength, or a modification to the structure of the biological product that does not result in a change in safety, purity, or potency. In most instances, the date of first licensure will be the initial date the product at issue was licensed in the United States.

3. Considerations in aBLA drafting

a. aBLA Modules and Which Ones Matter Most in Litigation

An aBLA includes multiple modules. The first module includes draft labeling and proprietary naming. The second and third modules provide information on the active drug substance, elucidation of the drug substance, manufacturing information for the drug substance, impurities, and drug stability information. These modules also include information on the formulation, including excipients, manufacture, and stability. Pharmacology, pharmacokinetics, and toxicology studies are included in these modules. Module 4 includes additional pharmacokinetic and toxicology studies.

Module 5 includes clinical study reports, including those from human trials. Comparative analytical data plays a vital role in the development of biosimilars. These investigations supply evidence to establish the structural and functional resemblance between biosimilar and reference products. Additionally, they assess the implications of any differences between the reference product and the biosimilar.

Clinical studies may demonstrate that the proposed biosimilar moves through the body in the same way and provides the same effects as the reference product. Other comparative clinical studies are sometimes conducted to address any uncertainty about whether the proposed biosimilar has any clinically meaningful differences from the reference product.[27]

During litigation, the drug substance, formulation, manufacturing protocols, labeling, and clinical trials sections could all be relevant, depending on the patents held by the RPS.

For those familiar with Hatch-Waxman litigation, the general five-module structure of BLAs and aBLAs will appear familiar. However, while ANDAs will often contain only limited clinical data in Module 5 (and sometimes omit Modules 4 and 5 entirely), aBLAs will contain all five modules. The need for all five modules for aBLAs is driven by the testing requirements for biosimilarity under the BPCIA, which are more rigorous than bioequivalence under the Hatch-Waxman Act.

b. Review of the Purple Book (Incompleteness of It)

Pharmaceutical companies seeking to develop small-molecule generic drugs can look to the FDA's publication *Approved Drug Products with Therapeutic Equivalence Evaluations*, which is commonly known as the "Orange Book," for certain patent information relating to drugs. Originator companies are required by the Hatch-Waxman Act to list patents they own or licenses that cover those drugs.[28] Generic developers can rely on the Orange Book to list the universe of patents that an originator might claim cover the drug itself during litigation[29] and gauge their risk and exposure in considering whether to pursue a generic product.

There is no equivalent reference guide for biosimilar applicants. Instead, the only information available to a biosimilar applicant is the information contained in the List of Licensed Biological Products with

---

27. *Review and Approval*, FDA, https://www.fda.gov/drugs/biosimilars/review-and-approval (last updated Dec. 13, 2022).

28. 21 C.F.R. § 314.53(b)(1) (2024).

29. Although the statutes and regulation governing the Hatch-Waxman Act require complete patent listings of applicable patents, the required patents are limited to select categories. *See id.* (limiting patent listing requirements to "drug substance (active ingredient) patents, drug product (formulation and composition) patents, and method-of-use patents"). Thus, the Hatch-Waxman Act does not require listing of method of manufacturing, intermediate, and delivery device patents. By contrast, patents in these categories are frequently included on the patent list exchanged via the patent dance under the BPCIA.

Reference Product Exclusivity and Biosimilarity or Interchangeability Evaluations, also called the "Purple Book." In contrast to the Orange Book, the Purple Book does not provide a list of the full universe of patents that may be asserted by the originator as covering the drug substance, drug product, and methods for using them. Recent amendments to the BPCIA have provided some information on this front, but some in the field continue to argue that information on relevant patents is still lacking.

On September 9, 2014, the FDA published the first edition of the Purple Book. The Purple Book began as two lists (one for the Center for Drug Evaluation and Research (CDER) and one for the Center for Biologics Evaluation and Research (CBER)) that keep track of each center's licensed biological products. This edition listed biological products, including any biosimilar and interchangeable products licensed by the FDA. Approved biosimilar and interchangeable products are listed under the applicable reference product. The Purple Book lists included the following information: (1) the date a biological product was licensed under section 351(a) of the PHS Act (42 U.S.C. § 262(a)); (2) whether the FDA evaluated the biological product for reference product exclusivity under section 351(k)(7) (42 U.S.C. § 262(k)(7)); (3) whether a biological product licensed under section 351(k) has been determined to be biosimilar to or interchangeable with a reference biological product; and (4) biosimilarity or interchangeability evaluations. It did not include any patent information. In February 2020, FDA released a searchable, online database that now replaces the CDER and CBER lists because information about FDA-approved biological products is available in the Purple Book database.

In December 2020, Congress enacted the Purple Book Continuity Act (PBCA) as part of the Consolidated Appropriations Act. The statute added paragraph 9 of subsection (k), which requires an RPS to provide FDA with copies of patent lists within 30 days of when they were first provided to biosimilar applicants as part of the "patent dance."[30] Likewise, FDA must be updated within 30 days of any subsequent or supplemental list of patents provided to a biosimilar challenger. Consequently, patent information is not available in the FDA database until such a biosimilar applicant emerges and a patent dance commenced. Additionally, the PBCA does not establish any obligation for product sponsors to continuously update patent information in the Purple Book, underscoring the book's limitations for understanding potential patent challenges under FDA statutes.

The lack of clear consequences for noncompliance presents another limitation on the PBCA. While the legislation indicates that the patent holder "shall" provide this information to FDA, it does not specify

30. 42 U.S.C. § 262(k)(9)(A)(iii).

consequences for failing to comply. It remains unclear what obligations would fall on the RPS if a biosimilar applicant opted out of participating in the patent dance.

Relating to exclusivity, the PBCA required the Purple Book to feature information about unexpired exclusivity periods for reference and interchangeable products, provided FDA had made a determination of eligibility for exclusivity. However, the exclusivity periods cover only the 12-year reference product exclusivity and exclusivity granted to interchangeable biosimilar products, and posting these exclusivities is contingent on FDA's eligibility assessment.

The disclosure of patents listed under section 262(*l*)(3)(A) or (*l*)(7) in the PBCA amendments have substantial strategic implications for the patent dance. An RPS has some discretion in selecting patents for inclusion on these lists. The sponsor includes patents that could reasonably be asserted against the specific biosimilar in question. The prior version of the BPCIA prompted broader patent lists to avoid limiting preliminary injunctive relief options.[31] However, the public disclosure of these patents in the Purple Book under the PBCA introduced new issues. Comprehensive patent lists in the Purple Book could expose these patents to preemptive challenges and might prompt biosimilar makers to design their products to avoid infringing the listed patents. Consequently, post-PBCA, RPSs may opt for narrower patent lists that align closely with a specific biosimilar at hand.

For biosimilar makers, the disclosure of patents in the Purple Book may discourage participation in the patent dance. During this dance, a biosimilar applicant exchanges confidential information for patent details from the RPS. The Purple Book's disclosure of certain patents could potentially expose confidential details of a prior biosimilar product as they may have been chosen for the exchange based on the BLA holder's review of the confidential aBLA. Additionally, an earlier biosimilar applicant could prevent later applicants from benefiting from the disclosure of the patent list in the Purple Book by skipping the patent dance.

The PBCA provided more information and transparency for biosimilars. However, compared to the Orange Book, the Purple Book remains somewhat "incomplete." First, the PBCA does not provide much help for companies seeking to expedite development of biosimilars. The RPS must only provide information on its patents to the FDA for listing in the Purple Book *after* it engages in the patent dance. Rather than encouraging companies to quickly develop biosimilars, the PBCA helps those developers who sit back and wait for others that are willing to proceed with the patent

31. *Id.* § 262(*l*)(3)(A).

dance. Compare this with the Orange Book, which provides complete patent information to all developers at the time of FDA approval of the RPS.[32]

In contrast to the Orange Book, the Purple Book will only list patents that the RPS alleges cover a specific biosimilar product. It is possible that the RPS might have a different patent list that it would assert against a different biosimilar. But under the PBCA, that different list of patents would not be listed in the Purple Book unless those patents are included in another 3(A) list against a different biosimilar. The extensive patent portfolios common with biologic products only exacerbate the problem. Where the patent landscape is vast, and the patents listed in prior lawsuits are specific to that particular biosimilar applicant's product and processes, it could take more aBLA filings—and more 3(A) lists—to reveal the full RPS patent portfolio.

The large numbers of patents that often cover the biologic products weigh in favor of more transparency. Yet, even with the passage of the PBCA, the Purple Book provides less patent information than the Orange Book for a given product. And while biosimilar developers can use earlier litigation to identify some RPS patents—that litigation may occur too late in the development process for the biosimilar applicant to design around troublesome patents.[33]

4. Detailed Statements under 42 U.S.C. § 262(l)(3)

One of the early statutory requirements for an aBLA applicant that has decided to participate in the so-called "patent dance" is that the applicant provide the RPS with a

> detailed statement that describes, on a claim by claim basis, the factual and legal basis of the opinion of the subsection (k) applicant that [any identified] patent is invalid, unenforceable, or will not be infringed by the commercial marketing of the biological product that is the subject of the subsection (k) application.[34]

This statutorily required "detailed statement" is also called the "3(B) statement."

a. Content of the Statement

The authors generally recommend that aBLA applicants present only their best defense for each patent in their detailed statement. Typically, this

32. Stacie Ropka & Ted Mathias, *Opinion: Purple Book Patent Listings Are Only a First Step*, Ctr. for Biosimilars (May 8, 2021), https://www.centerforbiosimilars.com/view/opinion-purple-book-patent-listings-are-only-a-first-step.

33. *Id.*

34. *Id.* § 262(*l*)(3)(B).

defense should be the strongest defense (i.e., the defense that is mostly likely to give the RPS pause before filing suit).[35]

The authors' recommendation is drawn from the body of case law governing detailed statements under the Hatch-Waxman Act of 1984. The Hatch-Waxman Act had more than 25 years of history at the time Congress enacted the BPCIA in 2010. While there are still relatively few judicial decisions interpreting the statutes and regulations governing BPCIA detailed statements, there is a significant body of case law concerning detailed statements under the Hatch-Waxman Act. The statutory language governing the BPCIA detailed statement is very similar to the Hatch-Waxman Act's detailed statement requirement for ANDAs containing so-called Paragraph IV certifications.[36] As a result, BPCIA applicants can look to court decisions under the Hatch-Waxman Act for some guidance on the content of their statements.

Hatch-Waxman Act decisions counsel that an aBLA applicant is not obligated to provide *every* defense in its detailed statement. U.S. district courts have repeatedly rejected the argument that ANDA applicants are limited to only the defenses raised in their notice letters.[37] These rulings will likely be persuasive under the BPCIA for a couple reasons. First, the language of the BPCIA detailed statement provision is similar to that of the Hatch-Waxman Act. Neither states that the detailed statement must include "all" or "every" basis for its patent challenge. Instead, both statutes use the conjunction "or," stating in the case of the BPCIA that the detailed statement should state why the patent is "invalid, unenforceable, or will not be infringed."[38] Second, U.S. courts allow extensive discovery, which will often reveal new, previously unknown defenses in a litigation. It makes sense that BPCIA applicants should be permitted to add defenses in view of such discovery just like other litigants.

Hatch-Waxman litigation has also exposed disadvantages in saying too much in detailed statements. The more defenses raised, the greater the possibility that the generic litigant will learn something new in litigation

---

35. *See* Yamanouchi Pharm. Co. v. Danbury Pharm., Inc., 231 F.3d 1339, 1346–47 (Fed. Cir. 2000) (noting that a Hatch-Waxman litigation "may become exceptional" justifying an award of attorney fees against the ANDA filer "if the ANDA filer makes baseless certifications").

36. 21 U.S.C. § 355(j)(2)(B)(i), (iv)(II) (requiring service of a "detailed statement of the factual and legal basis of the opinion of the applicant that the patent is invalid or will not be infringed" where the application contains a certification under 21 U.S.C. § 355(j)(2)(A)(vii)(IV)).

37. *E.g.*, Bausch Health Ir. Ltd. v. Mylan Pharms. Inc., No. 1:22-CV-20, 2023 WL 2726432, at *3 (N.D. W. Va. Mar. 30, 2023); Abbott Lab'ys v. Lupin Ltd., No. 09-152, 2011 WL 1897322, at *7 (D. Del. May 19, 2011); Abbott Lab'ys, Inc. v. Apotex Inc., 725 F. Supp. 2d 724, 728 (N.D. Ill. 2010).

38. 42 U.S.C. § 262(*l*)(3)(A)(b)(ii).

that causes it to rethink one of those defenses. Raising more defenses also increases the possibility of conflicting with the position of another applicant, again raising the possibility that an applicant will need to step back from a defense raised in its detailed statement. The courts have not always looked kindly upon generic applicants that change positions from those in the notice letter—as opposed to adding new positions. In one case, the Federal Circuit affirmed an award of more than $16 million in attorney fees against generic applicants who had "changed the focus of their invalidity arguments from those in their certification letters."[39]

In a related vein, parties serving detailed statements should state their positions on noninfringement, invalidity, and unenforceability without taking a formal position on claim construction wherever possible. Patent litigants have been known to take myriad different positions on claim construction of the same term. Just like Hatch-Waxman litigation, there are often multiple aBLA applicants challenging the same patent or related ones in BPCIA litigation.[40] To avoid the need to backtrack on positions taken in the detailed statement, an aBLA applicant should attempt to fully present its defense(s) without taking a formal position on precisely how particular claim terms should be construed. This preserves maximum flexibility on claim construction issues and avoids potential conflicts in the event that the aBLA applicant's case is consolidated with others' cases in subsequent litigation.

Other than the above special considerations, best practices for detailed statements overlap with those for opinions of counsel in patent cases generally. The detailed statement can be a persuasive piece of evidence in defending against an exceptional case claim or, in the event of an at-risk

---

39. *E.g.*, Takeda Chem. Indus., Ltd. v. Mylan Lab'ys, Inc., 549 F.3d 1381, 1384 (Fed. Cir. 2008); *see also Yamanouchi*, 231 F.3d at 1347 (affirming award of attorney fees against an ANDA filer where the "notice does not present a *prima facie* case of invalidity"); Otsuka Co. v. Sandoz, Inc., No. 07-1000, 2015 WL 5921035, at *7 n.6 (D.N.J. Oct. 9, 2015) (declining fees under 35 U.S.C. § 285 where "[t]he defendants argue, and this Court agrees, that the parties' main arguments of non-infringement, invalidity of the '528 patent, and unenforceability of the '528 patent remained the same throughout the course of the litigation."); AstraZeneca AB v. Mut. Pharm. Co., 221 F. Supp. 2d 528, 534 (E.D. Pa. 2002) (observing that courts "have determined that an unfounded or deficient notice can lead to a finding of willful infringement which constitutes an exceptional case which permits the award of counsel fees").

40. For example, Genentech and City of Hope sued multiple biosimilar applicants for infringement of common patents related to the drug Herceptin®. *E.g.*, Genentech, Inc. v. Pfizer Inc., No. 17-1672 (D. Del. filed Nov. 17, 2017); Genentech, Inc. v. Amgen Inc., No. 17-1407 (D. Del. filed Oct. 6, 2017); Genentech, Inc. v. Samsung Bioepis Co., No. 1:18-cv-1363 (D. Del. filed Sept. 4, 2018); Genentech, Inc. v. Tanvex BioPharma USA, Inc., No. 3:22-cv-809 (S.D. Cal. filed June 6, 2022). Similar litigation dynamics exist with other biosimilars, including proposed biosimilars to adalimumab, bevacizumab, etanercept, filgrastim, infliximab, pegfilgrastim, rituximab, and trastuzumab.

launch, a willfulness infringement claim.[41] Unlike reliance on an opinion of counsel, an aBLA applicant can rely on the detailed statement to defend the reasonableness of its positions without risking a privilege waiver. But the detailed statement must be well-grounded to be useful in this regard. Like opinions of counsel, a detailed statement should include an accurate and current statement of the relevant law and persuasive, fulsome analysis of the basis for the aBLA applicant's opinion that the patent is invalid, not infringed, or unenforceable.[42]

b. Notice Letters and Confidentiality

One important difference between the BPCIA and Hatch-Waxman Act is that the BPCIA does not require a formal notice letter or offer of confidential access (OCA) to the application. The Hatch-Waxman Act requires that the detailed statement is attached to a notice letter, which is required by FDA regulations to contain very specific content.[43] No such notice letter requirement exists in the BPCIA—just the detailed statement is required.[44] BPCIA detailed statements may thus be attached to a short cover letter or simply attached to an email.

The BPCIA also provides a different confidentiality scheme than the OCA mechanism in the Hatch-Waxman Act. Under the BPCIA's confidentiality scheme, an aBLA applicant generally can and should freely provide its full aBLA and additional documentation (if requested) and is assured of strong confidentiality protection.[45] By contrast, under the Hatch-Waxman Act, a generic drug applicant asserting noninfringement must provide an OCA to relevant portions of its ANDA. The parties often dispute the terms of the OCA exchange, sometimes failing to reach agreement in time to

41. *E.g.*, Abraxis Biosci., Inc. v. Navinta, LLC, No. 07-1251, 2009 WL 5174454, at *2 (D.N.J. Dec. 17, 2009) (declining an award of attorney fees under § 285 because "[a]lthough Defendant ultimately did not prevail at trial, the Court does not find that the non-infringement theory offered by Defendant in its Paragraph IV certification was so utterly devoid of support that Defendant's ANDA certification should be deemed 'baseless.'").

42. The Federal Circuit has held, in the context of willfulness, that an opinion of counsel "must be competent or it is of little value in showing the good faith belief of the infringer." Sunoco Partners Mktg. & Terminals L.P. v. U.S. Venture, Inc., 32 F.4th 1161, 1178 (Fed. Cir. 2022) (quoting Comark Commc'ns, Inc. v. Harris Corp., 156 F.3d 1182, 1191 (Fed. Cir. 1998)).

43. 21 C.F.R. § 314.95(c) (2024) (listing required contents of a notice letter under 21 U.S.C. § 505(j)(2)(B)(iv)).

44. *See generally* 42 U.S.C. § 262(*l*).

45. One note of caution is warranted. Under the PBCA, the holder of the reference drug product will provide information about the patents it believes could reasonably be asserted to FDA for listing in the Purple Book. If the BLA holder owns patents with very specific process or formulation requirements, the mere listing of those patents in the Purple Book may give competitors some information about a given aBLA product, particularly if there are few known biosimilar competitors. The aBLA applicant should carefully consider this possibility when deciding whether to engage in the patent dance.

exchange information before suit must be filed.[46] In some cases, the reference listed drug sponsor then publicly filed the detailed statement—negating the entire purpose of the OCA.[47] The result is that Hatch-Waxman detailed statements asserting noninfringement tend to omit to the greatest extent possible any discussion of confidential information in the ANDA.

Twenty-five years later, when Congress enacted the BPCIA, it chose not to carry over the Hatch-Waxman Act's malleable OCA procedure—and the problems associated with it. The BPCIA does not allow an aBLA applicant flexibility to set the terms and scope of its disclosures; it mandates simply that the aBLA applicant "shall provide the RPS a copy of the application . . . and such other information that describes the process or processes used to manufacture the biological product that is the subject of such application."[48] On the flipside, the BPCIA provides concrete protections for the confidentiality of the aBLA and its content, stating confidentiality protections "shall apply to the exchange of information described in this subsection." Thus, the confidentiality of the "information" in the aBLA is protected regardless of whether it is provided only in the aBLA itself or discussed in the detailed statement, allowing the parties to the BPCIA patent dance the benefit of fulsome disclosures via the detailed statement.[49]

II. Litigation and Beyond: Early Litigation Strategic Considerations

As the patent dance progresses, aBLA applicants should begin preparations for possible patent infringement litigation. Typically, the RPS will file a patent infringement action under the BPCIA within 30 days of reaching agreement with the aBLA applicant as to the patent list. This is because, if the RPS misses the 30-day deadline, its "sole and exclusive remedy . . . shall be a reasonable royalty."[50] If filed within 30 days, an RPS

46. *E.g.*, Lupin Atlantis Holdings v. Ranbaxy Lab'ys, Ltd., No. 10-3897, 2011 WL 1540199 n.7 (E.D. Pa. Apr. 21, 2011) (noting in passing the parties "dispute[d] whether Ranbaxy's offer to provide Lupin Atlantis with limited access was reasonable"); Takeda Pharm. Co. Ltd. v. Zydus Pharms. (USA) Inc., No. 18-1994, 2021 WL 3144897, at *6, *8 (D.N.J. July 26, 2021) (noting Zydus's OCA negotiations involved "email[ing]/call[ing] Takeda eight times" over the course of a month, yet, "Takeda did not accept Zydus' OCA or review its full ANDA before bringing suit").

47. *E.g.*, Nycomed U.S. Inc. v. Tolmar, Inc., No. 10-2635, 2011 WL 1675027, at *1 (D.N.J. Apr. 28, 2011) (permitting reference listed drug sponsor to publicly file Hatch-Waxman detailed statement).

48. 42 U.S.C. § 262(*l*)(2)(A).

49. *Id.* § 262(*l*)(1).

50. 35 U.S.C. § 271(e)(6)(B).

can seek additional remedies, such as injunctive relief or other monetary damages.[51]

Although patent infringement actions under the BPCIA share many similarities with actions under the Hatch-Waxman Act, there are two differences between them that are particularly important when considering early strategy. First, although Hatch-Waxman prohibits the FDA from approving a generic drug's ANDA for 30 months, there is no such bar under the BPCIA.[52] Accordingly, for actions under the BPCIA, the RPS must use the courts, and their injunctive power, to prohibit impending launches. Also, BPCIA litigants generally have a right to a jury trial, while Hatch-Waxman cases are generally tried before a judge.[53]

Although RPS-filed patent infringement litigation is a typical culmination of the patent dance, aBLA applicants should be aware of other avenues by which these matters may be resolved or the RPS's patents may be challenged. Options for adjudicating patents under the BPCIA, and some high-level considerations that counsel should keep in mind as they advise clients regarding prospective BPCIA adjudication in each, are discussed in the following sections.

A. The Who, What, Where of BPCIA Litigation in the District Courts: Venue and Personal Jurisdiction

The patent dance will frequently culminate in the RPS filing suit in the district courts for patent infringement. The basics of an action under the BPCIA resemble that of other patent infringement actions. Like patent cases generally, both venue and personal jurisdiction are driven by the identity of the parties. And, just like other patent cases, the litigation forum may impact timing, cost, and the outcome, so counsel should consider which forums are likely as early as possible and potentially take action to make sure it is ready for suit.

As one would expect, the RPS is typically the plaintiff in a BPCIA action. However, to the extent the RPS seeks to assert patents that it does not have exclusive rights over, the RPS would need to include the other right holders as parties. For example, in an action related to cancer therapy Avastin, the plaintiffs were (1) Genentech, the RPS of Avastin and

---

51. *Id.* § 271(e)(4).

52. 21 U.S.C. § 355(j)(5)(B)(iii) (stating "the approval shall be made effective upon the expiration of the thirty-month period beginning on the date of the receipt of the notice provided under paragraph (2)(B)(i) or such shorter or longer period as the court may order because either party to the action failed to reasonably cooperate in expediting the action").

53. Because BPCIA plaintiffs are typically seeking, at least in part, monetary damages, the parties have a right to a jury trial. *See* U.S. Const. amend. VII ("In Suits at common law, where the value in controversy shall exceed twenty dollars, the right of trial by jury shall be preserved . . . .").

owner of most of the asserted patents, and (2) City of Hope, a co-owner of two of the asserted patents.[54] Further, although Hoffmann La-Roche owned four of the asserted patents, Genentech did not need to include Hoffmann La-Roche as a party on the complaint because Genentech was the exclusive licensee of those patents with the sole right to enforce them.[55] Nonetheless, Pfizer's answer to the complaint asserted counterclaims against Genentech, City of Hope, and Hoffmann La-Roche, alleging: "Disposing of this action in Roche's absence would, upon information and belief, impair or impede Roche's ability to protect its interest in the four patents and leave Pfizer with a substantial risk of incurring double, multiple, or otherwise inconsistent obligations because of Roche's interest in the asserted patents."[56]

The defendant in a BPCIA action is typically the aBLA applicant. So who can be sued for infringement under the BPCIA? The answer is in the statute, which codified a new act of infringement in 35 U.S.C. § 271(e)(2)(C):

> *It shall be an act of infringement to submit . . . an application* seeking approval of a biological product . . . if the purpose of such submission is to obtain approval under such Act to engage in the commercial manufacture, use, or sale of a . . . biological product claimed in a patent or the use of which is claimed in a patent before the expiration of such patent.[57]

Thus, the statute states that the act of "submit[ting]" the aBLA is the act of infringement. This begs the question of whether other entities besides the applicant named in the aBLA can properly be sued for infringement. There is at least one early example in which a court looked beyond the named applicant to determine the "submitter" of the aBLA.[58]

In both the BPCIA and its predecessor, the Hatch-Waxman Act, the act of infringement that defines a cause of action is set out in 35 U.S.C. § 271(e)(2) and shares the same root language (i.e., "It shall be an act of infringement to submit . . . an application."[59]). The Federal Circuit has held that this language limits who may be sued for infringement under the Hatch-Waxman Act, stating that a party that "did not submit an

54. Genentech, Inc. v. Pfizer Inc., No. 1:19-cv-00638 (D. Del. Apr. 5, 2019), ECF No. 1.
55. *Id.*
56. Genentech, Inc. v. Pfizer Inc., No. 1:19-cv-00638 (D. Del. Apr. 29, 2019), ECF No. 14.
57. 35 U.S.C. § 271(e)(2)(C) (emphasis added).
58. Memorandum Opinion and Order, AbbVie Inc. v. Alvotech hf., No. 1:21-cv-2258 (N.D. Ill. Aug. 24, 2021), ECF No. 51.
59. 35 U.S.C. § 271(e)(2)(A).

ANDA . . . cannot be liable for infringement under § 271(e)(2)."[60] This limit makes sense in the context of the safe harbor of 35 U.S.C. § 271(e)(1). Under that statutory provision:

> It shall not be an act of infringement to make, use, offer to sell, or sell within the United States or import into the United States a patented invention . . . solely for uses reasonably related to the development and submission of information under a Federal law which regulates the manufacture, use, or sale of drugs . . . .[61]

For both the BPCIA and Hatch-Waxman Act, the line between protected activity under the safe harbor of § 271(e)(1) and infringing activity under § 271(e)(2) is thus the "submi[ssion]" of the application.

Despite the apparent simplicity of the statutory scheme's "submission"-based line for infringement, it is not always as simple as looking at the signatory of FDA's Form 356h to determine who "submit[ted]" the application. Often the signatory is one of several related corporate entities and it is not always clear which can be sued under the BPCIA. Where a related entity signs an application as an agent of the true applicant, the related entity may be joined in the suit.[62] However, some courts have dismissed non-submitting corporations even where they are related to the entity responsible for submitting the application.[63] Others have held that related entities can properly be sued, particularly where the entity had

---

60. Shire, LLC v. Amneal Pharms., LLC, 802 F.3d 1301, 1310 (Fed. Cir. 2015) (holding supplier of active pharmaceutical ingredient was not a proper defendant in a Hatch-Waxman litigation).

61. 35 U.S.C. § 271(e)(1); *see* Amgen Inc. v. Hospira, Inc., 944 F.3d 1327, 1337–39 (Fed. Cir. 2019) (noting application of safe harbor to biosimilars).

62. *In re* Rosuvastatin Calcium Patent Litig., 703 F.3d 511, 527–29 (Fed. Cir. 2012); *In re* OxyContin Antitrust Litig., Nos. 04-MD-1603 (SHS), 10 Civ. 6038 (SHS), 2012 U.S. Dist. LEXIS 151139, at *38, 46–47 (S.D.N.Y. Oct. 19, 2012). The signatory of the application is indicated in FDA Form 356h.

63. Oral Order, H. Lundbeck A/S v. Apotex Inc., No. 18-88 (D. Del. Feb. 26, 2019), ECF No. 197 (dismissing Sandoz AG as party to litigation); *see* Galderma Lab'ys, L.P. v. Teva Pharms. USA, Inc., 290 F. Supp. 3d 299, 617–18 (N.D. Tex. 2017) (holding that allegations as to the collective conduct of Teva USA and Teva Israel were insufficient to support a claim against Teva Israel); M2M Solutions, LLC v. Telit Commc'ns PLC, No. 14-1103, 2015 U.S. Dist. Lexis 102349, at *7 (D. Del. Aug. 5, 2015) (observing that "Plaintiff's decision to lump two defendants together in addressing its direct infringement claim . . . does not identify which particular defendant or defendants are responsible for which allegedly infringing products, process or method"); *see also* Bausch Health Ir. Ltd. v. Mylan Lab'ys Ltd., No. 21-10403, 2022 WL 683084, at *6 & n.12 (D.N.J. Mar. 8, 2022) (observing that "[b]ecause Plaintiffs have not demonstrated that Mylan API participated in preparing ANDA No. 215686, they have not established that it is a 'submitter' under § 271(e)(2)").

or will have "active involvement" in the development or marketing of the product.[64]

In one particularly unusual case, BLA holder AbbVie filed suit against the foreign parent of Alvotech USA—the party that had signed and filed the aBLA for Humira.[65] AbbVie alleged that the foreign parent, Alvotech hf., is the entity that will engage in the manufacturing and commercialization of the biosimilar and "created and prepared the information in the aBLA."[66] Taking AbbVie's allegations as true, the court concluded that Alvotech hf. "can be deemed a 'submitter,'" reasoning that Alvotech hf. was actively involved in preparing the ANDA and participated in the drug's manufacture or importation.[67] The court went on to conclude that Alvotech USA was not a necessary party.[68] Note that the court concluded this even though it might not have had proper venue or personal jurisdiction in the Northern District of Illinois had AbbVie sued Alvotech USA, a Virginia corporation.[69]

Against the backdrop of the Hatch-Waxman Act precedent existing to date, the following factors should be considered when deciding which entities may be sued in BPCIA litigation:

- First, consider whether the entity is named in the aBLA application and, if so, in what capacity. The party identified as the aBLA applicant in FDA Form 356h or signing FDA Form 356h for another related entity can expect that they may be named as a defendant. This is true even if the party is simply acting as an agent for another, related entity and signs the ANDA submission

---

64. Cephalon, Inc. v. Watson Pharms., Inc., 629 F. Supp. 2d 338, 343, 349 (D. Del. 2009) (non-ANDA submitters found to be proper parties where, inter alia, they would be "involved in the marketing and distribution" of the ANDA product); Helsinn Healthcare S.A. v. Hospira, Inc., No. 15-2077, 2016 U.S. Dist. Lexis 45826, at *3–4, 21 (D.N.J. Apr. 5, 2016) (declining to dismiss domestic subsidiary of the ANDA submitter that "markets, sells, and distributes drugs for Hospira in the United States," and "plann[ed] to 'manufacture, import, market, and sell the [ANDA] product'"); AstraZeneca UK Ltd. v. Watson Lab'ys, Inc. (NV), No. 10-915, slip op. at 9 (D. Del. Mar. 23, 2012) (finding involvement of non-ANDA submitter suggested it was "prime mover" in seeking FDA approval). These cases are arguably limited by the Federal Circuit's 2015 decision in *Shire*, as these holdings all follow from *Forest Laboratories, Inc. v. Ivax Pharmaceuticals, Inc.*, which was limited to its facts by *Shire*. *Shire*, 802 F.3d at 1310 (distinguishing Forest Lab'ys, Inc. v. Ivax Pharms., Inc., 501 F.3d 1263, 1271–72 (Fed. Cir. 2007)).

65. Memorandum Opinion and Order, AbbVie Inc. v. Alvotech hf., No. 1:21-cv-2258 (N.D. Ill. Aug. 23, 2021), ECF No. 51.

66. *Id.* at *3.

67. *Id.* at *8.

68. *Id.* at *10.

69. Memorandum in Support of Defendant Alvotech hf.'s Motion to Dismiss for Lack of Subject Matter Jurisdiction, Lack of Personal Jurisdiction, Failure to State a Claim, and Failure to Join a Necessary Party, AbbVie Inc. v. Alvotech hf., No. 1:21-cv-2258 (N.D. Ill. June 2, 2021), ECF No. 27.

in that capacity. The aBLA applicant should be mindful that these entities may be sued, but that the holder of the BLA may sue one or more of them selectively if it believes it can file suit in a more desirable venue by doing so. By contrast, an ingredient supplier identified in the aBLA is unlikely to be a proper defendant.[70]

- Second, consider what involvement an entity has in the development and marketing of the aBLA. The level of active involvement in the development and marketing of the biosimilar may impact whether an entity can be sued under the BPCIA.[71]
- Third, consider whether the entity is likely to have discoverable information related to the drug product. If that is the case, it is more likely that the entity has a level of involvement that may make it a proper party.[72]
- Fourth, consider which parties were named as defendants in prior aBLA litigation involving the named aBLA applicant. As a practical matter, a court may be less likely to entertain a motion to dismiss if the parties were previously named as defendants in prior, similar litigation and no dismissal was sought.

Where an entity believes it is improperly named as a defendant in BPCIA litigation, there are several options. The preliminary question the entity should ask is, "Does this matter to the client and, if so, why?" In some cases, the entity may be so closely related to the true aBLA applicant that it makes no difference whether both are named—filing a motion to dismiss may be elevating form over substance with little benefit to justify the cost of briefing on the issue. However, if the improperly named defendant impacts venue, a motion to dismiss may be the only option that will allow the true aBLA applicant to seek transfer to a more appropriate venue.[73] In other cases, there may be concern about setting precedent that the entity may be sued in future BPCIA cases. In such cases, a stipulated dismissal in exchange for the entity's agreement to participate in discovery

70. Shire, LLC v. Amneal Pharms., LLC, 802 F.3d 1301, 1310 (Fed. Cir. 2015).

71. *See supra* note 64 (collecting cases assessing whether an entity's role rose to the level of active involvement sufficient to make them an ANDA submitter).

72. *See, e.g., supra* note 64 (collecting examples).

73. *See, e.g.*, Memorandum Opinion and Order, AbbVie Inc. v. Alvotech hf., No. 1:21-cv-2258 (N.D. Ill. Aug. 24, 2021), ECF No. 51.

may meet both sides' objectives.[74] There can also be situations in which the entity is not involved with the aBLA, but expects to be unduly burdened by discovery if not dismissed from the litigation early. For example, some foreign countries have discovery restrictions that may make producing information just to prove noninvolvement unduly burdensome. In such situations, the entity can provide assurances of its noninvolvement, but the BLA holder may be reluctant to voluntarily dismiss an entity from the suit without something in exchange.

Once the proper parties are assessed, general patent litigation precedent governing venue and personal jurisdiction applies. Under this precedent, venue is determined pursuant to 28 U.S.C. § 1391.[75] Under the patent-specific venue statute of 28 U.S.C. § 1400(b), "[a]ny civil action for patent infringement may be brought in [(1)] the judicial district where the defendant resides, or [(2)] where the defendant has committed acts of infringement and has a regular and established place of business." "[T]he judicial district where the defendant resides . . . refers only to the State of incorporation."[76] Likewise, courts apply precedent applicable to personal jurisdiction in non-pharmaceutical cases when assessing personal jurisdiction under the BPCIA.[77]

B. Special Considerations for Declaratory Judgment Actions

1. RPS-Filed Declaratory Judgment Actions

The law is clear that the BLA holder can file a declaratory judgment action against an aBLA applicant either if the applicant refuses to engage in the patent dance or if the brand considers the applicant's proffer of

74. There is a large body of these types of dismissal orders littering the federal courts' dockets in pharmaceutical litigations. A few recent examples are collected here. *E.g.*, Catalyst Pharms., Inc. v. Lupin Ltd., No. 23-cv-1197 (D.N.J. entered Apr. 25, 2023), ECF No. 33 (stipulating to dismissal of Lupin Inc. in exchange for agreement to cooperate in discovery); Theravance BioPharma R&D IP, LLC v. Eugia Pharma Specialties, Ltd., No. 23-cv-926 (D.N.J. filed Mar. 15, 2023), ECF No. 12-1 (stipulating to dismissal of Accord Healthcare, Ltd. and Intas Pharmaceuticals, Ltd. in exchange for Accord Healthcare, Inc.'s consent to personal jurisdiction and venue and agreement to provide discovery from the dismissed parties); Heron Therapeutics, Inc. v. Fresenius Kabi USA, LLC, No. 22-985 (D. Del. filed Nov. 4, 2022), ECF No. 12 (stipulating to dismissal of Fresenius AG in exchange for agreement to cooperate with discovery); Novartis Pharms. Corp. v. Teva Pharms. USA, Inc., No. 1:22-cv-83 (D. Del. filed Mar. 15, 2022), ECF No. 7 (stipulating to dismissal of Teva Ltd.).

75. 28 U.S.C. § 1391(c).

76. TC Heartland LLC v. Kraft Foods Grp. Brands LLC, 137 S. Ct. 1514, 1519-20 (2017).

77. *E.g.*, Memorandum Opinion and Order, AbbVie Inc. v. Alvotech hf., No. 1:21-cv-2258 (N.D. Ill. Aug. 24, 2021), ECF No. 51.

information inadequate.[78] In practice, BLA holders have successfully maintained declaratory judgment actions even against applicants that have disclosed hundreds of thousands of pages of information, including information on the manufacturing processes and product.[79]

Considering RPSs' considerable leeway in electing to file a declaratory judgment action,[80] an applicant may choose to skip the patent dance altogether. Such a strategy would avoid the 200+-day delay that the patent dance presents. However, succumbing to a declaratory judgment action means that an applicant cedes control over the timing and scope (e.g., the asserted patents) of the litigation. Moreover, a biosimilar applicant may lose its right to file a declaratory judgment action based on a notice of commercial marketing, and a failure to participate in the patent dance may factor into a court's decision to enter an injunction against the applicant.[81]

2. Applicant-Filed Declaratory Judgment Actions

Biosimilar applicant-filed declaratory judgment actions are not likely viable, and have not yet survived motions to dismiss. Applicants that filed declaratory judgment actions before their aBLAs were accepted by the FDA have found their cases dismissed for a failure to establish a "case or controversy" sufficient to establish standing.[82] And applicants that have pursued declaratory judgment actions during the patent dance also faced

---

78. Sandoz Inc. v. Amgen Inc., 582 U.S. 1, 16 (2017) (providing that "[w]hen an applicant fails to comply with 42 U.S.C. § 262(*l*)(2)(A), § 262(*l*)(9)(C) authorizes the sponsor, but not the applicant, to bring an immediate declaratory judgment action for artificial infringement. Section 262(*l*)(9)(C) thus vests in the sponsor the control that the applicant would otherwise have exercised over the scope and timing of the patent litigation. It also deprives the applicant of the certainty that it could have obtained by bringing a declaratory-judgment action prior to marketing its product.").

79. *See, e.g.*, Genentech v. Pfizer, No. 19-cv-00638 (D. Del. Apr. 5, 2019), ECF Nos. 1, 14 (indicating that Pfizer produced the portions of aBLA to Genentech, sufficient to describe "Pfizer's Product and the processes to manufacture it").

80. *See, e.g.*, Candace Polser et al., *Declaratory Judgments Unavoidable for Biosimilar Applicants*, Law360 (Mar. 5, 2021), https://www.morganlewis.com/-/media/files/news/2021/law360_declaratory-judgments-unavoidable-for-biosimilar-applicants_5march21.pdf.

81. *See, e.g.*, Celltrion, Inc. v. Genentech, Inc., No. 18-cv-00274, 2018 WL 2448254, at *8 (N.D. Cal. May 9, 2018) ("[A] notice of commercial marketing only opens the door for an applicant to file a declaratory judgment action if the applicant complies with the rest of the statute. A notice of commercial marketing is no *carte blanche*, and Celltrion points to no authority that offers a contradictory interpretation."), *appeal dismissed*, No. 2018-2160, 2018 WL 7046651 (Fed. Cir. Nov. 30, 2018); *Sandoz*, 582 U.S. at 19-20 (stating that noncompliance with the patent dance may factor into imposition of an injunction under state law).

82. *See* Sandoz Inc. v. Amgen Inc., 773 F.3d 1274, 1282 (Fed. Cir. 2014) (affirming dismissal of Sandoz's declaratory judgment action filed on the same day Sandoz began a Phase III trial of its Embrel biosimilar); Celltrion Healthcare Co., Ltd. v. Kennedy Tr. for Rheumatology Rsch., No. 14-cv-2256, 2014 WL 6765996, at *4 (S.D.N.Y. Dec. 1, 2014) (dismissing Celltrion declaratory judgment action filed before Celltrion filed an aBLA for a Remicade biosimilar due to a lack of justiciable controversy).

dismissal. For example, applicant Celltrion proceeded with the patent dance until Genentech identified 40 patents associated with its Herceptin biologic. Celltrion then filed an action for declaratory judgment of patent noninfringement, invalidity, and unenforceability, accusing Genentech of providing allegations that were either "wrong" or a "panoply of vague allegations . . . simply intended to interfere with Celltrion['s] . . . entry into the market."[83] Although the court held that the patent dance was not a jurisdictional prerequisite, the court held that because Celltrion "did not complete its obligations under Section (*l*)(5), Celltrion may not file actions for declaratory judgement with respect to the patents at issue," and, thus, failed to state a claim.[84] Moreover, Celltrion—and others—have tried, but failed, to avoid dismissal by pointing to their notice of commercial marketing as triggering an alternative ground for jurisdiction.[85]

C. IPRs and PGRs

The Patent Trial and Appeal Board (PTAB) presents another option for adjudicating patents that may apply to biosimilars. As in other industries, IPRs and PGRs afford patent challengers a lower cost and quicker alternative to district court litigation. Unsurprisingly, these types of challenges—particularly IPRs[86]—have similarly dominated the biosimilar landscape, with one analysis concluding that, "[a]s of February 28, 2023, there have been 144 biosimilar-related IPRs encompassing 70 patents and 14 reference products, and there have been 46 BPCIA litigations related to 12 reference products."[87] The analysis further notes that "[w]hile most of the RPSs have faced both IPRs and litigations related to their patents, some biologic patents have only faced one type of challenge."[88]

An aBLA applicant should investigate the option of pursuing IPRs early on—likely before or during the patent dance itself. The PTAB—the

83. Celltrion, Inc. v. Genentech, Inc., No. 18-cv-00274 (N.D. Cal. Jan. 11, 2018), ECF No. 1 (related to Genentech's Herceptin); *see also* Celltrion, Inc. v. Genentech, Inc., No. 18-cv-00276 (N.D. Cal. Jan. 11, 2018), ECF No. 1 (related to Genentech's Rituxan).

84. *Celltrion*, 2018 WL 2448254, at *4–5.

85. *Id.* at *7; Amgen, Inc. v. Genentech, Inc., No. CV 17-7349, 2018 WL 910198, at *3–4 (C.D. Cal. Jan. 11, 2018) (discretionarily declining declaratory judgment jurisdiction), *incorporated into* 2018 WL 718418 (C.D. Cal. Feb. 2, 2018).

86. April Breyer Menon & Ha Kong Wong, Biologics HQ, The State of Biosimilars in 2023 (2023), https://www.venable.com/-/media/files/publications/2023/03/thestateofbiosimilarsin2023venable.pdf?rev=0c1dfb03e06f4612a8d5d339d8eb5d96 ("PGRs have not been a preferred way of resolving biosimilar-related patent disputes, with only three biosimilar-related PGR filings to date."). Among other things, PGRs can only be used to challenge a patent within nine months of the patent's issuance, limiting its use for many applicants. *See* 35 U.S.C. § 321(c).

87. Menon & Wong, *supra* note 86.

88. *Id.*

venue that considers IPRs and PGRs—may discretionarily deny a petition where the patent's validity is likely to be resolved by a district court near the PTAB's own projected deadline for a final written decision (i.e., one year after an institution decision)—even if the petitioner is not involved in the subject district court case.[89]

There are advantages of challenging a patent before the PTAB as compared to the district court, for an aBLA applicant. First, the patent does not enjoy a presumption of validity in an IPR or PGR, as it does in district court. Second, the burden of establishing unpatentability is lower before the PTAB as compared to in district court (i.e., preponderance of the evidence versus clear and convincing evidence). Further, the PTAB is composed of judges that will often have a technical background similar to the challenged patents. This can often be an advantage for the party with more technically complex arguments. However, be aware that an unfavorable PTAB final written decision precludes the petitioner from asserting in district court that a patent claim "is invalid on any ground that the petitioner raised or reasonably could have raised" in the IPR.[90]

Challenging patents, or threatening to challenge patents, via IPRs and PGRs can increase pressure on an RPS in settlement discussions.[91] This leverage exists even in the absence of district court litigation, and even before a petition for post-grant adjudication is filed, as applicants may offer not to file such petitions in exchange for a more favorable settlement. However, it is notable that "biosimilars have prevailed in litigation by

---

89. Apple Inc. v. Fintiv, Inc., IPR2020-00019, paper 15, at 9 (P.T.A.B. May 13, 2020). An example of the influence of a different applicant's cases can be found in the ANDA context, where the PTAB discretionarily denied institution of an IPR filed by Mylan at least partly because the validity of the patent was already at issue in a district court case against Teva. According to the PTAB, "the validity of claims 1–21 of the '906 patent is the only issue to be resolved at [Teva's] trial, and all claims are challenged as being obvious for reasons overlapping those of the instant Petition." Mylan Lab'ys Ltd. v. Janssen Pharmaceutica NV, IPR2020-00440, paper No. 17 (P.T.A.B. Sept. 16, 2020).

90. 35 U.S.C. § 315(e)(2).

91. *See, e.g.*, Confidential Settlement and License Agreement between Alexion and Amgen re SOLIRIS [redacted] (May 28, 2020), https://www.sec.gov/Archives/edgar/data/899866/000089986620000061/exhibit101-alexionamge.htm (reflecting a settlement entered into after Amgen filed three IPRs challenging Alexion's patents, but before Amgen had filed an aBLA application for an eculizumab biosimilar product).

proving non-infringement, not by invalidating patents," and "few biologic patents have been invalidated" in IPRs.[92]

D. Investigations at the International Trade Commission

Along with a district court action, an aggressive RPS might pursue a parallel action in the International Trade Commission (ITC) against a biosimilar applicant. Generally, ITC actions are premised on the importation, or imminent importation, into the United States of articles that infringe a patent, trademark, trade secret, or similar.[93] Thus, these actions are generally only available to domestic BLA holders against foreign biosimilar applicants.[94] Due to the importation and other requirements, ITC proceedings are unlikely to be a direct substitute for district court litigation.[95]

However, an RPS might initiate an ITC action in the event of purported trade secret theft, cases involving "skinny" labeling, or potentially so that the RPS can mitigate the BPCIA's timing for "second phase" litigation.[96] As one example, after filing two BPCIA cases (one under 42 U.S.C. § 262(*l*)(6) and one under 42 U.S.C. § 262(*l*)(8)) and a separate district court trade secret misappropriation case, AbbVie filed an ITC complaint against Alvotech, asking for a limited exclusion order and cease and desist

92. Menon & Wong, *supra* note 86 (stating "There have been nine BPCIA cases involving five reference products that have concluded with infringement and/or validity determinations by the court (7), or through stipulated judgments of non-infringement by the parties (2). In these cases, three were resolved in the RPS's favor with resulting damages (1) and permanent injunctions (2), and the remaining six resulted in a finding that the patents remaining at issue were not infringed by the biosimilar." And further concluding that 35.5 percent of biologic patents (22 out of 62) challenged in IPRs "had at least some claims invalidated or disclaimed" as of March 2023.). The USPTO's analysis concludes that, as of March 31, 2023, 160 biologic patents were challenged in IPRs/PGRs, and of those, 26 percent reached a final written decision concluding that at least some challenged claims were unpatentable. USPTO, PTAB Orange Book Patent/Biologic Patent Study: FY23 Q2 Update (2023), https://www.uspto.gov/sites/default/files/documents/orange_book_biologics_study_update_thru_march__2023_.pdf.

93. *See* 19 U.S.C. § 1337.

94. The complainant must establish there is an "industry in the United States" sufficient for the ITC to exercise jurisdiction. *Id.* § 1337(a)(2)–(3).

95. Allison Inserro, *When Can Biologic Patent Disputes Go before the ITC?*, Ctr. for Biosimilars (June 25, 2019), https://www.centerforbiosimilars.com/view/when-can-biologic-patent-disputes-go-before-the-itc.

96. *See, e.g.*, *id.*; Filko Prugo et al., *USITC: A Powerful Forum for Biologics Patent Owners*, Life Scis. Intell. Prop. Rev. (Oct. 10, 2018), https://www.lifesciencesipreview.com/americas/usitc-a-powerful-forum-for-biologics-patent-owners.

orders based on the alleged trade secret misappropriation.[97] In particular, AbbVie alleged that a former employee used its proprietary information in developing Alvotech's biosimilar candidate for Humira.[98] Although the ITC instituted that investigation, the parties entered a global settlement shortly thereafter.[99]

E. Be Prepared for Settlement

Most BPCIA cases settle early—few have gone to resolution on the merits. This tendency toward settlement is likely because the BLA holder seeks predictability as to the timing of generic entry. A notable example surrounds AbbVie's blockbuster drug Humira, a monoclonal antibody. Before the 2016 expiration of AbbVie's original patent on the active ingredient of Humira, AbbVie began filing numerous other patent applications, and ultimately obtained more than 130 patents.[100] As noted on the court's opinion, the last of these patents was set to expire in 2034.[101] However, in 2015, AbbVie sued prospective Humira biosimilar competitors, including Amgen, Samsung Bioepis, Mylan, Sandoz, Fresenius Kabi, Momenta, Pfizer, Coherus, and Boehringer Ingelheim.[102] AbbVie settled every case, and all of the parties agreed to entry dates in 2023.[103] The first-settling defendant, Amgen, obtained a January 31, 2023, entry date, while the others agreed to entry dates of June 30 or later—generally staggered according to the date of settlement.[104]

Because of the likelihood of settlement—or, at the least, settlement discussions—aBLA applicants should have a dedicated financial team

---

97. Settlement and License Agreement between AbbVie and Alvotech (regarding Humira) [redacted] (Mar. 8, 2022), https://www.sec.gov/Archives/edgar/data/1898416/000119312522074698/d193995dex1029.htm; News Release, ITC, USITC Institutes Section 337 Investigation of Certain Adalimumab, Processes for Manufacturing or Relating to Same, and Products Containing Same (Jan. 26, 2022), https://www.usitc.gov/press_room/news_release/2022/er0126ll1877.htm.

98. Dani Kass, *ITC Investigating Alvotech's Humira Biosimilar Imports*, LAW360 (Jan. 26, 2022), https://www.law360.com/articles/1459001/itc-investigating-alvotech-s-humira-biosimilar-imports.

99. Notice of Institution of Investigation, *In the Matter of* Certain Adalimumab, Processes for Manufacturing or Relating to Same, and Products Containing Same, Inv. No. 337-TA-1296 (Jan. 26, 2022), https://www.usitc.gov/secretary/fed_reg_notices/337/337_1296_notice01262022sgl_0.pdf; Settlement and License Agreement between AbbVie and Alvotech (regarding Humira) [redacted], *supra* note 97.

100. Mayor & City Council of Balt. v. AbbVie Inc., 42 F.4th 709, 711 (7th Cir. 2022).

101. *Id.*

102. Consolidated Class Action Complaint and Jury Trial Demand, *In re* Humira (Adalimumab) Antitrust Litig., ECF No. 109, ¶ 211 (N.D. Ill. Aug. 9, 2019).

103. *Id.*; *Mayor & City Council of Balt.*, 42 F.4th at 714.

104. Consolidated Class Action Complaint and Jury Trial Demand, *In re* Humira (Adalimumab) Antitrust Litig., ECF No. 109, ¶ 211 (N.D. Ill. Aug. 9, 2019).

ready to assess settlement alternatives.[105] To the extent the aBLA applicant is not the first to litigate, analysis of the prior settlements is crucial to identify trends and likely settlement options. In particular, case dockets and press releases may provide high-level information. For example, as to Humira, AbbVie issued a press release on September 28, 2017, announcing a "global resolution" with the first-settling defendant, Amgen, and describing settlement agreements wherein "AbbVie will grant to Amgen a non-exclusive license to AbbVie's intellectual property related to HUMIRA," and adding that "[t]he license period will begin on Jan. 31, 2023 in the U.S."[106] The press release further states that although "Amgen will pay royalties[,] . . . [t]he precise terms are confidential between the parties."[107]

Beyond public documents, an aBLA applicant's counsel may be able to obtain discovery into the RPS's actual executed settlement agreements. For example, in *AbbVie Inc. v. Boehringer Ingelheim International GmbH*, the District of Delaware ordered production of the adalimumab biosimilar settlement agreements AbbVie reached with Amgen, Samsung, Bioepis, and Mylan.[108] Boehringer argued that these agreements "are likely to be relevant to Boehringer's invalidity and unenforceability defenses," and argued that they "are routinely produced in patent litigation, with adequate confidentiality protections."[109] The court agreed, ordering AbbVie to "produce the settlement agreements subject to the protective order entered in this case, and subject to review by outside counsel only."[110]

As reflected in the Humira cases, early-settling aBLA applicants may be able to negotiate earlier entry dates. Note, however, that the BPCIA

105. In fact, this financial team should be identified and ready to go even *before* the aBLA applicant files its application. About six months after Amgen secured the first settlement in regard to Humira, AbbVie and Samsung Bioepis announced a "global resolution" of their own—three months before Samsung Bioepis even filed its aBLA for Hadlima, its Humira biosimilar. *See* Press Release, AbbVie, AbbVie Announces Global Resolution of HUMIRA® (Adalimumab) Patent Disputes with Samsung Bioepis (Apr. 5, 2018), https://news.abbvie.com/index.php?s=2429&item=123539 (stating that the U.S. Samsung Bioepis "license period will begin on June 30, 2023"); CDER, Approval Package for Application Number: 761059Orig1s (Hadlima Injection) (July 23, 2019), https://www.accessdata.fda.gov/drugsatfda_docs/nda/2019/761059Orig1s000Approv.pdf.

106. Press Release, AbbVie, AbbVie Announces Global Resolution of HUMIRA® (Adalimumab) Patent Disputes with Amgen (Sept. 28, 2017), https://news.abbvie.com/2017-09-28-AbbVie-Announces-Global-Resolution-of-HUMIRA-R-adalimumab-Patent-Disputes-with-Amgen.

107. *Id.*

108. No. 17-CV-01065-MSG-RL, 2019 WL 1571666, at *2 (D. Del. Apr. 11, 2019).

109. *Id.* More specifically, Boehringer argued that "the settlement agreements are relevant to the "'nexus' between the alleged commercial success of Humira and the allegedly inventive features of the asserted patents" (an element of nonobviousness) and to Boehringer's unclean hands defense based on AbbVie's extensive "overlapping and non-inventive" patent portfolio related to Humira. *Id.* at *3.

110. *Id.* at *4.

does not offer any regulatory incentive to the first aBLA applicant. This differs from the Hatch-Waxman regulatory scheme, which created an incentive to the first ANDA applicant to challenge the brand patents: eligibility for a 180-day period of generic exclusivity.[111] Nonetheless, it is possible that the Hatch-Waxman generic exclusivity incentive—supported by market incentives—has informed the settlement negotiations for aBLA applicants. In Humira, the first-settling party apparently negotiated 150 days (nearly five months) of exclusivity.[112] And as reflected in Humira, this type of most-favored-nation clause can be used by subsequent settling aBLA applicants to provide additional windows before subsequent parties enter.

Further, although negotiations will often focus on a specific entry date, settling aBLA applicants will want to consider how the agreement might allow for other events to trigger entry.[113] Of course, the impacts of an early loss of brand patent coverage should be considered, as would early entry by a competing aBLA applicant. Likewise, an early unexpected drop in the brand market share or revenue could be used to trigger earlier entry.

Other settlement considerations include the amount of any royalty (considering the royalty rate, the royalty base, and the royalty term), the timing and scope of non-U.S. launches,[114] the effect of any unbranded biologics sold by the brand under its BLA, and potentially agreements as to other products that the parties want to address.[115]

---

111. 21 U.S.C. § 355(j)(5)(B)(iv).

112. *See* Consolidated Class Action Complaint and Jury Trial Demand, *In re* Humira (Adalimumab) Antitrust Litig., ECF No. 109, ¶ 211 (N.D. Ill. Aug. 9, 2019).

113. *See, e.g.*, Confidential Settlement and License Agreement between Alexion and Amgen re SOLIRIS [redacted], *supra* note 91 (stating that the "'License Effective Date' shall be the earliest to occur of: (i) March 1, 2025; (ii) [redacted] or (iii) [redacted]").

114. Global settlements are not uncommon. *See, e.g.*, Press Release, Mylan N.V., Mylan Announces Global Settlement and License Agreements with Genentech and Roche On Herceptin® (Mar. 13, 2017), https://www.biosimilardevelopment.com/doc/mylan-announces-global-settlement-and-license-agreements-0001; Kelly Davio, *Pfizer Confirms It Plans to Launch Bevacizumab Biosimilar on December 31*, Ctr. for Biosimilars (Sept. 30, 2019), https://www.centerforbiosimilars.com/view/pfizer-confirms-it-plans-to-launch-bevacizumab-biosimilar-on-december-31.

115. *See, e.g.*, *Genentech and Amgen Settle Biosimilar Disputes*, Generics & Biosimilars Initiative (July 31, 2020), https://www.gabionline.net/policies-legislation/Genentech-and-Amgen-settle-biosimilar-disputes (describing an agreement over biosimilars to each of Herceptin and Avastin).

chapter 15

Licensing and Negotiations*

I. Introduction

Negotiation and licensing play a key role for both the reference product sponsor (RPS) and the biosimilar applicant in Biologics Price Competition and Innovation Act (BPCIA) litigation. Prior to litigation, the RPS and biosimilar applicant may engage in information exchanges for which careful negotiations are necessary. These exchanges can implicate the rights of third parties who have previously licensed their patents to the BPCIA litigants. Even when parties elect to forego the voluntary exchanges set out in the BPCIA prior to litigation, a comprehensive review of licenses held by both the RPS and biosimilar applicant is prudent prior to suit. This review—and any additional subsequent negotiations between patent licensors and BPCIA litigants—can ensure that the RPS and biosimilar applicant will be able to comply with the BPCIA statute as well as any competing license provisions.

Strategic client counseling about negotiation and licensing is also crucial to settlement. Settlement agreements in BPCIA litigation commonly include licenses executed between the RPS and biosimilar applicant. Familiarity with provisions commonly seen in these licenses is important for the RPS and biosimilar applicant to conduct settlement talks efficiently. Parties must also understand their obligations to comply with governmental reporting requirements for settlements in biologics litigation.

---

*Hassen A. Sayeed, M.D., O'Melveny & Myers LLP.

II. Third-Party Negotiation and Licensing Issues Prior to Suit

The BPCIA sets out a voluntary exchange schedule for litigation between the RPS holding the rights to the reference biologics license application (BLA) and the biosimilar applicant using the abbreviated regulatory pathway authorized by the BPCIA for approval of a biosimilar or interchangeable version of the RPS's product. These exchanges—commonly referred to as the "patent dance"—proceed in phases triggered by the acceptance of the biosimilar application by the U.S. Food and Drug Administration (FDA).[1]

If the RPS and biosimilar applicant engage in the patent dance, they must analyze issues relating to patent disclosure and confidentiality within limited windows of time, particularly with respect to any exclusive licensors. The relevant timing provisions of the patent dance that constrain this analysis are summarized in the following sections. However, as that discussion also makes clear, these issues arise even when the RPS and biosimilar applicant do not participate in the patent dance. If a biosimilar applicant elects to forego the patent dance disclosure process, the only remedy available to the RPS under federal law is to bring a declaratory judgment action for infringement.[2] In those circumstances, the importance of the RPS and biosimilar applicant having clarified their pre-litigation positions with respect to licensed patents can also be important.

A. Timing Restrictions in the Patent Dance

The patent dance begins when the FDA accepts the abbreviated BLA (aBLA) submitted by the biosimilar applicant. Within 20 days of FDA acceptance, the biosimilar applicant must provide the RPS confidential access to that application and "such other information that describes the process or processes used to manufacture the biological product that is the subject of such application."[3] The timing burden then shifts to the RPS, which must within 60 days after receiving this information provide the biosimilar applicant with (1) a list of all the patents that the RPS believes it could reasonably assert against the biosimilar applicant, or that a patent owner that has granted an exclusive license to the RPS sponsor could assert against a biosimilar applicant;[4] and (2) an identification of

---

1. The U.S. Supreme Court made clear subsequent to the enactment of the BPCIA that engaging in the BPCIA patent dance is optional. *See* Sandoz Inc. v. Amgen Inc., 582 U.S. 1 (2017).
2. *Id.*
3. *See* 42 U.S.C. § 262(l)(2)(A) (2022).
4. *See id.* § 262(*l*)(3)(A)(i).

patents, if any, that the RPS would be prepared to license to the biosimilar applicant.[5] Within 60 days of receiving this list, the biosimilar applicant must identify any additional patents that it believes could be reasonably asserted against it by the RPS in connection with the aBLA product.[6] This response sets the outside perimeter of the number of patents that could be asserted against the biosimilar in the first wave of BPCIA litigation.[7]

Completion of these exchanges initiates what the BPCIA describes as "patent resolution negotiations" between the RPS and the biosimilar applicant to identify which patents from their combined list, if any, should be the subject of the first-wave infringement action.[8] The RPS and biosimilar applicant must engage in "good faith" negotiations. The statute does not identify when these negotiations must begin or which party must initiate them.[9] The statute does, however, require that the negotiations conclude within 15 days.[10]

If negotiations end with an agreement on the patents that should be the subject of the complaint, the RPS can bring an action for infringement on those patents "not later than 30 days" after such agreement.[11] If no agreement is reached, however, the parties immediately pursue further negotiations to narrow down the list of patents to litigate. The narrowing negotiations begin with the biosimilar applicant advising the RPS of the number of patents that it believes should be the subject of the first-wave litigation.[12] Within five days of that number being communicated, the RPS and biosimilar applicant must simultaneously exchange the lists of patents that each party believes should be litigated.[13] The number of patents on the RPS list may not exceed the number previously identified by the

5. *See id.* § 262(*l*)(3)(A)(ii). The biosimilar applicant must respond to the license offer if made. *See id.* § 262(*l*)(3)(B)(iii).

6. *See id.* § 262(*l*)(3)(B)(i).

7. The biosimilar applicant must also provide other information during this time period, including a detailed responsive statement providing the factual and legal basis for its opinion that the RPS patents on either list are invalid, unenforceable, or will not be infringed by the commercial marketing of the aBLA product. *See id.* § 262(*l*)(3)(B)(ii). A more detailed description of the exchanges in the first wave of BPCIA litigation is provided in Chapter 7.

8. *See* 42 U.S.C. § 262(*l*)(4). There is also a supplemental disclosure process contemplated by the BPCIA. To the extent that the RPS receives or licenses additional patents after the patent dance has started, the RPS must identify those patents to the biosimilar applicant within 30 days of issuance or license. The biosimilar applicant must provide responsive contentions for these newly listed patents within 30 days of receiving notice from the RPS. Newly issued or licensed patents become the subject of second-wave BPCIA litigation. *See id.* § 262(*l*)(7).

9. *See id.* § 262(*l*)(4).

10. *See id.* § 262(*l*)(4)(B).

11. *See id.* § 262(*l*)(6)(A).

12. *See id.* § 262(*l*)(5)(A).

13. *See id.* § 262(*l*)(5)(B)(i)(I)–(II).

biosimilar applicant.[14] If the biosimilar applicant does not identify any patents, then the RPS may identify one patent.[15] After the simultaneous exchange, the RPS has 30 days to initiate an infringement action on the narrowed list of patents.[16]

B. Negotiating Disclosure of Licensed Patents

An RPS that owns its patents can elect to disclose them to the biosimilar applicant in the course of the patent dance. Given the complexity of biologics and their manufacture, however, it is not uncommon for an RPS to extensively in-license technology from others in the course of developing its product. To the extent that an RPS holds an exclusively licensed patent that it wishes to disclose, there are additional complications for the RPS to consider. The RPS must evaluate, for example, whether its license rights require it to provide notice to the patent owner of potential third-party infringement of the licensed patent. The RPS must also evaluate whether its license rights permit disclosure of the existence of the license to the biosimilar applicant in the patent dance, and whether the RPS must either notify or seek approval from the licensor to make such disclosure or offer sublicenses or cross-licenses. The RPS must also evaluate who has control of the licensed patent during the patent dance and in litigation, and whether it must cooperate with the patent holder with respect to patent dance, litigation, and settlement strategy. If the RPS is constrained from disclosing the licensed patent or asserting the licensed patent in a way that prevents engagement in the patent dance, the RPS should consider entering into negotiations with the patent owner-licensor to provide both entities with additional flexibility that will be useful in the event of litigation.

An RPS and its licensor should conduct these discussions as early and as quickly as practicable. When engaging in the patent dance, the RPS has only 60 days after receiving the aBLA and any manufacturing information from the biosimilar applicant to disclose any exclusively licensed patents that the RPS may wish to assert.[17] That limited window can leave insufficient time to conclude renewed negotiations concerning a constrictive license. Outside of the patent dance, the RPS can immediately assert against the biosimilar applicant without delay any patent that claims the BLA product or its use.[18] A lack of preparation and discussion in

14. *See id.* § 262(*l*)(5)(B)(ii)(I).
15. *See id.* § 262(*l*)(5)(B)(ii)(II).
16. *See id.* § 262(*l*)(6)(B).
17. *See id.* § 262(*l*)(3)(A)(i).
18. *See id.* § 262(*l*)(9)(C).

connection with third-party licenses could hinder the ability to make that assertion with the desired speed.

As originally enacted, the BPCIA did not make public the disclosure of patents in the patent dance. However, Congress subsequently authorized changes requiring an RPS to provide the FDA with the number and expiration dates of any patents (and any supplemental patents) provided to the biosimilar applicant in the patent dance list exchanges.[19] Those patent numbers and expiration dates are published and updated monthly by FDA in its searchable database of biological products and biosimilars, the "Database of Licensed Biological Products" (known as the "Purple Book").[20] These public disclosures can provide a follow-on biosimilar applicant with some ability to assess the scope of an RPS patent portfolio by reviewing what was contested in a prior litigation. The biosimilar applicant could use, for example, the U.S. Patent and Trademark Office (USPTO) Patent Center public database to determine which patents are assigned to the RPS and which are licensed to other entities that are presumptive licensors. However, the Purple Book listing is not a complete source of information in this regard. For example, an RPS may not have listed all the patents covering its reference product against a particular biosimilar applicant due to specific noninfringement defenses associated with the aBLA application. An RPS may also have purposely declined to disclose an in-licensed patent in a prior litigation in order to avoid a Purple Book listing, and thus avoid alerting a follow-on biosimilar about the existence of that patent and the need for a design-around strategy. Finally, the Purple Book may not include newly issued or newly in-licensed patents recently acquired by the RPS.

In contrast to the RPS, a biosimilar applicant is not obligated to disclose any of its own patents in the course of the patent dance. It is not uncommon, however, for a biosimilar applicant to have also developed or in-licensed patents during the development process for submission of its aBLA. These assets can be tools to assert in litigation. A biosimilar applicant might threaten or allege infringement of its own patents against the RPS in a separate action, for example, or against competing biosimilar applicants. The principles of disclosure and diligence remain the same for the biosimilar applicant as the RPS when exclusive licenses are involved. The biosimilar applicant should review any license agreements to which

19. *See id.* § 262(k)(9)(A)(iii).

20. *See Purple Book Database of Licensed Biological Products*, FDA, https://purplebooksearch.fda.gov/patent-list (last updated Jan. 29, 2024). FDA's role in publishing the list is ministerial and FDA does not consider the validity, enforceability, or potential infringement in publishing the information described in the Purple Book.

it is a party to determine whether it can disclose, assert, and potentially license its patents to the RPS or other biosimilars.

C. Negotiating Confidential Access to the aBLA

The BPCIA restricts access to the aBLA and manufacturing information to the RPS outside counsel and one in-house attorney.[21] Under the statute, the RPS can share the aBLA with third-party patent owners only where the RPS is an exclusive licensee, the patent owner has retained a right of assertion or participation in the case, and the patent owner agrees to the BPCIA confidentiality provisions.[22] These provisions include a patent prosecution bar under which any attorney who receives access to the aBLA is barred from engaging, "formally or informally, in patent prosecution relevant or related to the reference product."[23]

These statutory provisions can become complicated for litigants when there are in-licensed patents for the RPS. Under the terms of its license, the RPS may be obligated to consult with a patent owner to assess infringement by or assert infringement against the biosimilar applicant. However, the designated in-house counsel of the patent owner must agree to forego any prosecution that is related to the reference product before getting access to the aBLA. Resolving disputes between the patent owner and the RPS over this point—including a determination of what constitutes prosecution "relevant or related to" the reference product—may take time to resolve. In the patent dance, the RPS has only a 60-day time period to review the aBLA and manufacturing information and identify any patents that it can assert against the biosimilar applicant. Accordingly, the RPS would benefit from reviewing—and, if necessary, renegotiating—the terms of any licensed patents to ensure that the patent owner will not object to the BPCIA confidentiality terms if it wants to participate in litigation. The RPS and the patent owner should also be mindful that the biosimilar applicant should be expected (quite naturally) to actively surveil patent dockets during the course of the litigation and afterwards for violations of the confidentiality provisions. The reward for that vigilance—and the cost for the patent owner and RPS for poor safeguarding of the biosimilar applicant's information—is high. As a statutory matter, the BPCIA assumes that "any violation or threatened violation" of the biosimilar applicant's

21. *See* 42 U.S.C. § 262(*l*)(1)(B)(ii)(I)–(II).

22. *See id.* § 262(*l*)(1)(B)(iii).

23. *See id.* § 262(*l*)(1)(B)(ii)(I)–(II) (concerning outside counsel and in-house counsel prosecution bars); *id.* § 262(*l*)(1)(B)(iii) (concerning patent owner prosecution bars). The bar is not clear as to whether it is prospective only, or whether individuals with past relevant prosecution experience would also be barred. This subject would likely need to be negotiated by the parties.

confidential information warrants imposition by the court of "immediate injunctive relief" as an "appropriate and necessary remedy."[24]

D. Other Pre-Suit Issues to Be Negotiated

Other issues often arise requiring negotiation prior to initiating suit under the BPCIA. The specifics naturally depend on the terms of the license between the patent owner and the RPS, on the one hand, or between the patent owner and biosimilar applicant licensee on the other. A non-exhaustive list of these potential issues includes:

1. How costs, royalty payments, and insurance or indemnity payments arising from BPCIA litigation should be allocated between the patent owner and its licensee
2. Whether the RPS, patent owner, or both have authority to determine which patents can be asserted in the patent dance, and whether the biosimilar applicant, its licensor, or both have authority to determine which of their patents can be asserted in response or in other litigations
3. Who has the right to grant sublicenses or cross-licenses and what permissions are necessary to make those grants
4. What notice and consulting requirements, if any, must be met by the patent owner and the RPS prior to filing suit, or by the biosimilar applicant prior to entering or skipping the patent dance
5. What notice and consulting requirements, if any, must be met by the parties prior to settling a litigation
6. Whether the RPS or patent owner (or the biosimilar applicant or its licensor) has control of major litigation decisions, including selection of counsel

III. Negotiations and Licensing in Settlement

Negotiation and licensing strategy is just as important to ending a BPCIA litigation as to starting it. Similar to most civil litigation in federal court, the majority of litigations brought under the BPCIA to date have settled. Table 1 highlights selected BPCIA litigations.

24. *See id.* § 262(*l*)(1)(H).

TABLE 1. BPCIA Litigation Data for Selected Reference Products[25]

Settlements/ Voluntary Dismissal	Involuntary Dismissals	Noninfringement	Stipulated Judgment	Pending
24	2	4	3	1

There are some systemic reasons that make BPCIA settlement more likely than not. The cost and duration of complex patent litigation raise significant hurdles for both the RPS and the biosimilar applicant to achieve market certainty for the future. In any BPCIA litigation, the RPS needs to be prepared for multiple waves of litigation arising from repeated biosimilar challenges to a single reference product. These waves of litigation may proceed without the efficiencies that normally can be leveraged from related litigations because there is no guarantee that two BPCIA litigations brought against different biosimilars at different points of time will involve the same patents. Thus, the RPS may not be able to leverage its investments in discovery and expert preparation in a prior case against a new biosimilar applicant.[26] For the biosimilar applicant, which normally must challenge a reference product covered by multiple patents, the ability to launch a biosimilar product through litigation necessitates achieving victory on every patent asserted against it. In comparison, a plan to engage in selective litigation in order to improve positioning for later settlement negotiations can be cheaper and easier.

The timing of settlement talks in BPCIA litigation does not raise special issues. At the outset of litigation, uncertainty about the outcome is at a maximum and litigation expenditure is minimal. There is usually some benefit from engaging in settlement talks to define a benchmark for subsequent settlement discussions before the case gets too far underway. As with other patent litigation, parties will typically reengage in settlement talks during litigation when there is a shift in balance between the relative uncertainty of case outcome and litigation cost. Those shifts (and subsequent settlement discussions) usually occur at times that overlap with completion of the case phases defined in a BPCIA scheduling order, including the close of fact discovery, the close of claim construction, the close of expert discovery, the submission of pretrial order materials, the eve of trial (the well-known experience of "settlement on the courthouse steps"), during trial, and after trial but before final judgment or appeal.

25. Data current through August 2023.

26. The RPS may also face challenges to its patents in other forums, including in the form of a petition for inter partes review (IPR) filed at the Patent Trial and Appeal Board (PTAB) against one or more of the patents covering the reference product.

Each of these periods offers the parties a potential opportunity to explore settlement as an alternative to trial during a time when transparency into the likelihood of a favorable case outcome is changing and while fees and costs inexorably increase.

A discussion of some provisions that the RPS and biosimilar applicant should consider in connection with settlement can be found in the following sections.

A. General Settlement Provisions

Settlement term provisions in biosimilar negotiations implicate many of the same provisions seen in general patent litigation. A few of these general provisions are considered in the following subsections in more detail.

1. Parties to the Settlement

The question of which parties to name in a BPCIA settlement agreement is not always as simple as naming the parties to the litigation. Unlike generic pharmaceutical manufacturers in Hatch-Waxman cases, biosimilar applicants may have significant marketing and distribution partnerships to launch and sell their product. Accordingly, the RPS should consider naming the biosimilar applicant's distributors, suppliers, and marketing partners who might be acting in concert with the biosimilar applicant to market the aBLA product, and against whom claims of indirect, contributory, or joint infringement might be made. Conversely, the biosimilar applicant should consider naming subsidiaries and other affiliates of the RPS to avoid the possibility that the RPS may seek to escape the scope of the settlement by having an affiliate engage in acts that it is otherwise prohibited from pursuing under the agreement.[27] To avoid future litigation on the same product, the biosimilar applicant must also ensure that any third-party patent owners implicated in the litigation that have the authority to approve settlement by the RPS agree to the settlement terms. As a result, the biosimilar applicant may seek representations and warranties to confirm the RPS can enter into the settlement agreement. Alternatively, the biosimilar applicant may seek to directly engage the third-party patent owner through discussions with the RPS and ask the owner to be a signatory to the settlement agreement.

2. Scope of the Settlement Agreement

The settlement agreement between the RPS and biosimilar applicant can resolve a BPCIA litigation, but it can also serve as a truce to stop related

27. This issue may also be addressed through a meaningful definition of "affiliate" in the definitions section of a settlement agreement.

litigations or USPTO proceedings between the parties. It is not uncommon for biosimilar litigations to be occurring simultaneously in different forums (for example, a BPCIA litigation in district court and an inter partes review (IPR) petition at the Patent Trial and Appeal Board (PTAB)). The RPS and biosimilar applicant may find it useful to expand the negotiations over a BPCIA litigation settlement into a more "global peace" concerning the aBLA product.[28] A global peace may also include settlements and licenses in foreign markets, such as Europe or Japan. Alternately, they may agree to settle the BPCIA litigation but agree to continue to litigate their remaining disputes elsewhere.

3. Form of Dismissal

In the course of resolving the BPCIA litigation, the RPS and biosimilar applicant are likely to enter into negotiations over the form of the dismissal document. A filing with the district court in which the BPCIA litigation is proceeding will frequently involve a consent judgment or a stipulated dismissal filed on the docket, and a separate settlement or license agreement that is not filed. The consent judgment is the form generally preferred by the RPS because that form usually incorporates a public admission of the validity and infringement of the patents-in-suit, which can then be enforced against the biosimilar applicant in the event of breach of the underlying license or settlement. The biosimilar applicant generally prefers the more anodyne stipulated dismissal, which usually is more neutral in tone and does not include any admissions about the patents. When this is the form being considered, the parties typically debate whether the dismissal should be with prejudice (preventing the RPS or patent owner from bringing the action back to life) or without prejudice. Whether the RPS is able to negotiate the form of dismissal as a consent judgment, or whether a biosimilar applicant is instead able to successfully negotiate a stipulated dismissal with prejudice, will generally depend on the perceived strength of their respective cases and their negotiation skills.

4. Communications with FDA

Given the challenges inherent to obtaining aBLA approval, a biosimilar applicant might negotiate for provisions that limit the RPS from launching

28. In the event that litigants pursue this option of broader settlement negotiations, they should of course be aware of the unique jurisdictional rules where the other disputes are pending. For example, and in contrast to district court litigation, an agreement by the parties to terminate an ongoing IPR may not necessarily result in the PTAB agreeing to terminate the proceeding even upon a joint motion by both parties. Further, unlike district court litigation, the parties must submit a copy of any agreements relating to the settlement. *See* 35 U.S.C. § 317(b); 37 C.F.R. § 42.74 (2018). The parties can request that those agreements be treated as business confidential information. *Id.*

parallel regulatory challenges to block FDA approval of the aBLA. At the same time, the RPS might seek to retain the ability to communicate good faith safety or efficacy concerns relating to the reference product and its biosimilars to the FDA. The parties might negotiate a compromise wherein the RPS is permitted to file citizen petitions with the FDA that concern the reference product generally, but not directed toward any specific aBLA product. The exact details of a provision concerning FDA approval will depend on each party's perceived need for such a provision, and the perceived strength of their respective cases.

B. Negotiating Confidentiality of Settlement Agreements

Drafts and written negotiations relating to a settlement agreement should be routinely marked as covered by Federal Rule of Evidence 408. The final settlement agreement will typically contain a confidentiality provision, which can survive as long or longer than the term of the settlement agreement itself. The RPS and the biosimilar applicant should draft settlement agreements, however, with the understanding that any confidentiality provisions might not be fully maintained. Settlement agreements are not immune from production in subsequent related litigation. For example, a settlement agreement involving a license may be sought in connection with discovery requests directed to commercial success from other biosimilar applicants in BPCIA litigation on the same reference product. The settlement agreement may also be sought by private plaintiffs in antitrust litigation. Although production of the agreement may be made in litigation with certain restrictions attendant to a protective order, there are limits to that protection. If terms from an agreement are disclosed in public hearings or at trial, those terms are likely to become available to the general public.

Accordingly, the settlement agreement should memorialize a process for consultation between the parties to align on what information they would fight to keep confidential under circumstances where publication is possible. The agreement should also memorialize what provisions of a settlement might become public by mutual consent, such as in connection with part of an agreed-upon press release or a securities filing for public companies.

C. Specific BPCIA License Provisions

Settlements in BPCIA litigation generally include a negotiated license agreement between the RPS (and a third-party patent owner, where appropriate) and a biosimilar applicant. The terms of the license typically permit sales of the biosimilar product to occur after a specified entry date, with various conditions proposed around those sales. No case is exactly alike, and licenses obviously differ from case to case. However, certain provisions frequently arise in BPCIA licensing negotiations. These provisions are discussed in more detail in the following subsections.

1. Entry Date

The most debated term in any license between an RPS and biosimilar applicant will be the entry date upon which the biosimilar applicant can enter the agreed-upon market and sell the aBLA product. The entry date is often the first point on which the parties must agree in order to achieve a settlement. Although additional terms can be negotiated afterwards, it is often true that agreement on an entry date can amount to agreement in principle to settle. Both the RPS and the biosimilar applicant will need to model a variety of factors to determine an appropriate date. Factors commonly considered in this assessment include (1) the perceived strength of the patents-in-suit, and their perceived vulnerability at trial; (2) the benefits to the RPS and biosimilar applicant business of having certainty around the biosimilar market entry timeline as opposed to the uncertainty of litigation; (3) the time to market entry of the aBLA product and the booked revenue and future market value secured from that date for both parties; and (4) the savings in litigation costs by entering into settlement.

2. Pre-Launch Stockpiling Clauses

In order to begin booking revenue as of the entry date, a biosimilar applicant will need to have prepared supplies of the aBLA product ready to ship. Absent an agreement by the RPS to authorize this stockpiling, however, the biosimilar applicant would be liable for a claim of infringement.[29] Accordingly, a license agreement with a pre-launch stockpiling clause would permit the biosimilar applicant to manufacture, use, or import into the United States its aBLA product or infringing precursor material, or to use infringing processes to make that product or material, prior to launching the aBLA product into the market.

3. Entry Date Acceleration Clause

Securing an entry date by itself may not give a biosimilar applicant complete comfort in settlement. BPCIA litigations often involve multiple biosimilar applicants seeking FDA approval to market aBLAs directed to the same reference product. These litigations necessarily involve different accused infringing aBLA products, and they can also involve different patents. Moreover, an RPS is not obligated to settle litigations on the same

29. Pursuant to 35 U.S.C. § 271(a), anyone who "without authority makes, uses, offers to sell, or sells any patented invention, within the United States or imports into the United States any patented invention during the term of the patent therefor, infringes the patent."

reference product on identical terms. As a result, a biosimilar applicant that settles a litigation has no guarantee that a follow-on biosimilar applicant will not receive more favorable terms, including the possibility of entering the market earlier.[30]

Accordingly, BPCIA settlement agreements might include an acceleration clause that accelerates the licensed entry of a biosimilar if a follow-on biosimilar receives an earlier entry date through any of a series of events. These events can include settlement, market entry by virtue of an at-risk launch, or invalidation of a patent in the same or another forum (i.e., an IPR at the PTAB).

A sample entry date acceleration clause is as follows:

> For the purposes of this Settlement Agreement, the "Entry Date" shall mean the earlier of (a) [**the agreed-upon date from negotiations**]; (b) the date of a final decision holding that all asserted and adjudicated claims of the [**asserted patents in the litigation**] are invalid or unenforceable; or (c) the date on which a third party is authorized to launch a [**biosimilar version of the reference product**] in the United States under a license or other agreement with [**the RPS**].[31]

Several terms in this sample clause would of course require further negotiation. For example, the parties would need to consider whether the definition of the RPS should be expanded to include third-party patent owners for patents-in-suit, and whether those patent owners can provide the necessary authority for the RPS to enforce the clause. The parties would also need to define with precision the scope of a "final decision" concerning the disputed patents. It is not uncommon to define such a final decision as one from which no further automatic right of appeal can be taken. Given that appeals to the U.S. Supreme Court require a petition for a writ of certiorari and are not automatic, this definition usually means

30. An exception to this concern can occur in the form of interchangeability designations. Under the BPCIA, the first aBLA product designated as "interchangeable" with the reference product is eligible for a period of "first interchangeable exclusivity." During that time period, the FDA may not approve a second biological product as interchangeable with that same reference product for any condition of use. *See generally* 42 U.S.C. § 262(k)(6). Interchangeable biosimilar products may be substituted at the pharmacy for the reference product without intervention from the prescribing health care provider. A biosimilar that has achieved an interchangeable designation thus enjoys not only temporary protection from follow-on interchangeable biosimilar products, but also the benefits of substitutability against the reference product.

31. All sample clauses provided in this chapter are intended to be conceptual exemplars only. They are not intended to provide—nor should they be interpreted as providing—specific legal advice.

that a final decision results after an unsuccessful appeal by the RPS to the U.S. Court of Appeals for the Federal Circuit.

An additional consideration that arises in connection with these kinds of clauses is whether the "final decision" must include a decision of noninfringement with respect to the asserted patents. Biosimilar applicants may seek this broader definition of a "final decision" because it can serve to trigger the entry date acceleration clause more often. In contrast, the RPS will generally oppose this provision since noninfringement positions (like aBLA products) can vary dramatically between biosimilar applicants. An RPS is likely to take the view that a victory on noninfringement by a follow-on biosimilar due to design-around strategies should not result in an earlier entry by a biosimilar that settled for a later date based on its own beliefs about the weakness of its noninfringement position. One deciding factor in resolving this potential dispute may be whether the same patents will be disputed between biosimilar cases. The parties may be able to agree on different entry date acceleration provisions if there is a reasonable likelihood that different patents will end up being litigated against different biosimilars over time.

4. Royalty Clauses

License agreements between the RPS and biosimilar applicant can also involve royalty payments in recognition of the patents being licensed. Two common royalty structures are a flat royalty and a multi-tier royalty.

In a flat royalty, a flat rate is paid by the biosimilar applicant from its entry date until (usually) the final expiry date of the patents, regardless of how many other biosimilar entrants subsequently enter the market. This option does not incentivize biosimilar applicants to settle early, but the revenue can be used by the RPS as a predictable income stream and can be used to offset an earlier entry date. A sample flat royalty clause is as follows:

> In consideration for the license granted herein, [**biosimilar applicant**] shall pay to [**RPS**] royalties in an amount equal to [**flat rate**] percent on net sales of the [**aBLA product**] during the term.

There are a variety of ways to structure a multi-tiered royalty, but one option is to set a contingent royalty paid by the biosimilar applicant tied to the number of biosimilar entrants into the market (e.g., 50 percent royalty if only one biosimilar entrant, 25 percent if two biosimilar entrants, and no royalty if more than two biosimilar entrants). A sample multi-tier royalty clause is as follows:

In consideration for the license granted under Section X, [**biosimilar applicant**] shall pay to [**RPS**] royalties in an amount equal to the following rates on net sales of the [**aBLA product**] during the term:

On that portion of net sales of [aBLA product] that is sold:	Royalty rate
(a) From the Entry Date (or date of unlicensed launch by [**biosimilar applicant**]) until such time as there is one other third-party biosimilar product	Fifty percent (50%) of net sales of [**the aBLA product**]
(b) From the date that royalties cease to be owed under Section (a) until such time as there are two or more third-party biosimilar products	Twenty-five percent (25%) of net sales of [**the aBLA product**]
(c) From and after the date that royalties cease to be owed under Section (b)	No royalties payable

provided, however, in each case (b) and (c) above, if one or more of the third-party biosimilar products that triggered a royalty reduction under this section cease to be sold on a commercial scale in the United States during the term, then the applicable royalty rate shall reset to such royalty rate that was in effect prior to the commercial launch of such third-party biosimilar products.

Several terms in these sample clauses would require additional negotiation between the parties to generate agreed-upon definitions. In both the flat and multi-tier royalty clauses, for example, the parties would need to agree on an objective and verifiable definition of "net sales." For the multi-tier royalty, the parties would also have to agree on what constitutes sales of the aBLA product at a "commercial scale."

For both flat and multi-tier royalties, the parties should consider the duration of the royalties. The parties can agree to terminate royalties on a set date tied to the expiration of the licensed patents. However, the parties may also consider earlier terminations based on findings of patent invalidity or unenforceability.

Royalty term clauses should also take into consideration any tax implications. The biosimilar applicant entity paying the royalty and the RPS entity booking the revenue should evaluate jurisdiction and payment timing issues to try to maximize favorable tax treatment.

5. Most-Favored-Nation Clauses

As discussed earlier, acceleration clauses can be raised in negotiations between the RPS and a biosimilar applicant in connection with an entry date. However, a biosimilar applicant may seek additional reassurance that a follow-on biosimilar competitor will not receive any more favorable business terms on other points of negotiation. In such cases, the parties sometimes negotiate a general "most favored nations" (MFN) clause that provides such reassurance.

A sample MFN clause is as follows:

> In the event that [**the RPS**] grants to any third party any license, authorization, or other permission to make, have made, import, market, use, sell, or offer for sale any equivalent product in the territory on terms more favorable to the third party than the terms set forth in this agreement, then this agreement shall be deemed amended to extend such more favorable terms to the [**biosimilar applicant**]. [**The RPS**] shall notify the [**biosimilar applicant**] promptly in writing and in no case later than [**15 or some other number of**] days, following the execution of any such agreement to advise [**biosimilar applicant**] about the changes to this agreement in [**biosimilar applicant's**] favor resulting from this paragraph.

Obviously, among the terms that would need to be narrowed in negotiations in this sample clause is the definition of what counts as "more favorable" terms. It is crucial that the RPS and biosimilar applicant avoid ambiguity in negotiating this provision. It is generally useful to specify the terms to which the MFN clause would apply. Before entering into an agreement containing an MFN clause, it is also important to confirm that there are no other preexisting agreements to which the RPS or biosimilar applicant are parties that may conflict with the grants made by the MFN provisions.

6. No-Challenge Clauses

Resolution of the BPCIA patent litigation via a license does not necessarily prevent the biosimilar applicant from later challenging the litigated patents. The Supreme Court held decades ago in *Lear v. Adkins* that a patent licensee may challenge the validity of a licensed patent.[32] More recently, the Supreme Court clarified in *MedImmune, Inc. v. Genentech, Inc.* that a licensee may seek a declaratory judgment that the licensed patent is invalid, unenforceable, or not infringed without abrogating the license agreement to which it is a party.[33]

32. *See* 395 U.S. 653, 670–71 (1969).
33. *See* 549 U.S. 118, 137 (2007).

Resolution of this potential asymmetry can be resolved by inclusion of a no-challenge clause in a settlement agreement. Such a clause serves to limit challenges to the patents being resolved in the litigation and can be defined broadly to prohibit challenges in district court or other forums. The Federal Circuit has held that no-challenge clauses arising in litigation can be consistent with the Supreme Court's rejection of the licensee estoppel doctrine in *Lear*.[34] In *Flex-Foot, Inc. v. CRP, Inc.*, the Federal Circuit noted that the license in *Lear* "did not contain, and was not accompanied by, any promise by the licensee not to challenge the validity of the patent."[35] As a result, *Lear* did not involve "the important policy of enforcing settlement agreements and res judicata."[36] Endorsing the idea that an interest in settling litigation is more favored as a policy matter than "the technical requirements" of contract law, the Federal Circuit concluded that after

> an accused infringer has challenged patent validity, has had an opportunity to conduct discovery on validity issues, and has elected to voluntarily dismiss the litigation with prejudice under a settlement agreement containing a clear and unambiguous undertaking not to challenge validity and/or enforceability of the patent in suit, the accused infringer is contractually estopped from raising any such challenge in any subsequent proceeding.[37]

The Federal Circuit has also clarified after *Flex-Foot*, however:

> Each case must be examined on its own facts in light of the agreement between the parties. In the context of settlement agreements, as with consent decrees, clear and unambiguous language barring the right to challenge patent validity in future infringement actions is sufficient, even if invalidity claims had not been previously at issue and had not been actually litigated.[38]

34. *See* Flex-Foot, Inc. v. CRP, Inc., 238 F.3d 1362, 1368 (Fed. Cir. 2001).

35. *Id.*

36. *Id.*

37. *See id.* at 1370. The Federal Circuit has held similarly in prior cases as well. *See, e.g.*, Hemstreet v. Spiegel, Inc., 851 F.2d 348, 350 (Fed. Cir. 1988) (holding that a party must pay royalties under a settlement license agreement after the patent was held unenforceable in a different court because enforcing settlement agreements invokes a "public policy totally absent in *Lear*: the encouragement of settlement of litigation and the need to enforce such settlements in order to encourage the parties to enter into them").

38. *See* Baseload Energy, Inc. v. Roberts, 619 F.3d 1357, 1363 (Fed. Cir. 2010).

Accordingly, the RPS and biosimilar applicant would do well to focus on the specific language in a no-challenge clause to ensure that it will survive appellate review if challenged.[39]

7. At-Risk Launch

Settling a BPCIA litigation provides a biosimilar applicant an entry date upon which it can launch its aBLA product with a license. The inclusion of an entry date acceleration clause permits a biosimilar applicant to match earlier entry dates negotiated by other biosimilar applicants who have settled with the RPS. However, a biosimilar applicant might also seek the ability to launch if another biosimilar applicant were to launch its aBLA product without a license. This is particularly true if the biosimilar applicant has already provided its 180-day notice of commercial marketing and can thus launch at any time.[40] Such a launch would be "at risk" because it would be without a license from the RPS.

Multiple considerations go into the negotiation of an at-risk launch provision. First, the parties should define the third-party launch that would trigger an at-risk launch by the settled biosimilar applicant. An RPS might wish to limit the ability of a settled biosimilar applicant to launch at risk if there are material differences between the aBLA products of the settled biosimilar applicant and the third party. The parties can consider, for example, whether a third-party at-risk launch of a noninterchangeable aBLA product would permit a settled biosimilar applicant to launch an interchangeable aBLA product at risk. Likewise, the parties can consider whether a third-party at-risk launch based solely on noninfringement arguments would permit a settled biosimilar applicant to launch its aBLA product if those noninfringement arguments do not apply to the settled biosimilar applicant.

Second, the parties can negotiate procedural steps for a settled biosimilar applicant to launch at risk. For example, the parties can define time periods

39. The language of the settlement agreement approved by the Federal Circuit in *Flex-Foot* may be an instructive exemplar:

> The CRP Group agrees not to challenge or cause to be challenged, directly or indirectly, the validity or enforceability of the '913 patent and/or the '363 patent in any court or other tribunal, including the United States Patent and Trademark Office. As to the '363 and '913 patents only, the CRP Group waives any and all invalidity and unenforceability defenses in any future litigation, arbitration, or other proceeding. This waiver applies to any product made, used, or sold by the CRP Group or any of their assignees, successors or those who act for or in concert with any of them at any time during the life of either the '363 or '913 patents.

See Flex-Foot, Inc., 238 F.3d at 1364.

40. *See* 42 U.S.C. § 262(*l*)(8).

during which an RPS would be permitted to seek a preliminary injunction to block the settled biosimilar applicant from an at-risk launch. The parties can also negotiate time periods in which an RPS could appeal the denial of any preliminary injunctions against the settled biosimilar applicant.

Third, the parties can consider what happens as a result of an at-risk launch by the settled biosimilar applicant. For example, the parties can consider whether a judicial decision or settlement that enjoins the sales of the third-party aBLA product that triggered the at-risk launch would require the biosimilar applicant to also stop its sales. The parties can also consider whether the at-risk launch provision provides for damages, or a method for calculating damages, in response to any losses resulting from the at-risk launch. Finally, the parties can consider whether an at-risk launch by the settled biosimilar applicant voids the settlement agreement and any licenses provided therein.

IV. Antitrust Considerations

In *FTC v. Actavis, Inc.*, the Supreme Court held that anticompetitive effects of settlement agreements in patent infringement litigation may be found unlawful under the Sherman Antitrust Act.[41] The Court ruled that this determination requires a fact-intensive rule-of-reason analysis "because the likelihood of a reverse payment bringing about anticompetitive effects depends upon its size, its scale in relation to the payor's anticipated future litigation costs, its independence from other services for which it might represent payment, and the lack of any other convincing justification."[42]

In subsequent years, *Actavis* and its progeny have substantially affected the pharmaceutical industry and precipitated a number of lawsuits by private plaintiffs in the context of Hatch-Waxman litigation. Although a detailed discussion of antitrust law is beyond the scope of this chapter, it seems reasonable to conclude that BPCIA litigation is likely to be a space in which antitrust law and the legacy of *Actavis* will develop in the coming years.[43] The RPS and a biosimilar applicant would both be wise to seek antitrust advice in negotiating a settlement agreement. The review should include an analysis of any transfers of value (both cash and non-cash) from the RPS or patent owner to the biosimilar applicant, and preparation of objective justifications supporting those transfers under the rule of reason.

41. *See* 570 U.S. 136 (2013).

42. *Id.* at 159.

43. A more detailed discussion of antitrust law in the context of BPCIA litigation can be found in Chapter 11.

V. Filing Requirements for Biosimilar Settlements

The successful negotiation of a settlement agreement to end a BPCIA litigation comes with additional obligations. It is not enough to merely file a dismissal of the litigation after executing a settlement agreement. By law, BPCIA settlement agreements must be filed with both the U.S. Department of Justice (DOJ) and Federal Trade Commission (FTC). The governing statutes and the detailed procedures that the RPS and biosimilar applicant must follow when filing their settlements are described in more detail in the following sections.

A. Agreements That Must Be Filed

As originally enacted, the Medicare Prescription Drug, Improvement, and Modernization Act of 2003 (MMA) required Hatch-Waxman litigants (i.e., the patent-holding innovator and the challenger generic pharmaceutical company) to file their settlement agreements with the DOJ and FTC. In 2018, however, the MMA was amended to expand the scope of this requirement to cover agreements relating to biosimilars.[44]

As revised, the MMA requires that the text of an agreement between a biosimilar applicant and a "brand name drug company"[45] must be filed with the DOJ and FTC when it concerns three subject categories: (1) the manufacture, marketing, or sale of the reference product; (2) the manufacture, marketing, or sale of the biosimilar product for which the biosimilar aBLA was submitted; or (3) any of the time periods in the BPCIA that relate to the interchangeability exclusivity periods set out by the statute.[46] Agreements concerning these three subject categories must be filed prior to the date of the first commercial marketing of "the biosimilar biological product that is the subject of the biosimilar biological product application."[47] It is

44. *See* SUPPORT for Patients and Communities Act, Pub. L. No. 115-271, § 4004, 132 Stat. 3894, 3960 (2018) (codified at 21 U.S.C. § 355 note at §§ 1111–1118).

45. The 2018 MMA amendments likely refer to a "brand name company" instead of an RPS at least partly because the MMA reporting requirements arose originally in the context of Hatch-Waxman litigation. The term "brand name company" includes the holder of a new drug application in Hatch-Waxman cases. For BPCIA litigation, the term includes the RPS and the owner or exclusive licensee of patents included in the patent dance list sent by the RPS to the biosimilar applicant within 60 days of receiving the aBLA and the biosimilar applicant's manufacturing information. *See* 21 U.S.C. § 355 note at § 1111(7); 42 U.S.C. § 262(*l*)(3).

46. *See* 21 U.S.C. § 355 note at § 1112(a)(2). These categories would encompass settlement and license agreements. The MMA as amended also requires submission to the DOJ and FTC of agreements made between biosimilar applicants when their aBLAs refer to the same reference drug product, and when those agreements reference any of the BPCIA interchangeability exclusivity periods or "the manufacture, marketing, or sale of a biosimilar biological product." *See id.* § 1112(b).

47. *See id.* § 1112(a)(1).

not a sufficient excuse to fail to file an agreement because the parties did not reduce it to writing. The MMA provides that if any agreement required to be filed "has not been reduced to text, each of the parties involved shall file written descriptions of such agreement that are sufficient to disclose all the terms and conditions of the agreement."[48]

There is also a broader catch-all provision in the MMA. Parties are required to file the text of any agreements that "are contingent upon, provide a contingent condition for, were entered into within 30 days of, or are otherwise related to" an agreement relating to the three subject categories for which filing is mandatory.[49] The statute does not require that these other agreements relate in any way to the BPCIA litigation, its settlement, the reference product, or the aBLA product. All that is arguably necessary to trigger the catch-all is that the later agreement is "entered into within 30 days" of the settlement agreement.[50] All submitted agreements are treated as confidential and may not be made public "except as may be relevant to any administrative or judicial action or proceeding" or to Congress.[51] The submissions are also exempted from the disclosure requirements of the Freedom of Information Act.[52]

However, the MMA does specifically exclude certain agreements from the requirement to file with the DOJ and FTC. Parties need not file an agreement if they concern solely (1) purchase orders for raw material supplies; (2) equipment and facility contracts; (3) employment or consulting contracts; or (4) packaging and labeling contracts.[53]

B. Timing

The timing provisions for filings made under the MMA are generally straightforward. The statute requires that any required agreement "shall

48. *See id.* § 1112(c)(3).

49. *See id.* § 1112(c)(2).

50. The use of the disjunctive "or are otherwise related to" in the subsequent clause of the same sentence reinforces this interpretation. *See id.* The FTC encourages submission of anything a party believes "will assist the agencies in evaluating the agreement," and FTC staff can discuss issues with parties in advance of filing an agreement. *See* FTC, Frequently Asked Questions about Filing Agreements with the FTC Pursuant to the Medicare Prescription Drug, Improvement, and Modernization Act of 2003 (2019) [hereinafter FTC, Frequently Asked Questions], https://www.ftc.gov/system/files/attachments/competition-policy-guidance/mma_pharmaceutical_agreement_filing_faq_6-6-19.pdf.

51. *See* 21 U.S.C. § 355 note at § 1114.

52. *See id.* Joint stipulations of dismissal where there is no related settlement or license must also be submitted under the MMA. In addition, although outside the scope of this chapter, practitioners and parties should note that agreements arising from resolutions of disputes before the PTAB (e.g., a petition for IPR) that fall within the scope of the MMA subject-matter requirements must also be filed. *See* FTC, Frequently Asked Questions, *supra* note 50 .

53. *See* 21 U.S.C. § 355 note at § 1112(c)(1).

be filed with the Assistant Attorney General and the Commission not later than 10 business days after the date the agreements are executed."[54] However, the statute also requires that any agreement must also be filed prior to the date of the first commercial marketing of the aBLA product at issue.[55] In the event that the settlement permits the marketing of the aBLA product in fewer than ten business days from the execution date of the settlement, the agreements may need to be filed earlier to comply with the MMA timing provisions. The parties can also negotiate the relative timing of their marketing date and settlement execution date, if necessary, to avoid being rushed to make the filing compliance deadline.

The agreements are filed by email by each party and must include a cover sheet that can be found on the FTC website.[56] The cover sheet requests (1) the name of the filing party; (2) the date of the agreement being filed; (3) the other parties to the agreement; (4) the civil action to which the settlement relates; (5) the MMA subsection to which the agreement relates; and (6) an identification of whether the agreement relates to a previously submitted agreement.[57] The cover sheet also requires the name of the reference BLA number, the biosimilar aBLA number, the reference biologic product name, and the biosimilar product name.[58]

C. Penalties for Failure to Comply

Parties that fail to comply with the MMA's filing requirements can face severe penalties. The MMA mandates that "any brand name drug company . . . or biosimilar biological product applicant which fails to comply with any provision . . . shall be liable for a civil penalty . . . for each day during which such entity is in violation of this subtitle."[59] The daily statutory penalty of $11,000 identified in the statute was increased by regulations to account for inflation and is currently set at $18,293 per day.[60] The penalties may be recovered in a civil action brought by the United States

54. *See id.* § 1113.

55. *See* 21 U.S.C. § 355 note at § 1112(a)(1) (relating to agreements between an RPS and biosimilar applicant); *id.* § 1112(b)(1)(B) (relating to agreements between two biosimilar applicants).

56. The agreements are emailed to specific addresses at the FTC (mma@ftc.gov) and the DOJ (mma@usdoj.gov). *See* Fed. Trade Comm'n., *Pharmaceutical Agreement Filing Procedures Updated* (2019), https://www.ftc.gov/news-events/news/press-releases/2019/06/pharmaceutical-agreement-filing-procedures-updated.

57. FTC & DOJ, MMA Pharmaceutical Agreement Filing Cover Sheet (2019), https://www.ftc.gov/system/files/attachments/pharmaceutical-agreement-filings/mma_pharmaceutical_agreement_filing_cover_sheet_blas.pdf.

58. *See id.*

59. *See* 21 U.S.C. § 355 note at § 1115(a).

60. *See* 16 C.F.R. § 1.98(n) (2024).

or the FTC.[61] In addition, a U.S. district court may order compliance with the statute and "such other equitable relief as the court in its discretion determines necessary or appropriate."[62]

There is no requirement to wait to hear from FTC or DOJ before moving forward with the settlement agreement, and there is no approved timetable for review.[63] The FTC neither approves nor denies an approval to file an agreement between the parties.[64] Accordingly, after the parties file their agreement, they may proceed as if they have the government imprimatur to do so. That does not mean, however, that such an imprimatur exists. A lack of response to the MMA filing does not signify an implicit approval of the agreement or a lack of antitrust concern. If such a concern exists, the government will raise it on its own timetable.

61. *See* 21 U.S.C. § 355 note at § 1115(a).
62. *See id.* § 1115(b).
63. *See* FTC, Frequently Asked Questions, *supra* note 50.
64. *Id.*

chapter 16

The Future of BPCIA and Biosimilars*

This treatise is intended to provide practitioners with the lay of the land for the Biologics Price Competition and Innovation Act (BPCIA) and related biosimilars litigation. This chapter focuses on recent changes, and what is likely to come next: what amendments to the BPCIA are contemplated, how biosimilars litigation may evolve, and how the landscape is likely to evolve. Changes first discussed here will either drop out (if rejected or disapproved) or else move into the body of the treatise (if enacted or adopted) as further editions are released.

I. User Fee Regulations

The FDA User Fee Reauthorization Act of 2022 included the Biosimilar User Fee Act (BsUFA III), which allows the U.S. Food and Drug Administration (FDA) to collect fees from October 2022 through September 2027. These user fees are earmarked for speeding up the time it takes for regulators to review biosimilar applications, and hence to facilitate consumer access to biosimilars in the drug market. For U.S. government fiscal year 2024 (October 1, 2023–September 20, 2024), the initial and annual Biosimilar Biological Product Development (BPD) fee for investigational new drug (IND) applications is $10,000, with a reactivation fee of $20,000. For biosimilar approval applications, the fee is $1,018,753 for an application requiring clinical data and $509,377 for applications not requiring clinical data. Atop these fees is a program fee of $177,397.[1] These fees will escalate yearly through 2027, with the precise amounts to be published for comment in the middle of each fiscal year.

---

*David S. Bloch, Greenberg Traurig LLP, San Francisco, and Melissa Hunter-Ensor, Ph.D., Greenberg Traurig LLP, Boston.

1. 88 Fed. Reg. 48,855 (July 28, 2023).

A. The Inflation Reduction Act

In 2023, U.S. biotech companies innovating in the biologics space reaped $3.2 billion more in venture financing relative to their small-molecule innovator counterparts.[2] This investment differential likely reflects the excitement among venture capitalists surrounding the biologic market, and the growth of that industry. However, the high price of biologics and other medications creates an economic burden on the U.S. market. This burden can be addressed, at least in part, by encouraging the adoption of biosimilars, which are priced on average 30 percent less than reference products.[3]

In an effort to encourage the cost savings associated with biosimilars, the Inflation Reduction Act (IRA) was enacted by the U.S. federal government on October 1, 2022. Under the IRA, the Secretary for Health and Human Services (HHS) is required to undertake price negotiations with drug companies for drugs covered under Medicare Part D beginning in 2026 and under Part B beginning in 2028. These requirements are the subject of numerous lawsuits by branded drug companies who argue that the IRA is unconstitutional.[4] Guidance promulgated by the Centers for Medicare and Medicaid Services (CMS) in June 2023 indicates that biologics without generic alternatives or biosimilar equivalents will be subject to price negotiations. In determining whether a generic or biosimilar version of the reference product exists, CMS will consider the "totality of the circumstances." This will include analyzing FDA sources to determine whether generic or biosimilars have been approved, reviewing Part D claims data to assess utilization and sales, and whether any agreements exist between branded and generic drug manufacturers that would limit availability.

CMS issued a memorandum for implementation of the IRA in March 2023, with drug price savings beginning in 2026. Under the IRA, CMS will provide an 8 percent add-on payment rate for biosimilars to Medicare Part B-covered entities. This incentive is intended to promote adoption of biosimilars, but it is difficult to predict how this incentive will actually play out given the complexity of the third-party payer system where health

2. Isabel Cameron, *Inflation Law Drives Biologic Drugs to Outpace Small Molecules in US Venture Financing*, BioPharma Rep. (July 6, 2023), https://www.biopharma-reporter.com/Article/2023/07/06/inflation-law-drives-biologic-drugs-to-outpace-small-molecules-in-us-venture-financing.

3. Shanna Schneider & Nilesh Desai, *Capitalize on Biosimilars, Understand the Inflation Reduction Act*, Pharmacy Times (May 2023), https://www.pharmacytimes.com/view/capitalize-on-biosimilars-understand-the-inflation-reduction-act.

4. Sheryl Gay Stolberg & Rebecca Robbins, *Drugmakers Are "Throwing the Kitchen Sink" to Halt Medicare Price Negotiations*, N.Y. Times (July 25, 2023), https://www.nytimes.com/2023/07/23/us/politics/medicare-drug-price-negotiations-lawsuits.html.

systems may select on-formulary (branded or generic) products even where that biosimilar fails to carry an interchangeability designation. Moreover, Medicare drug price negotiation can negatively impact the biosimilar value proposition. Under the IRA, the price of a reference biologic can be negotiated 11 years after FDA approval. Such negotiation substantially reduces the price that innovators can charge for biologic products, thereby eroding the value provided by the entry of biosimilars into the market. The Congressional Budget Office estimates that the drug negotiation provisions of the IRA will provide about $98.5 billion in savings to Medicare over a ten-year period.[5]

The biosimilar delay provision of the IRA provides a delay in selecting reference biologics for price negotiation where there is a "high likelihood" that a biosimilar will enter the market within "two years of the publication date of the selected drug list."[6] The delay is intended to obviate any disincentive to biosimilar manufacturers contemplating entering a market where the reference product selected for price negotiation might otherwise be priced lower than competing biosimilar products. Applications for a delay request must be submitted by the manufacturer of a biosimilar product corresponding to a given reference biologic *prior* to the date that the list of drugs for negotiation is published.[7] For the application to be considered by CMS, the manufacturer of the biosimilar must be different from the manufacturer of the reference biologic, and there must be no agreement in place between the biosimilar manufacturer and the reference biologic manufacturer that would limit competition between the two products.[8] At the time the application is submitted, the manufacturer of the biosimilar will not be certain whether or not the reference biologic has been selected for price negotiation.

In determining whether to approve an application for biosimilar delay, CMS will consider whether there is a high likelihood of biosimilar market entry. This high likelihood of biosimilar market entry will be based on whether the FDA has approved or accepted for review an application of licensure for the biologic, and whether there is "clear and convincing"

---

5. Juliette Cubanski et al., *Explaining the Prescription Drug Provisions in the Inflation Reduction Act*, KFF (Jan. 24, 2023), https://www.kff.org/ medicare/issue-brief /explaining-the-prescription-drug-provisions-in-the-inflation-reduction-act/.

6. *Id.*; CMS, HHS, Medicare Drug Price Negotiation Program: Revised Guidance, Implementation of Sections 1191–1198 of the Social Security Act for Initial Price Applicability Year 2026 (2023) [hereinafter Medicare Drug Price Negotiation Program: Revised Guidance].

7. Juliette Cubanski, *FAQs about the Inflation Reduction Act's Medicare Drug Price Negotiation Program*, KFF (Jan. 31, 2024), https://www.kff.org/medicare/issue-brief/faqs -about-the-inflation-reduction-acts-medicare-drug-price-negotiation-program/.

8. Medicare Drug Price Negotiation Program: Revised Guidance, *supra* note 6, § 30.3.1.

evidence that the biosimilar will be marketed within two years of the selected drug publication date.[9] The CMS guidance states: "The clear and convincing evidence criteria will be satisfied if the Initial Delay Request demonstrates both (1) that patents related to the Reference Drug are unlikely to prevent the Biosimilar from being marketed and (2) that the Biosimilar Manufacturer will be operationally ready to market the Biosimilar."[10]

The price reductions provided under the IRA should promote the entry of biosimilars into the marketplace. The negotiated price reductions under the IRA applies only to Medicare—these price reductions may have no effect on the prices of biologics charged to stakeholders serving 80 percent of the non-Medicare patient market.[11] Nevertheless, by encouraging biosimilar entry, the increased competition under the IRA should also benefit private payers and their patients. The biosimilar delay provision also provides a benefit to innovators who have typically sought to extend market exclusivity using patent protection and patent enforcement. To the extent that patent holders are incentivized under the IRA to promote the entry of biosimilars into the marketplace, it may limit their desire to enforce patents against biosimilar manufacturers.

Pending biosimilar legislation focuses on two issues: speeding up the biosimilar approval process and encouraging adoption of biosimilars by medical practitioners.

1. Speeding Up Approval by Eliminating the "Interchangeability" Standard

The BPCIA, which was written by Rep. Richard Hudson of North Carolina, is designed with the Hatch-Waxman Amendments to the Food, Drug, and Cosmetic Act in mind. But the small-molecule pharmaceuticals covered by Hatch-Waxman are different in kind from the biologic products covered by the BPCIA. Biologic products include, for example, a "virus, therapeutic serum, toxin, antitoxin, vaccine, blood, blood component or derivative, allergenic product, protein, or analogous product,"[12] and similar large molecules, which may be used for the "treatment, prevention, or cure" of diseases. On average, a biological drug is more structurally complicated than a chemically synthesized one. That complexity, as well as the different processes used to produce biologics, means that the concept of

9. Cubanski, *supra* note 7.

10. MEDICARE DRUG PRICE NEGOTIATION PROGRAM: REVISED GUIDANCE, *supra* note 6, § 30.3.1 Comment and Response section.

11. Sarfaraz K. Niazi, *The Inflation Reduction Act: A Boon for the Generic and Biosimilar Industry*, 46 J. CLINICAL PHARMACY & THERAPEUTICS 1738 (2022).

12. 42 U.S.C. § 262(i).

equivalence (and pharmacological identity) has been replaced with the concept of *biosimilarity* (sufficient sameness at the molecular level that the reference and biosimilar drug are functionally interchangeable). Whereas small molecules are chemically synthesized, biologics are large molecules that are typically recombinantly expressed in a variety of organisms (e.g., bacteria, yeast, and mammalian cells in culture). Given the complexity of the manufacturing process, a reference product sponsor typically submits a biologic application under Public Health Service (PHS) Act section 351(a), which shows that its biologic is not only biosimilar to the reference product, but is "expected to produce the same clinical result as the reference product."[13] Moreover, the biosimilar has a similar safety profile where the risk associated with receiving the biosimilar is no greater than the risk associated with receiving the reference product.[14] In sum, the designation of a biologic product as "interchangeable" indicates that the biologic product will produce the same clinical results as the reference product and will be similar in efficacy and safety.

The BPCIA amends the PHS Act in a number of ways. First, it creates an expedited path for approval to biologics that are biosimilar to a previously approved biologic (also termed a "reference product"). This allows biosimilars to be approved via an abbreviated biologics license application (aBLA).[15] The aBLA can only be approved after the exclusivity period of the reference product has expired. Such approval cannot be given "until the date that is 12 years after the date on which the reference product was first licensed."[16] In addition, the BPCIA provides for the resolution of patent disputes relating to biologics under 42 U.S.C. § 262(*l*). Further, it expands the definition of "biologic products" to include all proteins that are not chemically synthesized.

Biosimilar-side companies have begun lobbying for a streamlined approval process for biosimilars—in particular, relaxing the measure of biosimilarity so that biosimilar products would not need to demonstrate clinical efficacy, but instead similarity of biochemical, biophysical, and biological function.[17] The same companies also advocate for scrapping the United States-only requirement of multiple-switch studies in

---

13. *Id.* § 262(4)(A)(ii).
14. *Id.* § 262(4)(B).
15. *Id.* § 262(k).
16. *See id.* § 262(k)(7).
17. Hillel P. Cohen et al., *Future Evolution of Biosimilar Development by Application of Current Science and Available Evidence: The Developer's Perspective*, 37 BioDrugs 583 (2023), https://doi.org/10.1007/s40259-023-00619-0.

order to obtain a designation of interchangeability (as opposed to mere biosimilarity).[18]

In response to these concerns, the Biosimilar Red Tape Elimination Act of 2023,[19] which was proposed by Sen. Mike Lee of Utah, would eliminate the separate interchangeability requirement[20] and instead deem all FDA-approved biosimilars "interchangeable" for purposes of the BPCIA. A similar effort in 2022 was not voted out of the Health, Education, Labor, and Pensions Committee.

Currently, companies hoping to market interchangeable biosimilar drugs must pay for additional clinical trials. During these trials, patients undergoing therapies switch back and forth between a reference biologic and a biosimilar. Biosimilars that meet the interchangeability standard must be shown to be as safe and effective as the corresponding reference biologic. The FDA began approving interchangeable biosimilars in 2021. In that year, just two interchangeable biologics were approved: SEMGLEE®, which is the interchangeable biologic for LANTUS®, a long-lasting form of insulin, and CYLTEZO®, which is the interchangeable biologic for HUMIRA®, a biologic for the treatment of autoimmune disorders. The approval process for interchangeable biologics did not pick up pace in 2022, when again just two interchangeable biosimilars were approved: CIMERLI® for LUCENTIS®, a biologic for the treatment of eye conditions, and REZVOGLAR® for LANTUS®.[21] Interestingly, the interchangeability standard is not recognized in Europe, where approved biosimilars are readily provided to patients. In fact, patient access to biologics increased by about 44 percent once biosimilars entered the European market.[22] It is hoped that the Biosimilar Red Tape Elimination Act of 2023 would rapidly increase patient access to cost-saving biosimilar drug products.

2. Encouraging Substitution of Biosimilars for Reference Drugs

The problem with establishing biosimilarity in biologic pharmaceuticals to the same level of confidence as establishing equivalence in small-molecule pharmaceuticals was in part the driver of the Advancing Education on Biosimilars Act of 2021,[23] which requires FDA to undertake outreach and educational efforts regarding the safety and efficacy of biosimilars.

---

18. *See id.*

19. S. 2305, 118th Cong. (2023).

20. 42 U.S.C. § 262(k)(4).

21. Alyssa Billingsley, *What Is an Interchangeable Biosimilar Drug?*, GoodRx (Mar. 3, 2023), https://www.goodrx.com/drugs/biologics/interchangeable-biosimilar-drugs.

22. Luke Halpern, *The Growth of Biosimilars Continues to Create Hope for Lower Drug Costs*, Pharmacy Times (Aug. 28, 2023), https://www.pharmacytimes.com/view/the-growth-of-biosimilars-continues-to-create-hope-for-lower-drug-costs.

23. Pub. L. No. 117-8, 135 Stat. 254 (2021).

Yet uptake is lagging, at least in Congress's view. Given concerns that biosimilars are not driving down biotherapeutic drug prices and are not being prescribed as widely as are generic small-molecule drugs, the Increasing Access to Biosimilars Act of 2023[24] proposes a three-year nationwide demonstration project within Medicare to facilitate access to biosimilars by providing a shared-savings reimbursement model in which providers receive an additional payment based on the cost savings of prescribing a biosimilar versus reference product. Widespread adoption of biosimilars is expected to provide $133 billion in savings to the economy by 2025.[25]

Whether this is a problem with the availability of attractive substitutes, a lack of competition, or resistance on the demand side is hard to say. However, 2023 offered an interesting real-world experiment, because 2023 is the year HUMIRA® biosimilars became widely available. HUMIRA® is the world's leading drug when measured in worldwide sales[26]—it is a highly effective and widely adopted monoclonal antibody approved for treating arthritis and certain skin disorders. The extent to which practitioners, patients, and insurers will embrace biosimilars the same way they have embraced abbreviated new drug application (ANDA)-side generics played out in real time in 2023, when nine biosimilars of HUMIRA® launched in the United States (one in January, seven in July, and one in November 2023). A tenth biosimilar, SIMLANDI®, launched in February 2024. Most of these were authorized by agreement following inter partes review (IPR) petitions, as opposed to BPCIA litigation. Thus far the results are mixed. CVS Caremark did not replace HUMIRA® with biosimilar equivalents in the CVS Caremark formulary until April 2024.[27] Critics contend that sophisticated pricing strategies and Byzantine reimbursement-and-rebate rules have prevented a more rapid adoption of HUMIRA® biosimilars.[28] Presumably these same barriers exist for other biosimilars, as well.

---

24. H.R. 1352, 118th Cong. (2023).

25. Skylar Jeremias, *The Increasing Access to Biosimilars Act of 2023*, Ctr. for Biosimilars (Mar. 29, 2023), https://www.centerforbiosimilars.com/view/the-increasing-access-to-biosimilars-act-of-2023-introduced-to-congress.

26. Cardinal Health, 2023 Biosimilars Report: Tracking Market Expansion and Sustainability amidst a Shifting Industry 5 (2023), https://www.cardinalhealth.com/content/dam/corp/web/documents/Report/cardinal-health-biosimilars-report-2023.pdf.

27. Press Release, CVS Health, CVS Caremark Accelerates Biosimilars Adoption through Formulary Changes (Jan. 3, 2024), https://www.prnewswire.com/news-releases/cvs-caremark-accelerates-biosimilars-adoption-through-formulary-changes-302025679.html.

28. Joshua Cohen, *Humira Biosimilars Not Gaining Traction Epitomizes Dysfunctional U.S. System*, Forbes (Dec. 4, 2023), https://www.forbes.com/sites/joshuacohen/2023/12/04/humira-biosimilars-not-gaining-traction-epitomizes-dysfunctional-us-system; *Humira Biosimilar Landscape: Still Waiting*, Biosimilars Council (Jan. 30, 2024), https://biosimilarscouncil.org/resource/humira-biosimilar-landscape-still-waiting/.

chapter 17

Canadian Drug Approval Process and Litigation*

I. Introduction

The goal of this chapter is to provide an overview of the statutory and regulatory mechanisms governing the drug approval process and related litigation under Canadian law. The chapter will begin with the statutory and regulatory framework of the drug approval process in Canada, including the Food and Drugs Act (FDA) and Food and Drug Regulations (FDR), the Patented Medicines (Notice of Compliance) PM(NOC) Regulations, and the various types of submissions required to seek market access. Following this, an overview of the mechanism for asserting drug-related patents will be provided, with a particular focus on complex biologics.

II. Biologics Statutory and Regulatory Framework and Approval Process

A. Statutory and Regulatory Framework

1. The FDA and FDR

The sale of drugs in Canada is governed by the FDA and the FDR. The term "drug" is defined broadly in the FDA as follows:

> *drug* includes any substance or mixture of substances manufactured, sold or represented for use in
>
> > **(a)** the diagnosis, treatment, mitigation or prevention of a disease, disorder or abnormal physical state, or its symptoms, in human beings or animals,

---

*John E. Norman and Andrew Medico of Gowling WLG (Canada) LLP, Ottawa, Ontario, Canada.

(b) restoring, correcting or modifying organic functions in human beings or animals, or

(c) disinfection in premises in which food is manufactured, prepared or kept; (*drogue*)[1]

The FDR specifies the requirements for the sale and advertisement of drugs in Canada for innovative, generic, and biosimilar drug companies. In particular, no innovative drug can be sold or marketed unless the Minister has issued a notice of compliance (NOC) to the manufacturer of the new drug in respect of their submission.[2] According to Health Canada, an NOC is "issued to a manufacturer following the satisfactory review of a submission for a new drug, and signifies compliance with the Food and Drug Regulations."[3]

Innovative, biosimilar, and generic drug manufacturers alike must file a drug submission to Health Canada for review in order to demonstrate the requisite safety, efficacy, and quality of their product. However, it is important to note that innovative, biosimilar, and generic drugs have different regulatory requirements to satisfy before their product is authorized for sale in Canada. Generally speaking, the review process can take between nine months to two years, depending on the nature of the product.[4]

2. The PM(NOC) Regulations

The PM(NOC) Regulations intersect with drug approval under the FDA and Division 8 of the FDR.[5] The PM(NOC) Regulations provide the regulatory mechanism for patentees' to assert their intellectual property against prospective generic and biosimilar drug competitors, which will be discussed in greater detail in the chapter.

1. FDA, R.S.C. 1985, c F-27, s 2.

2. FDR, C.R.C., c 870, C.08.002(1).

3. *Notice of Compliance (NOC) Database*, Health Can., https://www.canada.ca/en/health-canada/services/drugs-health-products/drug-products/notice-compliance/database.html (last modified Oct. 30, 2023).

4. *Drug Funding Review and Approval Process*, Ont. Ministry Health, https://www.ontario.ca/page/drug-funding-review-and-approval-process (last updated Nov. 20, 2023).

5. Health Canada, Guidance Document: Patented Medicines (Notice of Compliance) Regulations (2021), https://www.canada.ca/content/dam/hc-sc/documents/services/drug-health-product-review-approval/drug-products/guidance-documents/pm-noc-regulations-guid-ld-eng.pdf.

B. Health Canada Approval and Regulatory Process

1. Biologics, Biosimilars, and Interchangeables

a. New Drug Submission

In Canada, innovative pharmaceutical companies must file a new drug submission (NDS) with Health Canada for a new drug to demonstrate that it meets the required threshold for safety and efficacy in order to market and sell a product. The PM(NOC) Regulations define an NDS as "a new drug submission or an extraordinary use new drug submission as those terms are used in Division 8 of Part C of the Food and Drug Regulations, but excludes such a submission that is based solely on the change of name of the manufacturer."[6]

The following information is included in the NDS:

1. Product information
2. Chemistry and manufacturing
3. Investigational preclinical studies
4. Clinical studies
5. Research and development

Like innovators, biosimilars must also file an NDS to seek approval for their product. However, the requirements will differ. For a product to be eligible to be authorized as a biosimilar, it must satisfy the following criteria:

1. A suitable reference biologic drug exists (i.e., innovative comparison drug).
2. The biosimilar and reference biologic drug can be well characterized by a set of modern analytical methods.
3. The biosimilar, through extensive characterization and analysis, can be judged similar to the reference biologic drug by meeting an appropriate set of predetermined criteria.[7]

With regard to point 1 above, a suitable reference biologic drug exists if the drug (1) was originally authorized for sale based on a full quality, nonclinical and clinical data package; and (2) has been used in the post-market setting such that the demonstration of similarity will bring into relevance a substantial body of reliable data on safety, efficacy, and effectiveness.[8]

---

6. PM(NOC) Regulations, SOR/93-133, s 3(1).

7. Health Canada, Guidance Document: Information and Submission Requirements for Biosimilar Biologic Drugs (2022), https://www.canada.ca/content/dam/hc-sc/documents/services/drugs-health-products/biologics-radiopharmaceuticals-genetic-therapies/applications-submissions/guidance-documents/information-submission-requirements-biosimilar-biologic-drugs/information-submission-requirements-biosimilar-biologic-drugs.pdf.

8. *Id.*

The biosimilar manufacturer chooses the indications they seek for their product, not Health Canada.[9] The key is for the biosimilar manufacturer to establish that the biosimilar drug is highly similar to the reference biologic drug with no clinically meaningful differences. It can do so via clinical studies for one of the indications, which permits extrapolation of indications by Health Canada. Effectively, this authorizes the biosimilar to market and sell their product based on prior clinical trials, for each indication, conducted with the reference biologic drug to establish safety and efficacy of their biosimilar product.[10]

b. Abbreviated New Drug Submission

The regulatory approval process for generic drugs (i.e., small molecules) differs from that of biosimilars. Unlike biosimilars, generic drug companies must file an abbreviated new drug submission (ANDS) rather than an NDS to obtain market authorization. The FDR permits the filing of an ANDS in the following circumstances:

> C.08.002.1 (1) A manufacturer of a new drug may file an abbreviated new drug submission or an abbreviated extraordinary use new drug submission for the new drug where, in comparison with a Canadian reference product,
>
> > (a) the new drug is the pharmaceutical equivalent of the Canadian reference product;
> >
> > (b) the new drug is bioequivalent with the Canadian reference product, based on the pharmaceutical and, where the Minister considers it necessary, bioavailability characteristics;
> >
> > (c) the route of administration of the new drug is the same as that of the Canadian reference product; and
> >
> > (d) the conditions of use for the new drug fall within the conditions of use for the Canadian reference product.

2. Application Approval Process

As discussed earlier, a biosimilar (i.e., subsequent entry biologic) must obtain an NOC based on demonstrated similarity between its product and the reference biologic drug to obtain market approval. Therefore, an NDS will contain extensive data on the similarity of the biosimilar with the

---

9. *Biosimilar Biologic Drugs in Canada: Fact Sheet*, HEALTH CAN., https://www.canada.ca/en/health-canada/services/drugs-health-products/biologics-radiopharmaceuticals-genetic-therapies/applications-submissions/guidance-documents/fact-sheet-biosimilars.html (last modified Aug. 27, 2019).

10. *Id.*

reference drug. The required amount of clinical and nonclinical information required to demonstrate safety and efficacy is reduced by virtue of relying on the reference biologic drug, per *Teva Canada Ltd. v. Pfizer Canada Inc.*[11] With this in mind, the party seeking approval must demonstrate that the biosimilar and reference biologic drug can be assessed as highly similar in order to determine whether the safety and efficacy profiles are similar.

The manufacture of biologics is a complex endeavor that results in greater variability than synthesizing small molecules. For instance, the medium in which the protein-expressing cells are cultured can have a material impact on the function of the biologic drug. This is because a specific cell culture medium may result in post-translation modifications (i.e., glycosylation, phosphorylation, etc.) that are different from the ones found on the reference biologic drug. Further, using a different downstream manufacturing process may result in differing purity and contamination levels.

For these reasons, additional information is required about chemistry and manufacturing to ensure purity, quality, and consistency of the biosimilar product. For example, the biosimilar must demonstrate that specific processes are in place to ensure there is no contamination.

Given the differences between biosimilars and generic small-molecule drugs, many characteristics associated with the authorization process and marketed use for generic pharmaceutical drugs do not apply. Authorization of a biosimilar is not a declaration of pharmaceutical equivalence, bioequivalence, or clinical equivalence to the reference biologic drug.

C. The Patent Register

The Minister is obligated to maintain a register of patents that have been submitted for addition to the register and certificates of supplementary protection (CSPs) associated with any of the patents.[12] This register includes a listing of medicinal ingredients and their associated patents, the patent expiry dates, and other relevant information.[13]

However, not all patents are capable of being listed on the register. A patent is only eligible to be listed on the register if the patent contains:

1. A claim for the medicinal ingredient
2. A claim for the formulation that contains the medicinal ingredient
3. A claim for the dosage form
4. A claim for the use of the medicinal ingredient[14]

11. [2016] F.C.J. No. 1126, 2016 FCA.
12. PM(NOC) Regulations, SOR/93-133, ss 3–4.
13. *Patent Register*, Health Can., https://www.canada.ca/en/health-canada/services/drugs-health-products/drug-products/patent-register.html (last modified Apr. 6, 2017).
14. PM(NOC) Regulations, SOR/93-133, s 4(2).

Only patents listed on the Patent Register can be asserted against generic and biosimilar submissions under section 6 of the PM(NOC) Regulations.

Aside from the above eligibility requirements, there are also timing requirements for a patent to be listed on the Patent Register. A first person can, after filing an NDS or supplemental new drug submission (SNDS), within 30 days after the issuance of a patent that was issued on the basis of an application with a Canadian filing date preceding the filing of the submission, submit a patent list for inclusion on the Patent Register.[15]

D. Notable Differences between Small-Molecule and Complex Biologics Regulatory Approval Processes

As stated, biosimilars must file an NDS when seeking market authorization for their drug product. This is a more comprehensive submission than what their generic counterparts must file with Health Canada. In effect, biosimilars are treated as new drug products because of the complexity in manufacturing them and the potential for some level of variability between the biosimilar and the reference biologic product. To alleviate any concern stemming from this potential variability, biosimilars must provide clinical trial data on safety and efficacy. This also serves to demonstrate that the biosimilar drug is highly similar to the innovative drug and effectively works in the same manner.

III. PM(NOC) Litigation

A. Litigation Timeline and Section 6 Actions under the PM(NOC) Regulations

If a biosimilar drug manufacturer wants to obtain market access, it must either wait until the patents listed on the Patent Register in respect of the innovative drug expire, or it can allege that the listed patents are invalid or that approval of its proposed product would not infringe the listed patents. If they chose the latter option, the biosimilar must serve on the first person (i.e., the patentee) a notice of allegation (NOA) relating to the submission filed with Health Canada.[16] In the NOA, the second person (i.e., the biosimilar or generic) must include (1) a description of the medicinal ingredient, dosage form, strength, route of administration, and use of the drug in respect of which the submission or supplement has been filed, and (2) a statement of the legal and factual basis for the allegation, which

15. *Id.* s 4(6).
16. *Id.* s 5(3)(a).

statement must be detailed in the case of an allegation that the patent or CSP is invalid or void.[17]

Upon receipt of the NOA, the patent owner may bring an action against the biosimilar or generic in the Federal Court within 45 days for a declaration that the making, constructing, using, or selling of a drug in accordance with the submission would infringe any patent that is the subject of an allegation set out in the notice.[18] The issuance of a statement of claim triggers a 24-month stay under section 7(1)(d) of the PM(NOC) Regulations whereby the Minister is prohibited from issuing an NOC to the biosimilar filer until after the expiry of this period. This is a compressed timeline imposed by virtue of the PM(NOC) Regulations wherein section 6 actions must be adjudicated.

1. Pleadings and Responses

Where a defendant is served in Canada with a statement of claim, it has to file and serve a statement of defence within 30 days, or within 40 days if a notice of intention to respond is served in the interim.[19] If deemed necessary, a plaintiff may reply to a statement of defence within ten days after service of the statement of defence.[20]

2. Discovery of Documents and Examination for Discovery

The discovery process for actions under the PM(NOC) Regulations is governed by the Federal Courts Rules (FCR), like any other action brought in the Federal Court. Within 30 days after the close of pleadings, every party to the litigation must serve an affidavit of documents on every party, which includes relevant documents to the pleaded allegations in the case.

Under the FCR, a document includes

> an audio recording, a video recording, a film, a photograph, a chart, a graph, a map, a plan, a survey and a book of account, as well as data that is recorded or stored on any medium in or by a computer system or other similar device and that can be read or perceived by a person or a computer system or other similar device.[21]

A document is deemed relevant if the party intends to rely on it or if the document tends to adversely affect the party's case or to support another

17. *Id.* s 5(3)(b).
18. *Id.* s 6(1).
19. Federal Courts Rules, SOR/98-106, Rules 204(1) and 204.1.
20. *Id.* Rule 205.
21. *Id.* Rule 222(1).

party's case.[22] The parties also have an ongoing obligation for continued disclosure of any supplemental relevant documents.

Subsequent to serving the affidavits of documents, a party is entitled to examination for discovery, where typically inventors and corporate representatives are examined. During examination for discovery, the person being examined has to answer, to the best of their knowledge, information, and belief, any question that (1) is relevant to any pleaded unadmitted allegation of fact, or (2) concerns information about the name or address of a person who can be reasonably expected to have knowledge relating to the matter of the question being asked.[23]

3. Summary Judgment

A party to the litigation can bring a motion for summary judgment on all or some of the issues raised in the pleadings at any point after the defendant has filed a statement of defence but before the time and place for trial have been fixed.[24] A party who brings a motion for summary judgment has to satisfy the court that there is no genuine issue for trial with respect to a statement of claim or defence. If the court is satisfied that the issue is a question of law, the court can determine the question and grant summary judgment if necessary.

B. Section 8.2 Actions (Unlisted Patents)

Following receipt of an NOA relating to a biosimilar or generic submission, a first person or patent owner may bring an action to assert a patent that is not listed on the register in respect of the innovative drug, but that would nonetheless result in infringement by the making, constructing, using, or selling of the biosimilar or generic drug in accordance with the submission.

C. Section 8 Damages

Where an action brought under subsection 6(1) is discontinued or dismissed (or reversed on appeal), a biosimilar or generic may apply for an order requiring the patent owner to compensate them for any loss suffered by the delay to their market authorization. Plaintiffs in a section 6 action are jointly and severally liable to the biosimilar or generic for any loss incurred following the day on which the Minister would have issued an NOC in the absence of the action. In other words, the patent owner is

22. *Id.* Rule 222(2).
23. *Id.* Rule 240.
24. *Id.* Rule 213(1).

liable for holding the biosimilar or generic off the market to the extent that they would have been approvable.

IV. Advising Clients on Product Strategies, Global Considerations, and the Future of PM(NOC) and Biosimilars

A. Innovative Drug Product Counseling and Strategies

Under section C.08.004.1 of the FDR, pharmaceuticals containing an innovative drug are given an eight-year period of market exclusivity, whereby the Minister cannot issue an NOC to a subsequent entry biologic. An additional six-month pediatric extension is applied when results of clinical trials designed to gain knowledge of the drug in pediatric populations are included in an innovative drug manufacturer's NDS, or any SNDS filed within the first five years of the eight-year data protection period. Subsequent entry biologics are also precluded from filing a drug submission copying the innovative drug for the first six years of this eight-year period, also known as the six-year no-file period.

An important strategy for innovative drug companies is to seek the grant of all patents relevant to the drug that are eligible to be placed on the Patent Register before the end of the six-year no-file period. This ensures that when a biosimilar filer seeks market access and initiates the PM(NOC) Regulations, it must address all the patents on the Patent Register at the date of filing prior to being granted market approval. The Patent Register is said to "freeze" at this date for the submission being filed. It is also crucial to ensure that you put your client in a position to assert the strongest patent that provides the greatest exclusivity, including patents with a CSP. A CSP can only be issued in respect of patents related to a compound, a process, or a use involving a medicinal ingredient or a combination of all medicinal ingredients.[25]

It is also important to file any outstanding regulatory submissions so that the product label is up to date. Additionally, any potential problem regarding inventorship should be resolved prior to the expiry of this six-year no-file period.

Leading up to any litigation, innovative drug companies should verify that they have access to inventors when the biosimilar challenge comes. They should also seek documents that are relevant to the invention story and that underlie the examples in the patents that will be asserted.

25. Certificate of Supplementary Protection Regulations, SOR/2017-165, s 3(2).

B. Future of PM(NOC) Litigation and Biosimilars

The landscape with respect to the PM(NOC) Regulations and the litigation of complex biologics continues to evolve under Canadian law. Innovative pharmaceutical companies must balance the potential upside of enforcing their drug-related patents and extending market exclusivity with potential section 8 damages liability. This becomes particularly important as Canada moves towards mandatory biosimilar switching. If mandatory biosimilar switching is employed countrywide, it will likely increase an innovative drug's potential section 8 liability post-biosimilar market approval. This and other considerations continue to change the future of PM(NOC) litigation in Canada.

Index

B

R

About the ABA Section of Intellectual Property Law

From its strength within the American Bar Association, the ABA Section of Intellectual Property Law (ABA-IPL) advances the development and improvement of intellectual property laws and their fair and just administration. The Section furthers the goals of its members by sharing knowledge and balanced insight on the full spectrum of intellectual property law and practice, including patents, trademarks, copyright, design, and trade secrets. Providing a forum for rich perspectives and reasoned commentary, ABA-IPL serves as the ABA voice of intellectual property law within the profession, before policy makers, and with the public.

Books from the ABA Section of Intellectual Property Law (ABA-IPL)

ABA
AMERICAN BAR ASSOCIATION
Intellectual Property Law Section

Title	Regular Price	ABA-IPL Member Price
ADR Advocacy, Strategies, and Practices for Intellectual Property and Technology Cases, 2nd Ed. (5370231)	$149.95	**$119.95**
ANDA Litigation, 3rd Ed. (5370243)	$379.00	**$295.95**
Antitrust Issues in Intellectual Property Law, 2nd Ed. (5370263)	$149.95	**$119.95**
Arbitrating Patent Disputes (5370229)	$89.95	**$74.95**
Biosimilars Litigation and Client Counseling (5370267)	$169.95	**$139.95**
Careers in IP Law (5370204) (The ebook is complimentary with ABA-IPL Section membership)	$24.95	**$16.95**
Commercialization of IP Rights in China (5370241)	$119.95	**$95.95**
A Comprehensive Patent Practice Form Book (5370260)	$139.95	**$109.95**
Computer Games and Immersive Entertainment, 2nd Ed. (5370239)	$89.95	**$69.95**
Copyright Litigation Strategies (5370228)	$369.00	**$285.00**
Copyright Remedies (5370208)	$89.95	**$74.95**
Crash Course on U.S. Patent Law (5370221)	$39.95	**$34.95**
The DMCA Handbook, 2nd Ed. (5370234)	$79.95	**$64.95**
The Essential Case Law Guide to PTAB Trials (5370233)	$249.95	**$199.95**
The Essentials of Japanese Patent Prosecution (5370245)	$149.95	**$119.95**
Intellectural Property and Technology Due Diligence (5370236)	$219.95	**$179.95**
The Intellectual Property Law Handbook, 2nd Ed. (5620154)	$139.95	**$109.95**
IP Attorney's Handbook for Insurance Coverage in Intellectual Property Disputes, 2nd Ed. (5370210)	$139.95	**$129.95**
IP Protection in China (5370217)	$139.95	**$109.95**
IP Strategies for Medical Device Technologies (5370238)	$149.95	**$119.95**
IP Valuation for the Future (5370237)	$89.95	**$59.95**
The Law of Trade Secret Litigation Under the Uniform Trade Secrets Act, 2nd Ed. (5370242)	$369.95	**$295.95**
A Lawyer's Guide to Section 337 Investigations before the U.S. International Trade Commission, 5th Ed. (5370266)	$139.95	**$109.95**
Legal Guide to Video Game Development, 2nd Ed. (5370227)	$74.95	**$59.95**
A Legal Strategist's Guide to Trademark Trial and Appeal Board Practice, 4th Ed. (5370247)	$179.95	**$144.95**
New Practitioner's Guide to Intellectual Property (5370198)	$89.95	**$69.95**
Patent Claim Drafting Practice (5370259)	$179.95	**$144.95**